D1389856

The CIM Handbook of Strategic Marketing

The Chartered Institute of Marketing/Butterworth-Heinemann Marketing Series is the most comprehensive, widely used and important collection of books in marketing and sales currently available worldwide.

As the CIM's official publisher, Butterworth-Heinemann develops, produces and publishes the complete series in association with the CIM. We aim to provide definitive marketing books for students and practitioners that promote excellence in marketing education and practice.

The series titles are written by CIM senior examiners and leading marketing educators for professionals, students and those studying the CIM's Certificate, Advanced Certificate and Postgraduate Diploma courses. Now firmly established, these titles provide practical study support to CIM and other marketing students and to practitioners at all levels.

 The Chartered
Institute of Marketing

Formed in 1911, The Chartered Institute of Marketing is now the largest professional marketing management body in the world with over 60,000 members located worldwide. Its primary objectives are focused on the development of awareness and understanding of marketing throughout UK industry and commerce and in the raising of standards of professionalism in the education, training and practice of this key business discipline.

Books in the series

Below-the-line Promotion, John Wilmshurst

The CIM Handbook of Export Marketing, Chris Noonan

The CIM Handbook of Selling and Sales Strategy, David Jobber

The CIM Handbook of Strategic Marketing, Colin Egan and Michael J. Thomas

CIM Marketing Dictionary (fifth edition), Norman A. Hart

Copywriting, Moi Ali

Creating Powerful Brands (second edition), Leslie de Chernatony and Malcolm McDonald

The Creative Marketer, Simon Majaro

The Customer Service Planner, Martin Christopher

Cybermarketing, Pauline Bickerton, Matthew Bickerton and Upkar Pardesi

The Effective Advertiser, Tom Brannan

Integrated Marketing Communications, Ian Linton and Kevin Morley

Key Account Management, Malcolm McDonald and Beth Rogers

Market-led Strategic Change (second edition), Nigel Piercy

The Marketing Book (third edition), Michael J. Baker

Marketing Logistics, Martin Christopher

Marketing Research for Managers (second edition), Sunny Crouch and Matthew Housden

The Marketing Manual, Michael J. Baker

The Marketing Planner, Malcolm McDonald

Marketing Planning for Services, Malcolm McDonald and Adrian Payne

Marketing Plans (third edition), Malcolm McDonald

Marketing Strategy (second edition), Paul Fifield

Practice of Advertising (fourth edition), Norman A. Hart

Practice of Public Relations (fourth edition), Sam Black

Profitable Product Management, Richard Collier

Relationship Marketing, Martin Christopher, Adrian Payne and David Ballantyne

Relationship Marketing for Competitive Advantage, Adrian Payne, Martin Christopher, Moira Clark and Helen Peck

Retail Marketing Plans, Malcolm McDonald and Christopher Tideman

Royal Mail Guide to Direct Mail for Small Businesses, Brian Thomas

Sales Management, Chris Noonan

Trade Marketing Strategies, Geoffrey Randall

Forthcoming

Relationship Marketing: Strategy and Implementation, Helen Peck, Adrian Payne, Martin Christopher and Moira Clark

Services Marketing, Colin Egan

The CIM Handbook of Strategic Marketing

Editors: Colin Egan and Michael J. Thomas

Published on behalf of
The Chartered Institute of Marketing

Oxford   Boston   Johannesburg   Melbourne   New Delhi   Singapore

Butterworth-Heinemann
Linacre House, Jordan Hill, Oxford OX2 8DP
225 Wildwood Avenue, Woburn, MA 01801-2041
A division of Reed Educational and Professional Publishing Ltd

℞ A member of the Reed Elsevier plc group

658.8

British Library Cataloguing in Publication Data
A catalogue record for this book is available from the British Library

ISBN 0 7506 2613 5

Typeset by Avocet Typeset, Brill, Aylesbury, Bucks
Printed and Bound in Great Britain by Martins the Printers, Berwick upon Tweed

FOR EVERY TITLE THAT WE PUBLISH, BUTTERWORTH-HEINEMANN
WILL PAY FOR BTCV TO PLANT AND CARE FOR A TREE.

Contents

Introduction _____

In recent years the rise of global competition and the prevalence of continuous innovation have combined to redefine market structures, reshape industries and give customers unprecedented value and choice. In this area of consumer sovereignty there is a tremendous amount of pressure on organizations to adopt the principles of the marketing concept and to develop a much sharper strategic focus. For most companies, however, this strategic shift involves radical changes in fundamental business processes and profound transformations in organizational design and culture. To address this marketing 'fact of life' firms readily express their desire to become 'market driven' and they often demonstrate a strong determination to act 'strategically'. There is little doubt that companies are aware of the organizational challenges this entails and no claim is made that their strategic aspirations are not genuine. Serious concerns do arise, however, when one questions the existence of appropriate levels of organization-wide competencies which are essential for a 'marketing-led' company to exist and thrive. In a truly market-driven organization everybody does marketing and, logically, there is no need for a 'marketing' department. In reality, however, marketing is frequently marginalized as a functional activity and the marketing philosophy remains an ephemeral idea in many companies. The key to solving this dilemma is education and a shared vision of what is actually meant by marketing. If the marketing philosophy is to permeate the organization there is no doubt that the inspiration should emanate from senior executives. *The CIM Handbook of Strategic Marketing* addresses this audience and aims to develop their knowledge of how designing and implementing effective marketing strategies can considerably improve business performance.

The book

The CIM Handbook of Strategic Marketing aims to play a key role in disseminating the marketing philosophy throughout organizations. It is one of a series of handbooks which introduce the principles and practice of marketing to people at all levels in organizations, from senior executives to sales personnel. The texts within the series serve two key functions: (i) as a reference source to guide effective marketing practice; and (ii) as supportive material to managers and employees who are building their marketing competencies by attending training programmes. Taken together these twin roles will underpin the CIM Continuing Professional Development initiative, itself a reflection of the generic need for continuous improvement in contemporary business practice.

    The CIM Handbook of Strategic Marketing is written for senior executives responsible for shaping and managing the company's strategic direction. The strategic dimensions of marketing management are strongly emphasized, as is the critical importance of matching the company's capabilities with genuinely attractive market sectors. The guiding philosophy of this handbook is based on its strategic perspective and pragmatic outlook, twin themes which pervade the text and underpin its practical foundations.

The contributors

Each contributor was asked to reflect on key issues in their own field of expertise. As marketing experts with extensive academic and practical experience, each of the authors focuses here on a specific topic but always with reference to the broader *strategic* marketing context.

The homily

Economists have a superb 'get out' clause when making observations of what should or should not be done, what is right and what is wrong. The Latin phrase *ceteris paribus* has spared many blushes for economists who have been proved spectacularly wrong! Meaning 'other things being equal', it allows predictions to be made on the basis of clearly stated assumptions. Unlike the 'pure' sciences, the social science base of marketing (economics, psychology, sociology, cultural anthropology) can accommodate exceptions to the rule without necessarily breaking the rule. Fortunately, when the rule is broken there are quite sophisticated quantitative and qualitative techniques to explain why.

Strategic and marketing lecturers are often accused by their students of enjoying the 'benefit' of hindsight. In contrast, the essence of strategic marketing management is to deploy the skills of foresight, competencies which are grounded in the models, methods and frameworks introduced throughout this handbook. Marketing is a normative subject, quick to offer prescriptions about what firms should do if they wish to survive and prosper in a competitive environment. But, as you will see throughout this book, all contributors acknowledge the organizational constraints which can sometimes conspire to prevent the best marketing intentions from ever reaching fruition. In this sense, strategic marketing has two dimensions: (i) content, i.e. the actual strategies which are formulated; and (ii) process, i.e. the decision-making actions and activities which lead to the development of the strategies. These twin forces evolve in a particular context, i.e. a marketing environment which is in a constant state of flux, a turbulent and sometimes hostile place within which to devise competitive strategies. All these issues are addressed throughout this book. The philosophy of the handbook is based upon the premise that while strategic marketing decision making is difficult, it is entirely possible to employ structured and systematic methods to enhance competitiveness and deliver superior performance.

Networking

The editors would welcome feedback. Those who read this volume will respond to its propositions and observations in the light of their own experience with their industry/organization background. We, the editors, welcome your responses – all will be acknowledged in the next edition. We are as close as your laptop. E-mail us at:

ceegan@ibm.net
michaelt@market.strath.ac.uk

1

Market dynamics and marketing strategies

Professor Colin Egan, Leicester Business School

 Brainstorming the title for this introductory chapter to *The CIM Handbook of Strategic Marketing* generated fascinating alternatives, some of which were quite clearly unpublishable! 'Survival of the fittest in the twenty-first century' was considered but passed over. Despite this, the Darwinian principle of natural selection it alluded to was readily accepted as a useful metaphor for the contemporary business environment. 'Capitalism – and how to survive it!' came close. The ascendancy of market economics has had a dramatic impact on the nature and intensity of competition and, therefore, the requirement for a strategic perspective on markets and the marketing process. The internationalization of the world economy and the globalization of many industries are accelerating this requirement; markets which were traditionally parochial and cartel-like in nature are nowadays subjected to unprecedented levels of sophisticated rivalry.

In the end the more downbeat title of 'Market dynamics and marketing strategies' was chosen but its sobriety should not be misinterpreted. Markets *are* more dynamic now than ever before in the history of capitalism and the need for a strategic perspective on how to compete successfully in them has never been more acute. This theme of competitive intensity is ubiquitous in the chapters of this handbook and in the business and management literature more generally. We will begin our evaluation of the challenges this context poses with a definition derived from that published by the Chartered Institute of Marketing:

Strategic marketing management is the process of defining, anticipating and creating customer needs and of organizing all the company's assets and resources to satisfy them for the greater profit of the customer and the firm.

Four points are worthy of particular attention:

1. Marketing management is defined as a *process*, i.e. it is to be understood as a central part of the management function, not *peripheral* to it. It also suggests that marketing can be treated in a scientific, systematic and structured manner, a recurring theme in the chapters that follow.

2. The emphasis on *the greater profit of the customer and the firm* stresses that marketing is based on the fundamental principle of mutual gain, i.e. the creation of 'win–win' relationships between the firm and the customer.
3. The statement *organizing all the company's assets and resources* draws attention to the fact that companies have to strive hard for sustained competitive success. They must leverage their marketing assets, stretch their core competencies and exploit all available organizational synergies to prosper in a competitive environment where their rivals will be doing exactly the same things!
4. Note the emphasis on *creating* new needs. This issue provides the dynamic basis of strategic marketing in that it combines managing the present with shaping the future.

In the following section the context that embraces market dynamics is discussed as a precursor to the detailed discussion in this chapter of the foundations of strategic marketing. Cross-references are made to the remaining chapters of the book and caveats are discussed relating to the barriers that prevent the successful implementation of marketing strategies.

Assessing strategic priorities: strategic choice and long-term profitability

The following sections provide an overview with which to consider the two dimensions addressed in this chapter: (i) market dynamics; and (ii) marketing strategies. Market dynamics define the context wherein strategic marketing decisions have to be taken. In most marketing textbooks this context is described as the 'marketing environment', a typical representation of which is provided in Figure 1.1.

This figure categorizes the variables which create the market dynamics into macro- and microelements of the marketing environment. PLESCT analysis (political, legal, economic, social, cultural, technological) provides the starting point for evaluating the principal opportunities and threats which a company has to be aware of. Key considerations in the microenvironment are the market dynamics associated with customers, competitors and intermediaries, although, as we will see, the other factors also play a significant role in facilitation or hindering of effective marketing strat-

egy development. Outside of the shaded area labelled 'Strategic Marketing Management' in Figure 1.1, the firm has progressively less and less control over events and circumstances and, in an extreme case, it is completely at the mercy of the environment. In this Darwinian sense, it must adapt or die. The extent to which this doomladen scenario reflects the real world of marketing management is hotly debated by marketing academics, a discussion that will be encountered throughout the pages of this book. The assertion that a company has much greater control over *internal* decisions relating to product development, price setting, distribution channel management, service provision and marketing communications is less contentious. At the outset of our exploration of strategic marketing management, then, we can safely say that a company should constantly strive to maximize the efficiency and effectiveness of these *internal* decisions and so create a more powerful impact on the *external* environment. What can't be controlled can be influenced and this basic 'marketing fact of life' will form a pervasive theme throughout the chapters of this book.

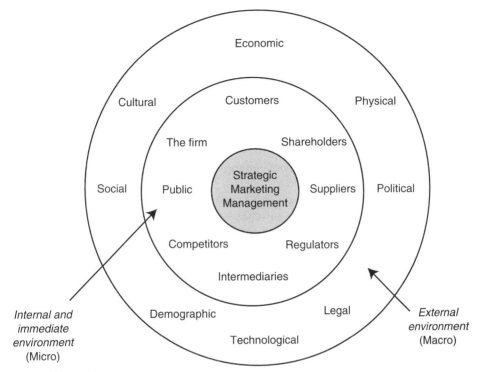

Figure 1.1 *The marketing environment*

Dimensions of strategic decision making

There are four key stages of strategic marketing decision making:

1. Sensing the need for a decision.
2. Choosing among alternatives.
3. Implementing the decision.
4. Evaluation and control.

It may sound overly simplistic but in practice firms often become so tied up with day-to-day operational activities that they rarely fully address the first part of this process, i.e. sensing the need for a *strategic* decision. Similarly, firms tend to pursue 'satisfactory' rather than 'optimal' strategic decisions, i.e. the alternatives from which they choose are quite narrowly defined around a relatively few options, a point addressed further towards the end of this chapter. A detailed discussion of the broad dimensions of strategic marketing planning is given by Malcolm McDonald in Chapter 8. The focus here is on the starting point which is a clear statement

of generic marketing objectives, goals which should be derived from a detailed evaluation of the macro- and micromarketing environment. It is critical, however, that marketing objectives acknowledge, and are consistent with, the other broad objectives which the company is pursuing. It must be emphasized strongly here that strategic marketing plans are not created or implemented in a vacuum. A broad range of factors must be taken into account when developing them.

Ultimately, however, and as indicated in our introductory definition, the principal objective of most commercial organizations is to secure long-term profitability. Figure 1.2 demonstrates this fundamental tenet of strategic marketing.

Titled 'Strategic Priorities', Figure 1.2 gives an overview of the determinants of long-term profitability drivers and it captures the broad range of strategic options available to a company as it considers its current market position and plans for the future. Note first the two generic challenges: (i) Be effective! and (ii) Be efficient!

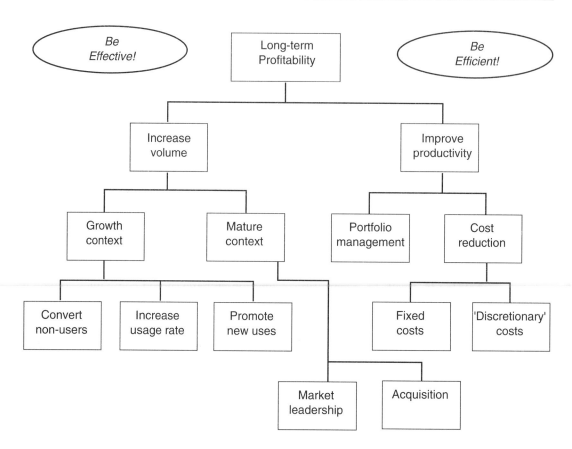

Figure 1.2 *Strategic priorities*

Market orientations: be efficient, be effective!

Peter Drucker provided the inspiration behind this apparently simple polarization of strategic goals. He described effectiveness as *doing the right things* and efficiency as *doing things right*. This is much more substantive than mere semantics. It must be acknowledged that *productivity gains* do constitute a major driver of long-term profitability and it is indisputable that companies should constantly strive to find them. Market leaders, for example, often become complacent and start to make frivolous expenditures, famously described by Drucker as 'Investments in Management Ego'. Having said this, an obsession with productivity can lead to a vicious cycle whereby the only way to improve profitability is to further reduce costs, a scenario which invariably leads to

customer value being eroded. As we will see, a *strategic* perspective on productivity enhancement focuses on portfolio management techniques to ensure that resources are not being squandered on weak products or business units positioned in unattractive markets. Furthermore, innovative solutions to 'trade-off' situations can considerably improve long-term performance. Examples here include flexible manufacturing systems and Just-in-Time inventory management processes.

The most successful firms over the long run are those that are both efficient and effective. Two important issues and one key danger arise from this contention.

First, strategies built on effectiveness must have an *external* focus. 'Doing the right things' requires that customer needs are met fully and in a fashion that is better than rival companies can achieve. Secondly, efficiency requires a sharply critical appraisal of *internal* operating procedures. The key danger relates to shifting market orientations since achieving a consistent balance of efficiency and effectiveness over time is extremely difficult.

The entrepreneurial spirit that underpins the birth of most successful companies is founded on effectiveness, an external focus that recognizes an opportunity to meet identified or as yet unidentified customer needs in a unique way. Over time, however, as companies become large and unwieldy, and as the ownership of the company moves towards 'grey' institutional investors and away from its original founders, the emphasis tends to shift towards efficiency, an internal focus that lends itself to accounting protocols and ratio management. A useful metaphor to illustrate this transformation is to characterize the life cycle of a sheep!

Down on the farm ...

When lambs are born they are masterful entrepreneurs, independent of mind and spirit and totally focused on two key goals: adventure and food. They will go to any lengths to explore new territory and break new ground. They will take their chances with any available sheep to procure milk and no amount of rejection or wayward kicks will deter their persistence or dampen their single-minded enthusiasm. Then they become sheep, one of the flock. Stupid, insular, flock-minded. Watch a group of sheep in a field. For no apparent reason one will take a random walk in a meaningless direction. The rest will follow, because that's what sheep do. So it seems to be with large companies! The entrepreneurial spirit is stifled, the enthusiasm and hunger long gone. In the strategic management literature there is a well-known strategic phenomenon, the industry 'recipe'. The leading companies in the industry all pursue virtually identical strategies, each claiming cost leadership, each claiming differentiation, all following each other in a bland and predictable fashion. For a hundred years the UK brewing industry provided the classic example, carving up the market via distribution and 'competing' with me-too products, me-too advertising and me-too cartel-based pricing. A similar background describes the insurance industry, the retail betting shop industry, the retail banking industry, the automotive industry, and so on. The classic example of the inherent dangers of this paradigm mentality is the Swiss watch business, a sector which created the technology for its own destruction (quartz) and mindlessly stepped aside as the Japanese consumer electronics industry deployed the technology and systematically destroyed the traditional industry.

As you will read throughout the chapters of this book, the follower, me-too type strategies which have served companies so well in the past are wholly inadequate for the competitive conditions which will characterize global markets in the twenty-first century. Returning to Figure 1.2, we can state that the most successful firms will be those who achieve an appropriate balance between being efficient and effective. In the following sections the range of options suggested in Figure 1.2 will be examined, examples given and links to other chapters in the book drawn out. Note that the overall goal is to improve long-term profitability, a fundamental objective of most definitions of marketing. There are two broad routes to enhancing profitability: (i) revenue generation; and (ii) enhanced productivity. Each is now considered in turn, beginning with productivity.

Improve productivity

Strategic marketing has an absolutely fundamental role to play in improving productivity. In a nutshell, enhanced productivity is about getting more for less, maximum output, minimum input. The ultimate strategic goal in market economies is the freeing up of resources so that they can be allocated in product/market segments where they will achieve the maximum long-run returns. It was this premise which gave birth to the strategy consultancy industry, including the Boston Consulting Group, famous for its matrix portfolio of cash cows (market leader, mature market), rising stars (market leader, high growth market), question marks (market follower, high growth market) and dogs (weak competitive position/mature market). The bandwagon rolled, and companies such as Shell and General Electric (GE) of the USA became famous in management circles as much for their portfolio planning techniques as for their oils and bulbs. A critique of the models is beyond the scope of this chapter (see McKiernan, 1992, for a comprehensive yet concise review), the goal here being to identify their role in the strategic marketing process.

Portfolio management

The basic principle of all portfolio management techniques is to ensure that resources are allocated in competitive market positions and withdrawn from segments that consume cash but provide low returns. This is captured in Figure 1.2 in the *portfolio management* category. In Chapter 5 Peter McKiernan provides a range of strategic possibilities for what he describes as 'end-game' scenarios, the point being that careful consideration should be given to otherwise arbitrary decisions regarding portfolio rationalization, particularly with regard to the weaker 'dog' market positions. With this caveat in mind, it can nevertheless be said that most companies have products or business units in their portfolio which drain scarce resources, fail to support other products or businesses and are never likely to make significant contributions to long-term profitability. Business unit closure or product deletion decisions are among the most difficult to take and they are often highly emotive, particularly when associated with failure. For this reason management often avoids the toughness of the decision making. Two outcomes are typical:

1. The product is a constant drain on resources, especially if 'just one more chance' is given to it. A classic example is IBM's OS/2 warp 4. With deeply wounded pride, the company made a

huge effort in late 1996 to recover lost ground against Microsoft's hugely successful Windows 95. The efforts predictably failed and little has been heard of the technology since. Every dollar spent, however, could have been invested more effectively elsewhere;

2. When a company finally acknowledges failure, the assets have no value. A good example of this was Rumbelows, the high street consumer electronics retailer. Originally the rental arm of parent company Thorn-EMI, the division floundered in open competition with discount out-of-town retailers such as Comet and the Dixons group. Furthermore, with its downmarket image, small store size and limited range, Rumbelows couldn't hope to compete with service-focused independents and upmarket department stores such as House of Fraser. Thorn-EMI continued to pump money into the division until its inevitable closure was announced. With little goodwill and no potential buyers, the division was simply closed down, its assets written off. Economists have a phrase to describe this scenario: *sunk costs*, let bygones be bygones. Strategists call it bad management. A good contrast is provided by Bass, who managed to secure £280 million for its uncompetitive (and declining) bingo hall chain, Gala, and £380 million for its betting shop chain, Coral, thus freeing up resources for investment into its growth-based internationalization strategy.

Cost reduction

A company's cost base is typically broken down into two categories: (i) fixed costs; and (ii) variable costs. In the long run all costs are fixed, so the two are combined in Figure 1.2. In recent years the biggest scope for cost reduction has been in outsourcing, i.e. to buy-in goods and services rather than making them or providing them internally. In the early days of outsourcing relatively mundane activities such as canteen catering were targeted. In the current business environment, however, a remarkable array of activities is outsourced, ranging from fundamental R&D technologies to 'rent-a-salesforce'. The following list indicates why this trend has accelerated so rapidly:

- The complexity of economic organization and the need to obtain economies from the division and specialization of labour.
- Technological development and complexity.
- Converging industries, most notably consumer electronics, telecommunications and computing in the emerging 'digital economy'.
- The need to remain flexible and responsive – capital expenditures can be controlled by hiring services that provide 'use' without 'ownership'.
- Time pressures (long lead-time to develop in-house expertise) and lack of available/appropriate internal resources.

There are numerous examples to illustrate the power of outsourcing. A notable case is that of Dell, the computer company which made a hugely profitable entry into an industry which was rapidly becoming a commodity goods sector and which saw low-cost Asian companies being shaken-out and upmarket differentiators such as IBM and Compaq haemorrhaging cash. Dell's formula was simple and highly effective. The value-added resellers used by companies such as Compaq were adding a large service value component, one which many customers no longer required in the 'plug 'n play', 'ready to run' era of personal computing. Dell sold direct, thus bypassing the fixed costs of distribution. The company acknowledged that the market would have to be provided with after-sales service but avoided the heavy cost of a large and expensive field engineer force. Dell's research suggested that most computer problems were people problems, i.e. that they could be resolved on the telephone, and the company set up a low cost, free-for-life 'tel-erepair' service system.

Dell recognized that genuine breakdowns would have to be dealt with rapidly and out-sourced the servicing to Honeywell Bull, a company with an established field engineer division. The fixed cost (field engineers) became a variable cost, i.e. Dell only incurred a charge when the computers broke down. This variable cost was reduced, in turn, by building reliable machines, reinforcing the TQM dictum that 'Quality is Free!'.

Other ways of reducing fixed costs are by using joint ventures, strategic alliances, partnership sourcing and the sharing of distribution assets. In general, as firms narrow down their resource allocation base to fewer and fewer core competencies, there will be many more examples of this type of marketing arrangement. Marks & Spencer focuses sharply on its retailing core competence and outsources its complex fresh food logistics requirements to specialist distribution companies such as Hayes and Excel Logistics; IBM has a joint venture with Toshiba to keep pace with developments in liquid crystal display technology for portable computing; British Steel outsources its information management systems to IBM, and so on.

From a marketing perspective, cost reduction via variable costs is highly contentious. For example, non-marketers typically regard advertising, employee training, service support and product development as variable or, more typically, as *discretionary* costs. These are given a separate category in Figure 1.2. Inverted commas are used to indicate the danger of treating these costs in an arbitrary fashion. Short-term profits can, of course, be greatly enhanced by removing marketing expenditures from this year's budget cycle. The erosion of market position that inevitably ensues, however, can be disastrous for long-term profitability. The following quote from *The Economist* (1990) stresses this point:

Coming out of the recession of the early 1980s, American companies swore never again to 'make the mistake' of cutting their advertising budgets in a slump. Going into the recession of the early 1990s, they are cutting quite sharply.

As Western firms in general were dramatically reducing marketing expenditures

Japanese companies were redoubling theirs, providing the foundations for a decade of prosperity.

In the chapters which follow you will read little about cost cutting, certainly not in any other than a derisory sense. A golden rule of cost cutting is that no costs should be cut which compromise customer value. The reality, of course, is that these are exactly the costs that are the most visible and therefore the easiest to target by managers who only think short term. It must be acknowledged, however, that this myopic management mentality essentially arises because mid-level executives are typically judged by short-term measures. Malcolm McDonald's discussion of the failure of British companies in the face of foreign competition (Chapter 8) pulls no punches in demonstrating this point. As one commentator famously noted, British manufacturing managers have inflicted a chronic dose of *anorexia industrialis* on the country's economic base. Thatcher and Tebbit were highly visible and easy targets for criticism as British manufacturing collapsed in the early 1980s. Meanwhile, the hordes of anonymous 'strategic' decision makers in the large manufacturing and engineering companies which provided the base of the UK's economic wealth quietly closed down the factories and, in many cases, killed the extraordinary brand heritage created by their companies' founders.

Increase volume

Marketing's principal role in driving profitability rests firmly on the *increase volume* side of the model shown in Figure 1.2. Having said this, we must also acknowledge that the market context constrains the strategic possibilities and imposes certain disciplines on marketing strategy development. This relates directly to the 'market dynamics' element of this chapter's title.

Increasing volume in a *mature context* essentially involves a zero-sum game, i.e. one firm's gain is another's loss. Two broad options for profitable success in these mar-

kets are *acquisition* and *market leadership*. A critical appraisal of acquisition-based growth strategies is presented later in this chapter.

The major driver of profitability in mature markets is *market leadership*. Experience curve effects plus the benefits of economies of scale and scope typically accrue to the market leader. The main point here, though, should relate to how market leadership is maintained. Most marketing textbooks refer to the advantages which successful firms build around their core product offering to *secure* competitive edge.

Augmenting the basic product

In his breakthrough study of competitive advantage, Michael Porter (1985) drew attention to factors which firms could manipulate to secure sustainable edge, characteristics he collectively described as 'drivers of uniqueness'. These were broken down into seven broad categories and they are presented here, updated with more recent developments in marketing theory and practice:

1. *Policy choices*, including product features, relative product performance, services provided, the intensity of marketing activities (e.g. the rate of advertising, distribution coverage, etc.), the content of an activity (essential in sectors such as professional services marketing and other 'knowledge-based' sectors), the technology employed in undertaking an activity, the quality of inputs procured for an activity, rules and procedures governing personnel actions (especially critical in all service businesses), the skill, experience and training levels of employees and information systems deployed in controlling business processes.
2. *Linkages*, both within a company's value chain (interfunctional co-ordination) and between organizations (with suppliers, e.g. JIT, EDI, extranet and with distribution channels, e.g. joint selling efforts, EFTPOS, etc.).
3. *Timing*, a critical factor in a context where

product, market and technology life cycles are shortening dramatically.

4. *Location*, especially for sectors such as retailing.
5. *Interrelationships*, including horizontal, vertical and lateral networks (See Chapter 10 for a detailed and contemporary evaluation).
6. *Learning* and *experience curve* effects, embracing the principles of first mover advantage.
7. *Vertical integration*, common in commodity-type sectors where upstream and downstream activities are strongly interdependent.

The important point to emphasize here is that, although most textbook discussions of marketing mix elements focuses on their tactical, controllable and operational dimensions, we must not neglect their strategic context. Furthermore, the examples listed in the seven categories above demonstrate that critical elements of a company's marketing mix are typically derived from external organizations. This can be through facilitative organizations such as advertising agencies or providers of primary functions such as industrial (OEM) suppliers and/or value-adding resellers. Having attained a position of market leadership the real discipline then required is maintaining it. Figure 1.3 shows a range of *entry barriers* which market leaders can draw upon to sustain and exploit their leadership position.

The goal of building a broad range of entry barriers is to protect the first mover advantages associated with innovation strategies (see Chapter 4) and/or to underpin market leadership. Many of the contributions to this book elaborate upon some of the entry barriers identified in Figure 1.3. For example, in Chapter 9 Leslie De Chernatony examines how to build and exploit brand reputation, a process which is fundamental to the segmentation and positioning strategies discussed by David Tonks and Graham Hooley in Chapters 6 and 7, respectively. In Chapter 10 Martin Christopher explores the impact of strategic marketing networks on securing sustainable competitive advantages while in the next chapter David Jobber will provide a

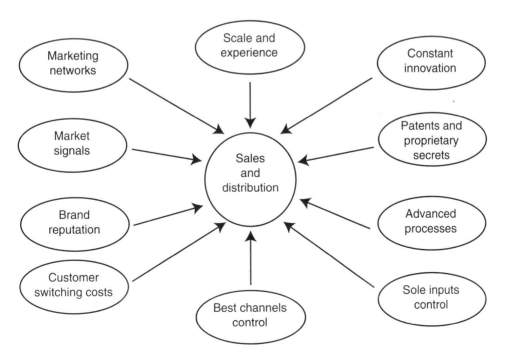

Figure 1.3 *Profiling powerful entry barriers*

strategic perspective on the role of sales and distribution in the marketing process.

It is only by considering entry barriers *in combination* that we can identify *sustainable* competitive advantages, whether these are based on innovation or not. For example, as the world's most profitable airline, BA has attracted a lot of attention from marketing and management commentators, particularly regarding its service and segmentation innovations. In explaining its success, however, does BA's market leadership derive from service-based reputation or a hugely dominant share of landing slots at Heathrow and Gatwick Airports, collectively the world's busiest? Richard Branson's highly innovative airline Virgin Atlantic would have a strong view on this question! Similarly, Microsoft saw off IBM's technologically superior OS/2 Warp 4 with Windows 95 because of its stranglehold on distribution, in this case, a dominant position with the OEM and branded PC companies. There was quite simply no route to market for IBM, regardless of the strength of their brand or however many patents had been filed for OS/2. Note that sales and distribution constitute the focal point of Figure 1.3. Zantac, for example, long dominated the US market for antacid ulcer treatment as a direct function of a powerful sales force, not a superior drug. Similarly, the 'alchopop' phenomenon in the UK was triggered by the entrepreneurial entry of the Australian brand 'Two Dogs' but is now dominated by Hooch, a copycat brand created by Bass to exploit its tremendous distribution clout.

Market signals as an entry barrier is more subtle than the others but can be equally powerful in underpinning market leadership positions. The following quote from Professor George Day provides a good example of how an innovative company defends the fruits of market leadership:

Few consumer goods companies dare attack Procter & Gamble head-on in their core markets. With a long history of aggressive retaliation and clear signals as to how they will react in the future, P&G keeps underlining their total commitment to the protection of their share position.

Like GE, P&G is an aggressive marketing organization, a characteristic it makes abundantly clear to its rivals via *market signals* and *aggressive retaliation*. The key words in the above quote are *total commitment*. Market leaders must be disciplined in defending their competitive advantage and must avoid resting on the laurels of complacency.

In Chapter 3 David Shipley examines how marketing strategies should evolve and be adapted as a market adapts over time. Peter McKiernan examines the particular case of the declining market in Chapter 5 while, in Chapter 4, Egan and Wong examine the role of innovation in strategic marketing management. The material in Chapter 4 should be consulted for a detailed evaluation of strategies for the *growth context* which is shown in Figure 1.2.

Key questions in strategic marketing

There are four broad questions that need to be addressed in strategic marketing management:

1. Where are we now?
2. How did we get here?
3. Where do we want to go?
4. How do we get there?

Each of these is now considered in turn.

Where are we now? *Strategic analysis and competitive positioning*

Before embarking on any strategic plan it is essential to have a clear grasp of the current competitive situation. The starting point is to address the question '*where are we now?*' and there are two key dimensions that must be considered: (i) strategic analysis; and (ii) market positioning.

Strategic analysis uses a range of tools, frameworks and models to evaluate the competitive situation a firm is in at any point in time. Porter's industry analysis (5 forces) and the traditional SWOT (strengths, weaknesses, opportunities, threats) analysis are very useful tools for understanding a company's current competitive situation. Portfolio models such as the Boston Box and the GE multifactor market attractiveness/business position matrix are commonly used to profile the range of competitive positions a company will typically have. Benchmarking is a powerful technique to assess a company's core competencies and the quality of its business processes. 'Best-in-industry' benchmarking studies compare a company's performance with a direct rival in the same industry, e.g. IBM PC company versus Compaq. 'Best-in-process' benchmarking studies break business operations down into process components and identify those companies that excel at each. For example, benchmark 3M on innovation, Procter & Gamble on marketing, Nissan on partnership sourcing, GE on market leadership, Hewlett Packard on human resource management, BA on customer service, etc. Another key aspect of strategic analysis is to understand the company's core competencies. These exist internally (e.g. marketing, R&D, people) and/or externally (e.g. distribution strength, alliances, etc.). Many companies seek to 'stretch' and 'leverage' these marketing assets, thus reducing the risk associated with investing in non-core activities (see Chapter 4 for examples).

Positioning is a critical dimension of market analysis since its starting point is an analysis of customers' perceptions of a range of brands *vis-à-vis* their ideal purchase criteria. Positioning analysis is undertaken after markets have been segmented and attractive segments have been targeted. For many companies the starting point of marketing objective setting is to either reinforce a strong position or to consider a variety of repositioning strategies. In Chapter 6 David Tonks examines market segmentation in some detail while in Chapter 7 Graham Hooley explores the broad range of issues associated with competitive positioning. Essentially, segmentation examines strategic decisions relating to market choice, i.e. *where* to compete. Positioning, meanwhile, examines deci-

sions relating to the tactical aspects of marketing management, i.e. *how* to compete. It is essential to understand the current range of market positions before future directions are determined.

How did we get here? *A historical profile of company history, company culture and industry characteristics*

Many standard texts on marketing and strategy ignore this question but companies should be fully aware of its significance. One of the greatest causes of marketing myopia is that companies tend to become trapped in a mindset of 'the way we were' at the expense of addressing the question of 'the way we *should* be to survive and prosper'.

Company history is a major barrier to strategic change. Analysts and planners should examine those factors that have shaped the firm's development over the years. A key area to address here is to profile the leaders who have played a key role in managing the company's growth and to consider their personalities and influences. The legacy of a charismatic leader can represent a significant barrier to adapting a marketing concept over time. A number of tools are available to facilitate the necessary task of internal evaluation. A *culture audit* reveals the attitudes and behaviours that permeate the organization. A *structural audit* assesses the degree of flexibility and responsiveness within the organization and identifies where rigidities and barriers to adaptation exist. A *political process audit* recognizes that rational marketing strategies can be blocked by 'coalitions of interest' which pursue their own agendas and goals. A *formal power base audit* deals with the more traditional 'organogram' definitions of power, i.e. it looks at the hierarchy to find out who reports to who and identifies which functions dominate in terms of policy direction. The *industry paradigm audit* is of vital importance even though it moves beyond organizational boundaries in its investigation of historical development. As discussed earlier, over time industries tend to conform to a 'recipe', i.e. a generic mix of technologies and routes to market which are relatively homogenous. When new technologies emerge *all* the industry players find it difficult to embark on the appropriate 'paradigm shift' and consequently allow new entrants to enter the market and capture significant market share. The final tool, the *political and economic context audit*, takes the industry audit a stage further and evaluates the broader macroenvironment context within which markets develop. For example, an industry which has traditionally operated within a tightly prescribed regulatory environment will need to adopt a radically different outlook when confronted by the liberalization of markets and the deregulation of industries. The composite insurance sector in the UK provides a good example. Large insurers such as General Accident, Norwich Union and Commercial Union all pursued very similar generic strategies. Deregulation in the Financial Services Act of 1988 caught the industry napping, allowing the subsidiary of Scottish bank, Direct Line insurance, to capture a huge market share.

Where do we want to go? *Strategic plans and time horizons*

There are three different planning time horizons:

1. tomorrow;
2. medium term (3–5 years);
3. long term (5 years plus).

There is also a pertinent caveat, a phrase coined by economist John Maynard Keynes: *'In the long run, we are all dead!'*

From a planning perspective this quote alludes to the limits of long-range planning, especially in a period of market turbulence where long-term forecasts are likely to be extremely unreliable. The solution to this problem is to remain realistic! More practically, scenario analysis and contingency planning can help to deal with uncertainty and, to some extent, shape the future in the company's best interests.

There are many tools available to facilitate marketing planning and these will be discussed throughout this book. In Chapter 8 Malcolm McDonald places these in a structured framework which clearly identifies the detailed tasks which must be undertaken to ensure that marketing strategies are correctly formulated and successfully implemented. The most successful strategic planning tools provide the ability to both evaluate current positions *and* to identify the best way forward. The GE multifactor screen, for example, is often called the 'directional policy matrix', i.e. it combines answers to the question of 'where are we now?' and gives insights into the question of 'where do we want to go?'.

Strategies for growth: examining product/market alternatives

Figure 1.4 illustrates one of the most useful tools for determining strategies for growth. Pioneered by Igor Ansoff, the recognition that competitive advantage arises at the product/market interface provides the cornerstone of an approach to strategic analysis which embraces situational analysis, directional policy, risk analysis, organic development, joint venture identifications, acquisition identification and portfolio management. Although Ansoff's growth matrix slipped out of fashion for a while, this was largely because it became over simplified in basic texts on strategy and marketing. In a later section we acknowledge the factors which underpinned the criticisms and indicate how they should be dealt with. The Ansoff matrix is used in other contributions to this handbook, demonstrating its versatility. Here the framework is used from a strategic perspective, exploiting its simple representation of the product/market interface to explore the complexity of the resource allocation decisions it points to.

The Ansoff matrix has four cells:

1. Current products in current markets
2. New products for current markets

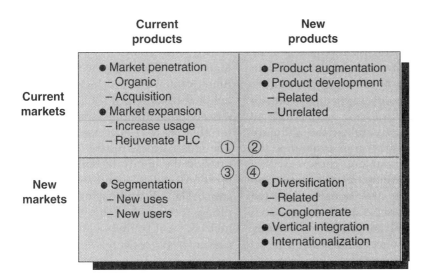

Figure 1.4 *Strategies for growth. Source: Adapted from Ansoff, I. (1987), Corporate Strategy, Harmondsworth: Penguin*

3. Current products for new markets
4. New products for new markets

Cell 1, current products in current markets, offers two broad strategies for growth. First, a strategy of *market penetration* involves taking share from rivals. In a mature market this can be achieved by expanding distribution coverage, offering service enhancements, dramatically reducing prices, increasing personal selling effort, increasing 'share of voice' in advertising, and so on. An important caveat needs to be added here. In the 'zero-sum' game context of the mature market there are rapidly diminishing returns to gaining an extra point or so of market share. Two solutions are available: (i) acquisition; and (ii) market expansion. Most *market expansion* strategies require product development and therefore fall within the remit of Cell 2. Having said this, creating new distribution channels (e.g. direct marketing), reducing costs so that prices can be cut sharply and raising customer awareness of the benefits derived from the product or service can often play a significant role in rejuvenating mature markets. David Shipley in Chapter 3 and Peter McKiernan in Chapter 5 examine the possibilities.

Another way of expanding the market is to encourage customers to increase their usage rate. Frequent wash shampoos are an example of a product category that has been created to ensure that customers wash their hair once a day instead of once a week! Kellogg is currently promoting the benefits of eating cornflakes in the evening, McDonald's now opens for breakfast, working its fixed assets harder. The computer industry is convincing its customers to use more and more memory when a few years ago, 20 MB hard disk storage and 1 MB internal memory was considered a luxury.

Cell 2, new products for current markets, profiles the options for growth emanating from product innovation. *Product augmentation* refers to relatively minor enhancements to the core offering, for example, packaging, warranties, installation service, training, etc. Some of these could act as revenue generators, others will work to enhance the overall perceived value of the total package.

Product development is a major preoccupation for many companies, either because they are undertaking R&D projects or contemplating doing so. There are two broad categories of product development: (i) related; and (ii) unrelated. Related product developments exploit and stretch existing technologies and/or develop new technologies from an existing core competence. Black and Decker, for example, stretched its small motor technology to create a broad range of electric tools for DIY enthusiasts. Similarly, Gillette upgraded its dry shaving technology to launch the Sensor shaving system, a significant improvement on the existing product. The software industry thrives on this approach, consistently enhancing core offerings by improving performance and/or adding new features. Unrelated product development is less common but can be very lucrative since it exploits a company's greatest asset, i.e. its customer base. For example, General Motors, Ford and Marks & Spencer have built substantial financial services businesses on the back of their core product offerings. Similarly, Gillette makes extremely high profits from supporting its shaver systems with a broad range of gels, after-shave balms, deodorants, etc. In Chapter 4 the principles of innovation which underpin these Cell 2 strategies are examined in depth.

Cell 3, *segmentation*, involves taking existing products into new market segments. Two broad strategies are common: (i) finding new uses for existing technologies; and (ii) converting non-users into customers. An example of 'new uses' is the application of CD technology as a data storage and retrieval device for personal computers. The pharmaceutical company Upjohn repackaged a blood pressure treatment as 'Regaine', a cure for male baldness. In its original application a 'nasty' side effect was excessive hair growth! Other pharmaceutical examples include Glaxo Welcome and SmithKline Beecham launching their two anti-ulcer drugs, respectively Zantac and Tagamet, as over-the-counter cures for serious heartburn. Examples of 'new users' include computer companies and software houses targeting segments such as small businesses, professional firms (e.g. accountants, lawyers) and small retailers who currently do not use electronic information processing methods. A similar example is the targeting of home users with multimedia PCs. Gillette made a

hugely successful entry into the previously untapped female wet shave market with the Sensor technology originally designed for men. In Chapter 6 David Tonks explores the principles of market segmentation, examining, among other things, how attractive segments can be identified and targeted.

Cell 4, *new products, new markets*, provides the final growth option. *Diversification* has two broad types: (i) related; and (ii) conglomerate. Related diversification involves stretching core technologies into new applications for new markets. A good example here is Honda developing its motorcycle engine technology into cars, lawn mowers and snow blowers. Japanese companies in general are prolific 'stretchers' of core technologies. Conglomerate diversification involves moving into completely new markets with completely new technologies. Synergies are often claimed to be the major motive, for example, GM-Hughes Aerospace, where a claim was made that core technologies were similar. Another major explanation of conglomerate diversification, i.e. the bringing together of unrelated businesses under one 'umbrella' company, is to spread risk across a broad range of product/market sectors. As we will see below, this strategic approach has come under severe scrutiny in recent years, not least among the investment community.

Vertical integration involves taking responsibility for upstream and/or downstream activities in the supply value chain. A brewer, for example, could own farms for hop growing and bars for beer retailing. A manufacturer of consumer electronics could own a semiconductor business and retail outlets. Horizontal integration was discussed with reference to Cell 1, i.e. a strategy of market penetration via acquisition. Where the technology, competition and customers are well understood then integration could be considered as related diversification.

Internationalization strategies provide a major growth opportunity. The reason why internationalization features in Cell 4 and not Cell 3 (current products, new markets) is because the adaptation requirements with respect to the marketing mix are typically so substantive that a whole new set of competencies are required for successful competitive performance. In Chapter 11 John Fahy explores the characteristics and challenges of international marketing and draws attention to the difficulties encountered in making appropriate adaptations.

The Ansoff matrix is extremely useful for profiling the range of options which are at the core of marketing strategy form the perspective of the business unit, i.e. the product/market interface. It is also a powerful tool to give an overview of the relative riskiness of alternative strategic projects.

Understanding risk and uncertainty

Strategists make a distinction between risk and uncertainty.

Risk describes scenarios where the alternatives are relatively well known and the probabilities of successful outcomes can be calculated. *Uncertainty* describes the 'black box' of the unknown. When dealing with uncertainty every decision is speculative. Returning to the Ansoff matrix we can evaluate the relative riskiness of alternative strategic projects.

Assessing the relative riskiness of alternative projects

Before exploring the issue of the relative riskiness of alternative marketing projects in this section a reference back to the Homily in the preface is worthwhile. The evaluation here carries the usual assumptions about markets and, in the section which follows, caveats with regard to the use of the Ansoff matrix for this type of analysis are offered.

Other things being equal, then, Cell 1 in the Ansoff matrix is the least risky. Companies pursuing this 'growth vector' are dealing with markets they know and technological processes they are familiar with. It must be acknowledged that in mature markets there are diminishing returns to the pursuit of an extra percentage point of market share, and such investments are likely to underperform

alternative marketing projects. Having said this, the knowledge associated with markets and technologies makes Cell 1 a priority for sustained investment, particularly where market leadership is enjoyed.

Cell 2 is riskier, particularly when the product development is in unrelated technologies. There is a myth in marketing that 80 per cent of all new products fail. In reality, 80 per cent of 'new to the market' products are likely to succeed (see Chapter 4 for definitions of new products and methodologies for enhancing new product launch success). What firms often define as new products are, in reality, 'new to the company' products, *not* 'new to the market products'. The greater risk associated with Cell 2 is the risk of *not* bringing the best technological solutions to meet existing customer needs. Cell 2 is the major source of marketing myopia, i.e. defining 'the market' with reference to the company's products rather than customer needs. Companies who do not deliver the optimal solutions to existing customer needs are extremely vulnerable to new entrants and/or technological substitutes. An obvious danger with Cell 2 strategies is cannibalization, i.e. taking revenues from existing products. But if cannibalization is managed effectively the approach can be very profitable. When Gillette launched the Sensor shaving system it took its first tranche of market share from the company's Contour product. But in doing so, it now earns up to 50 per cent more profit *per blade*. The Gillette cannibalization strategy also pre-empted the launch of a rival product from Wilkinson Sword, i.e. it combined both defensive and aggressive marketing strategies.

In general, Cell 3 is even riskier than the previous alternatives. Although the company is stretching its core competencies and, therefore, exploiting its knowledge assets, it may well find itself competing against new and unfamiliar rivals. By example, when Apple launched the Macintosh into the business segment it confronted IBM head on, a rival far more formidable than the computer industry minnows Apple were used to competing with in the home and educational segments.

Diversification dangers

Cell 4 is characterized more by uncertainty than risk, i.e. the probability of successful outcomes is based more on chance than calculation. Markets are unfamiliar and technologies are unknown. Most diversification strategies underperform, especially those that are unrelated. Vertical integration was very common in the past when markets were relatively stable and it was often a very successful approach. In today's markets, however, it can be seen in most sectors that specialization and *dis*aggregation is becoming the norm as companies increasingly focus on their core competencies and 'outsource' more and more business processes. Internationalization strategies are also fraught with peril. In many cases firms think they are pursuing a Cell 3 strategy, i.e. taking their present products to new markets. In practice, however, the adaptation requirements – even for quite basic elements of the marketing mix – tend to take the company well into the realms of uncertainty. A common characteristic of even the most successful domestic firms is 'export myopia', a syndrome which afflicts those companies who fail to deal with the nuances of international markets.

The Ansoff matrix can be used as a tool for situational analysis ('where are we now') and as a directional policy model ('where do we want to be'). It is excellent as a tool for profiling product/market alternatives and it does give a solid overview of the relative riskiness of different strategic options. Having said this, like any strategic planning models, the Ansoff matrix does have limitations, particularly in the way that the theoretical model is used in marketing practice.

There are two key caveats to take into account when using the Ansoff matrix as a tool for risk analysis or portfolio planning. The major issues concern the definition of the two matrix dimensions, i.e. 'market' and 'product'.

When considering 'market', account should be taken of the 'Four Cs', i.e. the *Customer segment*, the *Competition* serving the *segment*, access to distribution *Channels* and the broad set of issues relating to *Communications*. Regarding the latter, brand awareness is notoriously difficult to achieve in new markets, especially when well-established brands already exist. In Chapter 9 Leslie de Chernatony demonstrates, among other things, that building strong brands and establishing a company's reputation is a long-term exercise.

When considering 'product' the real issue to address is the technological processes that actually deliver the tangible goods, i.e. the core competencies that are essential to serve the target market segment. Bic's core competence, for example, is plastic extrusion, a technology it deploys in the mass manufacture of pens and lighters. Canon's core competence is optical lenses; Honda's is internal combustion engines and so on.

These expanded definitions of 'product' and 'market' serve to illustrate why many diversification strategies fail or severely underperform. When taking strategic decisions companies tend to fall into the trap of thinking that 'the grass is always greener on the other side of the fence'. In practice, however, the lush meadows are typically dominated by fierce and entrenched rivals willing and able to defend their territory.

Diversification strategies are often pursued with the intention of exploiting synergies, i.e. a situation whereby the whole is greater than the sum of its parts (normally expressed as $2 + 2 = 5$). In reality, however, these synergies are rarely exploited. The following quote from Professor George Day neatly summarizes the typical assumptions and problems associated with diversification strategies (Day, 1990):

So many diversification efforts fall short of their inflated expectations that the whole notion of synergy as multiplicative combinations of businesses is called into question. In theory, any activity a business excels at can be exported to a new arena. In practice, these prospective synergies are often illusions.

Many studies in organizational behaviour have demonstrated that senior executives tend to be more interested in expanding their 'empires' than in maximizing the profitability of the firm. Financial theory also warns against unrelated diversification, arguing that investors are likely to earn higher returns by building their own portfolio of investments rather than leaving such decisions to a relatively ill-informed board of directors.

How do we get there? *An evaluation of strategic options*

There are three generic options for implementing growth strategies: (i) organic growth; (ii) joint ventures and strategic alliances (including networks); and (iii) acquisitions.

Stretching core competencies: organic growth

Developing core competencies is often described as 'leveraging' or 'stretching' existing assets. A company's marketing assets are broad in scope, typically embracing product technologies, distribution channels and, very often, a highly regarded brand name. Companies such as Virgin, Cartier, Gucci and Dunhill have all grown their businesses by developing branded goods or merely licensing their name. The latter examples give an insight into what should be regarded as a company's major asset: its customer base. Today's sophisticated database technology allows companies to become much closer to their customers and, crucially, to understand their needs and preferences better. It has already been mentioned how Honda stretched its engine technology into motorcycles, cars, lawn mowers and snow blowers and how Black and Decker developed a broad range of DIY tools from its small motor technology. Additional examples abound. Canon stretched its optical technology into photocopiers and laser printer engines. Procter & Gamble uses its distribution channel assets and trade marketing skills to provide a conduit for a broad range of consumable products. 3M stretched its industrial adhesive technology into the now famous Post-it notes and, more generally, exploits its innovation competence in a broad range of industrial and consumer market sectors.

Organic development is similar to developing core competencies but is broader in scope. Essentially, it describes any growth strategies developed within the company and includes internationalization strategies, market segmentation strategies, market penetration strategies, and so on. The acid test of organic development is that the company makes investments in creating as opposed to acquiring business assets. Greater success is likely if the company exploits some existing marketing assets. Gillette, for example, has grown its business massively by supporting its shaver products with a broad range of toiletries. Similarly, Hewlett Packard sells laser and inkjet printers but has enhanced its profitability significantly by becoming a major consumables supplier, for example, ink cartridges, printer paper, laser toner, etc. It has also grown profits by selling 'Service Support Packs' for its hardware products. In a similar vein, a major thrust of IBM's growth in recent years has been based upon the provision of services, training and consultancy.

The two approaches discussed so far have dealt with *internal* development of business activities. Increasingly, however, firms are seeking *strategic alliances* and are creating *joint ventures* to enable them to survive and prosper in turbulent markets, i.e. they are using *external* links to secure competitive advantage.

An evaluation of the role of joint ventures and strategic alliances in marketing strategy development

There is a broad range of reasons why firms are seeking 'strategic partners' to cope with the risks and uncertainties of the contemporary business environment. The number of such alliances has escalated dramatically in recent years and in many cases old rivals are now beginning to collaborate.

The following list profiles the factors that are encouraging firms to increasingly seek *inter*organizational solutions for profitable growth:

- increased competitive pressure in the globalization process and the strategic need to gain scale and scope economies;
- the need to preserve strength in national markets while adapting to the local needs and demands of international markets;
- technology and knowledge transfer flows at ever increasing rates, in the process shortening product life cycles and forcing the need to share R&D activities between companies;
- sophisticated consumers are demanding more and more specialized packages, thus creating a supply-side need to combine the best technology with the best marketing;
- over capacity in traditional industries has led to many businesses repositioning in new markets and seeking partners to aid the transition;
- many groups have become over-diversified, thus forcing a need to restructure;
- threats of take-over or successfully completed take-overs have forced restructuring.

In general, when the marketing environment is discontinuous and turbulent, firms struggle to survive on their own and thus seek help from other organizations. Alliances and joint ventures are also commonly used to bypass otherwise impenetrable entry barriers. In Japan, for example, the distribution system is so complex that it is virtually essential for foreign companies to have a partner with access to marketing channel assets if they are to survive and prosper there. The foundations of the success of Disney, McDonald's and Toys 'R Us in Japan have all been built upon successful partnership strategies.

More generally, the importance of partnership by way of alliances and joint ventures is spreading to many areas of commercial activity. 'Partnership sourcing' and 'relationship marketing' are just two examples of how companies in a supply chain are working

much closer together to bring product to the market. The dramatic growth in 'outsourcing' provides a further illustration of the importance of strong interorganizational relationships. In Chapter 10 Martin Christopher examines the background to the growing use of strategic marketing networks in many business sectors and provides a range of examples to show the versatility of this approach.

A marketing perspective on mergers and acquisitions[1]

The final strategic option in the 'how do we get there' category is *mergers and acquisitions*. Recall from the discussion of the Ansoff matrix that a major problem with market development and diversification strategies is the lack of knowledge about the new competitive arena that the firm is entering. An obvious solution is to acquire this knowledge by taking over or merging with an established firm. A good example is provided by the British retailer Marks & Spencer. For years the company's organic development in North America had delivered very disappointing results. It then acquired the US firm Brooks Brothers to give more extensive market coverage and to allow the company to assimilate local knowledge.

Acquisitions are also commonly undertaken when a firm pursues a strategy of vertical integration. For example, many pharmaceutical companies have acquired distribution assets, particularly in the USA where 'managed healthcare' has given tremendous power to intermediaries in the supply chain. Merck's acquisition of Medco gave it direct access to this market power.

Mergers and acquisitions are also common when an industry is restructuring, a common occurrence when the rate of growth in an industry slows down. Such activity is described as horizontal integration. Another typical acquisition strategy is when a com-

1. This section adapted from Egan, C. (1998), 'Chasing the Holy Grail: a critical appraisal of "the brand" and the brand valuation debate', *The Journal of Brand Management*, 5(4), 227–244.

pany buys related and/or complementary business assets. IBM's acquisition of Lotus would fall into this category.

While there is some evidence for acquisition success the majority of the academic literature suggests that this strategic route typically underperforms. Despite the fact that growth via mergers and acquisitions is fraught with peril it remains a key strategic approach to building a portfolio of businesses. There are three broad categories of problems typically encountered with growth via acquisition: (i) 'quick fix' solutions; (ii) bid-premiums; and (iii) post-acquisition integration.

In many cases mergers and acquisitions are no more than a quick fix solution to recover from previous strategic sloppiness. Acquisitions are also perceived to be an easy way of entering markets and/or acquiring technologies. In practice, however, strategic marketing problems are long term in nature and are rarely solved by quick fix solutions, particularly when the following two problem categories are taken into account.

A second major problem with acquisition strategies is that firms pay too much. Bidding wars are common and stock market speculators are quick to 'talk up' the value of companies. Fuelling the escalating cost is that bidding firms are reluctant to lose 'face' once they have made their intentions clear, i.e. acquisitions can be considered as much a behavioural process as a rational economic strategy. For example, Ford paid in excess of $3 billion for Jaguar, the share price of the British car maker rising $15 per share as GM joined the fray and precipitated an auction environment. In this particular example it is widely regarded that Ford paid a huge premium to secure the Jaguar brand for a product/market segment the company didn't already compete in. Assume the pre-bid market capitalization of Jaguar was $1 billion: does this value the Jaguar brand at $2 billion? Hardly. The joke at the time was that you needed to be rich to own a Jaguar since you needed two in case one wouldn't start in the morning. The Jaguar brand was worth $2 billion to Ford, but it wasn't worth $2 billion in

any objective sense. The impact of such hugely inflated acquisition premiums is more likely to erode shareholder value than add any substantive net worth. Also, a basic tenet of economics is that all resource allocation decisions should be considered with reference to their opportunity costs, i.e. other projects foregone. There is little evidence that Ford executives factored in this cost, a sharp contrast to Toyota's 'Greenfield' development of Lexus.

The bid-premium problem has been particularly acute in the UK and the USA where the liquidity of the equity markets combines with an institutional investment base to create an extremely short-termist climate. By contrast, Japanese strategies, in the main, have tended to focus on stretching core competencies and leveraging established technological and marketing assets. Ironically, when Japanese companies have pursued the acquisition route there have been some spectacular failures, notably Matshushita's acquisition of MCA and Sony's of CBS and Columbia.

From a strategic marketing perspective, the key issue associated with the 'pay too much' syndrome is that funds for core activities such as product development and advertising are often substantially reduced as senior management perceive such investments as 'discretionary costs', i.e. as candidates for quick fix cutbacks. In the highly geared acquisitions of the late 1980s a major drain on marketing resources was caused by the high interest payments which had to be made, a problem which dramatically escalated as interest rates soared and a deep recession ensued. Of course, the first expenditures to be cut were advertising and product development, two key driving forces underpinning market leadership.

Firms often claim that the resources needed for high price acquisitions will be financed from subsequent synergies. Indeed, many acquisitions have cost-cutting agendas as their central rationale. Despite this, the synergies and cost-cutting potential rarely fulfil their pre-acquisition expectations, not least because of the final problem category associated with growth via acquisition. A broad set of *post-acquisition integration issues* plague acquisitive growth strategies. Different cultures, different systems, different remuneration policies, powerful unions and different legal structures are just some examples of the challenges which have to be addressed once an acquisition has been completed. The problem becomes acute with international acquisitions and also when large companies acquire smaller entrepreneurial firms. Furthermore, key staff are often lost, a major concern in 'knowledge-based' industries such as publishing and software.

Major changes are often required to integrate two previously independent organizations. Change is difficult enough to manage *within* an organization, let alone *between* organizations. The time required and the associated costs are often grossly underestimated, thus compounding the 'pay too much' syndrome. Post-acquisition integration tasks are among the most complex management challenges and very often firms have little or no experience of dealing with them.

Over and above the problems associated with post-acquisition integration it is generally acknowledged that 'good' acquisition opportunities are becoming increasingly scarce and/or expensive. Furthermore, this portfolio management approach to business management is very common but, as Professor Michael Porter (1987) has argued, 'is no way to conduct corporate strategy'. Porter's critique has emerged from a synthesis of his earlier observations on corporate strategy and competitive advantage and he makes a distinction between the two streams of thought which have substantive implications for strategic marketing management. Corporate strategy, he argues, 'concerns two different questions: what business the corporation should be in and how the corporate office should manage the array of business units'. Competitive strategy, on the other hand, 'concerns how to create competitive advantage in each of the businesses in which a company operates'.

Since strategic marketing management falls firmly in the latter category it seems clear that performance levels in achieving competitive advantages through implementing competitive strategies will have their limiting factors determined by strategic decisions made by senior management regarding corporate strategy. Indeed, in profiling the distinctive characteristics of competitive and corporate strategy, Porter found that the latter presented the most serious cause for concern, demonstrating that the corporate strategies of most of the companies he studied had dissipated rather than created shareholder value.

Caveats and pitfalls in strategic choice

The difficulties associated with acquisition strategies go some way towards explaining why 'soft' integration approaches such as joint venture creation and strategic alliance formation have become so common. Of course, mergers and acquisitions will continue to play a major role in most companies' growth strategies and the fact there are clear problems with this strategic choice should not preclude its consideration. Once problems have been recognized the marketing challenge is to identify creative solutions, not to hide away from difficult challenges. A simple golden rule applies: however a firm chooses to grow its business the strategic options adopted should not compromise customer value.

A key consideration with regard to question 4 (*How do we get there?*) is to ensure that the organizational issues addressed in strategic planning question 2 (*How did we get here?*) are fully understood. The strategic direction a firm wishes to pursue is often readily apparent. Creating the appropriate organizational structure and culture to successfully *implement* such strategies is a far trickier task, especially when the company and industry history are ingrained in an obsolete 'paradigm'. Before final decisions are taken it is essential that the company's historical 'baggage' is fully understood and that its potentially disruptive characteristics are countered. Nigel Piercy provides an in-depth analysis of the implementation issues associated with strategic marketing management in Chapter 13.

Rethinking marketing strategy in the era of global competition[2]

Michael Porter (1980) has published what has become one of the most widely disseminated books on competitive strategy. In this text he argued that in any particular industry there were three potentially successful generic strategies which could lead to superior business performance. These were: (i) overall cost leadership; (ii) differentiation; and (iii) focus.

Porter has been heavily criticized for presenting these as mutually exclusive options, although the critique itself is often flawed. Porter's principal concern in isolating the three approaches was to warn of the dangers of 'strategic sloppiness', whereby firms achieved neither differentiation nor cost leadership and so ended up being 'stuck in the middle'. Nevertheless, Porter is pretty unam-

biguous on exclusivity of generic strategic approach: 'Sometimes the firm can successfully pursue more than one approach as its primary target, though this is rarely possible'.

Given developments in flexible manufacturing technologies we can readily see the problem with Porter's 1980 contention. The combination of technological breakthrough and management learning has allowed firms to achieve the 'holy grail' of being able to offer higher value at lower cost, an irresistible combination for the well-informed buyer.

Porter's analysis drew heavily on US case studies and, in particular, examined market share and its cost relationships principally in the US market context. If we consider world market share as the key cost driver in the era of global competition a very different picture emerges. In the next section we examine the developing structure of global industries in the 1990s and, in particular, we profile the emerging 'super-league' of innovative global companies. The analysis presented links directly back to the 'strategic priorities' discussion earlier in this chapter, particularly with regard to the discussion of efficiency, effectiveness and the principles of market leadership.

---

2. This section adapted from Egan, C. (1995), *Creating Organizational Advantage*. Oxford: Butterworth-Heinemann.

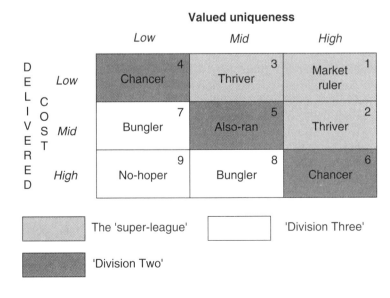

Figure 1.5 *Global competitive positions*

Profiling the super-league: strategic marketing in the era of global competition

The wholesale restructuring of international business has generated a general hypothesis that, early in the twenty-first century, most industrial sectors will be dominated by relatively few global companies. In Figure 1.5 we examine current and projected global competitive positions and, in the process, question the validity of Porter's generic strategies for the contemporary business environment.

For illustration purposes, imagine that Figure 1.5 depicts one global industry with nine firms competing for industry profits.[3] Firm 1 is the *Market Ruler*. It is enjoying the greatest profitability through a combination of higher revenues and lowest delivered costs. Firm 2, a *Thriver*, enjoys similar regard among buying groups but operates from a higher cost base than Firm 1. Its strategic intent is driven by process innovation and it constantly strives to dislodge Firm 1 from its coveted position by driving costs lower without compromising customer value. Firm 3 is also a *Thriver*. While it does not deliver the highest perceived value it does operate from a relatively low cost base, thus enjoying high margins. This company's strategic intent will be marketing mix innovation, i.e. enhancement of product, distribution, communication and customer service offerings to dislodge Firm 1 from its market ruling position. This constant jockeying for position through process and product innovation leads to the emergence of a 'super-league', a group of companies who develop an apparently impenetrable competitive position and enjoy strong profits to defend it. An output of their constant innovations is that they raise entry barriers, for example, through raising the capital intensity of production, securing the best distribution channels, attracting the best human resources, building large sales forces, raising customer service levels and committing to heavy advertising expenditures. Many Japanese manufacturing companies have progressed through this process, creating high capital intensity, focused factories and flexible manufacturing in a constant search for improved productivity and lower costs, a corollary of this process being zero defect quality levels and enhanced speed to market.

Firms 4, 5 and 6 are in the 'Second Division'. Firm 4 is a *Chancer*. Its competitive position is clearly Porter's original cost leader, i.e. the lowest cost producer in the industry or, more likely, it is a company among a group of low cost suppliers. This stance is risky because of the lower margins the company will earn and, more significantly, because of the fragility of this market position. Firstly, it will have to compete on price (because of its low perceived value) while, over time, all markets buy on value, i.e. consumers always seek to maximize their economic utility, a trade-off between value and price.[4] There can be only one cost leader in an industry whereas the scope for differentiation is as broad as managerial imagination. Secondly, other firms in the industry will constantly strive to drive down cost, thus removing Firm 4's flimsy advantage. Porter's original 'danger list' associated with the cost leader position remains applicable today:

- technological change that nullifies past investments or learning;
- low-cost learning by industry newcomers or followers, through imitation or through their ability to invest in state-of-the-art facilities;
- inability to see required product or marketing changes because of the organizational attention placed on cost;
- inflation in costs that narrow the firm's ability to maintain enough of a price differential to offset competitors' brand images or other approaches to differentiation.

3. The terminology and ideas presented in this section were inspired by discussions with Professor David Shipley, Trinity College, University of Dublin.

4. Peter Doyle, (1993), *Marketing Management and Strategy*, London: Prentice-Hall.

Firm 6 we also describe as a *Chancer*. It does have high perceived value but its wafer-thin margins threaten the stability of its position, with other firms constantly striving to raise their own perceived value. The danger for Firm 6 is of drifting into the *Bungler* box or, in the worst case, becoming a *No-hoper*. Firm 6's approach is similar to Porter's differentiation strategy and the potential pitfalls he identified for them remain valid today:

- the cost differentiation between low-cost competitors and the differentiated firm becomes too great for differentiation to hold brand loyalty;
- related to this, buyers sacrifice some of the features, services, or image possessed by the differentiated firm for large cost savings;
- furthermore, buyers' need for the differentiating factor falls, a common occurrence as buyers become more sophisticated and rivals erode the differentiators;
- finally, imitation narrows perceived differentiation, a common occurrence as industries mature.

Firm 5 is quite clearly 'stuck in the middle' in Porter's original sense:

The firm lacks the market share, capital investment, and resolve to play the low-cost game, the industrywide differentiation necessary to obviate the need for a low cost position, or the focus to create differentiation or a low-cost position in a more limited sphere.

Firms 7, 8 and 9 form the rump of our industry, a 'Third Division' who are extremely vulnerable to take-over or extinction. The above scenario is becoming a distinguishing characteristic of global industries.

Time, then, has taken its toll on Porter's original generic strategies, relegating them to a division two of good ideas. The super-league will dominate the global industry and create a virtuous cycle of investment and return. Occasionally a second division player will make a product or process breakthrough and enter the realms of the super-league, but in doing so they will have to raise the stakes and, as in sport, the odds are stacked against their survival chances. Instant relegation beckons!

Strategic marketing planning in perspective ▅▅▅▅▅▅▅

Marketing planning components provide the basis for day-to-day marketing decisions, giving details of the marketing mix programme along with budget requirements, plan schedules and detailed action plans. An effective *operational* plan should be a means to an end, i.e. a tool for ensuring that long-term marketing objectives are attained. In practice, however, the plan often becomes an end in itself, thus leading to a short-term tactical orientation with this, in turn, serving to compromise long-term market positioning strategies. This last point draws attention to the problematic links that exist between strategic marketing and the operational aspects of marketing management practice. Operations management and strategic marketing management are clearly strongly interdependent and, indeed, they actually compete for attention, skills, resources and money. A famous maxim, Gresham's law of planning, summarizes the key challenge: '*If left uncontrolled, operational activity suppresses strategic activity*'.

In Chapter 8 Malcolm McDonald develops a strong critique of this tendency and offers guidelines to restrain its occurrence. Here we briefly evaluate the benefits of strategic marketing planning before concluding the chapter with a discussion of the behavioural challenges that very often confront its successful deployment.

Profiling the benefits of strategic marketing planning ───────────

The following list summarizes the key benefits associated with strategic planning:

- highlights a company's strategic imperatives;
- helps to clarify marketing objectives;
- reduces risk;
- increases the probability of success;
- guides operational decisions;
- provides a strong sense of purpose.

In the first instance, the process of strategic planning forces companies to *highlight strategic imperatives*, i.e. to identify and prioritize key responses to opportunities and threats which arise from the macro and micro business environments. These are the issues that must be addressed in a timely fashion to ensure long-term survival. The more proactive a firm is in recognizing these issues the more likely it is to pre-empt serious threats and/or be responsive to 'strategic windows' (see Chapter 4 for a discussion of these 'windfall' opportunities).

A major benefit of the strategic planning process is that it helps to *clarify objectives*. Clarity of strategic thinking is essential for optimal marketing performance and the formulation of objectives based on a sharp interpretation of business environment dynamics provides the basis for competitive success. The remaining bullet points on the above list all derive directly from clarity in objective setting. In general, the strategic marketing planning process and the information gathering activities which underpin it serve to remove uncertainty and ambiguity from decision making. Where complete information is unavailable the use of strategic planning tools and techniques serve to plug the 'knowledge gaps', allowing assumptions to be made and scenarios to be developed. To the extent that strategic planning reduces uncertainty so it *reduces the risk* of decision making with this, in turn, *increasing the probability of successful strategic outcomes*. In the sense that 'marketing is science' we should use all the research evidence available and the models that the discipline has generated to ensure that strategic prosperity is not left to chance. Earlier in this section the important links which exist between strategy and operations were discussed. A major benefit of

strategic marketing planning is that clearly determined objectives and sharply focused strategies serve to *guide operational decisions*. Where strategic thinking is absent then tactical operations tend to be based on incremental planning, i.e. they are a function of what was done last year rather than what *needs* to be done for the future.

The final point on the above list is less tangible than the others but is an indispensable dimension of marketing strategy success. A key output of the strategic planning process should be a sense of mission, i.e. it must *provide a strong sense of purpose* throughout the organization. Important marketing strategy concepts such as 'shared values', 'strategic intent', 'find a common enemy', etc. all derive from this common, organization-wide' sense of purpose. Komatsu's famous goal to 'Encircle Caterpillar' or Honda's mission to 'Kill Yamaha!' are examples of a clearly determined strategic intent filtering through to create a very powerful organizational mission.

There is a lovely logic to many marketing principles, one that is so easy to demonstrate that the subject and its teachers often come under attack for being peddlers of common sense. The paradox here is that most firms are bad at *doing* marketing, i.e. at outperforming rivals in a sustained and systematic fashion. The next section goes some way to explaining why this is the case.

Is strategic marketing rational? Caveats and reflections

A major criticism of strategic marketing management as a discipline is that it is taught as a normative subject, i.e. it addresses what firms *should* do without considering organizational constraints preventing such rational choices being implemented. Traditional marketing thought is grounded in the *economic* theory of the firm. The realities of organizational life, however, require us to consider *behavioural* theories of the firm in tandem. In this section we examine major contributions to our understanding of the barriers to the successful implementation of marketing concepts.

Planning realities

The discussion of marketing that is presented throughout this book will consistently emphasize that a systematic, structured and, indeed, scientific, approach to strategic marketing management is possible. While this is undoubtedly true, it does not represent the norm in most firms. The following list presents a number of caveats to the proposition that strategy is rational.

- Bounded rationality
- Bounded discretion
- Muddling through

Bounded rationality is a major constraint that leads to 'satisficing' decision-making behaviour, i.e. a satisfactory as opposed to optimal strategic alternative is chosen. According to the economist Herbert Simon, three key characteristics of decision-makers explain why this is the case. First, the habits and skills which executives have developed over the years will deliver reflexive responses to strategic choice, in many cases prohibiting an objective evaluation of the full range of options. Secondly, the values and motives of the decision-maker will have an impact on strategic choice. For example, the executive is more interested in building his or her empire than selecting options that maximize the firm's profitability. Thirdly, it is often the case that the relevant information required to take the optimal strategic choice is unavailable or is not sought by the decision-maker.

Bounded discretion moves beyond the discussion of individual decision-makers to consider the broader context within which alternative strategic options are selected. In this scenario, optimal decision making is constrained by formal rules and policies, moral, social and ethical norms, legal restrictions and, finally, the basic values and culture of the organization.

One of the most memorable observations on strategic management practice was pre-sented by Lindblom (1959) in his article 'The Science of Muddling Through'. The basic idea is that strategies *emerge* over time as managers make a series of relatively low risk decisions that are limited in scope. This partly reflects the fact that different people will bring different agendas to the decision-making forum and, even if they agree on the proposed option, they will do so for different reasons. For this and other reasons, evaluation of strategic alternatives will concentrate on those options that most closely reflect the strategies already being pursued, i.e. strategic choice is *incremental* in nature. Although Lindblom's research was undertaken in public sector organizations, business strategy writers such as Henry Mintzberg and James Brian Quinn have observed that 'emergent' and incremental strategy development is also very much a feature of commercial organizations.

Dimensions of strategic marketing management: strategy, context and process

Figure 1.6 illustrates the three broad dimensions of strategic marketing management.

Strategy relates to the actual decisions which have been taken, i.e. it describes *what* firms are doing. A useful aspect of this model is that it accommodates good or bad strategies, i.e. it allows us to explain successful strategies and/or to analyse weak strategies. All firms have a marketing strategy, i.e. in its most basic sense 'strategy' relates to the resource allocation decisions which have been taken with reference to core competencies, market development and organizational development. This dimension of strategic marketing management is very visible and tangible: it can be observed and evaluated by 'outsiders'. As Figure 1.6 indicates, the strategy is the content of the marketing programme.

Much less visible but of fundamental importance is *Process*. This dimension covers those aspects of marketing management

Figure 1.6 *Dimensions of strategic marketing management*

which lead to the decisions that determine the particular strategy adopted, i.e. it considers *how* marketing strategies are formulated. The general assumption is that this is a rational process which employs tools and techniques of the type introduced in standard marketing textbooks. While this normative approach is desirable and, on the whole, empirically grounded, the *realities* of marketing strategy formulation are very often somewhat different, as we saw in the previous section. In the following sections we acknowledge that the strategic marketing decision-making process is often not undertaken in a systematic way and that there are significant hurdles to the adoption of the marketing concept. We then briefly consider the role of 'internal marketing' solutions to this core implementation problem.

Context demonstrates that marketing strategies are not formulated and implemented in a vacuum. It describes *where* strategies unfold and embraces a broad range of macro- and microenvironmental factors (see Figure 1.1). In an ideal world, context should provide the starting point for marketing strategy development. Many teachers of marketing nowadays introduce students to TOWS analysis rather than SWOT analysis, i.e. they argue that threats and opportunities of the *external* environment should form the basis of strategic analysis, especially in a fast-changing world. A focus on *internal* strengths

and weaknesses reinforces the inward-looking strategies associated with the disease of marketing myopia, i.e. the strengths a company has are no longer relevant. For example, the huge technological advantages enjoyed by Olivetti in precision mechanical engineering processes were useless in a world of software-based word-processing technologies.

For analysts the dimensions of strategic marketing illustrated in Figure 1.6 provide a simple yet comprehensive framework within which to interpret the complexities of managing for competitive success. The basic premise of most of the contributions to this handbook is that firms should adopt the marketing concept, i.e. they should identify customer needs and preferences and subsequently marshal all the company's resources and competencies to meet these requirements *fully* and *better* than rivals. In practice, however, there are substantial barriers to such normative prescriptions.

In the next section these hurdles to successful marketing strategy implementation are evaluated.

Barriers to the marketing concept

In his best-selling book on marketing management, Professor Philip Kotler draws attention to the barriers that prevent full and unfettered adoption of the marketing concept. He identifies three categories of problem (Kotler 1991):

1. Slow Learning
2. Fast Forgetting
3. Organized Resistance

Slow Learning argues that organizations are too cumbersome to correctly and quickly interpret market signals. New threats are not anticipated, opportunities are missed. In many cases, by the time the opportunity or threat is perceived, severe damage may have already been inflicted. The problem is particularly acute when the environment demonstrates discontinuity and when radical change is required. The behavioural forces at play are those associated with bounded rationality which were discussed above.

Fast Forgetting is common among many firms that have, in the past, been highly successful. In essence, firms forget what made them good, criteria that must have included, in competitive markets at least, being close to the customer and differentiated from the competition. The phrase 'success-induced-incaution' gives a clue as to the behavioural issues that underpin this particular hurdle to implementation of the marketing concept. Another word is complacency!

The first two points listed above can be interpreted as demonstrations of a general lack of environmental sensitivity, i.e. as an inability to recognize the *need* for change. In this sense the organization is too passive with respect to its environmental context.

Organised Resistance meanwhile, represents *active* resistance to change. This could take the form of a general preference for the status quo, a fundamental disagreement with the interpretation of market dynamics or structural problems with the implementation of necessary change programmes. As an example of the latter, General Motors struggled to stave off the competitive threat of the Japanese throughout the 1980s largely because unions feared the redundancies and job deskilling which this would entail and consequently pro-actively resisted change, thus reinforcing the company's lack of competitiveness. This is just one example of the many conflicting interests that abound in organizational life. In Chapter 12 this and other 'stakeholder' issues are addressed in detail.

As long as resistance to change permeates an organization there will be little chance of instilling an external, market-driven focus, i.e. adoption of the marketing concept. An important point to note here is that marketing should be seen as a company *philosophy*, not a business *function*.

Marketing is everything and everybody does marketing!

The following quote from Peter Drucker (Drucker, 1974) demonstrates why it is important that everybody in a company 'does marketing', i.e. is committed to an outlook or orientation wherein an external, customer-driven focus permeates the organization:

Marketing is too important to leave to a marketing department. Marketing is so basic that it cannot be considered a separate function. It is the whole business seen from the point of view of its final result, that is, from the customer's point of view.

Drucker's quote is all the more significant in the intensely competitive marketplace of the late 1990s. Customers now have choice and a high propensity to exercise it! Figure 1.7 demonstrates the principle of *market-driven management* alluded to in Drucker's quote.

Everybody in the organization should see the customers as their paymasters and should carefully consider their own role in delivering superior satisfactions. Having said this, without appropriate training and education it is unlikely that an organization will be able to instil the marketing philosophy throughout the company. *External* marketing strategies must be accepted *internally* if they are to be successfully implemented. In the next section the concept of *internal marketing* is introduced as a solution to the serious problem of organized resistance to the adoption of the marketing concept.

Figure 1.7 *Market-driven strategic management*

Internal marketing

The following list illustrates the key goals of internal marketing.

- To ensure that external marketing plans are successfully implemented.
- To combat internal resistance to the adoption of the marketing philosophy throughout the organization.
- To secure the commitment of senior executives to managing a market-driven organization.
- To secure the enthusiasm of personnel who have the responsibility for the implementation of marketing plans.
- To create what organizational theorists describe as an organic company, i.e. one which is responsive, flexible and adaptive within a turbulent business environment.
- To create a marketing culture, i.e. to shape the attitudes and behaviour of all employees, but especially those who operate on the interface between the customer and the firm.

Fundamentally, the objective of internal marketing is to secure effective *implementation* of

external marketing plans. As mentioned in the previous section, there is often intense *resistance* to the concept of marketing within the organization and the fundamental purpose of internal marketing is to play a crucial role in identifying the source of such resistance and to develop and implement action plans to overcome the problem.

Two key groups are the main targets for marketeers who want a marketing programme to be successfully implemented. First, the plan must be managed 'up'. The challenge is to secure the commitment of *deciders*, i.e. senior executives who will be responsible for sanctioning the project and approving the necessary resources. Secondly, the plan must be managed 'down'. Here the challenge is to ensure that the people responsible for *implementing* the marketing programme are fully aware of its objectives and are enthusiastic about its potential success. The importance of securing the commitment and enthusiasm of senior executives, deciders and implementors cannot be emphasized strongly enough. If a marketing strategy cannot be sold internally, it is highly unlikely to succeed in the external marketplace. In other words, if a strategy can't be implemented, it is not a strategy at all.

The last two points on the above list describe more general goals of internal marketing. A market-driven organization can be very *responsive* to changes in the business environment, being quick to stave off threats or to exploit strategic windows. When more people within the organization are included in the marketing process, environmental sensitivity is increased and the company is much more likely to be able to adapt to opportunities and threats in an appropriate way. The final point on the above list relates to company culture and focuses in particular on contact personnel, i.e. those staff who actually interact with customers (e.g. receptionists, sales reps, pilots, chefs, customer service support, etc.). Encounters between customers and employees have been described as 'moments of truth' which, broadly defined, means that the company's reputation is formed by customers' encounters with company representatives. It is absolutely essential that these staff are carefully selected and rigorously trained for the important task of being the external 'face' of the company. Their *attitudes and behaviour* should be shaped to reflect a culture of service excellence. You will recall from earlier sections and will read throughout this book that the provision of superior service is the most sustainable form of differential advantage. Internal marketing is the key to delivering a top class service culture.

To summarize, internal marketing is essential to ensure effective implementation of the external marketing plan. The ultimate goal is to convert *all* internal personnel to an external marketing orientation. The key to success is the identification of key internal customer groups and to understand where resistance to appropriate change is located. Finally, external differential advantage should be translated into a cluster of benefits for the company and the individual and a marketing programme should be developed to achieve the internal marketing goals.

In Chapter 13 Nigel Piercy introduces the concept of strategic internal marketing and demonstrates how this integrates with general issues in ensuring the successful implementation of competitive strategies.

A constant theme throughout this chapter has related to the importance of an external market focus for long-term commercial success, a thesis that permeates the chapters of this book. Paradoxically, however, success itself can induce a self-congratulatory, insular and inward-looking organization.

Reflections on strategic thinking: why nothing fails like success!

Exceptional success often creates a poisonous flow of complacency in organizations. They tend to suffer 'paradigm closure', i.e. they develop a world view which is based on a marketing concept which has been successful

in the past and is myopic regarding what is essential for the future. One of the most remarkable examples of what can happen when there is a failure to recognize environmental threats is that of the Swiss watch industry. It is generally believed that the quartz technology that threatened the precision engineering competencies of watch manufacturing was developed in Japan. In fact, as was mentioned earlier in this chapter, it was developed in Switzerland but was largely ignored.

In addition to 'substitute myopia', Swiss watch companies arrogantly underestimated emerging Japanese rivals (new entrants) and were dismissive of the notion of changing customer needs. The industry collapsed, seriously damaging the Swiss economy. A remarkable recovery was made, with industry consolidation and product innovation (including the 'Swatch' phenomenon) restoring Swiss fortunes. The man responsible for the turnaround, Nicolas Hayek, is determined to ensure that the industry does not repeat past blunders. Speaking to shareholders in the company's annual general meeting he gave the following warning:

The seeds of failure lie in success itself. We must be energetic and tireless, and every day fight against the beginnings of arrogance towards our customers. We must also be energetic and tireless against any tendency to become presumptuous, to rest on our laurels or fall back into old habits. This would be deadly for the enterprise.

For many companies the day-to-day 'hassles' of dealing with customers lead to a view which sees them as liabilities rather than assets. As Hayek indicates in the above quote, this is a sure way to corporate failure. The greatest asset a company can own is a loyal customer base and *everybody* in the organization should have a clear view of how their role enhances the satisfaction that delivers the loyalty. The greater the intensity of competition the more this basic marketing fact of life holds true.

Summary

This chapter has introduced two underlying concepts of the strategic marketing process:

1. The context of marketing, i.e. the market dynamics which are shaped by a broad range of macro- and microenvironment variables. It has been argued that these dynamics are more turbulent, more hostile and, on the whole, more discontinuous than in the past. The extreme intensity of competition in the context of the internationalization of the world economy is imposing a harsh discipline on firms who fail to keep pace with developments.
2. The organizational constraints which prevent companies from being effective, i.e. 'doing the right things' in the words of Peter Drucker. Rather than being flexible and responsive to a turbulent marketing environment many companies, especially large organizations, are riddled with internal functional conflicts and inter-divisional competition for scarce resources.

Despite its relative youth as a discipline, marketing concepts, frameworks and tools are now well understood, both by academics and practitioners. Marketing academics feel quite at ease prescribing what type of strategies will lead to superior competitive performance, a comfort level grounded in a huge base of knowledge relating to what does and does not work. The challenge for practitioners is to create organizations which can actually *implement* market-driven strategies. In this sense, true, sustainable, competitive advantage is organizational in character.

In the contributions which follow, many of the issues raised in this chapter are examined in more depth by contributors who are all experts in the topics on which they write. Each topic explored is done so from the perspective of the individual author and will reflect their scholarship and practical experience. Throughout the book, however, an emphasis on competitiveness and the requirement for a systematic and structured approach to strategic marketing for long-term survival provides a common theme.

References

Day, G. (1990), *Market Driven Strategy: Processes for Creating Value*. New York: Free Press.

Drucker, P. (1974), *Management: Tasks, Responsibilities, Practices*, London: Heinemann Professional Publishing.

Kotler, P. (1991), *Marketing Management: Analysis, Planning, Implementation and Control*. Englewood Cliffs, NJ: Prentice-Hall International.

Lindblom, C. E. (1959), 'The science of muddling through', *Public Administration Review*, **19** (Spring), 77–88.

McKiernan, P. (1992), *Strategies of Growth: Maturity, Recovery and Internationalisation*. London: Routledge.

Porter, M. E. (1980), *Competitive Strategy: Techniques for Analyzing Industries and Competitors*. New York: Free Press.

Porter, M. E. (1985), *Competitive Advantage: Creating and Sustaining Superior Performance*. New York: Free Press.

Porter, M. E. (1987), 'From competitive advantage to corporate strategy', *Harvard Business Review*, May–June, 3, 43–59.

The Economist (1990), 'Here we go again', 1 December, 46.

2

A strategic perspective on the marketing mix

Professor David Jobber, University of Bradford Management Centre

 This chapter examines a key element in marketing strategy development: the creation of an effective marketing mix. First, the classical marketing mix consisting of product, promotion, price and place (distribution) will be described. Each of these 4Ps as they are termed will be analysed from a strategic perspective. Then, the extended marketing mix which was developed for a services context will be considered. People, physical evidence and process are the additional variables that form the extended marketing mix. Finally, the key ingredients necessary for the development of a marketing mix that satisfies customers better than the competition will be analysed.

A key element in creating an effective marketing strategy is the choice of target market. A target market consists of a group of potential customers with similar characteristics (e.g. similar needs or price sensitivities) that a company has chosen to serve. The means by which it serves each target market is through its marketing mix. Although the creation of satisfaction among a group of potential customers involves making dozens of decisions, marketing decision making can usefully be categorized into four strategies: product, promotion, pricing and place (distribution).

These four strategies comprise the *classical marketing mix* otherwise known as the 4Ps. The objective is to blend the four strategy elements into a consistent package that satisfies the requirements of the chosen target market(s) better than the competition and in a way that meets the company's objectives be they profit or non-profit orientated.

Although understanding how to create individual product, promotion, price and distribution strategies is important it is the combination and integration of these strategies into a coherent whole that determines tʰ

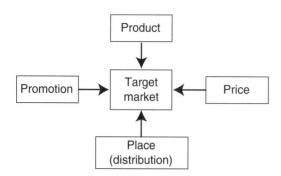

Figure 2.1 *The classical marketing mix*

degree of marketing success. Figure 2.1 summarizes the discussion so far. The key point is that each target market will have a uniquely blended marketing mix. As companies decide to target different groups of potential customers (market segments) so the marketing mix will need to be modified to accommodate their differing characteristics.

Practical tip

Identify the target markets that you serve. Each target market will differ in some way that affects the marketing of products and services to it. To what extent has your company developed a unique marketing mix that matches customer requirements better than the competition? Try to think of ways of better matching customer requirements.

A major consequence of the discussion so far is that companies need to understand the needs of their customers before they develop their marketing mix. Customer needs can be economic based such as performance, reliability or productivity, or psychologically based, for example the desire for a certain self-image, a quiet life or convenience. The link between customer needs and the marketing mix is shown in Figure 2.2. Through personal experience and/or marketing research, marketing managers must gain a full understanding of key customer requirements and provide the product, at the right price, where and when customers want to buy it and communicated in a manner that creates awareness and the right image for the target market segment. Without such an understanding, making marketing mix decisions will be like shooting in the dark with little hope that the resulting mix will achieve its objectives.

The next section examines in turn the key elements of the classical marketing mix to identify some of the key influences on decision making. Analysing each marketing mix element separately should not mislead the reader into believing that decisions can be made without reference to each other element in the marketing mix. As we shall see when exploring the key issues in developing an effective marketing mix, co-ordination and integration are necessary to blend together all of the 4Ps.

Product strategy

A product is anything that is capable of satisfying customer needs. Both goods and ser-

Customer needs

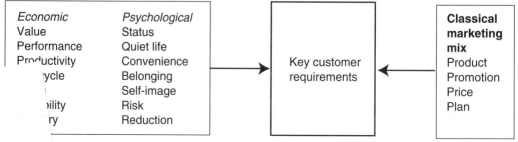

Customer needs and the classical marketing mix

vices are products with goods being tangible (e.g. a computer) and services intangible (e.g. a medical examination). Branding is the process by which companies distinguish their products from the competition. Brands are created by creating a distinctive name, packaging and design. Branding affects perceptions since it is well known that in blind product testing people may fail to distinguish between two products yet when the same test is carried out with the brands identified clear preferences become apparent.

Product strategy is the choice of what goods and services to market and the management of the chosen products over time. It also involves decisions regarding brand names, warranties, packaging, the services that should accompany the product offering, and how to build brands.

| | Products | |
	Existing	New
Existing Markets	Market penetration	Product development
New	Market development	Diversification

Figure 2.3 *Product growth strategies: the Ansoff matrix*

Practical tip

You may regard the product you supply as being essentially tangible. However, your customers may choose between competing offerings on the basis of accompanying services. Is there anything you could do to improve the services you supply with each product?

The choice of what goods and services to offer on the marketplace, from a strategic perspective, can be greatly aided by what has become known as the Ansoff matrix (see Figure 2.3). By combining present and new products, and present and new markets into a 2 × 2 matrix, four product strategies are revealed. As such it is a useful framework for thinking about the ways in which growth can be achieved through product strategy.

Market penetration: brand building is one way of achieving greater penetration of existing markets with existing products. Brand building can be achieved by such means as improved quality, better communications and positioning, and providing consistently high levels of brand investment rather than

making short-term cut-backs. The objective is to make existing customers more brand loyal (brand switch less often) and/or make new customers in the same market begin to buy our brand. Higher penetration can also be achieved by increasing brand usage through frequency (e.g. wash hair more often) or quantity (e.g. two teabags instead of one).

Product development: growth can also come from developing new products for existing markets. New products giving extra benefits based on new features can be the motor for increased sales and market share. Japanese camcorder manufacturers are consistently upgrading their products by adding features.

Market development: existing products in new markets is a third option. Moving into new international markets may be feasible or into new market segments.

Diversification: this strategy involves the development of new products for new markets and consequently is the most risky of the four options. Levi's ill-fated move into suits was an example of a diversification strategy that failed, whereas Heinz' development of a new service 'Weight Watchers' to support a new product range (low-calorie foods and drinks) proved successful.

A second key product strategy issue is how to manage brands and product lines over time. A useful tool for thinking about the changes that occur while a product is on the market is called the *product life cycle* (PLC). This states that a product passes through four stages: introduction, growth, maturity and decline (see Figure 2.4).

Practical tip

Think of ways in which your existing products could be marketed to new groups of customers. Also consider new products for existing markets and new products for new markets. Thinking in this way may reveal new opportunities for growth.

Introduction: when first introduced on to the market a product's sales growth is typically low and losses are incurred because of heavy development and promotional costs. Companies will be monitoring the speed of product adoption and if disappointing may terminate the product at this stage.

Growth: this stage is characterized by a period of faster sales and profit growth. Sales growth is fuelled by rapid market acceptance and, for many products, repeat purchasing. Profits may begin to decline towards the latter stages of growth as new rivals enter the market attracted by the twin magnets of fast sales growth and high profit potential. The personal computer market is an example of this during the 1980s when sales growth was mirrored by a vast increase in competitors.

The end of the growth period is often associated with *competitive shake-out* whereby weaker suppliers cease production.

Maturity: eventually sales peak and flatten as saturation occurs, hastening competitive shake-out. The survivors battle for market share by product improvements, advertising and sales promotional offers, dealer discount and price cutting; the result is a strain on profit margins particularly for follower brands. The need for effective brand building is acutely recognized during maturity as brand leaders are in the strongest position to resist the pressure on profit margins.

Decline: sales and profits fall during the decline stages as new technology or changes in consumer tastes work to reduce demand for the product. Suppliers may cease production completely or reduce product depth. Promotional and product development budgets may be slashed and marginal distributors dropped as suppliers seek to maintain (or increase) profit margins.

The PLC has a number of uses for product strategy. First, the stages emphasize the need to review marketing objectives and strategies in order to adapt them to changing market and competitive conditions. For example, *build* objectives which aim to increase sales and market share may be sensible in the

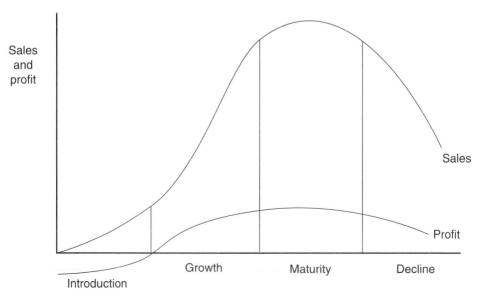

Figure 2.4 *The product life cycle*

introduction and growth stages. Once a product enters maturity, however, the costs of building may exceed the likely returns leading to a *hold* objective. In decline, products may be managed for cash until their eventual demise. Product strategy may also change over the product life cycle. The introduction of a new product may necessitate a basic design which becomes more elaborate during growth and maturity in an attempt to differentiate it as competition becomes more intense. Consistent with a 'managed for cash' objective, the product line may be rationalized during decline.

The PLC also emphasizes the need to prune product lines and replace them with new products. The danger is that management may become emotionally attached to star products of yesterday and be reluctant to terminate them. The PLC underlines the fact that management needs to face the harsh realities of commercial life and that most products will enter the decline stage eventually.

Third, the concept warns against the danger of assuming growth will last forever. It is easy during the growth phase to become over optimistic about future prospects leading to over investment in production facilities. The PLC reminds managers that growth will tend to be followed by maturity. Unfortunately, a limitation of the PLC is that it does not predict when growth will turn into maturity.

Finally, the PLC stresses the need to analyse the balance of products that a company markets from the perspective of the four stages. One danger is that a company with all of its products in the mature stage may be generating profits today but as they enter the decline stage future prospects may look bleak. The PLC provokes management into considering products as an interrelated set of profit-bearing assets that need to be managed as a portfolio.

Before leaving the PLC we should note a few limitations. First, the concept does not predict when products will move from one stage to the next. Second, stylised marketing objectives and strategies based upon the placing of products in particular stages may be

> ### Practical tip
>
> Examine your products from the point of view of the product life cycle. How many appear to be in the introduction, growth, maturity and decline stages. Too many products in the latter two stages, and too few in the first two stages may mean healthy profits now but an uncertain future.

misleading. Strategy should take account of all of the relevant factors not just the PLC stage. Finally, not all products pass through the four stages. Fads (e.g. skateboards) 'rise like a rocket and then fall like a stick' and classics (e.g. Cadbury's Milk Tray) have survived for decades with no indication that they may enter the decline stages. As such the PLC should be regarded as an aid to managerial decision making and a stimulus to strategic thinking. As a prescriptive tool it is undoubtedly blunt. Marketing management needs to consider all of the relevant issues before drawing up product marketing plans.

Promotion strategy

Promotion strategy is concerned with decisions which focus on the methods of communication with target customers. Key methods include advertising, personal selling, sales promotion (incentives to the consumer or trade which are designed to stimulate purchase), publicity, direct marketing, exhibitions and sponsorship. Marketing managers need to create the most effective promotional blend from these tools.

The starting point is not to ask 'should we spend an extra £200,000 on advertising or the sales force?'. A more fundamental question needs to be asked: what is our competitive positioning? This requires the choice of a target market (*where* we compete) and the creation of a differential advantage (*how* we compete). Once these decisions are taken more specific promotion decisions can b

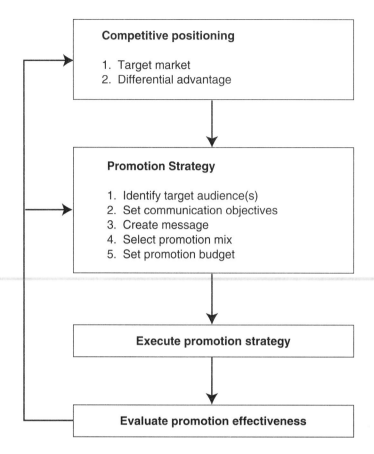

Figure 2.5 *Determining promotion strategy*

made, and the strategy executed (see Chapter 7 for a full discussion of competitive positioning). This sequence is shown in Figure 2.5. Each of the promotion strategy issues will now be examined.

Identifying the target audience(s): clearly the more we know about our target audiences the better we can communicate with them. Three questions that need to be asked are:

● Who are they?
● What are their choice criteria?
● What do they think of us?

nizational and consumer mar-
uying decisions are in the hands
on-making unit. The initiator
process of considering a purchase.
cer attempts to persuade others in

the group. The decider has the power to make the final decision regarding which product to buy. The buyer is the person who conducts the transaction including making payment. Finally, the user is the actual consumer of the product. The implication is that the key people taking on these roles need to be identified and communications directed at them since each has a role to play in the decision-making process.

An interesting fact about the decision-making unit is that different people who play differing roles may be evaluating supplier's products along completely different choice criteria. For example, in an organizational purchase a purchasing manager may be much more price conscious than an engineer who may be more concerned with technical issues. The choice criteria used by people need to be understood so that the correct

---

> ### Practical tip
>
> Think of a product which you market. Identify the target audience and the people who play each of the above roles in the decision-making unit. How do you communicate to them? Consider new ways of reaching them in a more cost-effective manner.

message can be communicated. For example, a salesperson would spend more time discussing cost efficiency to a purchasing manager, and more time discussing technical issues with an engineer. Choice criteria, therefore, influence the selection of the appropriate message to send to individuals.

It is also useful to know what the target audience think of our company and its products *vis-à-vis* the competition. This can reveal misconceptions which may be corrected through communications. For example, a significant proportion of the target audience may believe our product's performance to be inferior when in reality it is superior. Independently generated performance statistics could be communicated through advertisements, direct mail, salespeople, etc. to correct the misconception.

Setting communication objectives: promotional tools can be used to achieve a wide range of communication objectives. Awareness is an objective that can be achieved through all promotion tools although advertising is often used when the target audience is large. Stimulating trial is another objective which depends upon awareness but may also influence the choice of message. For example, Jameson, the Irish whiskey brand ran an advertisement which claimed 'You'll never know until you've tried it. Jameson, the spirit of Ireland'.

Communicators have a major role to play in positioning brands in the minds of target customers. Advertising is often used to generate positive associations (Aaker *et al.*, 1992) such as BMW 'The Ultimate Driving Machine' and Galaxy 'Why have Cotton

When You Can Have Silk'. Such perceptual positioning needs to have a clear message and to be credible so that people notice and retain the association. Once the association has been established the objective may change to reminding and reinforcing. Top-of-the-mind awareness and favourable associations are vital to maintaining market leadership of such brands as McDonald's and Coca-Cola.

> ### Practical tip
>
> Commission a market research survey to find out the positive and negative associations related to some of your key products/brands. You may be surprised at the number of misconceptions held by some people. Communications can be used to send the correct signals if the problem is acute.

Relationship building is another possible communication objective. Direct marketing can be used to develop, sustain and exploit personalized relationships with customers. Salespeople should be trained to foster close relationships rather than simply attempting to close the sale.

Creating the message: the choice of message will be influenced by what is important to the target audience (choice criteria) and the differential advantage of the product. The message should be clear, credible and consistently sent to the target audience. Television messages are often built upon the single-minded proposition since the brief duration of commercials mean that sending multiple messages may reduce the clarity of the communication. The flexibility of using salespeople to communicate with customers means that they can change the emphasis of the message they convey depending on the choice criteria of each individual in the decision-making unit.

Three processes are used by people to reduce the enormous number of messages into a manageable quantity. First, *selective attention* is used to screen out messages that are not meaningful or consistent with our experiences and beliefs. We are more likely to notice messages that relate to our needs and those that provide surprises such as a price reduction. Second, *selective attention* is the process where people distort messages according their existing beliefs and attitudes. Messages may be interpreted in ways very different to the communicator's wishes. By presenting evidence to support a sales message the scope for distortion is reduced. Finally, *selective retention* means that only a proportion of messages are retained in memory. Messages that are in line with existing beliefs and attitudes are more likely to be remembered than those that conflict. It is, therefore, important to understand those beliefs and attitudes for messages not to be too out-of-line with them. The exception is when convincing evidence can be drawn upon to support the new message. Under those circumstances it can be highly memorable.

Selecting the promotion mix: four factors have a major bearing on choice of promotion mix elements (e.g. advertising, sales promotion, publicity, personal selling, sponsorship, direct marketing and exhibitions). First, market size and concentration influences choice. If the market is large and geographically dispersed advertising or direct marketing is likely to be more cost effective than personal selling. However, for small, concentrated markets, personal selling may be feasible. Second, when customers require complex technical information, personal selling may be required. Where the key ingredient is brand image, advertising may be preferred. This often means that industrial goods companies spend more on personal selling than advertising while consumer goods companies often do the reverse. Third, resources can also affect choice. Where resources are limited the expense of a national advertising campaign may rule this promotional tool out. Other less expensive tools such as sales promotion or publicity may be preferred.

Finally, companies using a *push* strategy where the emphasis is on selling into channel intermediaries may opt for personal selling and trade promotions. Those favouring a *pull* strategy (where communication is direct to consumers), advertising, and consumer promotions may be preferred. By reference to these criteria marketing messages may select an appropriate blend of promotion mix tools. When implementing the strategy they must

---

Checklist 2.1

1. Do not under-emphasize the need to understand the target audience in terms of who they are, their choice criteria and how they perceive our company and brands *vis-à-vis* the competition.
2. Set clear communication objectives. These will guide later decisions.
3. Create a message based on what is important to the target audience. It should focus on our differential advantage.
4. Ensure that the promotion mix communicates a consistent message.
5. Do not use formula-based promotion budget methods. Take new communication needs into account.

ensure that the message projected is consistent between tools to provide a strong message to the target audience.

Setting the promotional budget: four methods may be used to set promotional budgets. First, the *affordable method* considers how much the company can afford and bases the budget on that figure. Second, the *percentage-of-sales* method bases the budget on a specified percentage of sales. This method keeps promotional expenditure in line with sales revenue changes. However, it pays no account of what might be the optimum budget given a set of communication objectives. The third method is called *competitive parity* and is based on how much competitors spend on promotion. An advantage is that it discourages price wars but the assumption that competitors know what is the correct promotional expenditure is weak.

Finally, the *objective and task* method begins with setting objectives, establishing the tasks required to achieve them, and estimating the cost of conducting the tasks. While this is a logical approach to promotional budgeting, in practice working out the relationship between objectives and tasks can be problematic. In reality, setting the promotional budget is a political activity with different functions within a company arguing their case (Piercy, 1987). One group may use 'affordable' arguments to keep the expenditure down, while another may argue that new communication requirements demand an increase in the promotional budget.

Pricing strategy

Pricing is a major element of the marketing mix because it is the only one that directly generates revenue. It costs money to design, develop and manufacture products, advertise and sell them (promotion) and transport and distribute them (place). Marketers, therefore, need to be very aware of the issues which affect pricing strategy.

Shapiro and Jackson (1978) discovered that three methods are used by managers to set prices. The first approach is to set prices on the basis of costs. The more a product costs to develop, manufacture and market the higher the price. Two methods tend to be used: full cost pricing (where all costs are taken into account) and direct cost pricing (where only direct costs which vary with output are used). These internally orientated methods suffer from a number of limitations (Fisher, 1976). First, full cost pricing leads to a price rise if sales fall as the same overhead (fixed costs) is being divided into smaller unit sales. Second, full cost pricing requires a sales estimate to be made before price is set. Since demand usually depends on price this a severely flawed procedure. Third, it focuses on internal costs rather than customer's willingness to pay. Fourth, direct cost pricing (where only direct costs such as labour and materials are taken into account) leads to losses in the long term since full costs are not covered. Finally, although it can be useful when the objective is to fill spare capacity, full cost pricing gives no indication of the best price attainable when business is buoyant.

Practical tip

Do you price any of your products or services using a cost-based method. Identify those which are priced by full or direct cost pricing. Are you really making the most profit potential from them? Could the market stand a higher price for some? Is there potential for advantageous market share gains by reducing the price of others? If so consider making price modifications.

The second approach used by managers to set prices is competitor-orientated pricing. This can take two forms: going-rate pricing and competitive bidding. When a product is not differentiated from the competition (e.g. a particular grade of coffee bean) the supplier may have to take the going-rate (market) price since customers may be unwilling to pay more for an identical offering. Such 'commodity' situations are anathema to a marketing-orientated approach which implies the search for competitive advantage. The message is that going-rate pricing should be avoided by differentiating through some other element of the marketing mix whenever possible. Better service, distribution, and communication may be possible and thereby justify a higher price. Some companies market their products through a competitive bidding process. Potential suppliers bid for a contract by quoting a price which is confidential to themselves and the buyer. Although statistically based competitive bidding models have been developed most suffer from unrealistic assumptions and data inadequacies. A key ingredient of pricing under competitive bidding situations is an efficient information system which provides data on past successful bid prices of competitors. Such information can be a useful starting point for future bids.

Practical tip

If you market products or services through sealed bid competitive tendering consider training your salespeople to find out from buyers the successful bid price for each contract. Store the information on computer so that it is available as input when you are next asked to tender for a contract.

Both cost-based and competitor-orientated pricing suffer from only taking a restricted number of issues into account. Marketing-orientated pricing, the third approach, has no such limitation. Marketing managers need to take into account a range of factors when setting prices. A key consideration is the value customers place on the product/service offering. The higher the value (which is linked to the extent of its differential advantage) the higher the price which can be charged. Price–quality relationships need also to be considered since customers' perceptions of quality can be influenced by price. This means that demand for a product can be lower with

a low price if quality perceptions are impaired. However, the focus of this chapter is on strategic perspectives of the marketing mix so we shall now examine in more depth the influence of two strategic influences on pricing strategy. These are positioning strategy and the setting of strategic objectives.

Positioning strategy: product positioning involves the choice of target market (*where* we compete) and the creation of a differential advantage (*how* we compete). The differential advantage needs to be clearly communicated to the target audience to create a distinct position in their minds. These decisions need to be taken before price is set (see Chapter 7).

Often management has a choice when selecting the target market for a new product. A usual scenario is the identification of a lower volume, price insensitive market segment and a higher volume price sensitive segment. In the ice-cream market, for example, a premium segment exists which has lower volume than the lower priced high volume market for standard quality ice-creams. Clearly the choice of target market has a fundamental effect on the price that can be charged. Similarly by creating a differential advantage within the chosen segment there is scope for setting a higher price than competitive offerings. In these ways, positioning strategy influences pricing strategy and places constraints on the price that can be charged. Setting price without reference to positioning strategy is fundamentally flawed since both target market and differential advantage are major influences on the pricing decision.

Practical tip

Choose three products or services that your company supplies. Identify their target market segments. Commission a marketing research study to identify the extent of their differential advantage over the competition (if any). Readjust prices to reflect the extra (or lower) value that your products/services provide.

Strategic objectives: the pricing of existing products should be consistent with strategic objectives. The value of setting them for products was established by the work of the Boston Consultancy Group (1977). The three strategic objectives that affect the pricing decision are *build*, *hold* and *harvest*. By explicitly deciding upon the appropriate strategic objective, pricing strategy and management reaction to competitor moves will be facilitated.

In price sensitive markets, a build objective implies a price lower than the competition. Our reaction to competitors who raise their price would be to not follow them if at all possible. Conversely a price fall would be matched. Where the strategic objective is to hold sales and/or market share, the appropriate pricing strategy is to maintain or match price relative to the competition. With a hold objective, a price rise or fall by a competitor would be matched.

A harvest objective focuses on the maintenance or enhancement of profit margin even though this may result in a sales and/or market share reduction. Products bound by a harvest objective will have premium prices. If the competition cut prices there would be much greater reluctance to follow them than if a build or hold objective were being used.

Conversely, price rises would be quickly followed.

Practical tip

Begin to think of your products/services in terms of the three strategic objectives: build, hold and harvest. Assign an objective to each of them (note that it may make sense to use product lines to do this). Manage your pricing strategy including reactions to competitive moves in line with your chosen strategic objective. You will find future pricing decisions much easier.

Developing clear strategic objectives aids pricing strategy for existing products as the above examples show. Marketing managers should resist the temptation of simply asking 'How much can I get for this product?'. The process should start by asking for new products 'How is this product going to be positioned in the marketplace?'. For existing products the question 'What is the most sensible strategic objective for this product?' should be asked. Once these issues are identified the pricing decision can be taken.

Checklist 2.2

1. Calculate costs but do not slavishly set prices on the basis of them.
2. For new products, determine the positioning strategy (choice of target market and extent of differential advantage) before setting price.
3. For existing products, set strategic objectives (build, hold or harvest) for each product or product line. Make each pricing decision consistent with the strategic objective.
4. Consider commissioning market research to measure the value which your products or services give to customers over the competition. This will be useful information when considering price changes.

Distribution strategy

Distribution is the place element of the marketing mix. Products need to be available in the correct quantities, in convenient locations and at times when customers want to purchase them. Suppliers must not only consider the needs of their ultimate customer but also the requirements of those organizations called channel intermediaries who help with the distribution of products to consumers. The choice of the most effective channel of distribution is a key question in distribution strategy. Other important issues in distribution strategy are selecting the most appropriate level of distribution intensity and the degree of channel integration (see Figure 2.6). Each of these will now be considered.

Channel selection: it is important to group the factors that affect channel selection. The most basic decision is whether to use channel intermediaries or supply consumers direct. Market, supplier, product and competitive factors will influence this decision.

Market-based considerations are buyer expectations and needs, distributor availability and demands and the location/concentration of customers. Buyer expectations may shape channel selection. Buyers may prefer to buy in a particular type of shop and in a convenient location. Failure to take these into account can lead to marketing failure. Buyers' needs may extend beyond the supply of the product to include information, installation and technical assistance. In some situations, distributors may have the expertise and commitment to fulfil these requirements. In others, the supplier may be in a better position to undertake these activities particularly when it has the resources to provide local service centres.

Unavailability or unwillingness of distributors to carry a product obviously influences the channel decision. In such circumstances direct distribution may be the only option. Where distributors are available the profit margins and commissions expected by them will also affect their attractiveness as intermediaries. Finally, the location and geographic concentration of customers also affects channel choice. Direct distribution is more likely when customers are more clustered, few in number and buy large quantities. Conversely a large number of geographically dispersed customers who buy small quantities is likely to favour the use of intermediaries.

A key supplier factor is the availability of resources. Lack of financial and/or managerial resources may mean that the expense of recruiting a sales force and setting up regional offices or servicing facilities is prohibitive. Distributors or sales agents may have to be used instead. Where suppliers lack the required skills to sell and service customers, intermediaries may be the only feasible alternative. Also, wide product mixes may make direct distribution cost effective whereas a narrow mix may require the services of a sales agent or distributor. Finally, direct distribution may be favoured when suppliers require control of operations. Using powerful intermediaries such as supermarkets may result in loss of market power on the part of suppliers.

Product issues also affect channel selection. Large complex products which require close personal contact between supplier and customer are often sold direct. The high prices charged also mean that direct distribution is economically feasible. The short supply chains required for perishable products also favour direct distribution as do bulky or difficult to handle products if there are storage or display problems.

Where the competition control traditional channels of distribution, a supplier may go direct or set up its own distribution network.

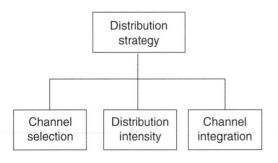

Figure 2.6 *Key elements of distribution strategy*

Suppliers should not unthinkingly accept traditional ways of distributing products.

Practical tip

Have another look at the way you distribute your products and services. Are there more innovative approaches that would give you a competitive advantage in the marketplace?

Distributive intensity: this requires the choice of intensive, selective or exclusive distribution. *Intensive* distribution involves the use of all available outlets to gain saturation coverage. Where consumers are reluctant to go to another outlet if the first does not stock the product intensive distribution can make sense.

Selective distribution involves the use of a limited number of outlets in each geographical area. Distributors prefer this method to intensive distribution since competition is reduced. The advantages to the supplier are clear working relationships and lower transportation costs. It is feasible when people are willing to shop around, thus making intensive distribution unnecessary.

Where only one channel intermediary per geographical area is used, *exclusive* distribution is practised. Restricting outlets lowers the

customers' bargaining power when buying a car for example. Close working relationships can be built up between supplier and intermediary. A distributor may demand exclusive distribution as a condition for stocking a product. Alternatively, suppliers may agree to exclusive distribution only if the distributor agrees not to stock competing products.

Channel integration: suppliers also need to consider the degree of channel integration they require to distribute their products effectively. Three options are: (i) independence between supplier and intermediary; (ii) franchising; and (iii) channel ownership by the supplier. Independence means that the supplier usually has no formal control over the intermediary and conflicts of interest can arise. However, where the supplier or retailer dominates the market with brand leaders it can hold considerable power which results in an administered marketing system. These days many retailers such as Marks & Spencer control the 'supply chain' system.

A franchise is a legal contract which specifies each member's rights and obligations. The supplier usually provides marketing, managerial, technical and financial services in return for a fee. The franchisee provides the energy and motivation of a locally owned outlet. Conflicts can still occur when the supplier may believe the outlet is not providing satisfactory standards of service or when the

---

Checklist 2.3

1. Review your channels of distribution for cost efficiency and customer effectiveness.
2. Do not slavishly accept traditional channels. Innovation can lead to competitive advantage.
3. Consider different levels of distributive intensity. For example exclusive distribution may be a luxury you can no longer afford.
4. Would you like more formal control of your channels or would this lead to less flexibility? Consider alternative levels of channel integration.

franchisee believes that marketing support is inadequate. A franchise is a form of a contractual vertical marketing system.

Channel ownership clearly gives the supplier control over the activities of the intermediary and provides a ready-made outlet for its products. However, purchasing intermediaries such as fast-food restaurants can be expensive and stretch the capabilities of management too thinly. However, the establishment of such corporate vertical marketing systems can be successful as in the oil industry.

The extended marketing mix

The analysis of the marketing mix so far has examined the classical 4P framework: product, promotion, price and place (Booms and Bitner, 1981). However, work in the services marketing area extended the marketing mix to include three additional variables – people, physical evidence and process (see Table 2.1). While the classical 4P framework is capable of accommodating these issues (for example, process could be considered part of the product offering) the importance of *people* (often representing the service), *process* (how the service is delivered to the customer) and *physical evidence* (the surroundings in which the service takes place) are so crucial to success in services marketing that they warrant individual treatment. Each of the additional variables will now be analysed.

People: one of the characteristics of services is the inseparability of production and consumption. Unlike the production and consumption of many physical goods (e.g. cars, televisions, soap powders) many services are produced and consumed simultaneously (e.g. a holiday, haircut, music concert). The people involved in the production of the service are an integral part of the satisfaction gained by the customer. The service must not only be provided at the right time and in the right place but also in the right way. This means that the selection, training, controlling and rewarding of staff who come into contact with customers is of immense importance to the achievement of high levels of service quality. Even in restaurants where the production staff do not come into direct contact with customers their presence in the same building means that their behaviour needs to be controlled: noise from the kitchen can be very distracting to those eating a meal. Without training and control, service providers can be variable in their performance leading to inconsistent service quality. A key issue is that the service provider adopts a customer-first attitude rather than putting their own pleasure and convenience in front of customer satisfaction.

Service providers also need to recognize that customer satisfaction can be impaired by the presence of other customers in the service interaction. This is so because the consumption of many services such as restaurant meals, music concerts and hotel accommodation takes place in the presence of other customers. The minimization of potential sources of inter-customer conflict needs to be achieved. For example, non-smoking areas in restaurants, air and rail travel need to be provided.

Table 2.1 *Elements of the marketing mix*

- Classical marketing mix
  - Product
  - Promotion
  - Price
  - Place

- Extension to the classical marketing mix
  - People
  - Process
  - Physical evidence

Practical tip
Consider your view on employing service staff. Are you too cost-focused? Low pay in service operations may result in lower service quality. Observe how your service providers perform. Supermarkets employ mystery shoppers to evaluate service quality. Identify training needs to improve standards of service at the customer interface.

Process: service providers need to consider how best to deliver the service to customers. For example, the process of delivering food to customers is very different in a restaurant to a fast-food outlet. The degree of self service needs to be thought out. Some customers prefer to serve themselves because it is quicker than waiting for the service to be provided by someone else. Many hotel breakfast bars are now self service for this very reason. Service providers must consider ways to reduce queuing (a common complaint in many banks). A trade-off needs to be made between the costs of employing extra staff and the length of queues. Flexibility in deploying staff to reduce queuing at peak periods also reduces the problem. Many supermarkets employ part-time staff at peak periods. Other service providers use differential pricing to encourage consumption during off-peak periods. Lower priced theatre seats for afternoon performances is one example. If queuing and delays cannot be avoided service providers should consider how the waiting can be made more tolerable by providing seats and free refreshments, for example.

Practical tip

Re-evaluate the delivery process that your company uses. Is there greater scope for customer involvement? What are the major problems as seen by your customers? What do they value highly? (channel resources here). What is of less importance to them? (take resources from here). Talk to customers or use marketing research to see your service operation from their viewpoint.

Physical evidence: this refers to the surroundings in which the service is provided and any tangible factors that facilitate the performance and delivery of the service. For example, the dress of waiters and the decor of the restaurant are used by customers as tangible clues to service quality. Since colour has meaning it can be used to create the ambience

desired in a service environment. For example, a feeling of calmness is provided by the use of pastel colours in passenger aircraft. Occasionally there can be conflict between efficiency and effectiveness in service operations. The desire to create greater potential output (efficiency) may tempt a restaurant owner to add more tables even though this leaves only the minimum of gaps between them.

Practical tip

Reassess the service environment you provide. Maybe the decor is a bit jaded. Perhaps the dress of your front-line service people is in need of replacement. Consider the impression it gives to your customers. Perhaps the expense will be worth it creating the right ambience for your customers.

Creating an effective marketing mix

Whether the 4 or 7Ps' framework is appropriate a key strategic consideration is the need to mould a marketing mix that creates higher customer satisfaction than the competition. Table 2.2 shows the guidelines for creating a marketing mix that brings strategic success. Customer needs must be understood and the marketing mix designed to match them. Effort should be put in to create a competitive advantage. Consistency between the elements of the marketing mix should be achieved. Finally, the marketing mix should take account of corporate resources (Jobber, 1995).

Understanding and matching customer needs: in Figure 2.1 the link between customer needs and the marketing mix was shown. Customer needs can be economic or psychological. Economic needs include high performance, high productivity, low life cycle costs, reliability and fast delivery. Psychological needs include status, the desire

Table 2.2 Guidelines for creating an effective marketing mix

1. Understand and match customer needs
2. Create a differential advantage
3. Blend the marketing mix variables to produce consistency
4. Ensure that the marketing mix matches corporate resources

for a quiet life, convenience and the feeling of belonging to a social group. The needs of individuals define their choice criteria which are used to evaluate one product offering against another. Consequently, the starting point for developing an effective marketing mix is to understand customer needs: only then can a marketing mix be developed which matches those needs and is successful in the marketplace because it reflects the choice criteria used by customers.

Creating a differential advantage: the usual way of creating a differential advantage is by marketing mix manipulation. Customers buy benefits not product features so it is important to design products that confer the desired customer benefits. By understanding customer needs and choice criteria, suppliers have an insight into the benefits customers are seeking. The key is to create a marketing mix that provides a greater bundle of benefits than the competition are offering. The result is a differential advantage, a reason to buy from us rather than our rivals. It can be derived from all elements of the marketing mix. Better product performance can lead to lower costs, higher revenues and enhanced status. Better distribution through location can provide more convenience and lower costs. More creative promotion can result in stronger brand personality and a better trained sales force can mean superior problem solving. Finally, lower prices can give better value, and higher prices can promote an image of superior quality. It is the search for differential advantage which separate the world-class marketers from the also-rans.

Blending marketing mix variables: each marketing mix variable should not be treated as a standalone element. They should be considered together to form a consistent blend. We have already discussed the need to take into account price–quality relationships. Price, then, should reflect where the product is to be positioned in the marketplace. Superior quality products may benefit from having a price that reflects that superiority. The promotional element of the marketing mix should be consistent with positioning strategy and the individual strands of promotion – advertising, selling, sales promotion and public relations – should themselves be sending a consistent message to customers. The selection of distribution channels should also reflect the overall positioning of the product. High class products (e.g. cosmetics) are usually sold in exclusive outlets to reinforce their upmarket positioning.

Matching corporate resources: the marketing mix must reflect the financial and managerial resources of the company. Whereas Laker Airlines had insufficient financial resources to compete with British Airways and TWA in a price war, Virgin Atlantic Airways' resources were bolstered by the resources of the Virgin Group of companies including the cash generated by the sale of Virgin Records. This gave them greater muscle in the marketing mix battle against British Airways. The marketing mix must also take account of the skills and competencies of the company's personnel. For example, a marketing mix strategy requiring excellent sales management and selling skills may be too ambitious for companies who are deficient in these areas. An alternative strategy, for example using the skills of sales agents or distributors, may be required as a result.

Summary

This chapter has provided a strategic perspective on the marketing mix. Each of the classical marketing mix elements – product, promotion, price and place (distribution) – have been analysed to show their contribution to effective strategy. The realization that this framework in services marketing may lead to the neglect of three additional variables – people, process and physical evidence – promoted the establishment of the extended marketing mix framework. Finally, this chapter provides guidelines for auditing the effectiveness of a marketing mix strategy. Does it match customer needs in a way that creates a differential advantage? Is it blended to produce a consistent package? Does it match corporate recourses (both financial and managerial)?

References and further reading ■

Aaker, D. A., Batra, R. and Myers, J. G. (1992), *Advertising Management*, New York: Prentice-Hall.

Booms, B. H. and Bitner, M. J. (1981), 'Marketing strategies and organization structures for service firms', in Donnelly, J. H. and George, W. R. (eds), *Marketing of Services*, Chicago: American Marketing Association, pp. 47–51.

Fisher, L. (1976), *Industrial Marketing*, London: Business Books.

Hedley, B. (1977), 'Boston Consulting Group approach to the business portfolio', *Long Range Planning*, February, pp. 9–15.

Jobber, D. (1995), *Principles and Practice of Marketing*, Maidenhead: McGraw-Hill.

Piercy, N. (1987), 'The marketing budgeting process: marketing management implications', *Journal of Marketing*, **51**(4), 45–59.

Shapiro, B. P. and Jackson, B. B. (1978), 'Industrial pricing to meet customer needs', *Harvard Business Review*, November–December, pp. 119–127.

3

Marketing strategies for growth, maturity and decline

Professor David Shipley, Trinity College, University of Dublin

 The rate of market growth is a major determinant of sales volume, competitive conditions, marketing strategy selection, costs, revenues, cash flows and profits. These relationships are modelled in the product life cycle (PLC) concept that holds that the sales of products pass through stages of growth, maturity and decline to cessation. Further and importantly, the changes in demand affect competitive conditions and other factors so that different strategies are required for the various life-cycle stages.

The PLC concept has attracted criticism as well as support but it is now solidly established as an important tool for market analysis and planning. Most marketing textbooks include a discussion of the concept and offer strategy prescriptions for the various demand stages. However, typically these are only generalizations. Moreover, most texts fail to stress the strategic significance of life-cycle changes while others overstate it and many do not provide an adequate coverage of the limitations of the concept. In particular, usually little detail is provided about the important influences on strategy selection apart from life-cycle conditions and very limited attention is given to the problems, risks and barriers to implementation of the strategies associated with the various life-cycle stages.

This chapter briefly reviews the PLC concept, its criticisms and its strategic importance. However, the main purpose of the chapter is to review the range of strategies associated with the PLC stages and to examine the external market and internal organisational conditions in which they are appropriate and the risks and problems that they can entail. The objective is to alert managers to the need to assess the full range of options and strategic influences before selecting strategies for growth, maturity and decline.

The product life cycle concept

The PLC concept was brought into the main-stream marketing literature by Levitt (1965) and is now widely documented and familiar to most marketing managers. For this reason, only a very brief review of the various stages is presented here to provide a setting for what follows. The classic PLC model is usually depicted as consisting of the four stages of introduction, growth, maturity and decline. The marketing literature depicts these as having different market conditions requiring firms to adopt different marketing behaviours. The following summary of these is drawn from the work of Doyle (1976), Hooley (1995), Jobber (1995) and Wesson (1974).

- **The introduction stage**: here sales are low and growing only slowly since awareness, interest and trial-buying rates are low among customers and channel members. However, rivals are few as second movers typically delay entry until the market shows signs of growing to viable levels. First movers usually incur negative cash flows due to low revenues and the need for heavy investment in product refinement, capacity expansion and marketing. At this stage the prime marketing objective is to expand the market by encouraging awareness, interest and trial. Hence, the strategy typically includes heavy trade and customer promotion while price is high if a skimming strategy is employed or lower than the eventual long-term level if a penetration strategy is used.
- **The growth stage**: in this phase, innovative customers have adopted the product and new segments enter the market so that sales and positive cash flows grow strongly. However, new rivals enter the market and competitive intensity increases. All firms pursue market growth strategies while first movers strive to hold market share and second movers seek to build it. Product quality is improved, product differentiation increases, promotion is heavy, channel incentives and coverage grow strongly and prices are lowered or raised depending on the initial price strategy.

- **The maturity stage**: at this stage repeat purchasing is established but all or most segments have been targeted so that sales reach a plateau at a high level. The number of rivals is at its maximum and market share fighting is intensive as the only means of growth. This often causes industry profits to decline as firms compete heavily on product differentiation, price, promotion and channel incentives. Often, some rivals are shaken-out of the market that enables profits to recover at least partially.
- **The decline stage**: here sales and industry profits are declining as customer needs change or as buyers switch to alternative products. These factors induce suppliers to reduce marketing expenditures sharply and market withdrawal occurs allowing the last one or two firms to enjoy considerable profits, particularly when the rate of decline is gradual.

These kinds of generalized descriptions are intuitively appealing. Moreover, it cannot be disputed that products do experience life cycles. In reviews of the PLC literature, much of it empirical, both Rink and Swan (1979) and Mercer (1993) concluded that life cycles do exist. However, there has been considerable debate among academics about the managerial applicability of the concept and whether it has a role to play in marketing planning. Some of the arguments are now presented.

Uses of the PLC concept

The PLC concept has two important applications for strategy planners. First, it does predict that market changes are inevitable. For example:

- sales growth ends when all customer segments have been saturated and all product uses have been exploited;

- decline occurs sooner or later;
- product sales ultimately cease;
- levels of competitive intensity vary;
- costs, revenues, cash flows and profits vary across the PLC stages.

For these kinds of reasons, the PLC concept forewarns managers of the necessity for constant vigilance and a willingness to apply strategic flexibility. Specifically, the adherence to the PLC concept helps managers to recognize that:

- ignoring the potential for market changes is dangerous in the extreme;
- adoption of a positive approach toward being strategically flexible is essential;
- short-term tracking and long-term forecasting of market conditions are necessary to identify and predict variations in sales trends and competitive intensity;
- planning and implementing contingency strategies to meet market changes is vital.

The second reason why the PLC concept is helpful to strategic planners arises because firms operate with multiple products in multiple markets or segments. Imbalance in the firm's portfolio of these product markets can prove disastrous. For example, if all of a firm's product-market segments were in, say, the introduction or early growth stages, it would not be possible to finance their growth out of retained profits. Similarly, if all of its products were in the maturity stage the firm would generate healthy short-term profits but encounter major problems of future continuation when maturity gives way to decline. Thus, effective portfolio management is required to ensure that firms have a balance of product-market segments in the late growth and maturity stages to generate sufficient short-term profits and others in the introduction and early growth stages to provide for their eventual replacement and the firm's long-term profitability. Meanwhile, some of the short-term profits from the more mature product-market segments will be allocated to fund the development of those in

the early PLC stages. Without an understanding of the PLC concept a balanced product-market portfolio would only materialize by chance.

Criticisms of the PLC concept ▄▄▄▄

Critics contend that the PLC concept has inherent flaws and limitations and these can involve major practical problems for managers.

First, there is no clear consensus about what the word 'product' refers to in the term 'product life cycle' (Doyle, 1994). It could be viewed as the product technology (for example, a motor car is a solution to the need for transportation), the product class (small saloon cars), the product form (small, hatchback, mini) or a brand (Ford Fiesta hatchback). Clearly, the demands for these product concepts are interrelated. However, they are affected by different driving forces and do not necessarily reach demand turning points simultaneously. For example, a brand could be launched, grow, mature, decline and die within a PLC stage of even a product form. It follows that, owing to their interrelatedness, managers can enhance the quality of strategic planning by tracking the PLC profiles of the product concepts defined at different levels of aggregation. The PLC patterns of all of them can be easily displayed on a single chart to enhance planning at all levels of product aggregation.

The second criticism of the PLC concept is that it is not possible to generalize about the shape of the PLC because such shapes vary across markets. Empirical studies have identified many different PLC patterns (Dhalla and Yuspeh, 1976; Rink and Swan, 1979). Examples include:

- fad products such as Ninja Turtles and the Rubik Cube exhibit an explosive growth curve, virtually no maturity period and very steep decline;
- seasonal products such as raincoats, soccer balls, fireworks, agricultural pesticides and outdoor paint are

characterized by seasonal peaks and troughs across all the stages of the PLC;

- some products follow a cycle–recycle pattern in which product sales grow, mature and decline and then repeat the entire profile, although sometimes at lower or higher sales levels. The sales of tea declined sharply after the introduction of instant coffee which was easier to prepare but then tea sales were rejuvenated with the advent of tea bags. Similarly, men's hairdressers experienced hard times when the Beatles pop group popularized the fashion of long hair in the 1960s. Later, when short hair became fashionable, the hairdressing business expanded again;
- many products exhibit a scalloped growth pattern in which growth occurs, early maturity is reached and then growth recurs. This can be repeated many times as new product uses and new segments are exploited before sales eventually settle into long-term maturity or decline. Examples include plastics, ceramics, man-made fibres and personal computers.

Many other PLC patterns have been identified. Nevertheless, the classical shape often does apply (Neidell, 1983) and rather than to invalidate the concept, the variety of patterns observed merely emphasises the need for careful sales monitoring and forecasting so as to identify turning points to guide appropriate strategic responses.

The third criticism of the PLC concept is that there are great difficulties in predicting the length of each stage and when turning points are about to be reached (Dhalla and Yuspeh, 1976; Hooley, 1995; Mercer, 1993). This arises partly because sales curves are seldom smooth. Rather, they contain numerous short-term peaks and troughs of varying magnitude. PLC analysis is primarily concerned with plotting the long-term sales trend but a particularly pronounced short-term aberration from this could confuse managers and cause them to conclude, incorrectly, that a long-term turning point had been reached. This could then lead to an inappropriate change in strategy. A related complication is that since the duration of stages cannot be predicted with certainty, plans may be made or resources allocated for periods that are longer or shorter than is strategically judicious. This problem can be alleviated somewhat by studying the life cycles of similar products in other markets. However, this can be misleading as PLCs are generally shortening and no two markets have identical characteristics (Doyle, 1994).

The fourth criticism of the PLC concept is the most powerful. It is concerned with the causal relationships among the stages of the PLC, the marketing environment and the marketing strategy. Adherents to the PLC concept accept that the stage of the PLC determines the strategy that should be adopted. This view is too strong and ignores the effects of environmental forces and the marketing strategy on the levels of sales within a PLC stage and even on the determination of which stage the PLC is actually in.

The stage of the PLC is only one of the environmental variables against which marketing strategies are formulated. Moreover, other environment factors strongly affect the shape or existence of a PLC. For example, the end of the Cold War caused the PLCs of many armaments products to go into swift decline. Similarly, social changes fostered the growth of fast-food restaurants while the introduction of facsimile machines spelled the end of the PLC for the telex industry for which they were a technological substitute. Yet further, even within a given PLC stage, other environment forces can affect the choice of strategy or the level of performance. For example, in a market exhibiting strong growth, supporters of the PLC concept would expect substantial profits to be available and urge firms to pursue growth strategies. However, profitability could be sharply constrained or negative if ferocious competition was occurring between multiple suppliers most of which were challenging for long-term market leadership. Any weaker firms lacking sustainable differential advantage might even conclude it to be strategically judicious to exercise a market withdrawal strategy.

Similarly, rather than the PLC stage suggesting the type of strategy to be applied, the marketing strategy can strongly influence the nature of the PLC stage and its shape, height and duration (Wind and Claycamp, 1976). For example, unless firms pursue innovation strategies there will be no PLC; the choice between a skimming versus a penetration price strongly influences post-launch sales growth; rapid product differentiation can steepen and extend the growth curve while over-pricing by multiple suppliers could even accelerate the onset of decline.

It needs to be recognized, therefore, that the stage of the PLC is not the exclusive determinant of strategy selection. Nevertheless, since demand elasticities and trends have important effects on marketing conditions and performance, it remains an important factor.

Determinants of strategy selection

The choice of a strategy from the range of alternatives available is affected by the current stage of the PLC and by its expected trend and duration. However, none of the strategies discussed in this chapter is exclusively appropriate for only one stage of the PLC although some of the strategies are obviously inappropriate for particular stages. While matters pertaining to the PLC are important influences on strategy selection it is essential that each in a wide range of other influences are also fully evaluated before forming strategic choices.

As is made clear elsewhere in this book, the prime imperative in strategy planning is to achieve and maintain a tight strategic fit between the marketing environment, the company's capabilities and the chosen strategy. Indeed, a key responsibility of strategy planners is to manipulate a *fit* between these three variables by selecting target markets in which key success factors can be met effectively by the firm's capabilities. Since the market environment is beyond the firm's control, when it changes the strategy and the organization need to be adapted or an alternative target market be selected so as to restore strategic fit.

In this context, the prime determinants of strategy reside in five sets of environmental and organizational factors.

- **Demand factors**: these include the nature of customer needs and suppliers' selection criteria, customer responsiveness to suppliers' offerings and whether needs are currently satisfied wholly, partly or not at all. Aspects of buyer behaviour are also important such as the degree of customer bargaining power, the nature of the buy class, the composition of the decision-making unit, usage and loyalty rates, etc. Finally the prevailing level of demand and how this and the other demand factors are expected to change over what remains of the PLC.
- **Competitive factors**: How many rivals are there, who are they and are there any dominant players among them? What are their objectives, key capabilities and strategies? What are their differential advantages and are these sustainable? Who competes on cost and who on differentiation? How are the various rivals vulnerable? What are their competitive intentions and how could all this change in the short, medium and long term?
- **Environment factors**: these include and impact on demand and competitive condition. They are usually grouped into macro and micro factors. The former includes economic, political, demographic, socio-cultural and technological factors. Apart from the behaviour and power of customers and direct competitors, microenvironment variables include the power of suppliers and channel members and the potential for and potential impact of new entrants and technological substitutes. Strategy selection depends not only on these conditions in the short term but on what they are expected to be like in the future.
- **Company factors**: strategy selection is clearly dependent on the corporate effectiveness of the company insofar as

these may concern growth versus stability, aggressive versus defence, high versus low risk, long-term versus short-term profits and so forth. A major consideration in this context concerns the achievement of a balanced product-market portfolio as discussed in relation to the uses of the PLC concept. Strategies must be formulated for the growth of some businesses and for the eventual replacement of those businesses currently managed for profit which finance them. Similarly, strategy selection should also take account of product interrelationships. These exist, for example, when the production, marketing and distribution of different products generate synergies or when the sales of one product depend on the availability of other products which are complements for them such as pistols and bullets. Also, of course, strategy selection must be realistic. That is, decisions must be based on the capabilities that the company has or can viably obtain. Key issues include the firm's finances, technological assets, image, human resources, information systems, costs, market shares, etc. Above all, perhaps strategy must be realistic in terms of the firm's potential market position with respect to sustainable differential advantage.

- **Risk factors**: potential strategies and performance objectives should always be weighed against the potential risks entailed. Financial and competitive failures are obvious types of risks. Other risks are less obvious. One such risk involves the possibility of damaging a strong image as may occur, for example, if a food producer launched a pesticide product or a university business school withdrew from the MBA market! Another form of risk becomes manifest when entry barriers forestall a growth strategy or a market withdrawal strategy is prevented by high exit barriers (Aaker, 1995). Finally, perhaps the least acceptable risk is that the company implements a strategy that prevents it from matching its opportunity costs. That is, the company selects a strategy that does not

represent the best use of its scarce resources. Examples could include a company continuing its presence in a market when more attractive new opportunities exist, or a firm redirecting its assets from a declining market which is later rejuvenated with profit levels exceeding those available in the new opportunity.

Strategies for growth, maturity and decline

Irrespective of the debate surrounding the value of the PLC concept, companies do need to launch new products and to manage them through periods of sales growth, maturity and decline. Strategies for innovation are addressed in the next chapter. In the remainder of this chapter a range of strategies for the PLC stages of growth, maturity and decline is discussed. It should be noted that while some of the strategies are mainly appropriate for one particular stage, most can have applications in two or even three of them depending on the conditions involving the factors discussed in the previous section.

Market expansion strategies

This option is the most appropriately deployed in the growth stage of the PLC. However, it also has useful applications during maturity for firms that are able to identify new segments. The strategy can involve attracting new customers into the market, building the usage rates of existing customers or exploiting new applications for the product.

Targeting new customers

This involves serving new segments. Various approaches can be adopted:

- **Geographical expansion**: this can be attempted by targeting new countries. For example, international growth has been successfully pursued in recent years by many retailers including Aldi (Germany),

Benetton (Italy), Ikea (Sweden) and Dixons (UK). Alternatively, geographical expansion can occur within a country as shown by Asda and Scottish and Newcastle Breweries in their drives into southern regions from their strongholds in northern England.

- **Targeting later adopters**: customer segments seldom enter a market simultaneously. Rather, their entrance is spaced out over time as their needs develop. For example, successively newly paired young couples enter the housing market sequentially. Alternatively, in-company marketing training has occurred for several decades in the UK. However, firms such as IBM United Kingdom and APV had other training priorities until recently and only began to buy marketing courses as their needs for them became apparent in the 1990s.

- **Repositioning in new segments**: this involves targeting new segments for existing markets, usually with a new marketing programme. For instance, positioning sportswear as fashion clothing in the leisure market greatly expanded the sales of rugby shirts, tracksuits, etc. Similarly, the repositioning of Lucozade as a fashionable young person's beverage greatly increased the sales of a product that had been historically marketed as a tonic for people recovering from illness.

- **Targeting new distribution channels**: hitherto unserved customers can be reached through new channels. Dell Computers reached a wider market for personal computers by distributing directly to customers while Daewoo entered the UK car market through its own low cost, low customer-hassle outlets. Alternatively, producers of lawnmowers attracted convenience shoppers by targeting supermarket chains in addition to traditional channels.

Building usage among current customers

Finding ways to induce existing customers to use or consume the product more heavily can substantially expand sales. Usual methods for this include measures to increase the frequency of use or to increase the amount used per occasion.

- **Increasing the frequency of use**: this can be encouraged by emphasizing the benefits of regular or frequent usage. For example, toothbrush manufacturers could promote avoidance of pain or bad breath as prime benefits of regular brushing. Alternatively, suppliers can motivate a greater rate of consumption by removing the negative factors associated with using the product. For instance, the introduction of low calorie spreads allayed fears of using yellow fats among health-conscious customers. Another option for suppliers is to offer incentives such as the scheme operated by Barclaycard Visa whereby customers are awarded a valuable number of points according to their total monthly expenditure and which can then be exchanged for prizes.

- **Increasing the quantity used per occasion**: this can be achieved through incentive offers. For example, many financial institutions vary the interest rates paid to investors directly with the size of their investments. Another approach is to encourage users to extend the duration of the usage experience. Many hotels do this by offering lower weekend rates to encourage mid-week business guests to extend their stay. Alternatively, adapting the product to fit environment change can also increase usage per occasion. In this way breweries introduced low-alcohol beers to enable consumers to drink more than a pint of beer before driving.

Targeting new uses

Introducing new applications for a product can both attract new customers and increase current usage rates. New uses can be exploited by identifying new purposes, times or locations for using the product.

- **Introducing new usage purposes**: the key to this is to identify new benefits of usage.

For example, aspirin was traditionally used as a painkiller but doctors now prescribe it for other purposes such as the prevention of blood clots. Similarly, soccer stadia are now used for other sports and pop concerts as well as soccer matches.

- **Introducing new usage times**: this can involve positioning products for usage at different times of the day, week, month, season or year. In recent years Kellogg has promoted Corn Flakes for use as a snack during the day or evening. The result was to increase usage among regular breakfast consumers and to attract new customers from among hitherto non-users. Likewise, public houses initially provided food at lunch times to attract lunch-hour drinkers. The food business was found to be profitable in its own right and is now offered by many publicans throughout the day and evening.

- **Introducing new usage locations**: targeting new places for customers to use products can involve different parts of a building or entirely different locations. Many homes now have several televisions or telephones in different rooms. Alternatively, advances in telephone technology now enable telephones to be used in non-traditional locations such as in aeroplanes, trains and cars.

Conditions favouring market expansion strategies

There is some variation in the conditions favouring market expansion depending on whether the approach to it involves new users, new uses or higher usage rates. Nevertheless, these approaches are advisable and/or more likely to succeed when:

- a short PLC is expected;
- the firm needs to spread high fixed costs;
- there are pockets of latent (unmet) demand;
- appropriate channels are available;
- the firm is a first mover;
- rivals are weak, inert or absent;

- the firm has sustainable differential advantage;
- necessary resources are available.

Risks of , and barriers to, market expansion strategy

Although growth through market expansion is attractive to most firms, strategies applied for its achievement sometimes fail. Various factors can account for this:

- some of the favourable conditions do not obtain;
- the firm has insufficient knowledge and/or incorrectly judges the opportunity;
- customers are not attracted by the product;
- the strategy is launched before the market is ready for it;
- the firm is beaten to the opportunity by a first mover;
- the firm moves first but loses to a more effective follower;
- the strategy costs too much for it to be viable;
- by allocating resources to the particular opportunity the firm may have to forego targeting a better one.

Market share expansion strategies

Share expansion is attractive since it increases volumes, lowers average costs via economies of scale and experience and provides other benefits. Strategies for share growth are very appropriate for the PLC growth and maturity stages.

Share growth often occurs as a result of short-term tactical skirmishes involving price cuts, channels incentives or consumer promotions. However, while such short-term gains are welcome, they are usually unsustainable in the absence of repetitive short-term tactical ploys which can be very costly. Instead of these it is far more strategically sensible to concentrate on building defensible long-term competitive strengths by planning strategies to provide *sustainable* differential advantage.

In the most fundamental terms, long-term share expansion requires that the firm either provides a more attractive product offering than its rivals or that it acquires its rivals. The economics of take-overs are beyond the scope of this chapter. What follows is a set of examples concerning how firms can develop long-term differential advantage:

- finding ways to maintain constant downward pressure on costs so as to be able to offer sustainably lower prices than competitors. Powerful cost drivers include:
  - gaining economies of scale and experience;
  - redesigning the product or the value chain to remove unvalued parts of the offering. Examples include Aldi, Motel 6 and Ryanair;
  - maintaining a very high capacity utilization to fully spread fixed costs. Alternatively, downsize as British Steel did some two decades ago;
  - forming strategic alliances to share the costs of R&D, capacity, channels etc;
  - removing all forms of waste from the production system;
  - occupying the least-cost products and distribution locations;
  - using advanced production technology as Nissan does;
  - adopting direct distribution or using direct marketing as IBM does in some markets.
- Supplying superior product offerings by:
  - developing superior quality products such as Rolls-Royce cars or uniquely different products such as Morgan cars;
  - developing technological substitutes such as when word processing was introduced to the detriment of typewriter sales;
  - adding valued product features as Apple did to make the Macintosh an easier-to-use product than its rivals;
  - exploiting packaging innovations as with the small sample can sizes of Dulux;
  - offering superior services such as help desks for information technology customers;

- providing more user convenience by building wider distribution coverage as Hertz did in car rentals;
- using more complete, honest or easily understandable advertising as is done for Ronseal varnishes and paints;
- exploiting non-price based ways to reduce the user's costs of ownership as when in 1997 Daewoo included three years' insurance, servicing, warranty and break-down coverage in the low price of its cars.

Since differential advantage is created by either driving down the customer's cost of purchase or ownership by raising his or her level of benefits, routes to building competitive advantage are limited only by management's imagination and resource availability. Generally, however, it pays to invest in creating multiple forms of differential advantage to raise competitors' costs of trying to gain equality or superiority.

Conditions favouring market share expansion strategy

Motivations for and opportunities to attempt successful share-building strategies are strengthened when:

- the firm has scope to increase economies of scale and experience;
- the firm wants to pre-empt a rival's attack or to divert its attentions from another product or market;
- the firm wants to win back lost share or punish a competitor for its previous aggression;
- customer needs are not being fully satisfied;
- rivals are weak, complacent and/or placid;
- the firm has sustainable differential advantage and adequate resources.

Risks of, and barriers to, market share expansion strategies

Although share growth would be attractive to most organizations, many share expansion strategies fail in the long term. Also, only one firm (occasionally two) can achieve market leadership in their markets. Risks and barriers include the following:

- some of the favourable conditions do not apply;
- customers are satisfied by and remain loyal to their current suppliers;
- other entry barriers may exist such as blocked channels, supply problems or customers are tied to long-term contracts;
- an alert, proactive and aggressive market leader continually innovates new customer benefits to deter others;
- rivals retaliate and retrieve their lost customers or raise the attacker's costs of holding them;
- an aggrieved rival retaliates by attacking others among the firm's products or markets;
- the benefits of winning are outweighed by the costs.

Defensive or hold strategies

Holding is most relevant in the maturity and early decline stages of the PLC. It involves firms defending their existing levels of market share, sales and/or profits against all-comers. The prime objective is usually to maintain current profitability levels and requires firms to invest just sufficient resources to maintain:

- competitiveness;
- customer loyalty;
- channels penetration;
- production capacity;
- all other holding requirements.

Conditions favouring defensive or hold strategies

Holding strategies are strategically sensible when:

- the firm has adequate resources and a strong competitive position in a strategically attractive market;

- particularly when it has a large share in a market that has reached maturity and further growth is either not possible or cost prohibitive;
- large profits can be taken from the product-market segment and used to support the development of others;
- it is strategically necessary to continue offering the product because it is a complement to other of the firm's products or is otherwise interrelated with other parts of the business;
- market decline is not swift or advanced.

Risks of, and barriers to, defensive or hold strategies

Defensive strategies do not always succeed as Caterpillar found out when it was attacked by Komatsu in bulldozers. Also, these strategies may involve problems:

- some of the favourable conditions do not apply;
- a more determined and innovative attacker possessing strong sustainable differential advantage may succeed;
- resources could be diverted from better usage in more attractive markets;
- the strategy will fail if permanent market decline occurs rapidly;
- the strategy usually fails under attack from a new technological substitute. For example, beer bottle sales were dramatically reduced with the advent of tin can beer packaging.

Profitable survivor strategies

Many experts would advise against investing in products in declining markets, but this approach can be attractive for such markets as well as in mature ones (Aaker, 1995). However, the rate of market decline should not be too rapid. The central thrust of the strategy is to force rivals out and then exploit the market as a monopolist or strong leader if one or a few rivals remain. The approach involves:

- signalling intent to capture or preserve strong market leadership;
- investing in product variety, price incentive, promotion, channel incentives and so on to raise rivals' holding costs and encourage their withdrawal;
- removing competitors by buying them or their brands;
- rationalizing the product range and investing only enough to hold position after rivals have withdrawn, thus maximizing profitability until the market ceases to be viable.

Conditions favouring profitable survivor strategies

Circumstances favouring this strategy include:

- market decline is gentle and/or some segments are expected to remain and support a lower but nevertheless viable sales volume;
- rivals are weak, fainthearted or concentrating on other opportunities;
- the firm has the necessary resources and sustainable differential advantage;
- the business is interrelated with others in the firm's portfolio.

Risks of, and barriers to, profitable survivor strategies

Obvious dangers of the strategy are:

- market decline occurs too rapidly to allow the firm to recoup its investment;
- success may be prevented or require prohibitively high costs if one or more competitors resist or themselves seek profitable survivorship;
- attention and resources may be diverted from better opportunities;
- a new substitute could fill the market for the product.

Harvest for profit strategies

Harvesting can be appropriate in the growth and maturity stages of the PLC if the firm considers that it lacks adequate resources to build sufficient sustainable differential advantage to gain a large market share. The approach is most commonly associated with market decline, however. In any event, harvesting is applied when firms recognize that the resources invested in the business can be used more effectively elsewhere and seek to withdraw from the market profitably. Features of harvest strategies are:

- acceptance that profitable suicide is the best solution to the firm's participation in the market;
- minimal investment in the business;
- possible price increases if more rapid withdrawal is required;
- maximization of positive cash flow and margins;
- orderly reallocation of resources to more attractive opportunities.

Conditions favouring harvest for profit strategies

Many managers have a natural aversion to harvesting a business, especially if they have been instrumental in building it hitherto. However, it is a sensible course when:

- resources have strategically superior uses elsewhere;
- the firm lacks and cannot develop sustainable differential advantage for the business;
- the market is in long-term decline, preferably at a slow or modest rate;
- there are no interrelationships between the business and others in the portfolio and no other barriers to exit.

Risks of, and barriers to, harvest for profit strategies

The problems associated with harvesting can be particularly powerful. They include:

- market withdrawal may be precluded if some of the favourable conditions are not present, especially if the product-market

segment shares strategic interrelationships with other parts of the business;
- the minimal levels of promotion and marketing activity could cause customers to lose interest in the product or to believe that it is no longer available and so accelerate the rate of sales decline beyond that planned by the firm;
- the above point may also apply in the case of channel members;
- brand managers and other employees may be demoralised by being required to administer the demise of a product that they have previously nurtured;
- managers may lack the specialist skills required for effective harvesting implementation which is very different from most other strategies;
- applying the strategy leaves the company open to attack by rivals, particularly any that may be pursuing profitable survivorship;
- if the market recovers and the firm adapts to a hold or build strategy it may find that its long-term position has been adversely affected by the shorter term period of minimal investment.

Divestment strategies

Divestment or liquidation strategies involve a more immediate market withdrawal than harvesting achieves. The usual objective here is to liquidate resources or reallocate them from product markets that have become strategically highly unattractive. Divestment might occur at any stage of the PLC but is most frequently associated with markets where decline is rapid and/or well advanced. For example, many coal merchants divested their businesses when legislation and technological substitution caused household and business users to convert from coal to other energy sources. Divestment can take the form of:

- cessation of production and liquidation of assets; or

- sell-outs to rivals or others who believe that they can manage the resources more effectively.

Conditions favouring divestment strategies

Divestment makes sound strategic sense when:

- the market is collapsing and not even niches within it can be sustained;
- harvesting is not viable;
- the market is not declining but the firm faces fiercely share-growth orientated rivals with overwhelming competitive superiority;
- the firm wishes to reallocate resources to more attractive uses.

Risks of, and barriers to, divestment strategies

Divestment strategies do play an important role in portfolio management. However, they are not without pitfalls:

- the market could revive or otherwise improve after the event;
- sudden deletion of a major product-market could cause customers, channels, financiers and the like to suspect that the firm is in difficulties generally and consequently treat it less favourably in their dealings;
- there may be high barriers to exiting the business:
  - the firm may be tied to long-term contracts;
  - the problem of interrelationships may exist;
  - the firm's technological assets may be of no use to other players and therefore have no resale value;
  - managers may resist the strategy;
  - divestment may be precluded by government if the product is of national strategic value. This could be relevant for example for some producers of medicines, arms, transport or energy.

Summary

All markets grow, mature and ultimately decline and this has important effects on sales volumes, competitive conditions and other strategically important factors. Many marketeers analyse this in terms of the prescriptions of the PLC concept. This concept does have important uses. In particular, it underscores the critical fact that strategic market analysis and organizational flexibility are essential and it helps to guide product-market portfolio decisions.

However, the PLC concept also attracts some criticism. Most notably in this chapter it is argued that the PLC alone is insufficient to determine marketing strategy selection. Moreover, other environment conditions and the marketing strategies pursued by firms have causal impacts on the shape, height and duration of the PLC sales profile. The first priority in strategy selection is to ensure a continuous strategic fit between the environment (of which PLC conditions are a part), the organizational capabilities of the firm and the strategy. This requires a full review of all relevant environmental and company conditions before an effective strategy can be chosen. Five sets of these factors were discussed in the chapter.

The chapter contends that very few types of strategies are uniquely appropriate for any one of the PLC stages. A range of these strategies has been reviewed along with the conditions in which they can be appropriate and the risks and barriers associated with them. Managers are strongly recommended to evaluate these in their own strategic contexts prior to making strategy choices, irrespective of the stage of the PLC.

References and furtherreading ■

Aaker, D. (1995), *Strategic Marketing Management*, New York: Wiley and Sons Inc.

Dhalla, N. and Yuspeh, S. (1976), 'Forget the product life-cycle concept', *Harvard Business Review*, **54**, January–February, 102–112.

Doyle, P. (1976), 'The realities of the product life cycle', *Quarterly Review of Marketing*, **1**, Summer, 1–6.

Doyle, P. (1994), *Marketing Management and Strategy*, Hemel Hempstead: Prentice-Hall.

Hooley, G. (1995), 'The life-cycle concept revisited: aid or albatross?', *Journal of Strategic Marketing*, **3**(1), 23–40.

Jobber, D. (1995), *Principles and Practice of Marketing*, Maidenhead: McGraw Hill.

Levitt, T. (1965), 'Exploit the product life cycle', *Harvard Business Review*, **43**, November–December, 81–94.

Mercer, D. (1993), 'A two-decade test of the product life cycle', *British Journal of Management*, **4**(4), 269–274.

Neidell, L. (1983), 'Don't forget the product life-cycle concept for strategic planning', *Business*, April–June, 30–35.

Rink, D. and Swan, J. (1979), 'Product life-cycle research: a literature review', *Journal of Business Research*, **7**, September, 219–242.

Wesson, C. (1974), *Dynamic Competitive Strategy and Product Life Cycles*, St Charles: Challenge Books.

Wind, Y. and Claycamp, H. (1976), 'Planning product line strategy: a matrix approach', *Journal of Marketing*, **40**(1), 2–9.

4

Innovation strategies for competitive success

Professor Colin Egan, Leicester Business School and Dr Veronica Wong, Warwick Business School, University of Warwick

In recent years the pressures for firms to innovate have grown tremendously. As markets develop over time the combination of sophisticated demand and intense rivalry forces companies to strive harder and harder just to keep pace with competitive dynamics. They do this in a broad range of ways, consistently seeking product and process breakthroughs to build or maintain a competitive advantage. In this chapter we examine the broad range of marketing issues which are bringing innovation to the top of the boardroom agenda for many firms. In a competitive marketplace the importance of innovation cannot be overstated in an environment where 'the survival of the fittest' is the watchword for corporate success. The following quote from Peter Drucker (1974), the doyen of management gurus, illustrates the central role of innovation in the contemporary business environment:

Because its purpose is to create a customer, a business has two – and only two – functions: marketing and innovation. Marketing and innovation produce results; all the rest are 'costs'.

An important point to make at the outset of this chapter relates to the distinction that should be made between invention and innovation. Invention is the *creation* of an idea and is typically based on technology breakthroughs. Innovation is the *commercialization* of ideas and embraces creativity in all elements of the marketing mix: *everything* provides scope for differentiation if an appropriate market-driven outlook is adopted. While invention is often more interesting for research scientists in R&D departments the strong evidence is that innovation strategies tend to be more profitable! Having noted this, it must be emphasized that a strong creative process and organizational responsiveness are essential to secure innovation success. As we will see, the trick is to innovate for first mover advantage, a process which combines speed to market and an ability to build entry barriers as the market develops and becomes more attractive to follower companies.

Profiling the context of innovation ■

Figure 4.1 identifies four dimensions of innovation:

1. Market context
2. Innovation strategy
3. Innovation process
4. Responsive organization

This chapter is mainly concerned with the first three of these dimensions, although the need for a flexible and responsive organization is emphasized throughout. In Chapter 13 Nigel Piercy deals with the broader issues associated with marketing strategy implementation, the fundamental principle being that if a strategy cannot be implemented, it is not a strategy at all.

In this section we profile the range of pressures which are forcing firms to give innovation an urgent strategic priority, i.e. we examine the *market context*. We can describe

these as the key drivers of innovation, i.e. those factors in the marketing environment which stimulate the development of innovation strategies. Some of these change vectors are gradual and can be identified in the range of business environment *trends* picked up by a company's marketing information systems. Others are a function of *discontinuities*, i.e. relatively quick changes that have no direct precedents. Collectively these trends and discontinuities present the firm with a broad range of opportunities and threats and they provide the context for the creation of marketing and innovation strategies.

The following list identifies key categories of 'innovation trigger' and the sections that follow explore each category in more detail, giving practical examples where appropriate:

- long-term growth and profitability;
- changing patterns of demand and basic customer needs;
- income growth;

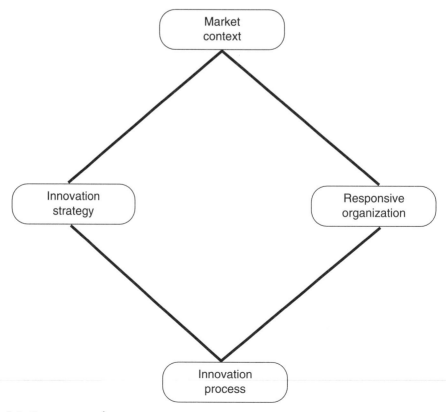

Figure 4.1 *Dimensions of innovation*

- intensifying competition;
- disruptive technologies;
- shortening technology and product life cycles;
- need to build a balanced portfolio;
- need to build reputation;
- stretch and leverage core competencies;
- market complementary products;
- exploit strategic windows;
- pre-empt rivals;
- copy rivals and disruptive technologies.

Long-term growth and profitability

Innovation and the ability to demonstrate and fulfil growth potential is the fundamental determinant of long-term profitability. The share prices of innovative companies invariably outperform inferior rivals, principally because smart investors see capital growth in the equities of those firms who invest in the future.

Changing demand patterns and basic customer needs

Markets are highly dynamic and demand patterns are in a constant state of flux as a direct function of the growing intensity of innovative competition and the emergence of new customer needs. On the demand side markets are fragmenting into smaller and smaller segments and customer preferences are becoming more heterogeneous. This, in turn, is forcing companies to adopt more focused segmentation strategies and to organize their operations to address the phenomenon of *mass customization*, a scenario where the individual customer is the segment. Marketing myopia provides the death knell for many a firm that fails to respond to *changing customer needs*, particularly when sharp, entrepreneurial rivals spot the opportunity. Henry Ford once remarked, 'You can have any colour you like, as long as it's black'. This was fine until the founding father of General Motors said simply: 'You can have any colour you like!' Customers seek variety and companies should protect their market positions by ensuring they provide the broadest choice.

Changing customer needs is not just an industrialized world phenomenon. In many sections of developing country societies there are clusters of demand for relatively upmarket products. India, for example, has a middle class of more than 200 million people who express preferences that parallel those in the advanced economies and, because of their relatively high incomes, have the resources to satisfy them.

Income growth

This pressure to innovate builds on the latter point and we must draw attention to the fact that this characteristic, like all those listed here, provides both opportunities and threats. In the advanced industrial economies, customers' expectations and aspirations have grown in line with their rising living standards. Firms failing to innovate to deal with this trend are seriously threatened by new entrants and technology breakthroughs. Similarly, as income levels in less developed economies are rising in general and not just, as in the India example, among the middle classes, so more and more citizens of those countries can afford a broader range of basic goods. Participation in international business has also earned many countries the foreign currency to be able to buy in a broader range of basic infrastructure products as they attempt to close their technology gap with advanced economies. Taiwan is a classic example of this, as is China which in many technologies is 'leapfrogging' its Western rivals in technology deployment.

Intensifying competition

This is a major driving force for innovation, particularly as new technologies make it easier for small and entrepreneurial companies to bypass the experience curves enjoyed by established market leaders. Developments in Internet technologies provide a classic contemporary example. Economists have always equated competition with innovation, particularly with reference to entrepreneurial behaviour.

Shortening technology and product life cycles

As firms constantly strive for both product and process innovations the time frames over which the leading firms can enjoy their advantage becomes ever shorter. New technologies are now rapidly transferred around the world and quickly transcend different industries. The 'digital revolution' is complicating matters and generating huge discontinuities, as are developments in 'parallel development', an R&D strategy where first, second and third generation technologies are developed in tandem, not sequentially.

Disruptive technologies

This is a phrase which has been coined to describe two key characteristics of contemporary marketing environments: (i) technology life cycles have dramatically reduced across a broad range of industrial sectors; and (ii) second and third generation technologies tend to be pioneered by industry outsiders, i.e. innovative rivals who oust the established firms. One of the most striking examples of this is the deployment of quartz technology for timekeeping. Swiss watch companies arrogantly underestimated emerging Japanese rivals and were dismissive of the notion of changing customer needs. The industry collapsed, seriously damaging the Swiss economy. In this case the Swiss invented the technology but were dismissive of its potential. The convergence of the telecommunications and computer industries around a digital platform is a good example of how traditional industry structures and their associated entry barriers are being shattered by disruptive technologies. In sectors ranging from banking to leisure and entertainment, digital technology is transforming the nature and intensity of competition and is providing unprecedented threats to the established firms in the traditional industries. A culture of innovation and continuous renewal is essential to deal with this threat.

Shorter life cycles

These provide the fundamental dynamic of modern markets, forcing the emphasis towards 'time-based competition'. Technologies now transfer rapidly around the world, thus making sustainable advantage extremely difficult to secure. In today's competitive climate, innovation is much more than technology-driven R&D. Having an emphasis on service support and a focus on emerging market development is just as important, and innovations should be pursued in all aspects of the marketing mix.

The need to build a balanced portfolio

Firms must always balance strong positions in existing markets with investments in future growth markets. In a later section we profile the particular characteristics and dynamics of mature versus growth markets. Suffice to say here, a balanced portfolio of current and potential product/market segments is essential for long-term competitive success.

Build reputation

A strong track record in innovation enhances the brand reputation considerably. 3M is widely regarded as a world champion innovator, consistently earning a high proportion of profits from recently launched technologies. The dull-sounding Minnesota Mining and Manufacturing has been transformed into an instantly recognizable global brand. 3M has exploited this powerful reputation, using the strap line Innovation in its corporate communications. In Chapter 9 Leslie De Chernatony provides a framework which demonstrates how companies can develop and maintain a strong brand reputation.

Stretch and leverage core competencies

In a world of scarce resources the ability to 'stretch and leverage' a company's existing competencies is a tremendous asset. Black and Decker stretched its small electric motor technologies to develop a complete range of DIY tools, thus creating a whole new category of product. Likewise, Honda 'packages' its combustion engine technologies into a diverse array of products, ranging from Formula 1 racing cars to snow blowers! In a classic example, Hewlett Packard developed a domineering position in the computer consumables and peripherals market by developing its core competence in inkjet and laser technology. It has built the latter competitive edge in alliance with Canon, a company that successfully leveraged its optical camera technology into photocopying machines and then into laser printers, the latter being a global market it now dominates.

Market complementary products

The ability to market a range of complementary products can be a tremendous source of profitability and should be a prime driver of innovation strategies. Gillette, for example, sells a hugely successful range of hygiene products to accompany its wet shaving products such as the Sensor. While Gillette was not traditionally a chemicals company, it uses its key core competence of distribution channel management to great effect in marketing gels, shaving foams and after-shave balms as complements to wet shaving systems.

Exploit strategic windows

This aspect of innovation requires an extremely responsive and flexible organization. A strategic window is a one-off opportunity often created by a discontinuity of some form in the marketing environment. Direct Line Insurance, for example, quickly exploited the 1988 Financial Services Act (which deregulated the insurance and banking markets) and was a first mover in adopting emerging database marketing technologies to successfully penetrate the UK market. As we will see, flexibility and responsiveness within the organization are critical for competitive success. A true measure of innovativeness is the ability to exploit these strategic windows, i.e. potentially profitable market gaps.

Pre-empt rivals

A truly innovative company aims to be first to market with new technologies and product concepts to gain 'first-mover advantages'. Japanese consumer giants Sony and Panasonic, for example, have traditionally been first to associate themselves with new technologies such as Camcorders and DVD machines, leaving their Western rivals trailing badly.

Copy rivals and off-set disruptive technologies

Very often established firms are slow to spot new customer trends and/or disruptive technologies. Furthermore, some companies purposefully pursue 'follower strategies'. Where marketing assets such as strong brand reputation and control of distribution channels are held this can be a very successful approach. Bass, for example, was not first to market with 'alchopops' but it quickly bypassed the original imported 'Two Dogs' brand by creating its own copycat brand, Hooch, and, crucially, by exploiting its dominant distribution position in the UK market. Similarly, Microsoft was able to rapidly catch up with Netscape in the Web browser market because of its absolute control of the desktop operating system market.

In sum, a complex and turbulent business environment has created a marketing context in which innovation strategies and organizational responsiveness are essential for survival and prosperity. In the next section we address this complexity by profiling the typical characteristics of different types of market structure and dynamics. The more we understand about the economics of markets, the better will be our strategic marketing and innovation response.

Profiling the nature and dynamics of demand

In the following sections we briefly revise some issues relating to marketing dynamics. Throughout this book a variety of authors have discussed models and frameworks which facilitate our understanding of what, at first sight, appear to be extremely complex phenomena. Here we profile alternative types of demand. Strategic marketing essentially boils down to success at managing the supply/demand interface. In a nutshell, if companies can understand the true nature of demand then they are far more likely to be able to take more sensible supply-side decisions.

Exploring the characteristics of demand

There are three broad types of market demand:

1. **Existing demand** is the type of demand which most marketing managers are familiar with. The common data in market research reports describes existing demand, for example, the size of market (units and/or value), the number of competitors and so on.
2. **Latent demand** is broadly defined as a situation where there is an obvious customer need that is not being currently met by a significant number of suppliers. This type of demand is very common in less-developed countries where there are clear needs but the relative lack of an ability to pay renders the market unprofitable to supply.
3. **Incipient demand** refers to needs that have yet to be identified. This type of demand is very common in advanced industrial economies where the pursuit of 'higher order needs' are matched by relatively high living standards and a general willingness to pay premium prices for new and novel products.

Contrasting mature and high potential markets

The following list profiles the typical characteristics of existing demand:

- mature context;
- clever customers;
- intense and sophisticated rivalry;
- excess capacity;
- price/margin erosion.

You will recall from Chapter 3 that the rate of growth in a market is a critical determinant of the type of marketing strategies which firms do or should develop. Existing demand tends to have low growth levels, i.e. these types of market are typically characterized by a *mature context*. The market will typically be very large and may well be growing at rates of up to 10 per cent. Despite such growth, the opportunities for unestablished firms will be limited. *Clever customers* refers to the fact that in mature markets customers are typically well informed about all the alternatives available to them, both in terms of alternative suppliers and alternative technologies. Given choice, customers will choose! Their expectations will also be being continuously raised, not least because of the *intense and sophisticated rivalry* that is a typical feature of mature markets. The shakeout phenomenon, whereby firms that haven't kept pace with the market's development have been acquired or have gone out of business, will already have occurred. The combination of these market characteristics leads to the problem of *excess capacity* and, consequently, *margin erosion*. Excess capacity is a particular characteristic of capitalist economies since individual producers will make investment decisions based on their own interpretations of market demand. Where lead times are long and the rate of growth in the market slows, there is invariably an 'overhang' of excess capacity. Market 'imperfections' such as government subsidies (for example, in the steel industry) can lead to long periods of chronic excess capacity, a scenario where the market forces which would force bankruptcy or industry restructuring are prevented from doing their job.

The principles of market leadership ___

There are three key marketing challenges for success in mature markets:

- market leadership;
- reinforce customer loyalty;
- process innovation (i.e. a focus on productivity gains).

The first marketing challenge is *market leadership*. As GE CEO Jack Welch once famously remarked, 'If you're one or two in a market in a downturn, you catch a cold. Any lower and you get pneumonia'. The second (and related) marketing challenge is to *reinforce loyalty* among the customer base. Repeat purchase customers are profitable customers, a factor reinforced by the plethora of loyalty schemes and relationship marketing programmes available today. The market leader in a mature market should constantly strive to identify *process innovations*, i.e. to drive down costs and thus enhance margins and combat the effects of price erosion. Increasingly, such innovations come from outside the traditional industry structure, a classic example being Direct Line Insurance who smashed the distribution entry barriers enjoyed by the UK's large composite insurers.

A range of marketing models and frameworks underpin the importance of market leadership in mature markets, including the Boston Box, the GE Multi-Factor Business Screen, the PIMS findings and so on. Similarly, as you will see in Chapter 9, market leadership is *maintained* by securing brand loyalty via an innovative and augmented product concept. Furthermore, as mentioned above, a common characteristic of mature market life cycles is *shakeout*, whereby industry consolidation leaves only a few firms with profitable market positions. This highly predictable phenomenon reinforces the market leadership message but it must be noted that

the disciplines of market leadership are often neglected by successful firms. In general, firms seem to be more capable of throwing away strong positions rather than building them! Great market leaders of the past (including IBM, GM, CBS, the Swiss watch industry, the UK motorcycle industry) have watched as rivals have exploited the complacency often associated with high market share positions.

The characteristics of high potential markets ___

The following list combines latent and incipient demand and profiles the typical characteristics of these types of markets. Although latent and incipient demand are fundamentally different, the market dynamics and marketing challenges associated with them are very similar:

- huge growth potential;
- few strong rivals;
- stupid companies;
- stupid customers!

The first characteristic is the *huge growth potential* available. Typical examples are multimedia PCs; dishwashing machines; Internet services; mobile telephones; infrastructure projects in South-East Asia; coal-fired power stations in China; a vast array of relatively basic product technologies in *mega-markets* such as Latin America, India and China.

When assessing such growth potential cross-country adoption comparisons are commonly employed. So, for example, European and US households have very high household penetration of colour TVs – in excess of 90 per cent. The equivalent figure for multimedia PCs is less than 20 per cent. Telephone lines per head of population in the newly industrializing nations are minuscule compared to those in advanced economies. And so on.

High potential, fast growth markets also tend to be more fragmented, i.e. there are *few strong rivals* with entrenched competitive positions. The key word here is 'strong'.

While there may be many companies competing none will dominate. This has been classically demonstrated in the cellular telephone market where the market was originally served by many small independent local agents. The entry of large companies such as Dixons Group and their partner Cellular Connections, alongside fast growing companies such as People's Phone, works to quickly 'mop up' the fragmented market.

Stupid companies, stupid customers and the core principles of innovation

Two key 'downside factors' are typical in high growth potential markets. First, *stupid companies*! Despite their obvious potential, incipient and latent markets are often ignored by companies who are blind to the opportunities they offer. A self-fulfilling prophecy scenario arises whereby because the market can't be 'seen', it is not developed, particularly by companies whose technologies can be readily substituted. Entrepreneurial new entrants, often with substitute process and/or product technologies, tend to be more able to exploit the potential and far less likely to suffer marketing myopia. Many examples of the latter abound, including the Swiss watch industry, mini-computer makers (such as Wang and Nixdorf), the big three US car companies in the 1970s, Olivetti in typewriters, IBM in PCs, and so on.

Perhaps the greatest challenge with latent and incipient demand is that posed by the existence of *stupid customers*! This statement is not meant in a derogatory sense. It just reflects a basic marketing fact of life that customers are not so good at articulating a desire for something they have yet to experience. This is changing slowly in industrial markets as customers take a more strategic approach to purchasing. Even here, though, a fear of technological obsolescence and general purchasing myopia present a difficult marketing challenge.

From a strategic marketing perspective, the challenge of latent and incipient markets is to be *first* and *fast*, i.e. to rapidly enter the market and to quickly build entry barriers as the market develops. It is a basic tenet of economics that attractive markets will always attract new entrants and that strong rivals will quickly emerge. As market and technology life cycles become increasingly shorter the requirement of rapid 'time to market' becomes acute. Substantial evidence exists which demonstrates that, with few exceptions, there are tremendous marketing and financial benefits associated with *first mover advantage*. The PIMS Database has shown that first movers typically gain both high market share and superior long-term profitability as the following list indicates (Doyle, 1989):

- pioneers typically win 29 per cent market share;
- early followers gain 17 per cent;
- late entrants only manage 12 per cent;
- pioneers typically earn 30 per cent more long-term ROI than followers.

The following list and subsequent evaluation illustrate why it is that first movers are typically so successful by examining the reasons why followers underperform:

- customer inertia;
- customer loyalty profiles;
- customer switching costs;
- first mover's experience curve cost advantage;
- first mover's aggressive defence of its market leadership position;
- first mover ties up best distribution channels;
- first mover enjoys generic associations.

Customer inertia refers to a general fact that, other things being equal, customers will not put the effort into switching brands just because a new supplier emerges. If the first mover is effective in developing the market it is highly likely that *strong customer loyalty profiles* will develop, i.e. customers enjoy strong brands and are likely to be highly satisfied with the first mover's offering. In the marketing literature there is a huge debate as to whether consumers tend to be brand loyal versus brand fickle. Loyalty profiles do vary depending on the type of market (e.g. consumer versus industrial) and its dynamics (e.g. emerging versus mature) but, as a general observation, if the first mover company continues to 'do the right things' as the market develops, it should be able to secure strong customer loyalty. This is particularly the case where customers will incur heavy *switching costs* in changing their supplier, a factor that the first mover can, of course, heavily influence. There are three categories of switching cost: (i) economic; (ii) psychological; and (iii) political. Economic switching costs include downtime, retraining, systems compatibility, etc. Many industrial firms build these factors in by linking capital goods with consumables, for example, Xerox with photocopiers (machine plus toner), Caterpillar (bulldozers plus spare parts), Rolls-Royce (aero-engines plus maintenance contracts and parts), Hewlett Packard (printers plus inkjet cartridges) and so on. Psychological costs indicate that buyers tend to be risk averse (e.g. 'nobody ever got fired for buying IBM', 'better the devil you know', etc.). More positively, the trend towards 'partnership sourcing', 'relationship management' and 'network marketing' build in strong emotional as well as economic ties (see Chapter 10 for a detailed discussion of these 'strategic marketing networks'). Political costs reflect internal powerplays within the decision-making unit and/or external dependencies such as reciprocal trading agreements. These are often very difficult to identify but are essential to acknowledge in developing marketing strategies.

The first mover will have the economic advantage of rapidly falling costs based upon its rapid descent down the experience curve, an edge that they should use to *aggressively defend* their market position via building entry barriers. One of the most powerful entry barriers is to tie up *distribution channels* by securing the best locations and becoming the preferred supplier to the trade. Another benefit the first mover enjoys is the *generic association* associated with the product, for example, Walkman, Post-it note, Hoover, Catnic lintels, and so on.

As markets become more competitive the benefits of first mover strategies are often short lived, principally due to rapid technology transfer which, in turn, leads to shorter market life cycles and rapid imitation by competitors. More generally, a broad range of pitfalls associated with pro-active first mover strategies has been identified in the literature. The following list provides a sample of the dangers:

- customer rejection;
- customer apathy;
- the technology is premature;
- market entry is premature;
- R&D project costs rapidly escalate;
- market development costs rapidly escalate;
- product development is deficient;
- poor market targeting;
- insufficient budgets, particularly for market development;
- inadequate cross-functional co-ordination.

Clearly, many of these are interrelated. Companies often underestimate the costs of innovation, both before and after launch, thus leaving inadequate resources to complete the project. Many of the issues listed above relate to poor timing, either because the company is not adequately prepared or because the customers are not ready for the product. The important point to note, however, is that all these issues *can* be addressed if appropriate preparation and planning is undertaken. Throughout this chapter we acknowledge the pitfalls associated with first mover innovation strategies but we aim to offer solutions to deal with the identified dangers. Remember the self-fulfilling prophecy syndrome: if the expectation is of failure then failure is highly likely.

Considering first mover strategies (alongside their pitfalls) from a tactical perspective, the marketing challenge is to develop communication strategies that inform, educate and demonstrate the advantages of the product to customers who might initially be reluctant to accept and/or understand the message. Furthermore, the power of word of mouth should be harnessed by seeking endorsement and testimonials from early adopters of the product (see the next section for a discussion of the role of early adopters in innovation strategies). The following quote from Sony founder Akio Morita concisely summarizes the point that it is the innovative company's marketing challenge to educate customers about the benefits associated with its products:

You must not expect the customer to understand the benefits of your technologies. That's your job!

Morita also notes that if Sony had listened to the customer too literally then the Walkman, one of the most successful mass-market products of all time, would never have been launched – potential customers could not possibly conceive the benefits of a non-recording tape recorder! It is in this sense that we describe customers as 'stupid', i.e. that it is the supplying company's task to educate and persuade them to change their routine purchasing habits. Extensive research has demonstrated that some customers are more open to being educated than others, particularly when a new technology is highly complex or is merely new to a particular society. A good example of the latter is the marketing of the contraceptive pill to a society such as the Philippines. Here the challenge was to educate the customers about contraception and how to use the pill rather than to inform them of how the technology worked.

In the next section we examine this critical element of the context of innovation in more depth. Once again, it is essential to assimilate the vast amount of research that has demonstrated how new concepts are adopted in markets if we are to increase the chances of our innovation strategies being successful.

The adoption and diffusion of innovations

Over the years researchers have documented how innovations are adopted and transmitted throughout societies. The cumulative research has delivered powerful insights into a process that embraces the economics of supply, the psychology of consumer behaviour and the sociology of group behaviour within society. Understanding how innovations are adopted can give companies a much greater chance of success when attempting to commercialize new ideas, especially those which, as discussed in the previous section, have no historical market precedent.

Innovation, product adoption and the diffusion of ideas within society

One of the most powerful concepts developed within the marketing discipline is the diffusion of innovation model. It includes concepts relating to economics (both supply and demand), cognitive and humanistic psychology, sociology and general societal trends. The diffusion model has two key components:

1. It is a *societal* concept grounded in sociology and observations of group behaviour. It explains how different groups come to learn about innovations, how innovations are adopted and how innovations are transmitted throughout society.
2. It is an *economics* concept which explains how the combined supply-side forces of competition and innovation drive market dynamics, deliver experience curve effects and ultimately determine market structure as a market matures.

Diffusion is a macro phenomenon, i.e. it explains how innovations permeate a particular society. *Adoption* is a micro phenomenon, i.e. it explains how individuals learn about and adopt innovations.

Extensive research has demonstrated that adopter groups have quite specific characteristics and, furthermore, that categories of adopters can be measured accurately. The following list shows the five main categories of adopter groups and, assuming that everyone in society ultimately adopts the innovation (100 per cent), it is clear that each adopter group accounts for a particular percentage of the total:

Innovators	2.5 per cent
Early adopters	13.5 per cent
Early majority	34.0 per cent
Late majority	34.0 per cent
Laggards	16.0 per cent

A detailed evaluation of each adopter category is beyond the scope of this chapter. We will give brief details of each and then give two applied examples of innovation diffusion.

Innovators typically have highly specialized knowledge regarding the particular technology in question. They are often visionaries, highly intellectual and prepared to take risks. They are non-conformist, ambitious and decisive. While being important for the take-up of new technologies they are not typically influential in whether or not the innovation goes beyond them and into society more generally.

The *early adopters* take a pro-active approach in searching for new ideas. This group are typically well educated and prepared to take risks. In consumer markets they are relatively better off and highly respected by the other adopter groups. They play a crucial role as *opinion formers* and are often critical in determining whether or not an innovation permeates throughout society. In industrial markets, early adopter groups will often be market leaders, new firms, fast growers, have younger senior managers and will typically outperform other firms in their sectors. Early adoption of new technologies in industrial markets can often have a dramatic effect on the economics of supply. Figure 4.2 shows a typical production function of a firm, i.e. the relationship between outputs and unit costs.

Economists describe this as the long run average total cost curve. It combines all fixed and variable costs and, in this example, any individual firm has to produce at least 1 million units to break even, i.e. it must operate at a minimum efficient scale to participate in the industry. Figure 4.2 shows the production function of General Motors (in the USA) in the early 1980s.

Figure 4.3 shows the economic impact of a technology process breakthrough.

The second curve is described by economists, with their usual candour, as the very

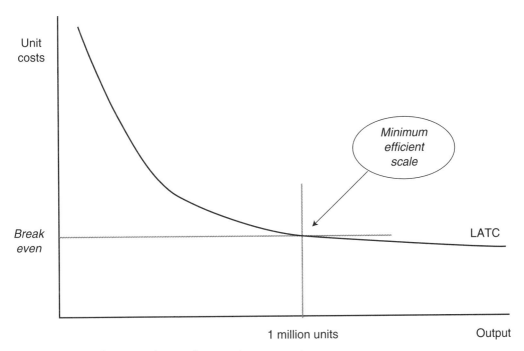

Figure 4.2 *An industry production function (automotive)*

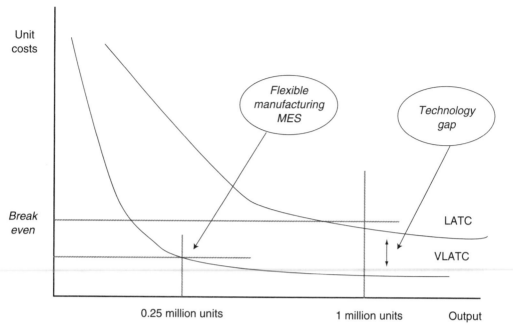

Figure 4.3 *The economics of a process breakthrough*

long run average total cost curve. The adoption of flexible manufacturing systems (robotics) has reduced the minimum efficient scale to 250,000 units, thus giving many more strategic options to the early adopter company while at the same time forcing follower companies to close the *technology gap* by the process innovation. General Motors spent $28 billion doing just this throughout the late 1980s.

As can be seen from the previous example, the *early majority* in industrial sectors *must* close the technology gap created by rival firms. Despite this, there will be many internal conflicts and a tendency towards the status quo. This will be particularly true where powerful trade unions resist the production process changes that are necessary. In consumer markets the early majority are *aspirers* and will actively seek endorsement, consciously or subconsciously, from the early adopters.

The *late majority* are typically consumers who are driven by price and availability and are generally sceptical regarding new ideas. Mass communications and distribution channels are essential to successfully service this market, as is a focus on productivity gains and cost leadership strategies. In industrial markets late majority companies are typically passive to market dynamics, short-term, finance driven and risk averse.

Laggards are traditionalists, apathetic to trends in society, cynical about new ideas and, indeed, may actually fear them. In industrial markets laggards are forced into end-game strategies, need alliances for survival and will be downsizing if they are not already bankrupt.

These classifications are obviously simplified generalizations and complicating factors such as decision-making unit composition will have a significant impact on family and organizational purchases. Nevertheless, the concept is very robust and has been proven to apply across all types of market sectors. The dynamic of innovation diffusion is fundamentally driven by how the twin forces of supply and demand interact over time. Figure 4.4 shows a generic example.

Initially prices are very high and the question to ask is which segment would derive enough value from the product or technology to justify the high price? As production expands economies of scale and experience begin to drive down costs. New entrants accelerate this

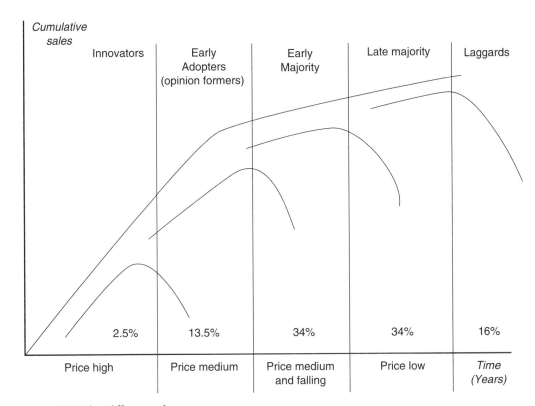

Figure 4.4 *The diffusion of innovations*

process and price falls, thus creating a value proposition for a new group of customers (the early adopters). Early adopters are opinion formers and two things occur: (i) they spread the word about the new technology; and (ii) the early majority aspire to the new technologies. As the market grows new entrants continue to arrive and costs once again fall, thus reducing market price levels and attracting a new group (the early majority). The market is now large, prices become low and the late majority enter, thus creating a mass market. Eventually the laggards may enter the market but this does not always happen.

Applied examples: (i) industrial robotics; (ii) consumer electronics

Figure 4.5 gives a specific example, that of industrial robots.

Innovators were those firms undertaking specialist applications, for example nuclear, defence, etc. Although the price was high the nature of the work under-

taken allowed the cost to be passed on.

Toyota and other Japanese companies were the early adopters in the continuous process-manufacturing sector. The early use of robotics technology was driven by a strong yen and chronic labour shortages. Japanese manufacturing generally then rapidly adopted robotics, giving them a significant global competitive edge and allowing them to achieve the manufacturing holy grail of providing extensive variety at low cost. In this example the implications for Western firms have been clear for all to see: the late majority are forced into catch-up mode while the laggards are heading for bankruptcy.

Figure 4.6 gives another applied example, this time CD players for the consumer market.

Again price is a major factor in triggering new groups of customers to enter into the market. Perceived value also changes for each group. The hi-fi freaks are interested in *sound* quality; the classical music lovers in *music* quality; the yuppies in *lifestyle*; the

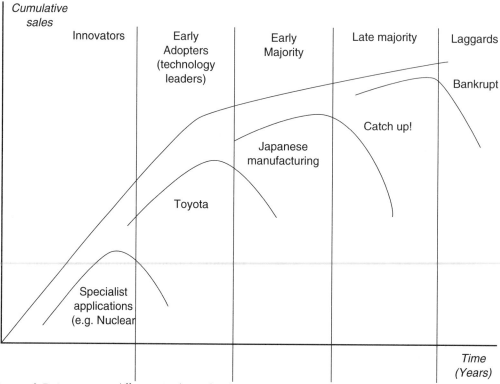

Figure 4.5 *Innovation diffusion (Industrial Robotics)*

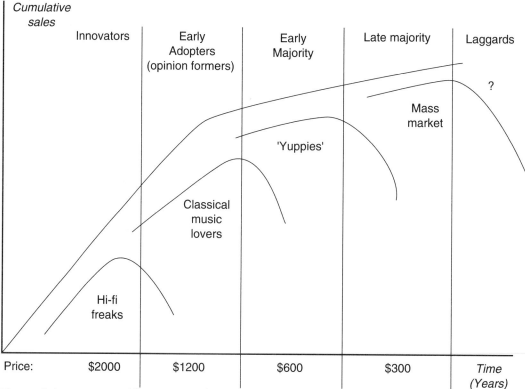

Figure 4.6 *Innovation diffusion (CD players)*

mass market in *price* and *availability*. Distribution channels also change over the cycle: *specialist* stores for the hi-fi freaks; *selective outlets* (music shops, department stores) for the music lovers; *intensive* thereafter.

A key question relating to the diffusion process is how quickly the cycle develops. Sometimes it is in the interests of manufacturers to slow down the process, for example, to cream high profits by using a skimming pricing strategy (see Chapter 2). On other occasions manufacturers might wish to build the market quickly, particularly if its characteristics lend themselves to rapid diffusion. The following list illustrates typical *diffusion accelerators*:

- The innovation has genuine differential advantages over existing products and technologies.
- The innovation is compatible with existing values and behaviours.
- The innovation has relatively low complexity.
- The innovation can be tried on a limited basis before a purchase is made.
- The customer benefits of the innovation are clear or can be easily explained.

These are self-explanatory and, clearly, those factors slowing down diffusion will be the reverse of the above list. Another key factor explaining slow diffusion is whether or not a single manufacturer holds patents and whether or not the technology is licensed.

This section on innovation diffusion concludes our discussion of the context of innovation strategies. Armed with this understanding of markets and their dynamics, it is now possible to evaluate in more detail specific types of innovation strategies.

Generic innovation strategies

The following list profiles alternative innovation strategies:

- create new positioning propositions;
- create new distribution channels;
- create new market segments;
- seek process breakthroughs;
- develop and launch new products.

Creating new positioning propositions is the most fundamental and often the most successful innovation strategy. Apple's early approach in taking computing to the home and education sectors is a good example of a company finding a market gap. Wang's early success was also based on this approach, targeting the smaller enterprises for mini-computers, a segment IBM largely ignored. Argos (originally the downmarket Green Shield Stamp outlets) successfully created a new high street positioning proposition, catalogue retailing. Famous authors Ries and Trout coined the phrase 'Positioning: the Battle for Your Mind', a statement which demonstrates how important it is to stand apart from the crowd in a cluttered and 'noisy' marketplace. The goal in this strategy is to exploit 'first mover advantage' or to exploit marketing assets such as strong brands or dominant channels to make the segment your own. The alchopop phenomenon is a classic example and, for Bass, it was a tremendous opportunity to expand sales in a mature market without cannibalizing its traditional beer and lager revenues.

One of the biggest barriers to market entry is restricted access to marketing supply systems. *Creating or adapting new distribution channels* is a key way to avoid this obstacle. Toys 'R Us established a strong position in Japan by exploiting a law change which allowed them to bypass traditional channel structures. Dell and Gateway 2000 attacked the expensive value added distribution channels of companies such as Compaq to establish strong market positions in the rapidly growing PC market in the late 1980s. Satellite TV companies such as QVC have transformed the possibilities for companies selling lower-end products to markets which are relatively price sensitive and where a dealer margin makes products uncompetitive. Database marketing systems and technologies attached to the Internet also provide tremendous possibilities for fast thinking firms to find new routes to market.

Tremendous innovation possibilities arise from *creating new segments* for existing technologies. This category can relate to segments within a particular market or with regard to opening up new geographic segment. Procter & Gamble, for example, created a huge market in Poland for vapour-rub medication, successfully launching its Vicks brand into a market which had strong latent demand for this established and relatively basic children's healthcare product. Similarly, Philips successfully launched its Philishave range in India, a market where dry shaving technology didn't previously exist. Staying with the shaving theme, Gillette's stretching of their male-derived Sensor technology to create a wet shaving system for women is a classic example of finding a new segment *within* a market (the USA), a success story it subsequently rolled out into the global marketplace. On the other side of the demographic equation, *Maxim*, *Men's Health*, *GQ* and *Esquire* collectively created a brand new 'middle-shelf' lifestyle magazine concept for men, a segment which traditionally only had the top shelf to look to for entertaining reading! As a final example, Psion's creation of the palmtop computer segment created competitive advantage over such marketing giants as Hewlett Packard, Sharp and Casio.

Seeking process breakthroughs is a major way that entrepreneurial companies can break into both new and established markets. Regarding the latter, incumbent firms tend to be locked into a particular 'paradigm', a recipe for doing business based on traditional production methods. Early adoption of robotics and flexible manufacturing systems have allowed Japanese and German companies to make inroads into apparently impenetrable markets. Similarly, US banks such as MBNA and Capital One have exploited the digital revolution and the convergence of telecommunications and computers to successfully penetrate the UK market for banking services using sophisticated database marketing systems. This software-driven process breakthrough allows the companies

to service a mass market without having to develop extensive retail or agency channels.

Note that the above examples do not necessarily involve the invention of new technologies and recall that innovation refers to creative ways of commercializing ideas which can relate to any element of the marketing process. Having said this, *developing and launching* new products still has a significant role to play, particularly for exploiting incipient demand.

Profiling 'new product' alternatives

The following list classifies the different types of new 'product' which are commonly launched as part of innovation strategies. Two factors are worthy of clarification here. First, these approaches are manifestations of the generic innovation strategies outlined in the previous sections. Secondly, an important caveat to note here is that not all innovations are product/technology based. As noted throughout this chapter, innovation equates with creativity and inspiration can be applied across the whole spectrum of marketing and strategic management.

- cost reductions;
- repositioning;
- improvements;
- line extensions;
- new lines;
- new to the world.

Cost reductions are innovation projects which aim to bring the same product to market but at a lower cost of production, thus contributing greater margins or allowing the company to compete on price. *Repositioning* product strategies make a new presentation of the same product and/or are targeted at a new segment. Bookmakers Coral, for example, are keen to reposition gambling as a more mainstream middle market activity and have invested heavily in store refurbishment and brand identity. In the process they hope to be able to attract a new segment – women – into betting shops and hence obtain greater revenue from the same fixed asset base.

Improvements are innovation projects that aim to give more features, higher quality and better performance, either with a view to charging a higher price or offering greater value at the same price. As an example of the former, Gillette invested heavily in its Sensor Excel technology to move many of its existing customers upmarket and away from its lower margin Contour and GII products. Honda is known to make relatively minor product improvements to its motorcycles every two weeks, thus building a cumulative competitive advantage which rivals are always chasing. More generally, the concept of *Kaizen* (continuous improvement) has given Japanese companies huge advantages in mass production industries, consistently allowing them to offer 'more for less', a superb winning formula in highly competitive markets. *Line extensions* stretch strong brand identities into new product categories, good examples being Lucozade into isotonic sports drinks, Black & Decker into a broad range of DIY tools, Gillette into male facial hygiene products. *New lines* are products that are new to the firm but not new to the market, a good example being Levi's Dockers brand of casual clothes. Levi's previous line extension into suits failed because of the strong association of the Levi brand with jeans. Creating a new identity exploited its manufacturing and distribution channel competencies and has proved to be a huge success. *New to the world* products are the riskiest and most expensive innovation projects, mainly because of the requirement to educate the market and to develop appropriate distribution channels in addition to making huge R&D investments. The potential rewards, though, are also great, and the opportunity to benefit from first mover advantage with new to the world product concepts is the strongest of all the innovation strategies. The marketing challenge with new to the world products is to understand the dynamics of market development and, in particular, to identify the potential market segments which are most likely to be the innovators and early adopters of the technology. As we saw in the previous section on the diffusion of innovation, there is a wealth of research evidence available to guide companies in addressing these issues.

Planning issues for innovation strategies

Innovators must make estimates to gauge the rate of adoption. We have already discussed the notion of shortening technology life cycles, rapid technology transfer and time-based competition. The following list builds on our previous discussion of diffusion accelerators and adds extra firm-specific dimensions which must be considered in developing innovation plans:

- the intensity of the customer's needs;
- the amount of customer learning required;
- the ability to demonstrate the innovation;
- the possibility of receiving third party endorsement and/or testimonials;
- the extent of the company's previous experience in implementing innovation projects;
- the existence of an effective planning process;
- careful preparation prior to the launching of the innovation project;
- the availability of suitable distribution channels;
- characteristics of the general marketing environment;
- the commitment of senior executives to the innovation process;
- the profiling of potential entry barriers.

An *intense need* for an innovation is a key factor in accelerating the launch cycle, a point that reinforces our earlier comments about basing innovations on genuine customer needs. The easier it is for buyers to *learn* about an innovation's potential, the more rapid will be its adoption. Taking into account the observation of Akio Morita above, it is essential to educate customers about the benefits associated with the new product concept. Two key ways of achieving this are via *demonstration* and *endorsement*. The latter is particularly powerful since it gives the impression of independence and objectivity from a *third party opinion former*.

As with all aspects of management, the likelihood of success increases with *experience*. As companies launch more products they should become more successful, avoiding the pitfalls and building upon positive experiences. Mini-case studies should be documented and circulated, 'awaydays' should be held and, more generally, companies should strive to become 'learning organizations'. Companies such as Honda, Canon, 3M and Hewlett Packard are exemplars of this art of organizational learning. *Effective planning* is essential for a speedy and successful launch. A campaign mentality should be fostered, critical paths and rate-limiting steps identified and contingency plans put in place. Marketing planning processes in general are discussed in detail by Malcolm McDonald in Chapter 8. In a later section of this chapter we identify key elements of the innovation planning process.

It is generally held that *careful preparation* provides the cornerstone of any marketing strategy and this is certainly true for innovations. Attention to detail and anticipation of all eventualities should provide the bedrock of the plan. Scenario forecasting techniques where a range of possibilities are profiled provide a powerful tool for predicting likely outcomes and, crucially, for preparing for all eventualities. Traditional quantitative forecasting techniques are very often useless for innovation projects that, by their very nature, have little or no historical data to project.

Channels' availability is a major consideration when planning any innovation programme. If appropriate channels cannot be found the innovator may have to accept responsibility for servicing the market itself, at least in the first instance. Developments in database technology, satellite/cable television, digital television and the Internet are making this increasingly possible, facilitating an efficient and effective direct route to early adopter customers.

Timing is critical for any innovation launch. Careful analysis should be made of the *general market environment* when the launch cycle is being planned. A caveat needs to added here. For some managers there will never be a 'right time' for launch and market conditions are frequently put forward as an excuse for inertia. A fundamental marketing 'fact of life' is that market conditions can be shaped by innovative and entrepreneurial actions by suppliers. As Peter McKiernan demonstrates in Chapter 5, apparently dull life cycles can be rejuvenated, extended and generally reshaped via innovative product and process breakthroughs.

Senior executive commitment is essential for innovation success and speedy launch cycles. It is a well-known adage of management that employees will do as their bosses do, not what they say. To elaborate, if top management demonstrate risk-averse behaviour subordinates will follow suit, even if the message coming from the bosses is positive with respect to innovative behaviour.

Recall that innovation has two principal components: *first* and *fast*, i.e. first to enter the market and fast in developing the market. From a marketing perspective the latter element forms the principal focus of innovation in the sense that it is the core of project implementation. A fundamental requirement in planning the implementation of innovation projects is to profile the potential for building *powerful entry barriers* to protect and build upon the first mover advantage. These were discussed in detail in Chapter 1.

So far this chapter has dealt with the importance of innovation in the current business climate and has introduced the principle of first mover advantage. We have also drawn attention to the organizational challenges and potential pitfalls of pursuing innovation strategies. In the next section we address the latter problems. Innovation is identified as a process, i.e. as an aspect of scientific management that can be modelled and understood in a systematic, structured fashion. This is the process element of innovation strategies identified in Figure 4.1.

The innovation process

A constant theme that permeates all contributions to this handbook is that strategic marketing management can be seen as a structured process which lends itself to formal planning techniques. This principle applies equally to innovation strategies. The core point is that enough theoretical research has been undertaken on the subject to understand what constitutes good and bad practice and countless practical examples are available for illustration.

In the following sections the components of the innovation process are considered in some detail. The factors that underpin innovation success are evaluated alongside the pitfalls which firms regularly seem to stumble across.

Profiling the innovation process

Figure 4.7 illustrates seven stages of the innovation process.

Note that we use the word 'project' when considering the development of the innovation idea. This emphasizes that innovation has a broad scope and should not be exclusively associated with 'product', i.e. it could relate to a communications programme, a logistics project, a channels strategy etc. The important point to emphasize is that as ideas develop through the process shown in Figure 4.7 the risks and costs associated with the project will typically increase, often dramatically. Once a project 'gets a life' the snowball effect of escalating costs can have a powerful impact on the potential success of innovation programmes.

A detailed evaluation of each of these stages is beyond the scope of this chapter although we will examine the first two elements in a little depth below. *Concept testing* embraces advanced technological feasibility studies and prototype development if the project is product based. Similarly, if the innovation is, for example, a distribution project, then detailed retail audits will be under-

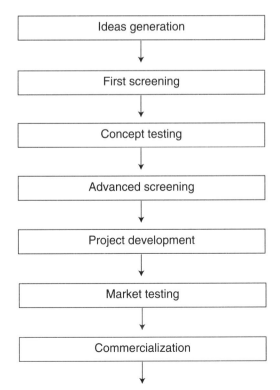

Figure 4.7 *The innovation process*

taken at this stage. *Advanced screening* is a critical stage of the innovation process. Here is the last chance to ensure that unviable ideas are taken out or that ideas that get the go ahead meet key corporate objectives. The following list gives examples of key measures that must be evaluated before full-scale project launch is commenced:

● potential volume;
● potential prices and revenue;
● expected investment needs;
● anticipated direct costs;
● projected cash flows;
● potential profitability;
● market dynamics;
● entry barrier possibilities.

Referring again to Figure 4.7, *project development* moves the innovation into its final phase of preparation. Production is prepared for ramping up and capacity plans are laid out. This stage is often carried out in parallel with *market testing* which may be undertaken on a regional basis or among a selected group of potential customers. *Beta testing* of software products is an example of pre-launch market testing.

Finally, the *commercialization* stage is arrived at. This last element provides the ultimate stumbling block for many firms. Even when the previous stages have been meticulously followed a failed launch can generate disastrous results. It will be recalled that the key to innovation success is the effective commercialization of an idea. Successful commercialization, in turn, requires a clear understanding of how innovations are actually adopted by customers and, moreover, how an innovation spreads throughout a society. These topics were discussed in detail in earlier sections of this chapter.

We will focus in a little more depth here on the second element of the innovation process, *first screening*, since this is where the major mistakes are typically made. Senior executives and other managers have no problem in the first phase of the innovation process, i.e. *ideas generation* and there are a broad range of creative and lateral thinking techniques

which can be utilized to generate hundreds of innovative ideas. A strategic perspective on project screening is typically neglected in the mainstream innovation literature.

Typical innovation errors and innovation error solutions

Two major strategic errors are common in the first screening element of the innovation process:

1. bad ideas go through;
2. good ideas are screened out.

Category 1 errors can often be described as investments in management ego. Partial information is used to move a project ahead and a power base is exploited to ensure that resistance to the programme is removed. In this scenario commitment is secured for a project which objective analysis would demonstrate as flawed. Such innovation programmes can be described as examples of a *pet project syndrome*, i.e. a scenario where a powerful manager pursues a project to meet his or her own objectives, not those of their company. Category 1 errors are very common in high technology companies. Considering the common term Research and Development (R&D), the emphasis tends to be on research (technology push) at the expense of development (market need and market development). The solution to Category 1 errors is to introduce a system of checks and balances, i.e. to ensure that powerful individuals cannot push through ideas without them having been objectively appraised by a cross-functional management team. Another solution increasingly employed by innovative companies is to shift the power base in the R&D function away from research and towards development. The market development team commission projects from the laboratory, projects that are based on their identification of genuine market needs. The laboratory then creates the products. Significant funds can still be put aside for 'blue sky' thinking but the majority of R&D is market focused.

Category 2 errors can be summarized in a simple phrase: *Whoops!* Put simply, it stands for: 'By the time we had realized there was an opportunity, it had gone'!; or, 'By the time we had recognized a threat, it was too late! Earlier in this chapter we emphasized the importance of speed in highly competitive markets. With Category 2 errors the problem is sluggishness. Firms that commit Category 2 errors tend to pursue follower strategies and commonly launch me-too products. As we have seen already, the market shares and financial returns are likely to be significantly lower than more innovative firms. Marketing myopia is strongly associated with Category 2 errors: GM and Ford were slow to launch smaller cars; Olivetti was slow to move away from typewriters; IBM missed a beat in the fast-moving PC business by allowing Compaq to bypass them into 32-bit technology; the Swiss watch industry allowed the Japanese to take significant global market share, etc.

Organizational issues associated with Category 2 errors relate to the way in which investments are made and how failure is handled. Excessive aversion to risk tends to lead to a 'wait and see' type mentality, a dangerous outlook in a fast-changing world. Often a blame culture develops in organizations, a scenario whereby individuals are quite literally scared of taking risks because failure will elicit excessive punishment and/or ostracism. As demonstrated earlier in this chapter, Category 2 companies earn the sort of mediocre margins associated with follower strategies and me-too products. They tend to become locked into a certain 'paradigm', a way of doing business strongly associated with a particular technology which is often divorced from genuine market needs. The following quote from Lee Iacocca, speaking in 1980 when Chrysler, the company he had recently joined, were on the brink of commercial disaster is illustrative:

I thought we were doing marketing. We have a corporate vice president for marketing, a top-notch sales force, a skilled advertising department and elaborate marketing planning procedures.

These fooled us. When the crunch came, I realized that we were not producing the cars that people wanted. We were not responding to new needs. Our marketing operation was nothing more than a glorified sales department.

The key phrase, 'we were not responding to new needs', neatly captures the typical characteristic of marketing myopia, i.e. a failure to be responsive to market dynamics. Customers not only had new needs, they also had new suppliers (the Japanese)! Iacocca also describes the common scenario whereby firms do 'marketing things', *not* strategic marketing management in the way it is outlined throughout the chapters of this book.

To summarize with respect to first screening: Category 1 projects escape rational screening, are vulnerable to rapidly escalating costs and are doomed to expensive failure. Category 2 errors screen good ideas out and the company is forced into 'me-too' type strategies, mediocre returns and, very often, commercial bankruptcy.

Explanations of innovation failure

The following list summarizes common pitfalls which companies stumble across in general, problems which are compounded in the more uncertain world of innovative concepts:

- poor quality market research;
- no valued differential advantage;
- product/technology driven focus;
- aggressive second movers;
- subjectivity in project appraisal;
- no balanced marketing mix;
- no distribution channel support;
- poor launch planning;
- poor marketing communications;
- the project compromises and/or conflicts with an established company image;
- weak inter-functional co-ordination on project development and launch.

Poor quality market research is perhaps the biggest culprit. Traditional research methods based on attitudinal surveys are not ideal for testing new innovation projects. In general, customers or potential customers are unable to articulate an opinion on concepts they have not yet experienced. With innovative concepts it is essential to include experimentation and *behavioural* research techniques into the market research process. Although this tends to be more expensive the greater cost – the cost of failure – should also be considered.

Numerous studies over the years have demonstrated that generic strategies of differentiation can lead to greater profitability. But to succeed, the differentiation embodied in the product concept must be *valued*. A famous story explains: 'If you build a better mousetrap the world will come running to your door'. The world's best-selling mouse catchers remain the wooden spring trap and the domestic cat! Many inventive mousetraps have been launched but none has delivered the core values of convenience, simplicity and, with reference to the cat, affection.

Recall the Category 1 error discussed above. An excessive *product/technology-driven focus* is often the major culprit, i.e. laboratory dreams are divorced from market potential.

The benefits of innovation are often readily outweighed by rivals who enjoy the luxury of existing strengths such as strong customer loyalty, tightly controlled distribution channels, powerful brand name, etc. *Aggressive second movers* frequently use these basic marketing assets to rapidly erode the early advantage of the innovative first mover. Microsoft's extraordinarily rapid destruction of Netscape's market leadership position in the Web browser market provides a classic example of an aggressive second mover leveraging existing market power.

No theory can ever replace the power of well-informed management judgement. Despite this, subjectivity is a major cause of innovation failure. *Subjectivity* backed by a strong power base is also a major cause of Category 1 errors. The tricky task is to exploit the value of management judgement and expertise but to impose 'checks and balances' and prevent strong hierarchical power bases being abused.

In Chapter 2 David Jobber introduced the notion of a 'blended' *marketing mix*. Many an innovation has floundered because the pricing strategy was flawed, the distribution channels were inadequate, the communications programme was weak, employees were not trained and so on. Linked to this, the lack of channel support is another major problem with innovation strategies. The supply chain constitutes the unit of competition and dealers and retailers must be convinced about the potential benefits of an innovative concept (see Chapter 10 for a discussion of how Procter & Gamble addresses this issue).

As mentioned earlier, *planning* is critical for the successful launch of an innovative concept, a topic that is examined in detail in Chapter 8. The newer the innovative concept, the greater the need for the *communications programme* to educate, demonstrate, persuade, etc. Advertising and other *passive* communications are inappropriate for demonstrating innovative concepts but are often heavily relied upon by companies launching new products. A company's reputation and *image* is potentially compromised by innovation failure. A failed technology or premature launch can significantly undermine the credibility of a firm, as can a product launch into a segment which has a different perceived positioning from the core brand.

Finally, organizational life is riddled with *interfunctional conflict* and feelings of internal competition. Taken together, these characteristics stifle innovation and entrepreneurial behaviour. As mentioned elsewhere, cross-functional co-ordination is crucial for inculcating the checks and balances essential for innovation success.

A major theme of the discussion thus far in this chapter has been the importance of first mover advantage for innovation success. This is fine, and an aggressive attacking approach to the marketplace does tend to secure competitive success. Having said this, it has also been demonstrated that many key barriers to innovation success are organizational in nature. As can be seen in Figure 4.1, a flexible and responsive organization constitutes a major component of innovation success. In the last section of this chapter we briefly highlight the importance of building an organizational culture which accommodates rather than constrains the innovation process.

Building an innovation culture ▄▄

The following list identifies critical success factors associated with the effective implementation of innovation strategies. It re-emphasizes the issue of speed and highlights the *internal* organizational issues that are essential to address for *external* innovation success:

- Build an innovation culture throughout the organization.
- Develop systems that reward creativity.
- Develop organizational learning processes to understand failure.
- Have a clear mission and an organization-wide sense of purpose.
- Create a lean, flat, responsive organization.
- Minimize bureaucracy.
- Create task forces and cross-functional project teams.
- Build checks and balances into the innovation screening process.
- Develop an organization-wide hunger for speed.

Organizational culture embraces attitudes, beliefs and behaviours. To secure innovative behaviour it is essential that attitudes are shaped in an appropriate manner. Leadership is critical and the notion of mission plays a powerful role. Honda's mission to 'Kill Yamaha!' led to a phenomenal burst of innovation and ultimate global market share leadership. Bureaucracy stifles innovation, as does the feeling that creative thinking is not recognized as valuable ('you're not paid to think').

A key factor in successful innovation strategies is the organizational ability to *facil-itate functional integration*. Project teams and task forces which draw on a cross-section of functions (e.g. R&D, operations, marketing, logistics, etc.) and divisions (for technology and resource sharing) are essential for improving both speed to market and innovation success.

The emphasis on developing an organizational *hunger for speed* embraces cultural and operational issues in what has widely become known in the literature and within companies as 'time to market' initiatives. The following aspects are central to achieving speed success:

- rapid and effective project screening;
- rapid and effective project development;
- short effective launch cycle;
- rapid market development.

The key words are *rapid* and *effective*. Speed is no good at all if it compromises effectiveness; equally, an obsession with effectiveness could well compromise speed. Business process re-engineering initiatives are often employed to find critical paths and reduce rate-limiting steps while at the same time testing for *total product integrity*. This last phrase was coined to describe how true innovation embraces both *product* and *process* design concurrently.

As mentioned earlier, a detailed evaluation of organizational issues in innovation success is beyond the scope of this chapter. This is not to say that they are unimportant or that they will not detract from innovation success if companies fail to address them. On the contrary, the biggest hurdle to the effective implementation of innovation strategies is an inability of companies to move from 'doing what we've always done' to 'doing what we need to do' for future success. Nigel Piercy looks at general issues in implementing marketing programmes in Chapter 13 while Malcolm McDonald examines the organizational challenges of strategic marketing from a planning perspective in Chapter 8.

Summary

Two statements can be made with reference to innovation from a strategic marketing perspective:

1. Successful innovation is essential for growth and long-term profitability.
2. Most firms are bad at successfully implementing innovation strategies.

In this chapter four key themes relating to innovation and competitive success have been identified:

1. The importance of understanding the context of innovation, particularly with reference to competitive dynamics and the way in which innovations are adopted by groups and diffused throughout society.
2. It is essential to take a strategic view of innovation, particularly with regard to finding genuinely 'new to market' innovation concepts.
3. Innovation should be regarded as a process, i.e. it should be managed in a systematic and structured fashion. Particular attention should be paid to project screening since this is where the major problems occur. Two types of mistake are very common: (i) bad ideas are allowed to go forward; (ii) good ideas are screened out.
4. As mentioned above, most firms are bad at successfully implementing innovation strategies. This is largely due to rigid bureaucratic organizational structures that stifle the flexibility and responsiveness required in turbulent business environments.

In conclusion, innovation provides the link between a company's current marketing performance and its long-term prospects. A sense of vision and a flexible organization is essential if the transition is to be successful.

References and further reading

Doyle, P. (1989), 'Building successful brands: the strategic options', *Journal of Marketing Management*, **5**(1), 77–95.

Drucker, P. (1974), *Management: Tasks, Responsibilities, Practices*, London: Heinemann Professional Publishers.

Trout, J. and Ries, A. (1979), 'Positioning: ten years later', *Industrial Marketing*, **64**(7), 32–44.

5

Strategies in the end game[1] _____

Professor Peter McKiernan, St Andrews University

 In this chapter, we shall explore the strategies open to organizations in the 'ageing' or end-game stage of their industry cycle. We begin by examining the life-cycle concept, its strengths and its limitations. Used wisely, it can help organizations predict patterns of future demand and so prepare themselves, strategically, for these outcomes. Their strategies will depend mainly on (i) the stability or instability of demand in the decline period; and (ii) the competitive position of the organization at the time. We will analyse the options thus available in a well-regarded framework developed by Michael Porter and Kathryn Harrigan. We then go on to extend this framework, adding finer detail where appropriate, by utilizing recent research work based on an alternative to the life-cycle concept, that of population ecology.

Life-cycle approaches to strategy ■

The life-cycle concept has enjoyed a long and useful reputation in helping marketeers and strategists analyse the dynamic evolution of products and industries. For instance, it was the framework that underpinned the vertical axis of business growth in the ubiquitous Boston Consulting Group grid when it was developed by Bruce Henderson and Alan Zakon for the Mead Paper Corporation back in the 1960s.

The concept is deceptively simple in form and inference. In brief, products and industry sales volumes are assumed to follow a four-stage biological cycle: introduction; growth; maturity; and decline (see Figure 5.1). Cash flow and profits have different cycles across the four stages from that of sales volume.

These latter cycles are important. Profit becomes positive only during the growth phase, peaking in maturity, and begins to recede in the decline phase – perhaps even turning negative. Cash flow, however, is significantly positive throughout both the mature and decline phases. These 'theoretical' profiles help analysts generate appropriate strategy options for organizations at each juncture in the life cycle. They also aid them in balancing the overall portfolio of products by ensuring the positioning of appropriate 'cash cows' in mature markets whose revenues can be utilized to support new product introductions and the growth of potential 'stars'. Strategies are thus related, in a pre-

---

1 This chapter owes much to the contributions of Porter, Harrigan, Hall and Taggart.

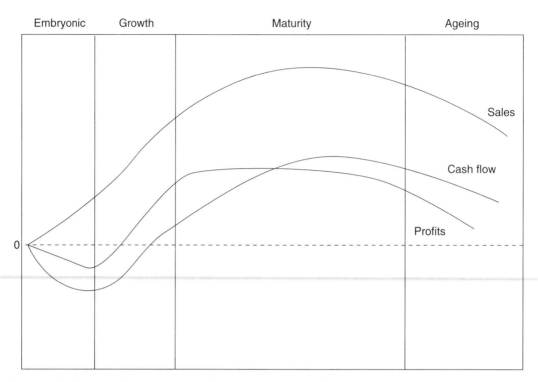

Figure 5.1 *Sales, cash flows and profits over the industry life cycle*

scriptive manner, to each stage of the cycle (see Figure 5.2).

Despite its simplicity and general utility, the life-cycle concept has come under heavy fire from its critics. They seem to have two main concerns outlined in the following text.

Shape and stage configuration

There is debate about whether or not the performance variables (sales, profit, cash flow) actually follow the natural evolution suggested by the shape of the life cycle. Such was

---

- *Introduction stage*: strategies emphasize a buyer focus, build on advertising and increased purchase frequency, high prices, product design, short production runs with high costs. This stage is characterized by few competitors, is high risk with low margins.

- *Growth stage*: buyer group widens, products differentiated by technical and performance characteristics, quality improvements, efficiencies in production and marketing with high advertising expenditure to create brand awareness, with mass distribution channels. This stage is characterized by many competitors, mergers, casualities, higher profits and falling prices.

- *Maturity stage*: focus on process efficiency, reduction in marketing and distribution costs, more product differentiation and market segmentation. Quality high, product standardized. Creative marketing to extend life cycle, packaging important. Mass production, long production runs, some overcapacity. This stage is characterized by price competition, shake-outs, cyclicality, lower prices and margins.

- *Decline stage*: sophisticated buyers, little product differentiation, variable product quality. Cost control by cutting advertising and marketing efforts, specializing channels, simplifying production lines, relying on mass production, reducing differentation and cutting R&D expenses. This stage is characterized by substantial overcapacity therefore more exits and fewer competitors, falling prices and lower margins.

Figure 5.2 *Suggested strategies at each stage of the life cycle*

its perceived relevance, this particular shape was incorporated into most marketing texts throughout the 1970s and 1980s. But, more recently, researchers have suggested that it is, perhaps, only one of thirteen possible trajectories that a product/industry could evolve along. They therefore question the 'homogeneity' of a life cycle. Critics, such as Porter, have asked serious questions about the structure of this 'grandfather of concepts':

- As stage duration differs widely from industry to industry, it is difficult to tell what stage an industry is in at any point in time and so it is impossible to use the life-cycle concept as a planning tool. For instance, economic depressions can mask the development stage of an industry.
- As some industries skip stages, passing, say, from growth straight to decline, and as others manage to be rejuvenated after periods of decline (e.g. motorcycles and bicycles in the UK in the 1980s), it is impossible to use the S-shape pattern consistently.
- As competition at each stage of the life cycle is different for different industries with some starting out fragmented and remaining so (electronic component distribution) and others becoming more concentrated (automobiles), it is impossible to take the broad strategy implications of each stage seriously.
- As organizations can alter the shape themselves through product innovations and creative marketing (e.g. BMX and mountain bicycles in the 1980s/1990s), why should they accept its evolutionary prescriptions in a reactive manner?.
- As the distinction between industries becomes more and more blurred (e.g. is a PC in the computing industry or telecommunications industry?), definitions become impossible and so life cycles pertaining to each could be meaningless.

True, the life-cycle pattern may have been the most common pattern of product/industry evolution but nothing in the concept allows us to predict when it will hold and when it will not. Hence, given this critique, it is difficult to understand why analysts and advisors hang on to the automatic strategy prescriptions of the concept for so long. In some cases, academic researchers were still espousing its virtues in the middle and late 1980s!

Prescriptive strategies

It is probable that the life cycle had run its course by the end of the 1980s. All the automatic strategy prescriptions, together with the typical characteristics of each stage, had been based largely upon data from the PIMS (Profit Impact of Marketing Strategy) source. A variety of samples and sampling methods were used in constructing the ingredients of each life-cycle stage, calling into question their consistency and durability. Moreover, the database was mainly made up of divisions of large organizations which, no doubt, had access to parental support and were constructed strategically, perhaps, by parental objectives and controls. Many facets of enterprise, ownership, flexibility and speed of response, that can form the basis of more creative strategies, were absent from the stage prescriptions.

Controversy also surrounded the nature of performance objectives at each life-cycle stage. The set of strategic variables at each stage differs with different objectives. For instance, inventories will be reduced to obtain a high rate of return on investment objective but increased to obtain a high market share objective. Thus, the important trade-off between long-term goals (market share) and short-term cash flow generation, each of which require different strategies, is ignored by the life cycle's prescriptive leaning. Moreover, strategies are also likely to vary with the type of business. Industrial product firms may differentiate on product quality and service to satisfy sophisticated buyers while consumer product organizations may rely more on market orientation actions (e.g. sales forces) to improve their lot. So effective strategies are likely to be a function of competitive posture, the nature of the environment, corporate objectives, the type

Table 5.1 *Criteria for classification of competitive position*

1 *'Dominant'*
  Dominant competitors are very rare. Dominance often results from a quasi monopoly from a strongly protected technological leadership.

2 *'Strong'*
  Not all industries have dominant or strong competitors. Strong competitors can usually follow strategies of their choice, irrespective of their competitors' moves.

3 *'Favourable'*
  When industries are fragmented, with no competitor clearly standing out, the leaders tend to be in a favourable position.

4 *'Tenable'*
  A tenable position can usually be maintained profitable through specialization in a narrow or protected market niche. This can be a geographic specialization or a product specialization.

5 *'Weak'*
  Weak competitors can be instrinsically too small to survive independently and profitable in the long term, given the competitive economics of their industry, or they can be larger and potentially stronger competitors, but suffering from costly past mistakes or from a critical weakness.

Source: Arthur D Little Inc.

of business as well as just life-cycle stage. As we now know, there are some strategies that have proven to be successful across each stage. Researchers have found that, where market share is the objective, differentiation (e.g. quality, product, value and price) leads industrial businesses to success whether in growth, maturity or decline.

The life cycle itself has had to undergo its own development. Care has been taken to investigate and improve the process and so overcome the difficulties mentioned above. The global consultancy firm, Arthur D. Little, was instrumental in developing a new matrix form by tabulating competitive position (see Table 5.1) against the life-cycle stage (see Figure 5.3).

Once a product/business is placed within the matrix (however subjective the decision), a more 'natural' prescriptive strategic objective is established, e.g. on market share, investment requirements or cash flow expectations. In turn, these suggest various strategic options (see Figure 5.4).

These two matrices then become the starting point of a well-structured, lengthy but organized methodology developed by ADL. Still, even in this form, there is a danger of restricting creative thinking in the generation of unique strategy options by feeling somewhat 'boxed in'.

This discussion of the life-cycle concept acts to warn us of any injudicious acceptance of both tools and techniques and, especially, of automatic strategy prescriptions. Any prescriptions in the end game based solely on the life cycle must be treated with great caution.

End game recognition and preparation

Inevitably, there will be some products or industries where overall demand growth begins to change irreversibly downwards. The context in the end game of shrinking demand is different from that of industry maturity and so requires the assessment of different strategic issues. The features of this context are:

Maturity

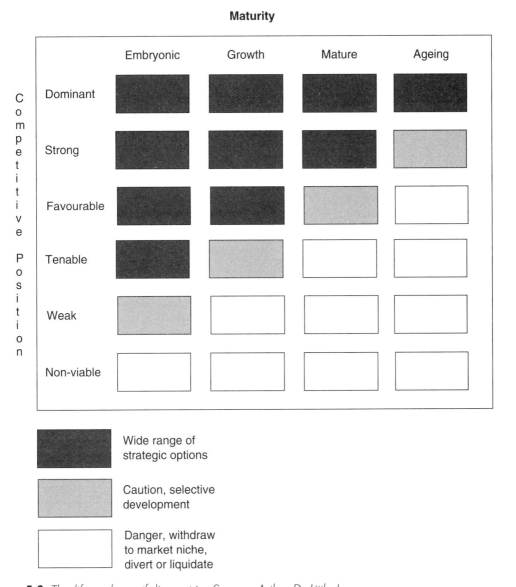

Figure 5.3 *The life-cycle portfolio matrix. Source: Arthur D. Little Inc.*

- excess capacity;
- lack of technical change witnessed by few new product introductions and stable process technology;
- competition shake-out;
- high average age of resource base;
- aggressive price competition in some sectors.

Given these conditions ahead, we first take care not to follow the traditional prescriptions of 'milking' or 'withdrawal' before we do further analysis and preparation; and second, we are encouraged to think proactively and, perhaps, optimistically, about the prognosis for our product/industry. These 'end-game' situations frequently contain contexts within which organizations can flourish with a finely tuned strategy. This phase can continue for decades and need not be dramatic. The example on page 91 illustrates that success can be achieved over long periods after the decline and eventual death of a product/industry. It has been estimated in

	Embryonic	Growth	Mature	Ageing
Dominant	All out push for share Hold position	Hold position Hold share	Hold position Grow with industry	Hold position
Strong	Attempt to improve position All out push for share	Attempt to improve position Push for share	Hold position Grow with industry	Hold position or Harvest
Favourable	Selective or all out push for share Selective attempt to improve position	Attempt to improve position Selective push for share	Custodial or maintenance Find niche and attempt to protect	Harvest or Phased withdrawal
Tenable	Selective push for position	Find niche and protect it	Find niche and hang on or Phased withdrawal	Phased withdrawal or Abandon
Weak	Up or Out	Turnaround or Abandon	Turnaround or Phased withdrawal	Abandon

Figure 5.4 *Strategic position in terms of market share suggested by the life-cycle portfolio matrix (see Figure 5.3) . Source: Arthur D. Little Inc.*

the USA and UK that about one-third of firms in declining businesses are capable of achieving returns on capital employed of over 35 per cent!

Although the end game can be of long duration and provide such high returns for some firms, it can also be characterized by intense competition, price wars, demand instability and supply problems which can make life tough for the unprepared. Hence, it is important to understand the factors influencing the dynamics of competition before successful strategies can be created for the end-game player. This analysis must begin early, while products/industries are still in the 'maturity' phase.

It is helpful to adopt the steps in Checklist 5.1 on the opposite page.

Market stimulation

Stagnation can set in cognitively in the minds of managers who have had years of stable or slowly declining sales in maturity. It may not be just the products that have nearly reached the end of their course! Some creativity, fresh eyes and a little risk can act to revitalize such markets where latent demand has yet to be tapped. Policies should be explored first before a final decision is made to accept that decline has set in for evermore. Such policies could be:

- **Ansoff-driven** – use the traditional Ansoff product-market matrix to explore new market segments (Texas Instruments' design for a calculator for women complete with

The last TV set containing vacuum tubes was manufactured in the USA in 1974. The legacy was a replacement tube market that fed over 20 years of production of TV sets since the 1950s. This was a sizeable market of price-insensitive demand, which enabled the six leading tube manufacturers, through efficient management, to continue in operation for a further two decades, reaping stable and high returns. In fact, price for the valves increased in the UK as they became more scarce – as this author found to his cost when, as a doctoral student in the late 1970s, he tried to re-furbish a VOX AC30 amplifier/speaker (the same model that the Beatles used).

TVs have clearly moved on but, in their progress, there lie the seeds of further decline and so of more end game opportunities. The cathode ray tube (CRT) is now potentially being replaced by liquid crystal display technology giving flat screen TVs with high definition pictures. These, too, may fall eventually from grace and be replaced by plasma versions. The huge installed base of CRT TVs should provide rich pickings for small firms in the repair and maintenance businesses for decades to come.

soft keys and colour tones) and new product opportunities (e.g. the multimedia chain has moved from vinyl records to cassettes to CDs). New applications for the same product or service (e.g. the use of baking soda as a deodorizer or miniaturization of washing machines and fridges for offices or student rooms in halls of residence) can often be created. Much of this can be achieved by a revitalized marketing effort, e.g. a change of distribution channels, an alteration in

Checklist 5.1

Can the market be stimulated?
Can decline be predicted?
Will demand conditions facilitate a favourable decline phase?
Can the exit barriers for all businesses be analysed, influenced and exit predicted?
What are the strengths and weaknesses of all the likely remaining competitors in addressing the residual pockets of demand?

pricing policy, or by giving the product away as a promotion to enhance other products.

- **Proactive lobbying** – influence local, national and regional governments to change the 'rules of the game'. They may be keen to subsidize key industries, e.g. tourism, at the national level or create electronic villages or towns or install airbags in cars (regional level). Good networking and diplomacy skills will still be essential, especially against a background of privatization.
- **Micro-marketing** – find niches in mature industries that are protected from competition due to the relative unattractiveness of the main industry. For instance, micro brewing pubs, which manufacture their own brands of beer, thrive amidst a mature beer market.

Predicting decline

A successful competitive posture in decline depends upon the amount or preparation an organization undertakes in late maturity. Over 60 per cent of industries within mature economies (Western Europe, Japan, USA) expressed slow, zero or negative demand in the late 1980s and early 1990s. Some of these are shown in Table 5.2. Many managers responsible for business in these mature industries fail to notice that demand is stagnant. Their focus is on revenues rather than unit volume. Rarely do they compare 'individual business output' with 'industrial output' and, consequently, these managements fail to predict the coming of the end game. There might be good explanations for this. For instance, if economies are experiencing an upward trend in their business cycle, man-

Table 5.2 *Industries suffering a levelling-off or decline in volume*

Adding machines	Leather belting for machines
Baby foods and baby products	Leather-tanning services
Barbed wire fencing	Mainframe computers
Basic petrochemicals	Manual typewriters
Beer	Millinery and millinery blocks
Buttons and hooks	Paper mills
Canned peas, other vegetables	Passenger-liner services
Cigars, cigarettes, pipe tobacco	Percolator coffeemakers
Commercial-passenger aeroplane propellers	Permanent-wave machines
Cork products	Petroleum refining
Corsets, girdles and brassieres	Gramophone records and players
Creamery butter, cheese, whole milk	Pocket watches
Nappies and rubber panties	Sewing machines
Electronic receiving tubes	Slide rules
Evaporated milk	Steam locomotives and passenger train cars
Farming machinery	Steam radiators
Fountain pens	Straight razors
Gas-lighting fixtures	Sugar
Hand-held irons and ironing boards	Trolley-car services
Hardwood flooring	Venetian blinds
Harpoons	Vinyl gramophone records
Hot breakfast cereals	Washboards
Lace and net goods	Whisky distilling
Lead pencils and crayons	Wringer washing machines

Source: Harrigan (1990)

agers in end-game businesses may be lulled into a false sense of security by frequent contact with managers of growth businesses. Their associated optimism and 'hubris' (e.g. business confidence, expansion by acquisition) may detain the decliners from taking immediate action to deal with their ailing business. (Similarly, economic depressions can be erroneously interpreted as the setting in of a decline phase.)

Correct and timely prediction of the decline phase is therefore critical. This will enable organizations to replenish, reinvest or rationalize their asset base and ensure that suitable general managers are employed if the decision is taken to remain in the industry. So, in preparation for the end game, organizations should be prepared to:

- Minimize investments or other actions that will increase exit barriers unless these are essential.
- Increase the flexibility of the asset base so that it can accept different raw materials or produce related products.
- Scan the industry for segments that will endure throughout the end game and occupy them early.
- Try to create customer-switching costs in these segments.

Hence, analysis of demand is essential in assessing the likely competitive dynamics of the decline phase; in deciding on whether to remain; and in deciding how to strategically reposition in order to compete successfully. If we are tuned into possible futures via, for instance, scenario planning, we have a better chance of avoiding unexpected shocks (e.g. oil price rises in the 1970s) which can make our progression into decline volatile and difficult.

Predicting demand conditions

Causes of decline need to be isolated before predictions on its rate and volatility, and the subsequent degree of competition, can be assessed. The general causes of decline can be split so:

- **Technological** – e.g. change, product obsolescence, substitutes, new raw materials.

- **Socio-demographic** – e.g. demographic trends (baby booms), conservation policies.
- **Fashion** – e.g. lifestyle changes, styling.

In general, technological declines are more predictable, especially when businesses have a good grip on the substitute technologies. Declines precipitated by socio-demographic and fashion changes tend to introduce a good deal of uncertainty into the prediction process.

Other variables

Besides the volatility of decline, other variables can be measured that highlight the likelihood of a favourable or unfavourable climate. These are, for example:

- **Managerial perception** – managers seeing the possibility of rejuvenation may hold on tighter and longer to their position, creating uncertainty and a higher degree of competition. On the other hand, a general acceptance throughout the industry of decline can lead to a more orderly process.
- **Structure of remaining demand** – if the remaining demand is price insensitive (e.g. premium products), it allows organizations to increase price to maintain profits in the face of decreasing sales. If a product has a direct substitute it becomes price sensitive and costs can no longer be fully covered by price issues. Any subsequent price war can be extremely destructive.

The above features provide only a partial determinant of the factors impinging upon favourable or unfavourable decline phases. This analysis needs reinforcement by careful study of the barriers that may prevent businesses from withdrawing easily from their current market position.

Predicting and influencing exit barriers

A timely exit from the industry can be thwarted by the existence of barriers which

Table 5.3 *Exit barriers*

Specialized assets (little or no alternative use)

Accounting loss treatments
- Poor performance undermines confidence in management's capabilities
- Valuation induces firms to prolong presence in industry

Strategic exit barriers
- Quality image, share customers, share physical facilities or other shared strategic facilities
- Centrepiece of related strategies impinging on corporate image
- Customers may be cut off, could harm firm in other businesses

Managerial exit barriers
- Emotional (prestige) investment on brands
- Turf battles (interdepartmental transfers)

Costs of exit
- Labour settlements
- Dismantling costs

Social barrier
- Effect on local economy
- Effect on unemployment rate
- Conservation issues

can become insurmountable for some businesses and strongly influence the extent of competition in the decline stage. Exit barriers manifest themselves in a variety of forms (see Table 5.3). Most critical are those barriers relating to specialized assets with little or no alternative use than to restrict a business's strategic flexibility. They can probably only be sold to competitors who wish to stay in the industry.

The manager's objective is to win the game of 'exit barrier manipulation'. The first move is to ease the way forward for their organization by lowering their indigenous exit barriers if analysis predicts extreme volatility and uncertainty in the end game and, consequently, they do not wish to participate (see Table 5.4). The second move is to influence the barriers to exit of their competitors (both to expedite their exit and to acquire their assets and customer lists and thereby increase market share), if analysis suggests that the end-game environment is going to be favourable for the businesses and they have decided to compete (see Table 5.5).

Predicting competitors' capabilities

Rafferty (1987), using the investment depreciation ratio[2] and the rate of cash flow[3], provides a detailed matrix-based analysis for studying competitors' financial exit barriers and hence their vulnerability to specific decline stage strategies. The former ratio, by measuring the level of investment in fixed assets, predicts the conservatism associated with a business's depreciation policy. The latter ratio gives an estimate as to the investment profile of a particular business by measuring the cash flows generated from its asset base. The result of combining these two ratios is a two-by-two matrix that positions all businesses in the declining industry relative to each other (see Figure 5.5). This display enables 'what if' type ques-

2 IDR = (DE – DI) GBV where DE = depreciation of fixed assets in the year, DI = disposal of fixed assets in the year, GBV = gross book value of assets at the beginning of the year.
3 RCF = (DE – DI) + TE + P GBV where TE = tax equalization and P = profits.

Table 5.4 *Lowering indigenous exit barriers*

Accounting
- Create reserves to offset the cost of write-off losses on disposal where allowed

Technological
- Trade-off highly specialized plant and equipment for more flexible assets that can take other raw materials and produce related products

Financial
- Lease. Do not purchase

Multinational
- Plan to move assets abroad on a scheduled basis, forcing 'jump-off' points of re-evaluation to fund new assets

Planning
- Routinely evaluate whether to exit from a business when it falls below a prescribed level. Unlock declining businesses from others

Source: Developed from Harrigan (1982)

tions to be asked about each firm's vulnerability to a specific decline stage strategy, for example:

B's strategic position is a strong one as investment levels are low while cash generation is high. Barriers to entry, in terms of the need to sustain specific returns on investment, are less demanding than those faced by company A. However, A's position is most vulnerable with low cash and high investments, exit barriers are formidable and probably insurmountable if faced with a rapid rate of market decline. Hence B could steal market share from A by leading a downward price spiral where A's ability to compete is handicapped by its need to maintain adequate ROIs. An inability to do so could have ramifications for its share price and cost of capital. C will do best to harvest its

position and may become the prime acquisition candidate as excess capacity dominates the declining market.

This type of analysis, coupled with a broader SWOT approach, can yield significant information for 'simulation' analyses of strategy choices and their effect on rivals. It also enables individual managers to analyse and identify the optimum strategy in their particular circumstances.

End game strategic options

Once we have completed our checklist in late maturity, we need to decide whether or not to compete in the end game or to exit. We need

Table 5.5 *Lowering competitors' exit barriers*

- Acquire their physical plant or assets
- Offer to service and supply replacement parts to their customers
- If a supplier appears eager to help a competitor, offer to purchase more from that supplier
- Alert regulatory agencies of competitors' transgressions, particularly in pollution control
- Start a price war providing strengths exit, e.g. if you face price insensitivity
- Go public in plea for their exit

Source: Developed from Harrigan (1982)

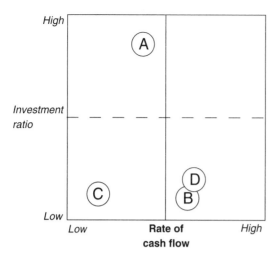

Figure 5.5 *Movement of cash flow against investment ratio. Source: Rafferty (1987)*

to make a major strategic choice. Such strategy selection means matching internal strengths and weaknesses to the end-game environment. The strengths and weaknesses in the previous stages of growth and maturity may no longer be appropriate for sustaining a competitive advantage in the decline phase. Success depends upon the ability to serve the residual pockets of demand that remain and the ability to handle the varying degrees of competition that may follow. The matrix shown in Figure 5.6 provides an approximate guide to strategy

	Competitive strength	
	High/Medium	*Medium/Low*
	Favourable	Harvest
Favourable	or	or
Industry decline structure	Niche	Divest quickly
	Niche	Divest
Unfavourable	or	
	Harvest	quickly

Figure 5.6 *Competitive strengths for remaining demand pockets. Sources: Adapted from Harrigan (1980) and Harrigan and Porter (1983)*

choice. This depends upon whether the prior analysis (in the checklist) established a highly certain, stable, orderly decline (favourable) or degree of volatility and rivalry between competitors (unfavourable). Table 5.6 provides a useful guide for judging the favourability of the declining industry. In the former case, indigenous strengths should lead to a drive for leadership position through investment; in the latter case, this strategy is likely to fail and rationalization and niche focus are probably the best prescription.

In these two circumstances, we can generate four generic strategies:

Leadership

Positive aggression to dominate the final revenues in the end game. This could include:

- **Market share gain** – through building by encouraging competitor exit or through buying up of competitors and/or their assets, e.g. White Industries became America's third largest appliance manufacturer by buying such names as Kelvinator, Westinghouse, Philco and Frigidaire from firms motivated to exit.
- **Raise the stakes** – through product/process improvements making it costly for competitors to stay around, e.g. Maxwell House introduced gourmet coffee in order to dominate yet another niche in the coffee business and so limit further opportunities for rivals.
- **Cognitive manipulation** – through extensive disclosure of credible marketing data illustrating the extent of decline which will force 'emotional' hangers-on to leave.
- **Servant strategies** – involving producing spare parts and private label goods for competitors making it easier for them to exit.

Niche

We can use analysis in late maturity to predict pockets of enduring demand and stable decline. We can also use leadership strategies to dominate the niche and build up entry bar-

Table 5.6 *Attractiveness potential of declining industry*

Demand conditions	Environmental hospitable	Attractiveness inhospitable
Speed of decline	Very slow	Rapid or erratic
Certainty of decline	Very predictable patterns	Great uncertainty, erratic patterns
Pockets of enduring demand	Several or major ones	No niches
Product differentiation	Brand loyalty	Commodity-like products
Price stability	Stable, price premiums attainable	Very unstable, pricing below costs
Exit barriers		
Reinvestment requirements	None	High, often mandatory and involving capital assets
Excess capacity	Little	Substantial
Asset age	Mostly old assets	Sizeable new assets and old ones not retired
Resale markets for assets	Easy to convert or sell	No markets available, substantial costs to retire
Shared facilities	Few free-standing plants	Substantial and interconnected with important businesses
Vertical integration	Little	Substantial
'Single product' competitors	None	Several large competitors
Rivalry determinants		
Customer industries	Fragmented, weak	Strong bargaining power
Customer switching costs	High	Minimal
Diseconomies of scale	None	Substantial
Dissimilar strategic groups	Few	Several in same target markets

Source: Adapted from Harrigan and Porter (1983)

riers to prevent invasion e.g. Cross and Mont Blanc have succeeded in the fountain pen market by positioning in the high price, high quality executive market.

Harvest

This is similar to a niche recovery strategy and emphasizes cost rationalization and minimum investment with the hope of maximizing revenue from the existing asset base. Harvest strategies can be fast or slow. The former attempts to maximize short-run cash flows and minimize investments by sharply reducing operating expenses. The latter attempts to maximize the flow of cash over longer periods by trying to slow down the decline. So investment in plant, equipment and R&D go ahead sharply while cuts in operating areas (e.g. marketing and after sales service) are only gradually reduced. Driven by short run horizons, a harvest strategy can often accelerate decline where competition is strong and firms battle for the rapidly reducing revenues. Employees can become utterly frustrated by the lack of long-term security making implementation of a harvest strategy difficult. Customers, too, can lose confidence if they suspect this strategy is in operation. Once the word is out that the company is not serious, aggressive competitors may move in and clean up. So harvesting should be disguised as much as possible. We should also spare a thought for managers who are charged with seeing the process through. Often, they can be demotivated and also lack the necessary recovery skills and expertise. Therefore, reward systems will have to be adjusted to ensure commitment. If this fails, 'specialists' may have to be hired on a contract basis – the kind of 'hatchet staff' infamous in corporate turnarounds.

One useful attribute of a harvest strategy, compared to one of divestment, is that, if decline has been predicted in error and sales take off, the strategy can be redeveloped and opportunities regained.

Divest

Again, analysis in late maturity is essential in order to make an early decision to remain in, or exit, the decline phase. If the decision is to exit then the earlier, the better, as the value of the assets will be greater near the top of the cycle. Potential 'leaders' of the decline phase, who may wish to purchase resources and customer lists to dominate the decline phase, should be approached. Divestment is not necessarily easy to manage. Exit barriers may be high (long-term contracts with suppliers/customers/employees, legal requirements to supply spares and service, government restrictions). In addition, as few managers willingly accept defeat and some

become the slaves of their emotions, there is a tendency to hold on, perhaps, too long. This is typical in many family businesses that may have survived on minimal wage costs and general family subsidization for years. Hence, some diplomacy and tenderness may be required for an efficient exit.

The strategies are illustrated in Figure 5.6.

This framework for strategic choice should facilitate an early strategic decision on whether to compete in the end game and how to do this. If this decision entails remaining in the industry, the strategy has to be forced through aggressively. Strong clear signals, say through capital investment early on in the decline phase, may be enough to nudge indecisive competitors to exit early, enabling market share to be captured and effective competition to be reduced. Significantly, in Harrigan's original research into 61 organizations in end-game situations, 92 per cent of them who followed the prescribed strategies in Figure 5.6 were successful, while 85 per cent of those businesses who did not follow them, failed.

Population ecology

Recently, the Harrigan/Porter model has been refined to include features stemming from the field of population ecology. Briefly, organizations occupy niches in their sectors. Two changes in the configuration of the niche can create the conditions for decline. Reductions in the size of the niche reduces the volume of business and so the number of companies that it can support. Changes in the shape of the niche, e.g. by consumer demand or technological innovation, affect the type of activity that it can support. Shapes undergo constant change so some part of an old niche may remain for a while until the transition to a new niche occurs. Such change can be either continuous or discontinuous. In the former, organizations can plan for the end game, in the latter, rapidity and crisis can make this impossible. We can bring together the two elements to analyse possible state in the end game (see Figure 5.7).

Configuration	Change	
	Continuous	*Discontinuous*
Niche size	Erosion	Contraction
Niche shape	Dissolution	Collapse

Figure 5.7 *Population decline model*

- **Erosion** – this is gradual over a long time e.g. IBM in mainframe computers; competition will slowly increase leading to downsizing; focused, cost-efficient organizations will win out.
- **Contraction** – this could be massive downsizing e.g. defence sector after the peace dividend; competition will increase dramatically; focused, cost-efficient players will win out.
- **Dissolution** – here, one niche slowly evolves into another e.g. vinyl records to CDs; competition increases moderately; broader, cost-efficient players will win out.
- **Collapse** – this could be complete eradication e.g. glass fibre wool with the advent of cheap double-glazing; competition will increase in the overlap between the old and new niches, but the overall level of competition in the new niche is likely to decrease due to the relatively rapid collapse of the original; focus or focus differentiators, who can move quickly between the old and new niches to gain first mover advantages, will win out.

The model predicts that:

- Specialist organizations are more prone than generalists to decline in niche shape, because of their narrow domains.
- Generalist organizations are more prone to experiencing decline due to reductions of niche size, because they are less efficient than specialist organizations.

The model explains why there are differences between the level of competition among organizations under different conditions of decline, why different types of organization do well in some conditions and not in others, and why variations exist in the types of organizations that are most threatened by the different conditions of decline. Hence, different organizations show a variety of strategic responses to decline, some more productive than others. The ecology model is much richer than its cousins as it is possible to assess the likely structural response of the organization as well as its strategic response. The latter, of course, will depend upon whether incumbent managers have correctly perceived the decline and timely responded; some may be blind and unresponsive (see Figure 5.8).

The ecology model, then, is a useful addition to our understanding of the behaviour of organizations in decline. It builds strongly on the contributions of previous work, although its reductionist nature means that it loses much of the richness of, say, a detailed industry analysis.

End-game research evidence

We witnessed previously how the research that claimed to justify the prescriptive strategies of the life cycle was flawed in a number of ways. Much more careful research was conducted in the 1980s to assess the viability of the strategic options in the end game. The results suggest that:

- much of the conventional prescriptions for strategy options in the decline phase are too general without a well-defined context;
- the adoption of an aggressive strategic posture in the early stages of decline, after careful analysis in late maturity, can yield high rewards;
- average profit and cash flow in the end game do not only depend on market structure (concentration); market share, number and type of customer or customer purchase amount and frequency are also important;
- capital intensity, employee ratios, marketing effort, cost structure and the

Configuration	Change	
	Continuous	*Discontinuous*
Niche size	*Erosion*	*Contraction*
	Structure:	Structure:
	Redistribution	Retrenchment
	Fine tuning	Substantial cuts
	Strategy:	Strategy:
	Offensive	Offensive
	consolidation	consolidation
Niche shape	*Dissolution*	*Collapse*
	Structure:	Structure:
	Incremental addition	Substitution
	New alternatives	Fast search for alternatives
	Strategy:	Strategy:
	Create new domain	Create new domain
	Substitute domains	Substitute domains

Figure 5.8 *Population ecology and strategic response*

extent of R&D do not differ much with market structure, market share or customer profile;
- the really influential variables for good profit and cash flows are:
  - strong product market reputation
  - low capital intensity
  - high relative product quality
  - low purchase and/or manufacturing costs
- high cash flows are as a result of high profitability, not the running down of the capital base, market share, sales force or R&D expenditure;
- in fragmented markets, low advertising expenditure is beneficial to both profitability and cash flows but, in concentrated markets, pricing is the key variable;
- interestingly, there was not a lot of difference between the profits and cash flows of successful businesses in the decline phase and those businesses in growing markets.

Example Two provides a good example.

Hostility

Throughout the decline phase, companies should be prepared for a certain degree of hostility, as competitors fight for diminishing shares of the cake. Research in this area is helpful as a guide to (a) the problem of what behaviour to expect in hostile markets and (b) strategies that seem to be effective in such contexts.

Process of hostility

Potter (1991) has described a study of the hostility process conducted by the Windermere Consulting Company in the USA. There are six phases:

- **Phase 1: margin pressure** – created by overcapacity and predatory pricing. Customers gain and competitors seek protected niches which eventually follow the same pattern.
- **Phase 2: share shifts** – leaders can hold high prices for too long. Faced by competitors with lower price points, they

**Example Two
Dundee jute industry**

Dundee in Scotland was famous for the three Js: jute; jam and journalism. These three sectors dominated the city's economy in the nineteenth and early twentieth centuries. The jute sector was made up of a number of family firms, many of which had grown by acquisition of other local firms. However, in the 1960s and 1970s, cheap imports of jute from India and Bangladesh, coupled with a switching by major carpet manufacturers to polypropylene rather than jute as a carpet backing in the UK, decimated demand for local producers. Clever firms bought up the assets and customer lists of competitors, thus signalling their intent early. The sector concentrated rapidly as competitors exited.

Hence, a few firms were able to capture greater market shares than before and, using the increased revenues so generated, invested in new machinery to produce (a) the polypropylene substitute and (b) high-end quality jute that could not easily be produced by the Indians or the Bangladeshis due to the skill and technology involved. The end game was dominated by them for decades thereafter

eventually concede but not after loss of considerable share, e.g. IBM and Compaq as leaders, and Dell at a lower price point in PCs. Other courses of share shift include a quality upgrading, where some companies simply deliver better products/services (e.g. UPS, FedEx), and acquisitions to obtain scale economies.

● **Phase 3: product proliferation –** competitors fight it out with upgrades and bundles (e.g. PCs and software with fax modems, etc; low sodium, low fat, low salt foods, etc.). Others can offer the bare product features to undercut the 'bundlers' on price, e.g. Easyjet (UK) and Southwest Airlines (USA). The result is hectic competition.

● **Phase 4: self-defeating cost reductions –** pressure to maintain margins leads to self-defeating cost reductions. Restrictions on investment mean a failure to match product/service quality improvements. Reputations become damaged and are difficult to reinstate (British Leyland,

General Motors, Chrysler and Fiat to name a few in automobiles). Distribution channel cuts can also destroy market position.

● **Phase 5: consolidation and shake-out –** first, internal pruning and cutting reduces the resource base. Second, mergers and acquisitions act to 'mop up' weak competitors. Finally, global consortia are formed, e.g. BT and MCI in 'Consort'.

● **Phase 6: rescue –** most firms eventually concede to the dramatic repercussions of their actions, markets settle down with fewer suppliers to become 'controlled' oligopolies with three or four key players controlling about 80 per cent of the market. Price competition is replaced by an acceptance of existing shares and things stabilize. The rescue phase can take up to 20 years to bring about, quicker if external factors, e.g. currency depreciation, (which may stimulate export growth) have a direct impact.

Successful hostility strategies

Research shows that leading performers in hostile environments can actually outperform the all share indices of their relevant stock markets. Their strategies follow common characteristics, despite the industry covered, and tend to be continuous and long term in nature. Namely:

- **Lowest delivered cost position** – relative to competition, coupled with an acceptable delivered quality and a pricing policy aimed at gaining profitable volume and market share (e.g. Ford, General Motors, Whirlpool, Miller).
- **Highest product/service quality differential position** – relative to competition, coupled with both an acceptable delivered cost structure and a pricing policy to gain margin sufficient to fund re-investment in product/service differentiation (e.g. Michelin, John Deere, Mercedes Benz).

Caterpillar (earth moving equipment) and Philip Morris (cigarettes) managed to achieve both positions successfully. Interestingly, most companies developed strategies unique to their own resource base and context rather than blindly following prescriptive advice such as 'milk, harvest and divest'. For instance, they continued to invest in core businesses rather than diversify.

Subject to careful analysis in late maturity, a decisive choice and a judicious strategy selection our optimism about end-game performance may well be justified.

Summary

So, contrary to a generally held opinion, the end game can and does prevent rewarding opportunities for proactive organizations. It is not the graveyard that most people think it is. With large installed bases, competitors exiting, technology more or less stable, accumulated wisdom and low investments, the gap between the revenue and cost lines can be as large as any other period in the life of organizations. The key to this appears very simple. It matters about how well companies are informed about the nature of change ahead when sitting comfortably in mature markets. This means continued awareness of industry, technological, government and consumer trends. It is about reading the emerging patterns and writing stories about, and sending postcards from, possible futures. Scenario planning can help here. Once read, then proactivity must follow quickly. Announce your intentions early and either dominate the end game or exit early while assets still command a reasonable price. As the great sage said: 'Don't get stuck in the middle'.

References and further reading

Harrigan, K. R. (1980), 'Strategies for declining businesses', *Journal of Business Strategy*, Fall, 20–34.

Harrigan, K. R. (1982), 'Strategic planning for end game', *Long Range Planning*, **15**(6), 45–48.

Harrigan, K. R. (1990), 'Will you be the last iceman?', *Sales and Marketing Management*, **142**(1), 62–67.

Harrigan, K. R. and Porter, M. E. (1983), 'End game strategies for declining industries', *Harvard Business Review*, July–August, 111–120.

Rafferty, J. (1987), 'Exit barriers and strategic position in declining markets', *Long Range Planning*, **20**(2), 86–91.

Exploring the principles of market segmentation _____

Dr David Tonks, The Management School, The University of Lancaster

This chapter starts from the premise that market segmentation provides a foundation for strategic marketing as higher-level analysis and decision making. Market segmentation therefore works as the keystone for building particular marketing strategies.

The chapter provides explanation of the need for market segmentation and recommends procedures for developing marketing strategies based on market segmentation. A framework for evaluating market segments is provided together with assessments of the standard market segmentation variables. The material in this chapter leads into the associated strategic activities of positioning.

Throughout, the main reference point is market segmentation of larger consumer markets in the UK.

Market segmentation and strategic marketing ▬▬▬▬▬

Segmentation (market segmentation) can be seen as a descriptive technique and even as a business philosophy but its major role is as a process which underpins strategic marketing where the guiding imperative should be marketing action. The essential principle behind the segmentation process is to make sense of complex markets where there exists a diversity of needs, wants, desires and choices. A broad definition of segmentation can be given as:

Segmentation is the process which identifies and evaluates groups of customers who have distinctive buying behaviour.

Strategic marketing has been likened to a process of 'adaptive search'. Working within a coherent marketing strategy is crucial when a company is searching and adapting in a complex market structure. Given that customer orientation should be the focus of all marketing activity, the process of segmentation converts the marketing concept, through strategic marketing, into an operational reality. Marketing strategy could consist exclusively of segmentation together with positioning and, in some circumstances, segmentation might determine marketing objectives and corporate purpose.

Strategic marketing is concerned with the bigger issues of medium- and long-term allocation of marketing resources. Segmentation will run through all marketing activity and tactical manoeuvres such as short-term adjustments to prices or advertising spend will be made for particular segments but these should be seen as consequences of marketing strategies based on segmentation principles.

Simple and sophisticated models designed to facilitate marketing strategy indicate the importance of segmentation. For example, any use of product life-cycle analyses, product-market expansion matrices, portfolio analyses and brand mapping requires segments to be identified and evaluated in some way. Strategic marketing thus revolves around segmentation.

In an ideal world, your job as manager would include setting goals and acquiring the resources to achieve them. But you don't live in an ideal world because there are people like you in it (Scott Adams).

Fragmentation of markets ▬▬▬

Segmentation is far from new. Markets have always been diverse and the process of segmentation is one of the older rituals of trade. What has altered is the extent of the diversity, the pace of change and the formality of the process.

J. B. Say was a French economist (1767–1832) who usually receives credit for the claim that 'Supply creates its own demand'. J. B. Say proposed that it is impossible for total production not to equal total demand because it is the act of production

that creates the potential demand for products. The idea is now seen as crude which is hardly surprising since this early proposition concerned a less complicated world of 'suppliers' markets' where needs and wants were basic, incomes were modest, products were commodities, distribution and communication links were primitive, technology was simple and the pace of change was slow. Segmentation certainly took place but it was a straightforward and often personal process.

Nowadays most markets are 'buyers' markets' where demand very much determines supply and companies must be market driven if they are to survive. Such demand is usually subtle in nature and this is why the need for segmentation is so acute. Even a basic consumer product such as salt is now differentiated with various product forms and brands targeted to particular segments. For example, on the shelves of any large supermarket in the UK, there will typically be at least six brands of salt covering iodised salt, reduced sodium salt, rock salt, coarse crystal sea salt, and fine crystal sea salt – as well as cooking salt and standard table salt.

In the UK, there was certainly a period when the emphasis in consumer marketing was on volume production and on what has been termed 'mass marketing' but changes over the last 40 years have located segmentation as a central and formal fixture in marketing strategy.

On the supply side, there has been a general intensification of domestic and international competition. Competitive pressures require companies to pay closer attention to customers in spite of the distance that usually exists between them. Competitive pressures have also resulted in supply cost reductions and the real cost of most products has dropped considerably over the last 20 years. This means that new segments have access to products that in the past were only available to a selected few. As well as – or perhaps because of – competition, continuing advances in manufacturing techniques and improvements in distribution and communication networks have assisted the implementation of segmentation to the point where 'micro-marketing' or 'mass customization' is now occurring and the relationship between the supplier and the customer moves from being remote to being highly personal once more, albeit through a formal planning process. The growing importance of direct marketing is an obvious example. Heinz is planning to increase its direct marketing database of households to 8 million, covering some 30 per cent of the UK, and intends to collaborate with owners of non-competing databases such as those of retailers built up from loyalty cards schemes and other methods. Another example would be the jeans market, already highly segmented, where it is now possible to order tailor-made jeans.

On the demand side, consumer markets are becoming increasingly fragmented. The principal influences on the demand side are pluralism and prosperity.

Pluralism

Economic, political, technological and socio-cultural forces all have some bearing on the fragmentation of consumer markets and they all mesh with one another but it is the socio-cultural factors which have the direct link. While there may be certain mainstream socio-cultural patterns that endure, the general trend in recent years has been towards greater individualism and from that greater variety in needs and wants.

For example, traditional structures such as the extended family, the world of work, state institutions and the church can all provide a sense of collective identity. Arguably, they are weakening structures or, at least, they and their influences are changing. Such changes, and they are myriad, affect the orientation of the individual. Some individuals, particularly younger people, are attracted to the proliferation of sub-cultures that provide comfortable allegiances and coherent meaning. The idea of predetermined identities at stages in life has changed with a portfolio of roles and behaviours being consciously

adopted over time, resembling a series of projects. Well-educated and more sophisticated individuals are likely to be motivated by the desire for experience, self-identity and self-realization. Furthermore, the modern consumer is better informed, is alert to overt marketing activity and is less passive when compared with the consumers of only 20 years ago. Such modern consumers have greater freedom of choice and are less bound by convention or utility.

A dominant feature of the UK and of the Western world is socio-cultural pluralism. One perspective is that as a new millennium arrives, there will be a continuing 'balkanization' of societies and of cultures, particularly popular cultures. Another perspective is that society is becoming 'atomized' but if that is too extreme a position, the general trend has certainly been entropic with the birth of many new tribes and the demise of socio-cultural absolutes. Such changes in society and culture and the spawning of new segments are non-linear. They are unpredictable and unstable.

Prosperity

Increases in disposable income allow the needs and wants of diverse groups of individuals to find expression. Most individuals and most segments have sufficient income for the basic necessities. Additional income provides freedom for self-expression and greater choice. Increasing prosperity facilitates not only greater consumption but also different consumption. As a result of increased purchasing power, a wider variety of products are called forth. At the same time, the distribution of capital and income causes further variation in discretionary spending.

These trends on the demand side can be expected to continue. In the absence of major political or economic upheaval, societies and cultures will become more complex and more fragmented in terms of values, beliefs, ambitions, desires, needs, wants and subsequent choices. It also seems likely that disposable incomes will continue to rise.

The same can be said for the influence of supply side trends but technology deserves special attention. Technology will continue to have a great impact on marketing processes. The last decade has seen the extensive diffusion of cheap and powerful business hardware and software. Systems for collecting marketing information are being improved continuously and commercial agencies now offer large and highly detailed databases for markets, segments and consumer behaviour. Developments such as EPOS (Electronic Point of Sale) and EFTPOS (Electronic Funds Transfer at Point of Sale) will generate even more information on segments and buying behaviour. New innovations in communication and distribution such as interactive TV and transactional marketing via the Internet will facilitate segmentation as well as creating new segments. In addition to the direct impact of IT on marketing and the process of segmentation, there is the powerful knock-on effect of technological advance in other functional areas such as manufacturing. CAM (Computer Aided Manufacturing) allows for small batch runs at relatively low incremental costs. The implications for segmentation are enormous.

Socio-cultural pluralism and rising disposable incomes are the main driving forces behind the need for segmentation. Markets are generally 'buyers' markets' where the consumers enjoy sovereignty and have very diverse needs and wants. Market segments are diverging rather than converging. Marketing strategy has to manage this diversity and it does so by using segmentation that allows the diversity to be recognized, understood and supplied.

Market segmentation as a process

The underlying principle and also the key function of segmentation is to make sense of consumer diversity and, from that, to provide a foundation for marketing strategy. There are few markets where the absence of any real differences in buying behaviour removes the need for segmentation.

The UK resident population now includes around 47 million adults. In an ideal world, each of these individuals might be seen as a segment for consumer products. Small businesses with well-defined geographical catchment areas may be able to treat a neighbourhood population as a collection of unique customers. The local garage or hairdresser may be in such a position. However, for most larger companies marketing consumer goods, working realities mean that there is a need to deal with segments of the population which share common characteristics but which are also geographically dispersed.

Segmentation can be seen as a 'bottom-up' or 'lumping' process where customers are

Checklist 6.1

How is segmentation incorporated into your marketing strategy?
What are the determinants of the market structure in which you operate?
How diverse are the needs and wants of your customers?
Are those customer needs converging or diverging?
What will happen to your market over the next ten years?

aggregated according to their similarities. It can also be seen as a 'top-down' or 'splitting' process through the disaggregation of a mass. The latter tends to be the popular view and operationally this may be easier. However, given that customer needs and wants should determine marketing activity then the preference would logically be for aggregating customers rather than disaggregating the mass, i.e. the total market. Either way, the segmentation process can cover any one or a combination of classifying, describing, explaining, predicting and evaluating market segments, each of which contains customers who are similar. Various marketing operations including sales force organization and distribution logistics will require some of these activities but segmentation as strategy will necessitate all of them if the exercise is thorough and the purpose is to develop sound positioning and subsequent implementation plans.

The process of segmentation within strategic marketing is illustrated in Figure 6.1. An array of distinctive and worthwhile segments is the outcome and this allows positioning to begin. In turn, positioning leads to implementation and monitoring with respect to target segments. Figure 6.1 provides the structure for the rest of this chapter.

This segmentation process shares the ultimate concern of marketing strategy, which is that of effective and efficient resource utilization. The company will be more successful by concentrating its efforts on particular segments instead of attempting to be all things to all people and segmentation leads to what is called the 'rifle' approach rather than the 'shotgun' approach. Using a rifle approach, there is a focus through positioning on some particular target market or target markets. The shotgun approach scatters its fire in a rough and general direction towards a large market or towards many segments.

The illustration provided in Figure 6.1 is a fairly accurate representation of what should happen with a formal, analytical, data-driven procedure but it is important to recognize that in practice, the process may be less tidy. Some examples may be needed here.

First, strategy development, like any other marketing activity, is an art as well as a science. Within the company, the impact of

Figure 6.1 *Segmentation as a process*

visionary or politically powerful individuals can be considerable. Inspiration may be as relevant as analysis in the identification of segments. Segmentation solutions that are known to be expedient might also be necessary.

Second, a formal, analytical procedure for segmentation assumes that adequate, timely and accurate data is available. This is not always the case and in times of change, such as with new products or with fickle segments, the available data may be very limited and judgement replaces analysis. There is always an element of risk.

Third, companies do not necessarily work through this kind of process from beginning to end in a linear fashion. Circumstance will cause the process to be iterative and sometimes the starting point will not be at the beginning with a blank sheet of paper.

Fourth, in circumstances of extreme change, such as when radically innovative products alter the market structure, the company might create the segments.

In the customer-driven company, there are consequential effects of adopting segmentation as a central fixture in marketing strategy. For example, there may be implications for marketing organization. With targeted segments, it may be preferable to organize marketing activity around the segments rather than around products or brands. Following on from this and when accounting for marketing activity, productivity analysis by seg-

ment becomes a requirement and when identifying the capital value of marketing activity, reference to the segments is needed in addition to measurements of brand values. Drastic upheavals in organizational structures and procedures can be very undesirable but it makes sense to consider the further implications of adopting market segmentation as the basis for strategic marketing.

Defining the market

Before considering the ways in which a market could be segmented, the market of interest should be clearly defined and this is not as simple as it might first appear. Industry convention, the perceptions of managers and available data can be influential and this applies equally to the selection of segmentation variables. Once a method is implemented, it can become institutionalized and shapes the way in which markets are conventionally understood. In this way, the markets and market segments that are chosen become important because they are believed to be important. Also, when major change is taking place, such as with an innovative product launch, market definition may be speculative.

Defining markets according to some broad characteristic displayed by consumers can have an immediate and intuitive appeal, but this usually falls down at the level of practi-

Checklist 6.2

In practice what does segmentation mean to you?
Is segmentation an explicit element within your marketing strategy?
From your experience, is segmentation something other than an analytical process?
Is your marketing function organized around segments?

cal significance. For example, a company marketing a brand of bottled lager could define the market of interest as the 'Youth Market', those within an 18–24 age group, but the plethora of goods and services which are bought by a market so defined means that it becomes a vague notion.

The essential purpose behind consumption or ownership makes sense as a way of defining markets, particularly generic markets. In the case of alcoholic drinks, the market might be defined by the fundamental need for 'escape'. An advantage of this approach is that it is less restrictive in terms of locating opportunities and threats but it is also vague and ambiguous.

A common method for delineating consumer markets is according to existing products, product groups and brands. This hypothetical company marketing bottled lager could make reference to the 'beer and lager market' with specific reference to brands available as draught or in cans and bottles such as Tetleys, Banks, Stones, Carlsberg, Heineken, Castlemaine, Becks, and so on. Associated with this method, there is an in-built idea of the 'choice set', those products or brands which are known to exist as alternatives but a danger is that classic 'marketing myopia' sets in where potential threats and opportunities are neglected because of the narrow product-based conceptualization of the market. With the example of bottled lager, the market definition might

encompass competing alcoholic drinks to include not only beers and other lagers but also ciders, fruit-flavoured alcoholic drinks such as Hooch and Memphis Mist, and whisky brands such as Bells – all of which are now being marketed heavily to the 'Youth Market'.

In practice, a number of alternative methods for defining markets are used. More distant competing products could be considered and the net is cast wide such that a brand of bottled lager is seen as existing in a market defined as 'All recreational drinking'. At other times, close substitutes are the main issue and the market of interest has a much tighter definition. To use the same example, the focus of attention could become 'bottled lagers for young people'.

Identifying the market segments ∎

The initial stage of defining the market of interest reveals different ways of tackling segmentation. The market of interest could be defined in terms of underlying needs or wants such as 'escape' or 'recreation', or it could be understood according to broad consumer characteristics, as with the 'Youth Market'. A combination of the two might also be used. These alternative approaches are also encountered with the identification of segments.

Checklist 6.3

How is your market defined?
What is your generic market?
What kinds of benefits are sought by customers in your market?
What is the choice set in your market?

For making sense of diverse markets, a crucial distinction has to be drawn between what will be called 'behaviour' variables and 'general' variables. Behaviour variables have a direct concern with the way customers are inclined to purchase and consume. 'Benefits sought' would be an example of segment identification using a behaviour variable and a segment within a market defined as 'bottled lagers for young people' might be identified as one which 'seeks peer group approval'. In contrast, general variables identify through providing descriptions of segments and they are not directly related to predispositions or actual acts of purchase and consumption. From this, a segment identified using general variables could be 'males, aged 18–24'.

The distinction between general and behaviour variables is extremely important for a clear appreciation of segmentation as a basis for strategy. Both behaviour and general variables can be used for identifying and understanding market segments but it is the behaviour variables that should always come first in any segmentation analysis that has a strategic purpose.

To give an illustration of this important distinction, the options for marketing strategy are often articulated using a product-market expansion matrix that considers the alternative combinations of existing, modified and new products against existing, associated or new segments. No matter what kind of movement might be contemplated, including that of doing relatively little by seeking penetration with existing products and segments, it will be necessary to have an appreciation of relevant aspects of buying behaviour in the segments. Behaviour variables, either implicitly or explicitly, will be of primary concern. As for the radical option of new products in new segments, it will be essential to have measures of the desired benefits among segment members.

Simply classifying a population using demographics or any other general variable may be interesting and may provide some perspective on market structure but the approach has no strategic significance unless it is linked to behaviour. The classic trap is a mass of data which describes market segments in general terms but which has little significance because the behavioural characteristics have been given insufficient attention. In contrast, it will often be possible to segment for strategic purposes using only behaviour variables. The general variables do have an important purpose but this is only when they are used in conjunction with behaviour variables.

Establishing evaluation criteria

Before segmentation variables can be considered and selected, there are two initial evaluation stages. The first concerns a preliminary assessment of the practicalities of the segmentation exercise. The second establishes the criteria for evaluating the intrinsic appeal of the segments.

Preliminary assessment

It may be unwise or impossible to embark on a formal segmentation exercise. The main consideration here is cost, which can be considerable, well before any thought is given to the costs of implementing target marketing. For the smaller organization operating in confined markets where familiarity, experience and intuition are paramount, the costs of a segmentation exercise may be prohibitive. In the case of more sophisticated segmentation techniques, the costs of these may well be outside available budgets. A preliminary assessment could indicate that the segmentation task has to be simplified.

This prompts a related issue. Few segments are static and this means that segmentation should be a continuous activity, analysing and monitoring on a regular basis rather than providing a one-off snapshot. There will be recurrent expenses associated with segmentation.

Segment evaluation criteria

Assuming that the segmentation exercise is seen as viable, there are standard criteria for

---

> **Practical tip**
>
> Data availability can be a serious problem in segmentation and it works both ways. Markets can be over-segmented, resulting in information fatigue and few tangible outcomes. Always consider the likely volume, the likely costs and the likely accuracy of data that might result from a segmentation exercise.

evaluating segments but chief among all of them is the need for segments across which there are significant differences in a relevant aspect of behaviour. This has to be the acid test. If this condition is met, then the other criteria can be applied.

Segment discrimination

Segmentation should aggregate customers so that a diverse market can be understood in terms of distinctive, homogeneous segments. If the segments are not distinctive, then there is little point in proceeding. For example, with popular and staple food products such as baked beans, all consumers could be roughly similar irrespective of which segmentation variable is chosen. Given the diversity of needs and wants, this will be unlikely for most product groups and brands, but while differences might exist they could be seen as insignificant.

So, the segmentation exercise should result in a set of segments across which *within-group* variation is minimized and *between-group* variation is maximized. Ideally, the segments should be mutually exclusive in that any one customer belongs clearly to one segment and not to any other. This raises a couple of questions.

First, segmentation looks at similarities and differences but some assessment has to be made of what degree of difference or of similarity is significant and from this, how many segments are required and with what degree of precision. Second, a dangerous

assumption to make is that all change takes place at the classification boundaries. In practice, segments will frequently overlap to some extent.

Segment information

It may well be that sufficient data is available to identify a clear-cut segment that has particular and relevant buying behaviour but if further segment information is difficult or costly to obtain, then the extent to which that segment can be approached will be very restricted. Without appropriate information that begins with segment size and segment growth rate it becomes impossible to take the segmentation exercise any further.

Segment size

The intrinsic worth of a segment will be a function of segment size. A segment may simply be too small to warrant any special marketing effort. Markets can be over-segmented or they might be too small in the first place to justify any attempt at segmentation. Brands have what might be called a 'critical mass' and it may be self-evident that this would never be attained.

> **Practical tip**
>
> The 'Pareto Rule' would suggest that 80 per cent of your business comes from 20 per cent of your customers. There may be a 'gap in the market' but is there a 'market in the gap'?

Segment access

An extremely important requirement of a segment is that it can be reached. The segment should be accessible in terms of communicating with and distributing to the segments but with some approaches, there may be no suitable channels. If this is the case, then the operational significance becomes limited or non-existent.

Segment stability

If the segment has a short life cycle or is in other ways unstable, this will normally reduce its appeal because of the need to hit a moving or vanishing target. Many segments are characterized by rapid change, and a volatile segment that is known to exist today may have disappeared in only a few years.

Segment sensitivity

Customers in the identified segments should be sensitive to marketing action. If they are immune to product differences, advertising, price changes and distribution methods then the practical implications will be limited. Ideally, it will be possible to assess why a segment behaves in a certain way and to predict how the segments will respond to changes in marketing stimuli. With appropriate data and analytical procedures, it may be possible to develop resource allocation models built on the identified segments.

Segment complexity

Some analytical techniques for segmentation are highly complex. Because the methods are complicated, so too are the resulting segments even if the attached labels are intelligible. This could be of concern in some situations. It may be important to know why a given segment behaves in a certain way and with multivariate methods, such as factor analysis and cluster analysis, the input variables will have degrees of significance which are hard to locate.

Segment acceptability

Included under this criterion are all the 'non-rational' evaluations that might be made of different approaches to segmentation and of the resulting segments. Some segmentation methods are regarded as being appropriate by the industry, the company or the manager and the effects of such perceptions can be considerable.

Selecting segmentation variables ■

The market is defined, the broad approach to the segmentation exercise has been considered, the preliminary assessment has been completed and the segment evaluation criteria have been established. Now, it is possible to select the appropriate segmentation variables.

Behaviour variables should always come first in all segmentation exercises and particularly for segmentation as strategy. Behaviour variables identify segments

Checklist 6.4

Which variables do you see as conventional for your market?
What kinds of variables do you use for segmentation?
Why do you use these variables?
How comprehensive and accurate is your existing segment information?
Which variables do you think are more appropriate for strategic decisions?
What costs do you associate with a major re-assessment of possible segments?
What are your criteria for evaluating possible segments?

according to the activities and responses of customers or the determinants of those activities and responses. Behaviour variables have also been termed 'product related', 'behaviouristic' and 'situation specific'. There are three categories of behaviour variables and these are given in Figure 6.2.

Brand behaviour

Benefits sought
Preferences
Perceptions
Usage rate
User status
Readiness stage
Usage occasion
Loyalty status

Media and shopping behaviour

Media habits
Shopping habits

Marketing sensitivity

Response inclinations

Figure 6.2 Segmentation using behaviour variables

Behaviour variables – brand

In this category are those behaviour variables that directly concern the consumption or ownership of the brand. Different segmentation exercises will have differing objectives but when marketing strategy is being considered, benefits sought, preferences and perceptions are fundamental because these determine all subsequent brand behaviour. The brand has attributes that should match what a segment prefers according to the benefits they seek and according to the ways in which the brand attributes are perceived.

Benefits sought can be multidimensional including the obvious functions of the product but also the psychological and social benefits that are thought to flow from ownership or consumption. With high involvement products, it may be essential to untangle the sets of meanings that accrue from ownership and consumption. Benefits sought determine preferences in the sense of how different product attributes are rated or how competing products are assessed. How consumers perceive the available brands defines what they really are.

The more radical strategic shifts require measures of benefits sought, preferences and perceptions. Other behaviour variables will be used according to the particular emphasis behind the segmentation exercise. For example, the introduction to the UK market of a brand of bottled lager might identify segments according to the benefits sought of 'high alcohol content' or 'flavour' or 'peer group approval'. The attributes of the brand and the perceptions held would be compared with competing brands in the choice set.

Usage rate can be a very important and more objective measure for strategic purposes. Usage rate refers to the volume of consumption and the categories light, medium and heavy are standard. Such a classification of usage is often used in conjunction with user status and this can be split into non-users, potential users, first-time users, regular users and former users. With more routine, low-involvement products and when dramatic strategic change is not contemplated, usage rate and user status might be the primary segmentation variables. To pursue the same example, the market segment for this brand of bottled lager could become 'current heavy users who seek peer group approval'.

Readiness stage refers to the point the consumer or potential consumer has reached in the buying process and this is often understood as including the stages of awareness, interest, trial and then purchase. The market segment could be potential users who are aware of and who are interested in the brand, but have yet to use it.

Usage occasion refers, quite simply, to when and where the brand is used, or consumed. There could be a distinction between bottled lagers drunk at home and those that are drunk in pubs and clubs.

Loyalty status is a measure of likely brand switching. Standard measures are 'solus' users who use one brand exclusively, 'most often users' who prefer one particular brand and 'minor' users who have no particular preferences. Consumers who buy and drink bottled lager could be promiscuous, in the sense that they have no particular brand preferences and will happily switch between alternatives in the choice set.

Behaviour variables – media and shopping

Media and shopping habits are different kinds of behaviour variable. They do not concern brand behaviour but are specific to the need to communicate with and distribute to segments. Knowing that a segment is inclined to read certain newspapers and magazines, or to watch particular TV programmes means that communications can be directed effectively to that segment. Similarly, if the segment is known to buy in certain outlets, it becomes possible to establish a distribution policy.

A key segment for this brand of bottled lager might be identified as 'current heavy users who seek peer group approval, who are not brand loyal, who read tabloid newspapers and who buy and drink in pubs and clubs'.

Behaviour variables – marketing sensitivity

The third subset of behaviour variables are those which measure sensitivity to marketing activity, or 'response inclinations'. As well as being a requirement of segments, the sensitivity of segments can be a direct way of identifying segments. Marketing activities in the familiar areas of product, price, promotion and place are used to stimulate or even control consumers in the segments and the consumers will have degrees of sensitivity to any changes. The concept of demand elasticity may allow precise measures of the likely impact of changes in price, advertising and so on.

Behaviour variables can be used individually or, more likely, they are used in combination to identify and reach a segment. A segment within the market defined as 'bottled lagers for young people' might now be identified as:

- Seeks peer group approval
- Prefers high alcohol content
- Current heavy users
- Not brand loyal
- Reads tabloids and 'men's' magazines'
- Visits the cinema frequently
- Drinks in pubs and clubs
- Price sensitive

Once the segment is pinpointed in this way, the next step is to apply the evaluation criteria. With this illustration, two criteria are satisfied in that through the use of behaviour variables alone, the segment can be accessed and there is some indication of how behaviour might be altered. Data will be required to determine if this segment is distinctive, of adequate size and sufficiently stable to warrant special attention.

Practical tip
I keep six honest serving men (They taught me all I knew) Their names are What and Why and When And How and Where and Who.
'The Elephant's Child', *Just-So Stories*, Rudyard Kipling

General variables

General variables are not immediately concerned with behaviour. They identify and describe segments – using general measures. Various terms are used for general variables including 'customer', 'descriptor', 'indirect descriptive', 'non-product related' and 'general customer characteristics'.

General segmentation variables are popular and with good reason. For a segment to be of practical relevance, it must be possible to locate and communicate with the segment and also distribute to it. This is where the use of behaviour variables alone can present problems. For example, knowing the media and shopping habits of 'current heavy users of bottled lager' might be insufficient and this segment identification has to be coupled with suitable general variables so that the segment can be better understood and more easily reached. Superimposing general variables facilitates access to the segments. That is, a segment that is identified as 'current heavy users of bottled lagers in Yorkshire and Humberside' is of greater interest as far as precision and access are concerned. Furthermore, when searching for potential users, the known profile of current users can be used to locate new customers who share the same general characteristics.

Some segmentation exercises might appear to begin with the general variables. What happens with this kind of approach is that there is some behavioural consideration in the background, such as 'all users' or 'usage rate', and then various general variables are applied to see whether or not they can discriminate the extent of usage. For example, the interest might be in the segment identified as 'current heavy users of bottled lager' and that primary segment is then analysed using general variables to see if these current heavy users are more or less inclined to belong to, say, specified age groups. Obviously, the discrimination requirement becomes very important here because if behaviour does not vary with the selected general variable, then there is little point in using that general variable. To pursue the chosen example, if 'current heavy users of bottled lager' are distributed equally across all adult age groups, then for strategic purposes, age is not of much value as a general segmentation variable.

General variables used in the segmentation of consumer markets can be placed into four categories and these are *geographic*, *demo-* *graphic*, *lifestyle* and *geodemographic*. Summary comments are provided below.

Geographic and demographic

Most geographic and demographic variables present few problems in terms of what they are and what they measure. They are commonplace for classification and for description of patterns. Their use in market segmentation has been standard practice for many years. The more common variables in these two categories are given in Figure 6.3.

Geographic	Demographic
Standard planning regions	Age
TV regions	Sex
Nielsen regions	Ethnic group
Urban/rural	Family size
	Family life cycle
	Income
	Occupation
	Social grade
	Education
	Religion
	Nationality

Figure 6.3 *Segmentation using geographic and demographic variables*

Critics point to the lack of discriminatory power of geographic and some demographic variables but the fact remains that for many applications, these variables are sufficient because for certain product groups and brands, data is abundant, there is good discrimination, and analysis is easy to comprehend and relatively cheap.

Family life cycle might be less obvious as a demographic variable. Family life cycle usually takes account of age, presence of children and income, all of which will determine family needs and the disposable income of the family unit. Moreover, decision making is often collective rather than individual so it makes sense to use the family as a reference point. One example of a family life-cycle segment would be the 'Pre-family Stage' which consists of adults under 35 without children.

Good correlations have been found between family life cycle and patterns of consumption and ownership. Family life cycle strikes a compromise between the simplicity but unreliability of single demographic measures and the greater complexity of more sophisticated methods. Critics of family life-cycle analysis point to the changing structure of family life and the declining importance of the traditional nuclear family. The growth in single parent households and the rising proportion of working women are often cited as examples.

Social grade has been one of the more popular demographic variables for segmenting consumer markets and deserves a special mention. In the UK, social grade is measured according to the occupation of the head of household and six categories are created. A typical grade 'A' household is described as having a head of household who is 'a successful business or professional man, senior civil servant or has considerable private means'. This category includes doctors, dentists, solicitors, university professors, newspaper editors, commercial airline pilots, stockbrokers, advertising executives and bank branch managers.

The supporters of social grade claim that it offers good or at least reasonable discriminatory power across a wide range of consumer goods and services. In addition, social grade is a fairly simple notion that is easily understood. The use of occupation to classify consumers does not present any great conceptual or methodological problems. Social grade is not only popular, it is also institutionalized and this means that information on the resulting segments is readily available when compared with other methods.

However, it is often argued that needs, wants and the ability to pay are not linked as they once were with occupation. The opponents of social grade see it as a rough measure, a blunt instrument that lacks the precision of alternative methods for establishing connections with buying behaviour.

Lifestyle

Early attempts to link personality with consumer buying behaviour had limited success but together with work on motivation, these approaches led to psychographic analysis and then to the creation of lifestyle as a general segmentation variable. Psychographic analysis lies behind lifestyle segmentation but the terms *'lifestyle'* and *'psychographics'* are now seen as interchangeable.

Lifestyles are *learned* as a consequence of numerous influences including culture, family, social grade, reference groups and peer groups. The underlying concern is with the personal characteristics and the social values that have been internalized by the individual and from this, outcome measures include the adopted orientation towards consumption, work and leisure. Lifestyle has been referred to as 'Patterns in which people live and spend time and money' which is appropriate because, in practice, lifestyle is usually measured according to activities, interests and opinions – known as the AIO framework. The fragmentation of consumer markets is reflected in the proliferation of lifestyle segments identified by various companies using this and other frameworks.

The appeal of lifestyle is that buying behaviour, particularly for high involvement consumer products, is likely to show a strong correlation with such segments. Lifestyle is also a highly evocative notion that can add to its appeal. The usual problems with lifestyle are that it lacks clarity because the data is elusive or the method of analysis is obscure and involves a degree of subjectivity that is unacceptable. Also, the stability of lifestyle segments and their accessibility can be significant problems. An interesting example of lifestyle analysis is the segment identified as 'Generation X' which contains young people often enjoying high disposable income for clothes and entertainment. The difficulty is that 'Generation X' is seen as being highly self-aware and also highly cynical such that traditional marketing activity is seen as transparent and false.

Geodemographics

Recent advances in segmentation have been information-led. The collection of relevant data and the conversion of that data into valuable information using new technology and sophisticated information systems has driven rather than facilitated some of these advances.

Geodemographic analysis is based on two simple principles. First, two people who live in the same area are more likely to have similar characteristics than two people selected at random. Second, areas can be identified in terms of the characteristics of the populace they contain, using demographics and other measures. Geographical areas can then be placed in the same segment even though they are geographically distant. The recent evolution of geodemographics has been extensive and now, there are 13 agents for census data, this being a major input into the well-known systems such as MOSAIC, ACORN and SuperProfiles.

The MOSAIC system creates 12 summary segments further subdivided into 52 typologies. The segments are assigned names which reflect their dominant characteristics and each segment is provided with a thumbnail description such that the MOSAIC group 'High Income Families' is described as being: ' ... found in the more affluent and leafy suburbs, where only professionals and wealthy business-people can afford the premium prices of large, owner-occupied housing'.

There are two significant advantages associated with geodemographics. First, the segments derive from a range of census and non-census variables rather than a single measure so a more complete picture of the consumer is obtained. Second, the locational characteristic of geodemographics via the postcode system allows these segments to be identified on the ground and, if appropriate, to be contacted. However, geodemographic analysis is complex and there have been many technical questions about the procedures used. Also, geodemographics can be very costly for unproven benefits.

With the example of bottled lager, the choice set approach to defining the market may have isolated the competition to fashionable, imported bottled brands such as Becks, Stella Artois, Labatt, Miller, Budweiser and Cerveza. Given this, the key segment for a new, fashionable brand might be 'current heavy users' of these existing brands and this segment is further described using a number of general variables to give a profile that might be:

- Male
- Aged 18–24
- Pre-family life-cycle stage
- Social grade A/B
- Generation X lifestyle
- MOSAIC group 'High Income Families'

This kind of profile can be very useful for obtaining a better understanding of 'current heavy users', for developing suitable promotional themes and for accessing the segment. However, of prime importance is the extent to which the segment profile is distinctive. If light users, former users and non-users of these brands have the same profile then the acid test of 'discrimination' is not satisfied.

Industrial markets

The reference point for this chapter is segmentation of consumer markets but much strategic marketing has to be seen in the context of industrial, or business-to-business markets. As with consumer markets, both behaviour and general variables can be used and again, it is the behaviour variables that are more important for the purposes of strategy. Volume has always been an important segmentation variable in these markets but only recently has there been a move towards more explicit and more detailed segmentation analyses for the purposes of strategic marketing. Segmentation variables for industrial markets are provided in Figure 6.4.

Customer size, SIC category and location are the more common general variables and the others all concern some aspect of behaviour. End-use as a kind of behaviour

Process
End use
SIC codes
Customer size
Order size
Frequency of purchase
Size of purchase
Buying habits
Buying situation
Buying process
Buying criteria

Figure 6.4 *Variables for segmenting industrial markets*

variable and geographic location as a general variable are often encountered in the segmentation of industrial markets.

As well as segmentation of the consumer market, segmentation of key retail accounts could be very relevant to the company intending to market a fashionable bottled lager. While the end-user is of ultimate concern, there is little point in marketing the ideal brand for a selected consumer segment without satisfactory relationships with intermediaries.

Using market segmentation

Segmentation makes sense of diversity and provides a foundation for marketing

strategy. These are the two important principles.

The *process* of segmentation is concerned with identifying and with evaluating. Many segmentation variables can be used. Given the multidimensional nature of consumer behaviour it is not surprising that simple methods, using one or two single variables can have limited success. It is unlikely that a segment can be identified adequately in terms of, say, usage rate and age.

The *choice* of a mix of behaviour and general variables for marketing strategy will be determined by the issues raised above and by immediate circumstance. Different segmentation variables will be appropriate for different purposes. For example, 'readiness stage' and 'media habits' will be important for decisions on advertising. However, targeting and positioning follow on from segmentation as the most important strategic activities. Targeting and positioning are covered elsewhere in this book.

Once the possible segments have been identified and evaluated according to their intrinsic worth, they must be assessed in terms of their attractiveness to the company. The chief concern when targeting and positioning will be to acquire differential advantage in the trade-off between satisfaction of segment requirements, economies of scale, and the strength of the company relative to the competition. Those segments that meet

Checklist 6.5

Which behaviour variables are used for segmenting your market?
Which general variables are used for segmenting your market?
Why do you use these variables?
Do the resulting segments meet your segment evaluation criteria?
Which alternative segmentation variables are available and appropriate?
Do you segment intermediaries in the supply chain?

Table 6.1 *Brand target segment*

Behaviour	General
Seek peer group approval	Males aged 18–24
Current heavy users	Generation X
Not brand loyal	Social grade A/B
Drink in pubs and clubs	MOSAIC group 'High Income Families'
Visit the cinema frequently	
Price sensitive	

the evaluation criteria must be assessed on the probability of each segment to provide a satisfactory return and the conventional outcomes are marketing strategies that can be termed undifferentiated, differentiated and concentrated. Once a target market has been located and the desirable positioning has been established, implementation, monitoring and correction follow.

teria established for evaluation. In particular, there is discrimination, the segments are accessible and the segment is known to be sensitive to changes in marketing activity. If the segment is sufficiently attractive to the company, then positioning is likely to be constructed around the primary behaviour variables.

Practical tip
However beautiful the strategy, you should occasionally look at the results. Winston Churchill

Typical variables for positioning will include benefits sought, preferences, perceptions and usage rates coupled with a suitable selection of general variables. This provides more accurate portraits of consumer segments, it allows more comprehensive explanations to be made and it facilitates access. The hypothetical brand of bottled lager is now seen to be competing in a market defined by a brand choice set. Benefits sought and usage rate are the primary segmentation variables and these are backed up with other measures of behaviour. They are also supported by a mix of general variables that are known to be strongly associated with the behaviour variables. From this and by way of example, a target segment for this brand could be as shown in Table 6.1.

With appropriate data, a segment identified in this way is more likely to meet the cri-

Summary

- Segmentation is central to marketing strategy.
- Segmentation makes sense of diversity.
- Segmentation provides the foundation for marketing strategy.
- Segmentation is best seen as a process.
- Segmentation identifies and evaluates suitably distinctive groups within a total market.
- Markets are becoming increasingly fragmented.
- Markets have complex needs and wants.
- A definition of the market of interest is required before segmentation begins.
- Segmentation variables can be classified as behaviour and general.
- Behaviour variables include benefits sought, preferences, perceptions, usage rate, user status, readiness stage, purchase or usage occasion, loyalty status, media habits, shopping habits and response inclinations.

- General variables include geographics, demographics, lifestyle and geodemographics.
- A segmentation exercise can be expensive.
- The intrinsic worth of a segment is determined by discrimination of behaviour, segment information, segment size, segment access, segment stability, segment sensitivity, segment complexity and segment acceptability.
- Segmentation for marketing strategy starts with a behaviour variable.
- Benefits sought, preferences and perceptions are commonly used for segmentation which has a strategic purpose.
- Other behaviour variables and an appropriate mix of general variables are used to support the primary segments.
- Once segments have been identified and evaluated according to their intrinsic worth, positioning for particular target segments can begin.

References and further reading ▬

Books that concentrate on the topic of segmentation include:

Dibb, S. and Simkin, L. (1996), *The Market Segmentation Workbook*, London: Routledge
Hooley, G. J. and Saunders, J. (1993), *Competitive Positioning: The Key to Marketing Strategy*, London: Prentice-Hall.
McDonald, M. and Dunbar, I. (1995), *Market Segmentation*, Basingstoke: Macmillan Business.

Internet – Information on segmentation is now becoming available via the Internet, particularly at US sites. One site that is typical of recent developments is that of SRI Consulting at:

http://future.sri.com/vals/valshome.html

CD-ROM – Useful material on segmentation is now available on CD-ROM. For example, CCN Marketing provides a 'Multimedia Guide to MOSAIC', one of the major geodemographic systems, and the Multimedia Marketing Consortium has a series of CD-ROMs including 'Segmentation, Positioning and the Marketing Mix'.

7

Competitive positioning ⎯⎯⎯⎯⎯⎯⎯⎯⎯⎯

Professor Graham Hooley, Aston University Business School

 This chapter explores two central issues in marketing today:

1. The identification and selection of target market or markets that the organization will seek to serve.
2. The creation of a competitive advantage in serving those chosen markets.

Together these choices constitute the competitive positioning of the firm in its marketplace and all major decisions should be geared up to achieving and reinforcing that positioning.

Effective positioning requires a thorough understanding of the market (both customers and competitors) together with a clear view of the competencies and assets the firm can bring to bear in that market. These competencies and assets arise through the firm itself as well as, increasingly, through the alliances and networks it operates in.

The chapter will explore ways of analysing the competitive environment and of categorizing assets and competencies. It will conclude with guidelines for creating and maintaining defensible positions in the marketplace.

Competitive positioning is at the heart of modern marketing. It recognizes that successful management is about making choices concerning which customers to serve and how to serve them. In the increasingly crowded and competitive markets of today companies that attempt to be all things to all customers run the danger of being nothing to any. Especially where smarter competitors target more effectively, creating closer relationships with key customers or customer groups, those firms that offer standard products across whole markets are finding themselves increasingly vulnerable.

Two particularly relevant trends are discernible in modern markets. First, customers are becoming increasingly demanding of the products and services they buy. Customers demand and expect reliable and durable products with quick efficient service at reasonable prices. They also expect the products and services they buy to meet their needs.

And here lies the big opportunity for companies smart enough to realize it. Different customers have different wants and needs. Most markets are segmented in one way or another (see Chapter 6) and hence marketers have an opportunity to select segments where their offerings most closely align with those needs and where they can focus their activities to create a competitive advantage.

The second major trend, one that particularly differentiates the 1990s from the 1980s, is that customers are less prepared to pay a substantial premium for products or services that do not offer demonstrably greater value. While it is undeniable that well-developed and managed brands can command higher prices than unbranded products in many markets (see Chapter 9) the differentials commanded are now much less than they were and customers are increasingly questioning the extra value they get for the expense. Marlboro cigarettes are a case in point. On 2

April 1992 ('Marlboro Friday') Philip Morris announced a one-fifth reduction in price of its market leading brand of cigarettes to defend market share against aggressive US rivals. The brand had lost substantial market share to these lower priced competitors. Customers were simply not convinced that Marlboro was worth the premium price it had been charging. The implications are clear. Differentiation needs to be based on providing demonstrably superior value to customers.

Figure 7.1 presents an overall framework for assessing the positioning options open to a company. Positioning is seen in the context of the market environment in which the firm operates and the capabilities of the firm itself. Positioning decisions are the result of a creative assessment of the marketplace in the overall context of the wider macro-environment, leading to a definition of the key market targets aimed for, coupled with a clear

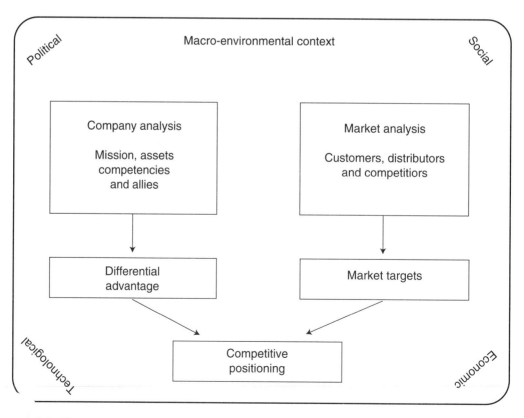

Ə **7.1** Competitive positioning

understanding of the company itself and what it can bring to the market which is of value to customers.

The changing macro-environment

To claim that 'the only constant is change' is trite but true in today's business environment. The recent Royal Society for the encouragement of Arts, Manufactures and Commerce (RSA) Inquiry into 'Tomorrow's Company' identified a number of major changes taking place in business markets (see Example One).

A logical approach to assessing the likely impact of the macro-environment on the firm's options is to work through the major sets of factors in sequence, noting likely changes and attempting to assess their impact. One such framework, *PEST* analysis, identifies four main components of the macro-environment for consideration:

Example One
The changing business environment

The Interim Report of the RSA Inquiry into Tomorrow's Company identified a number of major changes taking place in the wider business environment. Some of the most significant are listed below:
The pace of economic change is accelerating. During the Industrial Revolution it took 60 years for productivity per person to double. China and South Korea have done the same in 10 years.

- There is an explosion in innovation and new knowledge generation that is also accelerating. Every year as much new knowledge is generated through research and development as the total sum of human knowledge up to 1960.
- Competitive pressures are intensifying. Computer manufacturers, for example, need to reduce costs and improve product performance by around 30 per cent per annum to remain competitive.
- Manufacturing can now take place almost anywhere. Companies are constantly seeking more efficient manufacturing options and that typically means sourcing from wherever makes economic sense.
- New organizational structures are emerging as firms seek to make themselves more competitive. Firms have reorganized, reduced overheads, delayered, merged, created alliances and partnerships in attempts to create advantage in the marketplace.
- International trade is being liberalized through the GATT and WTO but there are still massive regional trading blocks within which regional, nationalistic, ethnic and religious groupings seek to retain individual identity.
- Company actions are becoming increasingly visible, especially their effects on the environment. Customers are demanding more both economically and environmentally.

(RSA Inquiry: Tomorrow's Company, Interim Report, 1994)

- **Political environment** – the impact of politics on the business environment through legislation, encouragement or constraint on business activities. Especially where the firm is operating in non-domestic markets the political climate needs to be understood and any potential changes in it forecast along with their likely effects. Western firms entering newly emerging markets in Eastern Europe, for example, have sometimes been frustrated by the political structures and systems facing them. Rover, a British car manufacturer (now owned by the German company BMW) and an early investor in Bulgaria, withdrew from the market in 1996 following frustrations in dealing with government bureaucracy.

- **Economic environment** – closely related to the political environment is the economic situation in the chosen markets. The state of the economy can have a major impact on many businesses through its impact on the purchasing power and confidence of potential customers. For example, the economic trough of the early mid-1990s had a dramatic effect on the fortunes of firms in the construction and housing industry. Major players such as Tarmac and Wimpey found that they could no longer operate as highly diverse organizations and began to focus their activities on their core businesses. In an innovative deal Tarmac swapped its loss-making house-building division for Wimpey's poorly performing quarry business in March 1996. Each was then able to focus more effectively on businesses it had real strength in.

- **Social environment** – changes in demography, age distribution of population and life styles can create opportunities and challenges for marketers. As noted by the RSA (Example One) a significant trend is the increasing level of environmental awareness of many people and the subsequent increasing demands on business to act in ethical and environmentally sensitive ways. The pressure put on Shell, for example, to

change its plans for decommissioning the Brent Spar oil platform show the power of the consumer and environmental lobbyists in this regard.

- **Technological environment** – firms need to be aware of, and act on, technological change. Breakthroughs in technology seem to take place at ever-faster rates making the innovations of yesterday the obsolete products of tomorrow. For example, as more customers opt for mobile telephone systems, increasingly using satellite technology, the strengths of the telecommunications giants, built on their physical copper cable networks, will become less important and sustainable as a basis for competitive advantage.

Just as water supply companies cannot change weather patterns most macro-environmental factors are outside the control of individual firms. Few companies have the ability to significantly influence political, economic, social, and technological processes. Most need to ensure they understand and predict the changes going on. Water companies need to predict both weather patterns (supply of water) and demand so that they can then put strategies in place to ensure demand is met.

While companies need to operate within the bounds and conditions of the macro-environment they may have some (limited) ability to influence it. The UK government's Private Finance Initiative (PFI), for example, which is designed to introduce private sector financing into public investment and infrastructure projects, is championed by a board including representatives of the construction and other industries. Similarly, most expenditure on scientific research is applied in nature and conducted in commercial companies such that their efforts will directly affect the technological environment in which they, and other firms, operate in the future.

No company can ever hope to understand every aspect of the macro-environment in which it operates. There will always be surprises and shocks as new technological breakthroughs emerge, or political disconti-

**Example Two
Encyclopedia Britannica**

Encyclopedia Britannica (EB) went from peak US profits in 1990 to severe difficulties in 1996 as it failed to fully appreciate the impact of computer technology, particularly the CD-ROM, on its business. The business had been built through a highly motivated and successful sales force selling encyclopedias to middle-class families (often bought by parents for their children's education) at around $1500 each.

Then along came home computers, with CD-ROM players and encyclopedias such as Encarta at less than $100. The new entrants may not have had the depth of coverage of EB but they were in a format the children enjoyed using, offered the opportunities for multimedia display (video and audio clips, animations), were more easily updateable, and, perhaps most crucially, offered middle-class parents a justification for the purchase of often expensive home computer systems that in many cases were used primarily for games purposes!

With the advent of the 'information superhighway', the World-Wide Web and Internet the holding of large amounts of data on individual PCs may become a thing of the past, posing potential problems (and, of course, opportunities) for the marketers of CD-ROM based encyclopedias.

Source: Professor David Cravens, address to the British Academy of Management conference, Aston Business School, September 1996.

---

nuities occur. What is important, however, is to spot and act on more of the trends and changes than competitors.

Competitive market analysis

At the more specific level companies need to understand the dynamics of the competitive markets in which they operate. This involves analysing customers, distributors and competitors.

Customer analysis

A fundamental question for any business is 'who is the customer?'. This may seem a simple question to answer but in some circumstances may not be clear-cut. In education, for

Practical tip

- Work through a PEST analysis of the main factors in the macro-environment that are likely to impact on your business in the future.
- Get others in your company (from their own different perspectives) to do the same.
- Highlight the critical issues and examine how much control you have over them.
- How can you gain more control of the important issues?

example, who is the customer? The student? The ultimate employer? The funder(s) such as government, parents, sponsors? Society as a whole? In hospitals who is the customer? The patient? The GP fund-holder? The government? The tax payer?

In practice all the above may be important to the purchase of products and services, though not all should necessarily be considered customers. Marketers find it helpful to differentiate various actors in the purchasing situation depending on the role they play in that process. Five key roles have been suggested: initiators, influencers, deciders, purchasers, and users.

Initiators are those who start the purchase process. These may be hungry children who scream for food, initiating the search by a provider for a suitable meal, or a town council deciding they need a bypass around a busy town centre. Increasingly, companies are attempting to communicate early in purchasing processes with initiators so as to get their goods or services on the agenda, especially where scarce resources are concerned.

Influencers affect the purchase process either directly or indirectly. Direct influence may be exerted through specific recommendations, advice, suggestions, etc. Business consultants may be experts in particular processes and recommend the adoption of new systems by their clients. Friends may offer advice on the purchase of a new car on the basis of their experiences in the market. Indirect influence may come through use of similar products and services by individuals or organizations seen as 'opinion leaders' or trendsetters. Seeing role models, such as professional footballers or catwalk models, adopting particular products can influence the choice of admirers.

Decision-makers/deciders hold the resources that are committed to purchase. In household purchases, such as groceries, a new car or a holiday, the decision-maker(s) will typically be the individuals with the power to commit the expenditure. For different purchases different members of the family may be designated 'decision-maker'. At school a child may be decision-maker as to how cash provided for purchase of food at lunch time is spent, whereas the decision on

what model of car to purchase may be taken by the eventual driver of the car, and decisions on where the family will spend their holidays could be made by all members together. In a business purchasing situation the purchase decision, to buy a specific product or service, will be made by the employee or manager with discretion to spend that resource.

The actual **purchase** may be made by the same individual or individuals who made the purchase decision or by an agent acting on their behalf. In family food purchases the decision as to what to buy may be made by one individual while another actually goes to the shop to make the purchase. In businesses a professional 'buyer' may be employed to get the best possible deal once the decision has been made as to what to buy. Retailers, for example, employ professional buying teams to ensure they get the best deals when purchasing raw materials or products for sale onto their ultimate customers.

Finally, the **user** may be different to all the above. The individual or individuals who will actually use the product or service are generally thought of as the ultimate customer. These are the family members who eat the food, the drivers and passengers who are moved through the use of the car, and the family members who go on holiday. In a business setting the users may be shop floor workers who use supplied raw materials or managers who receive services.

Each of the above roles may be undertaken by the same person or different people, at the same time (for example, in the case of impulse purchase of sweets) or over a long period (for example, in the purchase of a hydroelectric dam). Most important for any firm is to understand who or what takes on what roles at the different stages of the buying process so that suitable communications can be targeted to the right people at the right time.

Segmenting the market

Central to understanding customers and their needs is segmentation. Where there are different requirements in a market there is an opportunity to segment the market and target offerings more effectively. There is no one way to segment a market. A limitless number of ways are possible (see Chapter 6) and it is ultimately down to the creativity of individual companies and their managers to decide what segmentation scheme is most appropriate for them. Different competitors are quite likely to segment the market in different ways and there is no one 'best' or 'right' method.

Where competitors segment by one method it can often be profitable to explore different ways of segmenting. Indeed, segmentation is one of the key creative aspects of marketing. Not accepting the status quo and being prepared to look for different ways to segment the market is the hallmark of an innovative and creative company. Where competitors segment the market by age try segmenting by product usage. Where competitors segment by volume of usage try segmenting by customer benefits sought. The number of ways to segment a market are limited only by the creativity of the managers looking at the market.

Distributors

In addition to understanding the ultimate customers for their goods and services, firms

---

Example Three
Toshiba Notebook Computers

In 1995 there were around 10 million notebook PCs sold world-wide compared to 50 million desktop machines and servers. Sales for 1996 are predicted to be around 12.5 million and by the end of the decade over 20 million annually. At an average price of around $2500 the market to the end of the decade will be worth around $200 billion.

Toshiba is the market leader for notebook PCs with around 20 per cent market share. It segments the market into three main segments:

- The performance segment, where it positions its Tecra range offering the same specifications and capabilities as desktop PCs but with the added benefit of reasonable portability.
- For the more mobile user it offers its slimline Portege range. These products are designed to offer 'Ultimate Portability' and are lighter than the Tecra, sacrificing some of the capabilities of the latter.
- The final segment is the 'value for money market' where price is more important. Here Toshiba offers its Satellite range with, again, fewer capabilities but at a budget price.

Toshiba's strategy is to offer 'faster cycle time in development and production' introducing new features to make their products technological leaders. To facilitate this they make their own components including chips, hard drives, flat screens and batteries. They have deliberately focused on notebook PCs, avoiding the more crowded desktop market and focusing all their efforts on leading the notebook market.

Source: *The Guardian*, 20 June 1996

Example Four
The Skoda Felicia

The domestic automobile market is highly competitive with many large manufacturers attempting to plug every conceivable gap in the market.

In an attempt to identify an under-served market segment Skoda is targeting its new model, the Felicia, at what it calls the 'disillusioned generation' carrying negative housing equity and worries about the future, for whom price and value for money rule, and the image, styling and badging of the car are far less important.

The segment is termed OPTIEs – Over-mortgaged, Post Thatcherite Individuals. These consumers see property, money and job as less important than family, health and relationships. Impressing people with their cars is a low priority for them, they believe cars are over-hyped and over-priced and that if you take the badge off it's hard to tell one make from another.

The Felicia is positioned to appeal to this segment as 'sensibly stylish with honest intentions' and priced at £5999. It was jointly developed with Volkswagen and poster advertisements show the VW logo in the background to reassure customers of the quality of the product.

Source: *Marketing Business*, August 1995

need to examine the distribution options open to them to physically get their offerings to those customers. Many firms use distribution intermediaries such as wholesalers and/or retailers who can offer efficient access to customers. Increasingly, however, firms are going direct to their customers through direct marketing.

In grocery marketing the leading supermarkets now account for over 75 per cent of all food sales compared with only 35 per cent in 1970. At the same time the local food shops have declined from 47 per cent of the market to 14 per cent. This concentration of retailer power in the hands of a few supermarket chains has major implications for the way in which the food manufacturers do business. Where the balance of power was firmly in the court of the brand manufacturers in the past, now the supermarkets themselves have the power to make or break brands through their listings policies. Customers are increasingly store loyal rather than brand loyal.

As with segmentation there is no single distribution channel or approach that is 'correct' and innovative marketers will seek new and unique ways of distributing their products and services.

Competitor analysis

The third main set of actors to consider in market analysis is competitors. Most firms operate in a competitive market where there are rivals. Some may be more powerful than others but all are ignored in the development of strategy at your peril. Today's minor players in a market may become the major players of the future.

**Example Five
Choice Organics**

Choice Organics, for example, distribute organically grown vegetables in London. Initially the firm sold their produce through supermarket chains. Customers were attracted to organically grown vegetables because they thought they were not only healthier for them but also better for the environment (fewer insecticides used in growing).

By the mid-1990s, however, customer demand for organic food was beginning to wane and supermarkets increasingly put appearance requirements (such as conformity in size, shape, colour) on food supply that could not be met by organic growers. Choice found that they were having to reject half of their produce on cosmetic grounds.

The firm decided to market their vegetables direct to the customers and set up a distribution service in London which took customer orders by phone and then delivered direct to the customer's door.

Source: 'The Marketing Mix in Action', 1995, video published by TV Choice Ltd

A starting point in competitor analysis is to identify who the significant competitors are. Competition may take place on many levels: direct competition for sales with companies offering similar products or services, indirect competition for scare resources such as raw materials, distribution listings or skilled staff.

Direct competition for sales may take place in several ways. First there may be competition between products of the same form. Diet Coke, for example, competes at the product form level with Diet Pepsi (both are diet colas) as it is clearly offering the same combination of product features and customer benefits. At the product category level Diet Coke may also compete with other soft drinks such as 7-Up and regular Coke providing a similar, but not identical, set of benefits. The generic competition is with other beverages, such as juices, beers, wines, etc. Finally, Diet Coke also competes at the budget level against other ways in which the customer might choose to spend the (limited) budget available for leisure consumption (e.g. fast food, confectionery, video hire and such like).

In some product fields competition at the product form level may be most significant, in others at the budget level. When choosing a skiing holiday, for example, the major competition may not be between resorts but with the purchase of a new washing machine for the home!

Competitor analysis should seek to identify the level of competition currently most significant and predict whether (and how) this is likely to change. Often the most useful starting point for this type of analysis is the customer.

Firms can learn from other firms though. Analysing successful competitors to see why they are successful, then copying and improving on their success factors, identifying unsuccessful competitors to see what they get wrong, then overcoming or avoiding these pitfalls, and by looking to other markets (non-competitors) to see what best practice ideas and approaches can be adapted and used in their own markets.

A major concern in competitor analysis is to identify the likelihood of new competitor entry together with the possibilities of substitute product launch. As noted above, fixed cable telephone operators now face serious competition from mobile phone operators who have been able to leapfrog their long-established cable assets and provide superior services (mobility). Encyclopedia Britannica initially failed to respond to the threat to its core business posed by technological change and product substitution.

Practical tip

Work through an analysis of your main competitors using the following sequence:

- Ask your customers what is important to them in their choice of supplier for the goods and/or services you provide to them.
- Ask your customers to identify who else they might, or already do, do business with. Who else offers similar goods and services?
- Ask your customers to rate your performance alongside that of your competitors on the factors important to them as customers.
- Identify those factors where you outperform your competitors (areas of competitive advantage) and those where you fall short (competitive disadvantage).
- Assess how you can further exploit your areas of advantage, and how you can minimize the threats posed by competitors.

Company analysis

For any positioning strategy to be effective it needs not only to be externally orientated in recognizing what customers want and where competitor offerings are placed, but also based on the resources of the firm. A self-analysis by any firm should seek to uncover both the assets (resources) of the firm that can be deployed and the capabilities (competencies and skills) of the firm in deploying those resources.

Mission

A starting point in self-analysis is to question the purpose of the organization. Why does it exist? What is it setting out to achieve? The need to have a common, shared and understood purpose to guide the strategy is not only important for commercial firms but also for non-profit making organizations. The British Labour Party, for example, recently revised its aims and purposes, redefining its 'mission' in a redrafting of Clause IV of its constitution. Indeed, it is arguably more important for non-commercial organizations to know what they want to achieve than commercial ones where mission often gets distilled to 'make a profit'.

Simply having a goal (social, financial or otherwise) is not enough, however, and all organizations need a set of guiding principles as to how they will achieve those goals. These value statements increasingly form part of the mission specifications of leading firms and can have a significant impact on the positioning decisions taken. They may dictate the sorts of markets that the organization will consider operating in and the ways in which it will do business. Ethical or moral issues may guide the selection of options from the choices open to the firm.

Marketing assets and competencies

Successful positioning is based on real strengths and assets of the firm. It is useful here to distinguish marketing assets and competencies. Marketing assets are any properties that can be exploited in the marketplace to create or sustain a competitive advantage. They range from recognized brand names, through unique use of distribution channels, to information and quality control systems. These assets are the resource endowments the business has created or acquired over time and now has available to deploy in the market.

Competencies are skills and capabilities that are used to deploy the assets to best effect in the market. Day (1994) refers to them as:

the glue that binds the assets together and enables them to be deployed advantageously. They are complex bundles of skills and knowledge exercised through organizational processes to co-ordinate activities and exploit assets.

Marketing assets

There are three main types of marketing assets (see Hooley and Saunders, 1998): customer-based; distribution-based; and internal assets.

Customer-based assets are those assets that are directly valued by the customer and give a reason for purchase of the company's offerings. Often they exist in the mind of the customer and are essentially intangible, but no less valuable, in nature.

Company name, reputation and individual brand names are prime examples of customer-based marketing assets. Company brands such as IBM, Kodak and Sainsbury convey very clear images to their customers. The Virgin brand has been successfully used by Richard Branson in the marketing of records, videos, computer software, air travel, cola, insurance and most recently clothing. On each of these products the name 'Virgin' conveys the corporate values of a young, go ahead, no-nonsense company with the interests of consumers firmly in mind. Interestingly, while the products are diverse the target market aimed for is remarkably uniform across products.

In the late 1980s firms began to recognize the value of their brand names when a number of high profile takeovers showed the prices acquirers were prepared to pay for the rights to market and use high profile band names. Perhaps most famous was the acquisition of the York-based confectionery group Rowntree by its Swiss competitor Nestlé for a reputed six times the book value of the physical assets or three times the pre-bid market capitalization. Nestlé were paying for the KitKat, Quality Street, Smarties, Rolo and Yorkie brands that had been built over many years and were substantial customer-based assets (see Chapter 9 for a full discussion of brands).

Country of origin can also convey significant value in the minds of customers. For many Japanese customers, lamb reared in New Zealand benefits from their image of the country as 'clean and green', unpolluted with wide-open spaces (a real premium in crowded downtown Tokyo!).

Central to customer-based assets is the relationship between the company and its customers. This may be a direct relationship, as is often the case in business-to-business markets and high value consumer markets such as banking and insurance, or a 'proxy' relationship built through the brands sold. The ultimate asset for any company is a core of loyal customers who will purchase again and again. In the final analysis a brand is simply a way of building a relationship with more remote customers where one-to-one relationship building is uneconomic or impracticable. Hence the emphasis in FMCG on brands, while business-to-business marketers emphasize personal relationships.

Distribution-based assets lie in the physical network created to link supplier with customer or the processes created to facilitate that link. In car rental, for example, Hertz has built up a wide network of pick-up and drop-off centres, especially in the USA. These assets create customer benefits of ease and convenience in using the Hertz service. Other firms have created unique distribution channels for their products to differentiate them from competitors. These channels are then available, as assets to be exploited for new product launches, demonstrations, etc. Direct home selling of products such as cosmetics (Avon), home brewing (Mr Brewer), kitchenware (Tupperware), personal computers (Dell), and even sex aids (Ann Summers) is increasingly common.

Internal marketing assets include people, systems and processes that can be used to good effect in the marketplace. The most important asset in any company is the people. It is the people (managers and employees) that put the other assets to work and ultimately interface with the customers. Well-organized and controlled systems can ensure quality delivery, with 'zero' defects and hence low rework, and cost advantages.

Information systems can often be utilized to find out more about key customers and to help plan marketing campaigns more closely tailored to individual customer needs. Safeway, the supermarket chain, recently launched a store loyalty card (ABC) which customers use to collect bonus points which can be redeemed for free goods. The card has two main purposes. First, it is intended to create greater store loyalty giving shoppers an incentive to shop more regularly at Safeway to take advantage of collected points and offers. Second, and perhaps more significantly for the store, it provides on computer detailed records of the purchases of each registered customer which can then be interrogated for marketing purposes. The effects of special offers can be gauged, brand loyalty patterns can be assessed and brand complimentarity examined. Crucially, the data gives Safeway buyers an information edge over their suppliers when negotiating product supply. Such information systems are increasingly being used as a basis for direct marketing, communicating with customers on a one-to-one basis with offerings tailored to their individual needs.

Capabilities and competencies

Day (1994) identifies three main types of competencies: outside-in; inside-out; and spanning and integrating competencies.

Outside-in competencies are those skills and abilities that enable a business to understand its customers and create closer linkages with them. They include market sensing skills, or the abilities of the firm to assess and judge changes in its markets. Specific skills include the ability to conduct and interpret marketing research, and the capability of disseminating that information to those who need to know within the firm. Also relevant are customer bonding and linking skills which help build closer links with key customers.

Inside-out competencies are the internal capabilities of the firm and its employees that might be deployed in the marketplace to provide better products and services to customers. They include financial management, cost controlling skills, technological skills, logistics management, manufacturing processes and human resource management.

Spanning and integrating competencies bring together the inside-out and the outside-in to ensure delivery of appropriate products and services to customers. They include customer order fulfilment (which is achieved through understanding customer wants and needs [outside-in] and using internal systems and procedures to ensure delivery [inside-out]). Perhaps the most significant spanning and integrating capabilities are the abilities to set competitive, yet profitable, prices and the development of new products. Both require a clear understanding of market needs coupled with internal, technical capabilities.

Strategic alliances

Not all assets and capabilities may be vested in the focal firm. Increasingly companies are creating alliances and networks with others that enable them to leverage further assets and competencies of partner firms. Alliances can offer four main sets of assets and competencies: access to new markets; access to managerial competence; access to technological competence; and economic benefits.

Access to new markets might be provided through the networks and reputation of the partner firm. Western firms entering the newly emerging markets of Central and Eastern Europe, for example, have typically done so through alliances, joint ventures or acquisitions with local firms that know the market, have some existing market presence on which to build and, perhaps most crucially, understand how to do business in the very different market environment. In essence the local firm provides market knowledge and existing relationships that can add to the fund of assets and competencies of the foreign partner.

Alliances may provide further managerial competencies above access to markets. These may include technical skills in dealing with local technologies, and human resource skills in dealing with local staff.

In strategic alliances technological competence can be gained through technology transfer and the sharing of core skills and processes. Alliances may be created to allow both partners to share in the enhanced technical abilities of the partnership.

Economic benefits of alliances include the sharing of risks and costs (especially with new product development), taking advantage of locational assets, volume and scale opportunities and access to funds.

Taken together marketing assets and competencies/capabilities are the basis on which any competitive positioning is built. Ideally, firms are seeking to build their positions on the basis of assets and competencies that are superior to the competition's and difficult to duplicate. They are also seeking to create or acquire assets and competencies that can be

exploited in many other situations (e.g. extend their brand name into new markets, exploit their technology in new industries, use their networks in different ways). A critical issue for the future is how different assets and competencies can be combined to create new products and services (Hamel and Prahalad, 1994).

Building and maintaining defensible positions

As has been argued above, competitive positioning is about making choices that ensure a fit between chosen target markets and the competencies and assets the firm can deploy to serve those chosen targets more effectively. While there are, in reality, an infinite number of different ways in which firms might position themselves in their markets these can be summarized on the basis of the emphasis they give to four main dimensions of differentiation.

Figure 7.2 shows these four main dimensions. Positioning may be based on price, quality (or more correctly, grade), service, or innovation. While individual firms may choose to position on more than one dimen-

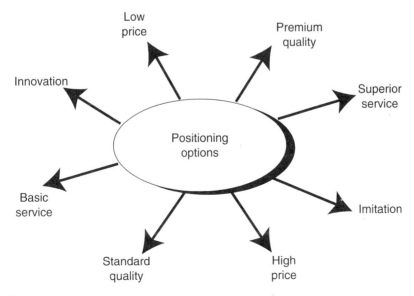

Figure 7.2 *Positioning options*

Position	Customer groups	Assets and competencies	Strategic focus
Price	Price sensitive customers	Cost control services, TQM processes, procurement, information systems	Internal efficiency
Quality	Premium demanding customers	Market sensing, quality control and assurance, brand and reputation, supply chain management	Superior quality, image management
Innovation	Innovations and early adopters	New product service development, R&D technical skills, creative skills	First to market
Service	Service seekers	Market sensing, customer linking, service systems, skilled staff, feedback systems, continuous monitoring	Augmentation of the basic product

Figure 7.3 *Positioning strategies*

sion simultaneously they often find that they are contradictory. For example, offering a higher grade of product is generally incongruent with keeping costs, and hence, prices as low as possible. Indeed, charging low prices for a high-grade product may create confusion in the minds of customers. The key to creating sustainable positions is to ensure that they are built on the marketing assets and competencies of the firm. Figure 7.3 shows the assets and competencies necessary for each positioning strategy.

Price positioning

For a low price positioning to be sustainable requires that costs are kept in check and are at least as low or lower than competitors. If there is no cost advantage price wars may put the instigator at a financial disadvantage and the whole positioning strategy may not be sustainable. Positioning as the low price supplier requires strong inside-out and spanning

capabilities. Effective cost control systems (through activity-based costing) are needed not only within the firm's own operations but also within suppliers. Procurement of raw materials and other factor inputs is organized around keeping costs to a minimum. Distribution logistics are similarly managed for minimum cost.

While the low price position is a viable option for some firms (e.g. KwikSave in grocery retailing) there is a constant need to work at keeping costs down, especially when new competitors enter the market with new operating methods or unique assets that can be used to undercut the costs of incumbents.

For a price positioning strategy to be successful in the marketplace also, of course, requires the existence of a viable, price sensitive customer segment. In most markets there are customers who will buy primarily on price. In the 1990s, however, it became clear that such customers also expect a base level of service and product quality such that rock bottom prices alone are unlikely to be good enough reasons to buy.

Finally, it should be noted that some firms position at the other end of the price spectrum. They deliberately price their products and services more highly than competitors to create an exclusivity for their offerings. High price positionings are usually accompanied by higher quality, branded offerings (e.g. Harrods department store in Knightsbridge).

Quality positioning

Positioning as a high quality (grade) supplier also requires effective internal control systems, especially quality assessment and assurance. Beyond control, however, it also requires technical competence, particularly in engineering and manufacturing where physical products are produced. Most significantly, however, it requires a clear view of what constitutes 'quality' in the eyes of the customer. That entails the outside-in capabilities of market sensing and customer bonding. Also important in delivering high quality products and services is supply chain management, ensuring that the inputs are of the required quality, not simply the cheapest available. Marks & Spencer has a reputation for building long-term, demanding relationships with their suppliers to ensure that the products they put their labels on are of the required quality. To provide high technical quality requires specific expertise.

Often critical to a quality positioning are the marketing assets of brand image and reputation. Image and reputation can take years to create and once established need to be nurtured and, when necessary, defended vigorously.

To customers quality is manifest through better reliability, durability and aesthetic appearance. For quality positionings to be viable customers must be prepared to pay for

Example Six
Betty's Tea Rooms

There are four Betty's Tea Rooms in Yorkshire and one Taylor's. Together they sell 2 million cups of tea each year. They don't advertise but people flock in their thousands and are prepared to queue for seats. The atmosphere is elegant, sophisticated. Waiters and waitresses are formally dressed in the style of Victorian servants. The tea is perfect and the cakes are delicious. The pastries range from exotic Amadeus Torte to local Yorkshire curd tarts.

The company was started in Harrogate, Yorkshire, by a Swiss confectioner, Frederick Belmont, in 1919. The company's bakers and confectioners still train in Lucerne.

The company has built on its brand asset by opening related gift shops on the premises, selling confectionery suited to the tourists who visit. They also sell their products by mail order. More recently they have marketed Yorkshire Tea which has become a major brand in the beverages market.

Source: Kotler, Armstrong, Saunders and Wong, 1996, Principles of Marketing, Hemel Hempstead: Prentice-Hall Europe.

Example Seven
Dyson Dual Cyclone vacuum cleaner

In the early 1990s a new vacuum cleaner was launched onto the UK market. The Dyson Dual Cyclone operated in a different way to conventional cleaners in that it creates a cyclone of air (faster than the speed of sound) and does away with the conventional bags to collect the dust. On conventional cleaners the pores of the bags gradually fill so that the cleaner works less well when half full. The Dyson cleaner claims three times the performance of conventional vacuum cleaners but, at around £200, costs up to double the price.

Manufacturers of conventional vacuum cleaners were unimpressed by the new product as they derive good ongoing profits from the sale of the disposable dust bags (that market alone being worth around £100 million per annum). They fought to keep the Dyson from conventional outlets and Dyson eventually hit on the idea of selling through mail order catalogues (a further innovation in the vacuum cleaner business). Despite the price disadvantage the Dyson had achieved 25 per cent market share within three years of its launch.

superior quality as there are usually higher costs associated with offering a higher quality product. In the automotive industry German manufacturers such as Mercedes, BMW and Audi have successfully positioned their offerings at the high quality end of the spectrum through superior design, technical engineering skills ('Vorsprung durch Technic' – leading through technology) and attention to quality control through the manufacturing process.

Innovation positioning

Where markets are changing rapidly, especially as a result of technological developments, there may be opportunities to position on the basis of innovativeness, or speed to market. In the personal computer market, for example, leading firms such as Toshiba (see Example Three) are constantly improving on their products and building in technological advances to

keep their products ahead of their competitors.

The key competencies required include excellent new product development skills together with both technical and creative abilities. These are combinations of inside-out and spanning competencies. Once new product ideas have been crystallized, however, it is important to test them out on customers to avoid the launch of highly innovative, but essentially unwanted, products (such as the Sinclair C5 electric car).

Service positioning

Positioning on the basis of offering superior service, or rather service clearly tailored to the needs of the target market, is increasingly being used. Variations in the nature and level of service offered, coupled with differences in requirements across customer groups, mean that service positioning can be viable and attractive for more than one company in a market. Critical to providing superior service are market-sensing skills that can identify what level/type of service is required, customer-bonding skills that build closer relationships with key customers, service systems that assist the service providers in delivering service to customers and monitoring skills that can regularly assess the customer satisfaction with the level and type of service provided. Most critical of all to providing superior service are the people, or staff, that actually provide the service. Selection, training, motivation and reward of service staff are areas that need high priority in firms seeking to establish a competitive edge through service provision.

There has now been a great deal of research published both in the USA and in Europe (see, for example, Berry and Parasuraman, 1991) looking at the nature of 'service' and what constitutes excellent service in the eyes of customers. The consensus of this research is that customers typically measure their experiences against some benchmark of the service they expect to receive. The quality of a service provision, and subsequently the level of satisfaction of the customer, is directly related to the difference (or 'gap') between expectations and experiences.

Expectations are created in a number of ways. Prior experiences of the service provider, or of similar providers, are often the starting point. When customers eat in a new restaurant, for example, they often judge the experience based on other restaurants they have visited. Verbal comparisons are common: 'it was more relaxed than...', 'the food was better than at ...'. In addition to customers' own prior experiences their expectations are also often affected by the opinions of others, friends, relatives, colleagues, who have related their own experiences. Depending on the standing of these opinion makers in their esteem they can have a significant influence on expectations, and even deter trial a particular service in the first place. A third major determinant of expectations are the promises the company itself makes prior to customers using it. These promises, by way of advertising messages,

sales pitches and general image created through pricing strategies and the like, set standards that the company is expected to live up to. Pitching them just right can be difficult. Promising too little may result in failing to attract the customers in the first place (who may be seduced away by more attractive competitor promises), promising more than can be delivered may result in dissatisfied customers.

Against expectations customers then evaluate the performance of a service provider. Again, research has shown a number of factors that customers typically take into account when evaluating the service they have received. The most enduring, and easiest to remember, classification is the **RATER** model: **R**eliability; **A**ssurance; **T**angibles; **E**mpathy; and **R**esponsiveness.

- **Reliability** is the ability of the provider to perform the promised service dependably and accurately. In other words, it is conformance to specification – doing what you said you would do when you said you would do it. How many times have you gone to pick up your car after a service and been told 'it'll be ready in five minutes'? An hour later and you're still drinking cold, stewed coffee from the reception filter machine.
- **Assurance** stems from the knowledge and courtesy of employees and their ability to convey trust and confidence. Customers want to be assured that the chef in the restaurant can cook, that the garage mechanic can fix the car, and that their accountant will not end them up in jail.
- **Tangibles** are the appearance of physical features, equipment, personnel, reports, communications materials and so on. No matter how good the doctor, for him to appear in the surgery dressed in a rubber suit and flippers won't generally instil confidence in his ability to cure your ailments.
- **Empathy** is the provision of caring, individualized attention to customers. It is the quality good doctors have of being able to convince you that they really care

about you, rather than just see you as a barrier over the next 15 minutes to getting out for their lunch.

● **Responsiveness** is the ability of the organization to react positively and in time to customer requests and requirements. This typically requires flexibility as customer requests can often be unexpected. It should also be noted that what constitutes fast response in the mind of one customer may be unacceptably slow for another. The highly responsive organization will need to predict where possible, but build into its systems and operations slack capacity to respond to the unpredictable.

understand how their customers judge service, what dimensions are important to them and how they are manifest. They then need to put in place strategies and systems to ensure their staff can deliver superior service.

The above five main approaches to positioning are by no means exhaustive and certainly not mutually exclusive. Positioning options are many and varied, and in the final analysis limited only by the creative imagination of marketing managers. Looking at a market afresh, resegmenting on new criteria, and combining assets and competencies in innovative ways are essential to finding new opportunities for the future.

These five main dimensions of servicequality have been found in many different service situations, from banking to restaurants, construction to professional services. The relative importance of each might vary, and the way in which each is manifest in any situation might be different, but time and again these factors have been shown to be relevant.

Firms seeking to create a service edge, to position themselves as offering superior service to that of competitors need first to

---

Practical tip

How well do you understand the way in which your customers judge the service you provide to them?

● Using the RATER framework ask your customer to evaluate the service you provide them with. Ask them how important each element is.
● See which you are under-performing on (especially those that are important to customers) and those where you may be achieving overkill and hence squandering resources.

Summary

● Competitive positioning is concerned with the development of long-term strategy. It is not just a fix for a short-term problem.
● Effective positioning, positioning that both differentiates the firm from competitors in a way of value to chosen customers and is sustainable, requires a clear understanding of market needs together with the resources, assets and competencies, of the firm.
● Positioning decisions then need to be made such that target customers and resources are optimally matched.
● As markets become more cluttered, and customers become more demanding, so we can expect greater fragmentation of markets and hence more opportunities for sharper positioning and tailoring of products and services more specifically to individual customer requirements. One-to-one marketing is both ultimate segmentation and ultimate positioning.

References and further reading

Berry, L. L. and Parasuraman, A. (1991), *Marketing Services : Competing through Quality*, New York: The Free Press.

Day, G. S. (1994), 'The capabilities of market-driven organizations', *Journal of Marketing*, **58**(3), 37–52.

Hamel, G. and Prahalad, C. K. (1994), *Competing for the Future*, Boston: Harvard Business School Press.

Hooley, G. J., Saunders, J. A. and Piercy, N. F. (1998), *Marketing Strategy and Competitive Positioning*, 2nd edition, Hemel Hempstead: Prentice-Hall International.

8

Market-driven strategic planning ———————

Professor Malcolm McDonald, Cranfield School of Management

 A search through the literature on marketing excellence reveals a fascinating array of findings and advice. None the less, from the more iconoclastic, such as Tom Peters, to the more sober and serious, such as Philip Kotler and John Saunders, there is a remarkable commonality and agreement about what constitutes marketing excellence. These common elements are shown in Table 8.1.

Table 8.1 *Key elements of world class marketing*

1 Profound understanding of the marketplace
2 Creative segmentation and selection
3 Powerful differentiation positioning and branding
4 Effective marketing planning processes
5 Long-term integrated marketing strategies
6 Institutionalized creativity and innovation
7 Total supply chain management
8 Market-driven organization structures
9 Careful recruitment, training and career management
10 Vigorous line management implementation

Even a cursory glance at this list reveals a very heavy emphasis on understanding the market and on being market driven. Indeed, increasingly organizations are writing phrases such as market driven, customer responsiveness and the like into their publicly promulgated mission statements.

Before getting into too much depth about what market-driven strategic marketing planning is, readers should try, or at least think carefully about, the answers to the following questions regarding the deliverables from the strategic marketing plan:

● can you list your key target markets? (in order of priority);

can you describe (quantitatively and qualitatively) the value that is required by each of your key target markets?;

- in each of these key target markets, can you describe how your organization creates better value than your competitors?;
- do the relevant senior people in your organization understand and support the above three points?;
- does your strategic marketing plan spell out how your organization is going to create superior profits? (sustainable competitive advantage);
- are all the relevant functions in your company organized in a way that is supportive of delivering the value required by the customer?

In this author's experience of working with some of the world's leading organizations, the scores given by directors and senior managers in response to these questions are generally low, which is an indication of the difficulty of implementing the blindingly obvious desire for any organization to run a truly market-driven organization.

Key to it all, of course, is the need to produce a professional strategic marketing plan, something which, alas, still eludes many organizations.

The purpose of this chapter is to explain how to produce a truly market-driven strategic plan. It will give some essential background information, will describe what it is and will then examine some of the principal barriers that get in the way of market-driven strategic planning, indicating how these can be overcome. Finally, the chapter will give some advice on how organizations can become more market driven.

Introducing strategic marketing planning

'A good big 'un will always beat a good little 'un'. So say the aficionados of the noble art of pugilism. They are undoubtedly correct in what they say, because their experience confirms this to be true. However, there are two very important, unspoken, assumptions which colour this thinking. These are that the contest is limited to the confines of a boxing ring, and conducted under the Marquis of Queensbury Rules.

Given these conditions, the heavier fighter will always triumph over his lighter-weight adversary. David would never have been able to overcome Goliath, had such a handicap been imposed upon him. Nor would Drake have defeated the vastly superior Spanish Armada.

Both of these apparently disadvantaged competitors owed their success to doing the unexpected. They refused to play the game on their opponent's terms and slog it out, toe to toe. Instead, they turned their lack of physical strength into a strategic advantage of nimbleness, speed of attack and surprise.

In essence, strategic marketing planning is an approach to business which, like the stories above, can enable even the smallest competitor to survive successfully. However, as we shall see, there is no simple 'magic formula' that can be administered. There is no marketing equivalent of Aladdin's lamp, which can make an organization's dreams come true.

Strategic marketing demands a perceptive and intelligent analysis of both the company and its business environment. The resulting plan then requires equal proportions of perspiration and inspiration to make it come alive, and be brought to fruition.

Strategic decisions are concerned with:

- the long-term direction of the organization, as opposed to day-to-day management issues;

- defining the scope of the organization's activities in terms of what it will and will not do;
- matching the activities of the organization to the environment in which it operates, so that it optimizes opportunities and minimizes threats;
- matching the organization's activities to its resource capacity, be it finance, personnel, technology or skill levels.

Strategic management is characteristically dealing with an uncertain future and new initiatives. As a result of this, it is often the harbinger of change. Organizations build their business strategies in a number of different ways. There are six accepted strategy-forming models:

- **A planning model**. Strategic decisions are reached by use of a sequential, planned search for optimum solutions to defined problems. This process is highly rational and is fuelled by concrete data.
- **An interpretative model**. The organization is regarded as a collection of associations, sharing similar values, beliefs and perceptions. These 'frames of reference' enable the stakeholders to interpret the organization and the environment in which it operates, cultivating the emergence of an organizational culture particular to that company. Strategy thus becomes the product, not of defined aims and objectives, but of the prevailing values, attitudes and ideas in the organization.
- **A political model**. Strategy is not chosen directly, but emerges through compromise, conflict and consensus seeking among interested stakeholders. Since the strategy is the outcome of negotiation, bargaining and confrontation, those with the most power have the greatest influence.
- **A logical incremental model**. Strategies emerge from 'strategic subsystems', each concerned with a different type of strategic issue. Strategic goals are based on an awareness of needs, rather than the highly structured analytical process of the

planning model. Often, due to a lack of necessary information, such goals can be vague, general and non-rigid in nature until such a time when events unfold and more information becomes known.
- **An ecological model**. In this perspective, the environment impinges on the organization in such a way that strategies are virtually prescribed and there is little or no free choice. In this model, the organization that adapts most successfully to its environment will survive in a way that mirrors Darwin's natural selection.
- **A visionary leadership model**. Strategy emerges as the result of the leader's vision, enforced by his/her commitment to it, his/her personal credibility, and how he/she articulates it to others.

It is unlikely that an organization will use a pure version of any of these models. In all probability, its strategic decision-making model will be a hybrid of some of them. However, it is possible that one or two of these will predominate and thereby give strategic decision making a distinct 'flavour'.

While these various models help to explain the different flavours of strategic decision making, at first sight they appear to have little in common. Closer examination shows that this is not the case. All of them see the organization and the environment as inseparable, even though the point at which the balance is struck varies from model to model. For instance, in the ecological model, the environment looms large, whereas in the incremental model, the organization appears to receive most consideration.

Another common theme is that strategies are perceived as necessary to help the organization to cope with changes in the environment. Again, the various models infer and accept different degrees of uncertainty in the environment. Thus, the ensuing strategies exhibit different degrees of flexibility. For example, the planning model assumes that the environment is more or less stable over the strategic time frame, or that any changes can be anticipated with some certainty. In contrast with this, the logical incremental model tests the environment continually, and is prepared to revise strategies if they are seen to be unsuitable.

While academics cannot seem to agree on a single, best approach, company executives have to get on with strategy formulation as best they can, using a combination of experience, intuition and hope. One of the earliest PhDs in the domain of marketing planning (McDonald, 1982) came to the conclusion that the process they go through is some sort of a logical sequence, leading to the setting of objectives, and the formulation of strategies and tactics for achieving them, together with the associated financial consequences. The formality of this process will be a function of the degree of product/market complexity, organizational size and the degree of environmental turbulence. In other words, the degree of formality will be driven in part by the dominant decision-making model in the organization.

Strategic marketing planning obviously cannot be discussed in isolation from the above strategic planning modes and it is likely that the way in which an organization's marketing planning is carried out will be a microcosm of the principal mode of the total process.

What is strategic marketing planning?

The overall purpose of marketing planning, and its principal focus, is the identification and creation of sustainable competitive advantage. Yet, after 50 years of research, teaching and writing about the subject, it seems that marketing planning is still one of the most enigmatic of all the problems facing management as they brace themselves for whatever challenges the coming years hold.

In simple terms, marketing planning is a logical sequence of activities, which leads to the setting of marketing objectives and the formulation of plans to achieve them. In small, undiversified companies this process, if it exists at all, is usually informal. In larger more complex organizations, the process is often systematized.

Usually, the planning process involves a situation review, the formulation of some basic assumptions about what constitutes the strengths and weaknesses of the organization, a comparison with how these weigh against the opportunities and threats posed by the business environment, setting objectives for what is sold and to whom, deciding how the objectives are to be achieved, and costing out and scheduling the actions necessary for implementation.

Apart from helping the organization to cope with increasing turbulence, environmental complexity, more intense competitive pressures, and the sheer pace of technological change, a marketing plan is generally accepted as being useful for the organization, for managers, for non-marketing functions, and for subordinates:

- to help identify the source of competitive advantage;
- to instil an organized approach to business development;
- to develop specificity;
- to clarify roles and improve co-ordination;
- to ensure consistent relationships;
- to inform;
- to provide a context for their contributions;
- to monitor progress;
- to get resources;
- to set objectives and strategies;
- to gain commitment.

The strategic marketing planning process – the steps

Figure 8.1 illustrates the several stages that have to be gone through in order to arrive at a marketing plan. This illustrates the difference between the process of marketing planning and the actual plan itself, which is the output of the process.

Each of the stages illustrated in Figure 8.1 will be discussed in more detail later in this chapter. The arrows joining up all the steps are meant to indicate the reality of the planning process, in that it is likely that each of these steps will have to be gone through more than once before final programmes can be written.

We can now look at the marketing planning process in more detail, starting with a look at the marketing audit. It is important to remember that at this stage we are describing the process only, rather than what should actually appear in a marketing plan. So far we have looked at the need for marketing planning and outlined a series of steps that have to be gone through in order to arrive at a marketing plan. However, any plan will only be as good as the information on which it is based, and the marketing audit is the means by which information for planning is organized.

What is a marketing audit?

There is no reason why marketing cannot be audited in the same way as accounts, in spite of its more innovative, subjective nature. A marketing audit is a systematic approach of all the external and internal factors that have affected a company's commercial performance over a defined period.

Given the growing turbulence of the business environment and the shorter product life cycles that have resulted, no one would deny the need to stop at least once a year at a particular point in the planning cycle to try to form a reasoned view on how all the many external and internal factors have influenced performance.

Sometimes, of course, a company will conduct a marketing audit because it is in financial trouble. At times like these, management often attempts to treat the wrong symptoms, most frequently by reorganizing the company. But such measures are unlikely to be effective if there are more fundamental problems that have not been identified. Of course, if the company survived for long enough, it might eventually solve its problems through a process of elimination. Essentially, though, the argument is that problems have first to be properly defined.

The audit is a means of helping to define them.

External and internal variables

Any company carrying out an audit will be faced with two kinds of variables. There is the kind over which the company has no direct control, for example economic and market factors. Second, there are those over which the company has complete control: the operational variables, which are usually the firm's internal resources. This division suggests that the best way to structure an audit is in two parts, internal and external. Table 8.2 shows areas that should be investigated under both headings. Each should be examined with a view to building up an information base relevant to the company's performance.

Many people mistakenly believe that the marketing audit should be some kind of final attempt to define a company's marketing problem, or, at best, something done by an independent body from time to time to ensure that a company is on the right track. However, many highly successful companies, as well as using normal information and control procedures and marketing research throughout the year, start their planning cycle each year with a formal, audit-type process, of everything that has had an important influence on marketing activities. Certainly, in many leading consumer goods companies, the annual self-audit approach is a tried and tested discipline.

Occasionally, it may be justified for outside consultants to carry out the audit in order to check that the company is getting the most of its resources. However, it seems an unnecessary expense to have this done every year.

Objections to line managers doing their own audits usually centre around the problem of time and objectivity. In practice, a disciplined approach and thorough training will help. But the discipline must be applied from the highest to the lowest levels of management if the tunnel vision that often results from a lack of critical appraisal is to be avoided.

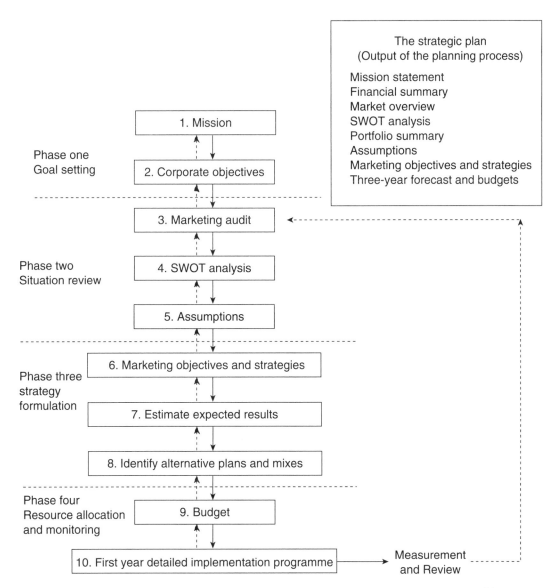

The strategic plan
(Output of the planning process)

Mission statement
Financial summary
Market overview
SWOT analysis
Portfolio summary
Assumptions
Marketing objectives and strategies
Three-year forecast and budgets

Phase one
Goal setting

1. Mission

2. Corporate objectives

Phase two
Situation review

3. Marketing audit

4. SWOT analysis

5. Assumptions

Phase three
strategy
formulation

6. Marketing objectives and strategies

7. Estimate expected results

8. Identify alternative plans and mixes

Phase four
Resource allocation
and monitoring

9. Budget

10. First year detailed implementation programme

Measurement
and Review

Figure 8.1 *The ten steps of the strategic marketing planning process. Source: McDonald (1995)*

SWOT analyses

The next question is: what happens to the results of the audit? Some companies consume valuable resources carrying out audits that produce very little in the way of results. The audit is simply a database, and the task remains of turning it into intelligence, that is, information essential to decision making.

It is often helpful to adopt a regular format for the major findings. One way of doing this is in the form of a SWOT analysis. This is a summary of the audit under the headings of internal strengths and weaknesses as they relate to external opportunities and threats.

The SWOT analysis should, if possible, contain no more than four or five pages of commentary, focusing only on key factors. It should highlight internal strengths and weaknesses (measured against those of the competition) and key external opportunities and threats. A summary of reasons for good or bad performance should be included. It should be interesting to read, contain concise

Table 8.2 *Conducting an audit*

External audit	Internal audit
External audit	**Internal audit**
Business and economic environment	*Marketing operational variables (own company)*

External audit

Business and economic environment

- Economic
- Political/fiscal/legal
- Social/cultural
- Technological
- Intra-company

The market

- Total market, size, growth and trends (value/volume)
- Market characteristics, developments and trends
  - products
  - prices
  - physical distribution
  - channels
  - customers/consumers
  - communication
  - industry practices

Competition

- Major competitors
- Size
- Market shares/coverage
- Market standing/reputation
- Production capabilities
- Distribution policies
- Marketing methods
- Extent of diversification
- Personnel issues
- International links
- Profitability
- Key strengths and weaknesses

Internal audit

Marketing operational variables (own company)

- Sales (total, by geographical location, by industrial type, by customer, by product)
- Market shares
- Profit margins/costs
- Marketing information/research
- Marketing mix variables as follows:
  - product management
  - price
  - distribution
  - promotion
  - operation and resources

statements, include only relevant and important data and give greater emphasis to creative analysis.

Where relevant, the SWOT analysis should contain life cycles for major products and for market segments, for which the future shape will be predicted using the audit information. Also, major products and markets should be plotted on some kind of matrix to show their desired position over the full planning method.

It is important to remember at this stage that we are merely describing the *process* of marketing planning as outlined in Figure 8.1. The format of the strategic marketing plan itself (i.e. what should actually appear in the written plan) is given in Table 8.3 later in this chapter.

Assumptions

Having completed the marketing audit and SWOT analysis, fundamental assumptions on future conditions have to be made. It would be no good receiving plans from two product managers, one of whom believed that market was going to increase by 10 per cent and the other who believed it was going to decline by 10 per cent.

An example of a written assumption might be: 'With respect to the company's industrial client, it is assumed that industrial over-capacity will increase from 105 per cent to 115 per cent as new industrial plans come into operation, price competition will force price levels down by 10 per cent across the board; a new product will be introduced by our major competitor before the end of the second quarter'. Assumptions should be few in number. If a plan is possible irrespective of the assumptions made, then the assumptions are unnecessary.

Marketing objectives and strategies

The next step is the writing of marketing objectives and strategies. This is the key to the whole process and undoubtedly the most important and difficult of all stages. If this is not done properly, everything that follows is of little value.

It is an obvious activity to follow on with, since a thorough review, particularly of its markets, should enable the company to determine whether it will be able to meet the long-range financial targets with its current range of products. Any projected gap has to be filled by new product development or market extension.

The important point to make is that this is the stage in the planning cycle at which a compromise has to be reached between what is wanted by various departments and what is practicable, given all the constraints upon the company. At this stage, objectives and strategies should be set for three years ahead, or for whatever the planning horizon is.

An objective is what you want to achieve; a strategy is how you plan to achieve it. Thus, there can be objectives and strategies at all levels in marketing, or advertising, for pricing, and so on.

The important point to remember about marketing objectives is that they are concerned solely with products and markets. Common sense will confirm that it is only by selling something to someone that the company's financial goals can be achieved, pricing and service levels are the means by which the goals are achieved. Thus, pricing, sales promotion and advertising objectives should not be confused with marketing objectives.

As already stated, the latter are concerned with one or more of the following:

- existing products in existing markets;
- new products for existing markets;
- existing products for new markets;
- new products for new markets.

They should be capable of measurement, otherwise they are not worthwhile. Directional terms, such as 'maximize', 'minimize', 'penetrate' and 'increase' are only acceptable if quantitative measurements can be attached to them. Measurement should be in terms of sales volume, value, market share, percentage penetration of outlets and so on.

Marketing strategies, the means by which the objectives will be achieved, are generally concerned with the '4Ps':

- **Product**: deletions, modifications, additions, designs, packaging, etc.
- **Price**: policies to be followed for product groups in market segments.
- **Place**: distribution channels and customer service levels.
- **Promotion**: communicating with customers under the relevant headings, i.e. advertising, sales force, sales promotion, public relations, exhibitions, direct mail, etc.

Having completed this major planning task, it is normal at this stage to employ judgement, experience, field tests and so on to test out the feasibility of the objectives and strategies in terms of market share, sales, costs and profits. It is also at this stage that alternative plans and mixes are normally considered.

General marketing strategies should now be reduced to specific *objectives*, each supported by more detailed strategy and action statements. A company organized according to functions might have an advertising plan, a sales promotion plan and a pricing plan. A product-based company might have a product plan, with objectives, strategies and tactics for price, place and promotion as required. A market- or geographically based company might have a market plan, with objectives, strategies and tactics for the four Ps as required. Likewise, a company with a few major customers might have a customer plan. Any combination of the above might be suitable, depending on the circumstances.

There is a clear distinction between strategy and detailed implementation or tactics. Marketing strategy reflects the company's best opinion as to how it can most profitably apply its skills and resources to the marketplace. It is inevitably broad in scope. The one-year plan that stems from it will spell out action and timings and will contain the detailed contribution expected from each department.

There is a similarity between strategy in business and the development of military strategy. One looks at the enemy, the terrain, the resources under command, and then decides whether to attack the whole front, an area of enemy weakness, to feint in one direction while attacking in another, or to attempt an encirclement of the enemy's position. The policy and mix, the type of tactics to be used, and the criteria for judging success, all come under the heading of strategy. The action steps are tactics.

Similarly, in marketing, the same commitment, mix and type of resources as well as al guidelines and criteria that must be all come under the heading of strategy. ample, the decision to use distributors but the three largest market areas, in company sales people will be used, is a strategic decision. The selection of particular distributors is a tactical decision.

The following list of marketing strategies (in summary form) covers the majority of options open under the headings of the 4Ps:

- **Product**:
  - expand the line;
  - change performance, quality or features;
  - consolidate the line;
  - standardize design;
  - positioning;
  - change the mix;
  - branding.
- **Price**:
  - change price, terms or conditions;
  - skimming policies;
  - penetrations policies.
- **Promotion**:
  - change advertising or promotion;
  - change selling.
- **Place**:
  - change delivery or distribution;
  - change service;
  - change channels;
  - change the degree of forward integration.

Formulating marketing strategies is one of the most critical and difficult parts of the entire marketing process. It sets the limit of success. Communicated to all management levels, it indicates what strengths are to be developed, what weaknesses are to be remedied, and in what manner. Marketing strategies enable operating decisions to bring the company into the right relationship with the emerging pattern of market opportunities which previous analysis has shown to offer the highest prospect of success.

What should appear in a strategic marketing plan

A written strategic marketing plan is the backdrop against which operational decisions are taken. Consequently, too much detail should be avoided. Its major function is to determine where the company is, where it wants to go and how it can get there. It lies at the heart of a company's revenue-generating activities, such as the timing of the cash flow and the size and character of the labour force. What should actually appear in a written strategic marketing plan is shown in Table 8.3. This strategic marketing plan should be distributed only to those who need it, but it can only be an aid to effective management. It cannot be a substitute for it.

It will be obvious from all this that not only does budget setting become much easier and more realistic, but the resulting budgets are more likely to reflect what the whole company wants to achieve, rather than just one department.

The problem of designing a dynamic system for setting budgets is a major challenge to the marketing and financial directors of all companies. The most satisfactory approach would be for a marketing director to justify all marketing expenditure from a zero base each year against the tasks to be accomplished. If these procedures are followed, a hierarchy of objectives is built up in such a way that every item of budgeted expenditure can be related directly back to the initial financial objectives.

For example, if sales promotion is a major means of achieving an objective, when a sales promotion item appears in the programme it has a specific purpose which can be related back to a major objective. Thus every item of expenditure is fully accounted for.

Marketing expense can be considered to be all costs that are incurred after the product leaves the factory, apart from those involved

---

Table 8.3 *What should appear in a strategic marketing plan*

---

1 Start with a mission or purpose statement outlining the *raison d'être* of the organization.

2 Next do a financial summary which illustrates graphically revenue and profit for the full planning period.

3 Now do a market overview:
Has the market declined or grown?
How does it break down into segments?
What is your share of each?
Keep it simple. If you do not have the facts, make estimates. Use life cycles, bar charts and pie charts to make it all crystal clear.

4 Now identify the key segments and do a SWOT for each one:
Outline the major external influences and their impact on each segment.
List the key factors for success. These should be less than six.
Give an assessment of the company's differential strengths and weaknesses compared with those of its competitors. Score yourself and your competitors out of 10 and then multiply each score by a weighing factor for each critical success factor (e.g. CSF 1 = 60, CSF 2 = 25, CSF 3 = 10, CSF 4 = 5).

5 Make a brief statement about the key issues that have to be addressed in the planning period.

6 Summarize the SWOTs using a portfolio matrix in order to illustrate the important relationships between the key points of your business.

7 List your assumptions.

8 Set objectives and strategies.

9 Summarize your resource requirements for the planning period in the form of a budget.

---

in physical distribution. When it comes to pricing, any form of discounting that reduces the expected gross income – such as promotional or quantity discounts, overriders, sales commission and unpaid invoices – should be given the most careful attention as marketing expenses. Most obvious marketing expense will occur, however, under the heading of promotion, in the form of advertising, sales salary and expenses, sales promotion and direct mail costs.

The important point about the measurable effects of marketing activity is that anticipated levels should result from careful analysis of what is required to take the company towards its goals, while the most careful attention should be paid to gathering all items of expenditure under appropriate headings. The healthiest way of treating these issues is through zero-based budgeting.

We have just described the strategic marketing plan and what it should contain. The tactical marketing plan layout and content should be similar, but the detail is much greater, as it is for one year only.

In the last section in this chapter the planning process is put into the context of different kinds of organizational structure, and the design and implementation of systems are described.

A recipe for commercial success? ■

Taken all round, marketing planning appears to provide numerous benefits for the organization and for this reason ought to be very well accepted as part of its standard operating procedures. However, such a state of affairs falls far short of the truth.

Greenley's (1987) study of marketing planning identified only seven UK empirically based studies into the marketing planning practices of commercial organizations. The remaining mass of publications are largely prescriptive and amount to little more than logically deduced theories based on ungrounded assumptions (what Glaser and Strauss (1967) refer to as 'exampling'). Most of the empirical studies concluded that few companies actually practice the theory of marketing planning so prolifically written about by so many.

But, even more disturbing, those who recognized the need for a more structured approach to planning their marketing and who turned to the formalized procedures found in prescriptive texts, rarely enjoyed the claimed benefits of marketing planning. Indeed, the very opposite sometimes happened, in that there were actually dysfunctional consequences, which brought marketing planning itself into disrepute.

This will come as no surprise to those keen observers who have noted that some companies who plan their marketing meticulously, fare badly, while their cavalier and inept (in marketing terms) contemporaries do well.

It raises the question about whether there is, or whether there has ever been, a relationship between marketing planning and commercial success.

The claimed benefits of better co-ordination of interrelated activities, improved environmental awareness, better communication among management, better use of resources, and so on, appear to be there for the taking, and there is a relationship between marketing planning and commercial success, as the work of McDonald (1982), Thompson (1962), Kollatt *et al.* (1972), Ansoff (1977), Thune and House (1970), Leighton (1966) and others has shown. It is just that the contextual problems surrounding the process of marketing planning are so complex and so poorly understood, that effective marketing planning rarely happens. What these problems are and how they can be overcome will be dealt with a little later.

The fact that financial performance at any one point in time is not necessarily a reflection of the adequacy or otherwise of planning procedures (since some companies just happen to be in the right place at the right time, usually in growth industries), should not deflect us from this fundamental truth. Those who want to know what marketing planning can add in a situation where a company has a well-established position, and where success to date has not been based on any particularly rigorous approach to marketing planning, should remember that all leadership positions are transitory. No industry based in the UK should need reminding of that today. The rapid and systematic demise of the UK's world leadership position is an insult to the founding fathers of British industry.

It is easy to forget the financially driven management of the 1960s and 1970s who milked dry the results of the endeavours of their entrepreneurial forebears. Rationality to them meant only short-term profits on a product-by-product basis, and if this meant raising the price or deleting the product, who cared as long as the end-of-year profit and loss account came out right? Regard for competitive position, market share, promotion, customer franchise, R&D and the like (all of which, of course, are funded from revenue) seemed irrelevant in those halcyon days of high growth.

Nor should we fool ourselves that this sad state of affairs has changed. A study by Wong, Saunders and Doyle, (1986) of Japanese and British companies in the UK concluded that 87 per cent of British firms still have profit maximization as their short-term goal, while 80 per cent of their Japanese competitors have market share growth as their major short-term goal. It is a sad reflection on our business schools in the UK that so many of our top industrialists still behave like vandals in the way they manage their marketing assets. It is little wonder that so many of our famous industries and names such as Dunlop, British Leyland and countless others, have had to suffer the humility of near bankruptcy, and it is a pity that so many more will have to suffer the same fate before we come to our senses and see that marketing planning is crucial to our long-term survival and prosperity.

Whatever the shape or size of the company, marketing's contribution to business success lies in analysing future opportunities to meet well-defined needs. This means that products and services need to provide the sought-after benefits in a superior way to those of competitors.

Organizational barriers to strategic marketing planning

A preference for 'short-termism'

A Chinese philosopher is quoted as saying: 'Even the longest journey must start with a single, small, step'. It was never envisaged that the step itself constituted the whole trip; it was merely a temporary position en route.

Unfortunately, many companies don't plan where they are going, they do the equivalent of taking one step, then look around before taking another. Sometimes, this journey is in the same direction, sometimes even backwards. Without having a destination to aim for, direction is relatively unimportant.

Nobody will claim that it is easy to identify one's long-term strategic objective, say, three years hence. The task is made extra difficult by the turbulent times in which we live. Yet without doing this, the next one-year step is likely to be irrelevant to the longer-term interests of the company.

It is easy to understand the appeal of short-termism. Most managers prefer to sell the products they find easiest to sell to those customers who offer the least line of resistance. By developing short-term, tactical marketing plans first and then extrapolating them, managers merely succeed in extrapolating their own shortcomings. It is a bit like steering from the wake – OK in calm, clear waters but not so sensible in busy and choppy waters! Preoccupation with preparing a detailed one-year plan first is typical of those many companies who confuse sales forecasting and budgeting with strategic marketing planning – in our experience the most common mistake of all.

Already companies led by chief executives with a proactive orientation that stretches beyond the end of the current fiscal year have begun to show results visibly better than the old reactive companies with only a short-term vision.

Figure 8.2 shows the old style of company in which very little attention is paid to strategy by any level of management. It will be seen that lower levels of management do not get involved at all, while the directors spend most of their time involved in operational/tactical issues.

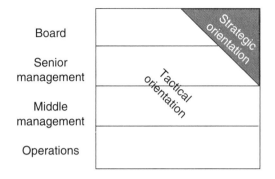

Figure 8.2 *Old-style company: levels of management and strategy*

Figure 8.3 shows another company with a similar management hierarchy. The difference between the two is striking. Here, instead of the strategic orientation just constituting a small part of the chief executive's job, many lower levels of management are also involved in strategy formulation.

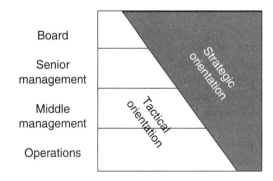

Figure 8.3 *New-style company: levels of management and strategy*

The lesson to be learned is simple:

Develop the strategic marketing plan first. This requires greater emphasis on scanning the external environment, the early identification of forces emanating from it, and developing appropriate strategic responses. All levels of management should be involved in the process.

A strategic plan should cover a period of between three and five years. Only when this has been developed and agreed, should the one-year operational plan be put together. Never write the one-year plan first and extrapolate from it.

Isolating the marketing function of operations

One of the most common causes of the failure of marketing planning is the belief that marketing is something that a marketing person 'does' in their office. The appointment of a marketing supremo is often a last-ditch attempt to put things right when all else has failed. The trouble is, the new person comes along and, irrespective of their knowledge and skills, quickly finds that all the power is vested in other functions, particularly for product development (the technical people), price (the accountants), customer service (the distribution department) and selling (the sales director). This leaves some bits of the promotional mix for the new person to play around with. Hence the new executive is powerless to influence anything of significance and quickly fails.

Line managers look on the new department with disdain and see requests for information, strategies and plans as a time-consuming task likely to have little impact on their real and more pressing problems.

This has much to do with the general misunderstanding about what marketing really is. Without a corporate driving force centred around customer satisfaction (i.e. a marketing orientation), arguments about where to put marketing are, of course, pointless, but even when top management is jolted into a realization of the need to take account of the customer, the most frequent mistake is to separate out marketing from operations as if it had the plague.

This is not the place to argue about organizational issues, such as line versus staff, centralization versus decentralization, although the principles are clear:

For the purpose of marketing planning, put marketing as close as possible to the customer. Where practicable, have both marketing and sales report to the same person, who should not normally be the chief executive officer.

Confusion between the marketing function and the marketing concept

The author's close contact with about 2,000 senior managers a year confirms his belief about the depth of ignorance that still abounds concerning what marketing is.

1. **Confusion with sales**. One managing director aggressively announced to the assembled seminar audience 'There's no time for marketing in my company 'til sales improve!'. Confusion with sales is still one of the biggest barriers to overcome.
2. **Confusion with product management**. The belief that all a company has to do is to produce a good product to succeed also still abounds, and neither Concord, the EMI body scanner, nor the many thousands of brilliant British products that have seen their owners or inventors go bankrupt, will convince such people otherwise.
3. **Confusion with advertising**. This is another popular misconception and the annals of business are replete with examples such as Dunlop, Woolworth and British Airways who, before getting professional management in, won awards with their 'brilliant' campaigns, while failing to deliver the goods. Throwing advertising expenditure at them is still a very popular way of tackling deep-rooted marketing problems.
4. **Confusion with customer service**. The 'have a nice day' syndrome is currently having its heyday in many countries of the world, popularized of course by Peters and Waterman in *In Search of Excellence*. The banks are among those who have spent millions training their staff to be charming to customers while still getting the basic offer fundamentally wrong – the banks are still closed when the public most needs them open. Likewise, in British Rail, while it helps to be treated nicely, it is actually much more important for passengers to arrive on time.

The principle then, is as follows:

Marketing is a management process whereby the resources of the whole organization are utilized to satisfy the needs of selected customer groups in order to achieve the objectives of both parties. Marketing, then, is first and foremost an attitude of mind rather than a series of functional activities.

Structural barriers

Closely linked with the issue of marketing powerlessness, is the issue of organizational form or structure.

The most typical organogram is the one that is based around corporate functions such as personnel, finance, production, distribution, operations and marketing. While the traditional reasons for this type of organization are clear, there is little doubt that it can be very difficult to get people who are loyal to their own 'tribe' to think of subjugating their own goals to the broader goals of customer satisfaction. This is clearly the role of top management and has a lot to do with corporate culture, to be discussed below.

While the team building approach has gone a long way towards overcoming this kind of organizational barrier, of much more importance is to get the task of defining strategic business units (SBUs) right.

A strategic business unit:

- will have common segments and competitors for most of its products;
- is a competitor in an external market;
- is a discrete, separable and identifiable unit;
- will have a manager who has control over most of the areas critical to success.

But SBUs are not necessarily the same as operating units, and the definition can, and should, be applied all the way down to a particular product of customer or group or group of products or customers, and it is here that the main marketing planning task lies.

The problem remains of getting organizational support and commitment to the marketing planning process, but this is discussed later.

Organize company activities around customer groups, if possible, rather than around functional activities and get marketing planning done in these strategic business units. Without excellent marketing planning in SBUs, corporate marketing planning will be of limited value.

Lack of in-depth analysis

Even from well-respected companies, the most common complaint concerns lack of adequate information for the purpose of analysis. On deeper investigation, however, it nearly always turns out to be a case of too much information, rather than too little. Frequently, the real problem is lack of proper analysis. At a recent conference for a builder's merchanting company that had increased its net profit before tax by 60 per cent for the second year running, one of their chief executives did not know the answer to any of the following questions:

How much of the profit increase is due to:

- market size growth?
- market share growth?
- price increases?
- cost reductions?
- productivity improvements?

Faced with such massive ignorance, it was clear what would happen to this company the moment construction industry trading conditions worsen.

The methodology for developing marketing intelligence systems has been comprehensively covered in the literature during the past 20 years, yet it is clear that, in Britain at least, industry has a long way to go to get even the basics right concerning trends in:

- the environment;
- markets;
- competitors;
- internal strengths and weaknesses.

It is also clear that, even if an organization has an adequate intelligence system, rarely is there a formal marketing audit undertaken by all SBU managers as a required activity at a specific time of the year as part of an agreed planning process.

The principle then, is as follows:

For an effective marketing audit to take place:

- checklists of questions customised according to level in the organization should be agreed;
- these should form the basis of the organization's MIM;
- the marketing audit should be a required activity;
- managers should not be allowed to hide behind vague terms such as 'poor economic conditions';
- managers should be encouraged to incorporate the tools of marketing in their audits, e.g. product life cycles, product portfolios, and the like.

Confusion between process and output

Confusion between the management process itself and the output of the process (the marketing plan) is common. In most cases, plans are too bulky to be of any practical use to busy line managers and most contain masses of data and information which rightly belongs in the company's marketing information system or audit, and whose inclusion in the marketing plan only serves to rob it of focus and impact.

The SWOT device (strengths, weaknesses, opportunities and threats), while potentially a very powerful analytical device to give impact to the ensuing assumptions, objectives, strategies and budgets, is rarely used effectively.

A SWOT should:

- be focused on each specific segment of crucial important to the organization's future;
- be a summary emanating from the marketing audit;
- be brief, interesting and concise;
- focus on key factors only;
- list differential strengths and weaknesses *vis-à-vis* competitors, focusing on competitive advantage;
- list key external opportunities and threats only;
- identify and pin down the real issues, it should not be a list of unrelated points;
- the reader should be able to grasp instantly the main thrust of the business, even to the point of being able to write marketing objectives;
- follow the implied question 'which means that ...?' to get the real implications.

This leads to a key point that needs to be made about this vital part of the marketing planning process.

Information is the foundation on which a marketing plan is built. From information (internal and external) comes intelligence. Intelligence describes the marketing plan, which is the intellectualization of how managers perceive their own position in their markets relative to their competitors (with competitive advantage accurately defined – e.g. cost leader, differentiation, niche), what objectives they want to achieve over some designated period of time, how they intend to achieve their objectives (strategies), what resources are required, and with what results (budget).

Lack of knowledge and skills

As we have seen, it is a matter of great disappointment to academics that many of the components of a typical marketing syllabus are rarely used by practising marketing managers, at least in industrial goods organizations. Indeed, in the author's experience, even experienced marketing managers with marketing qualifications often fail to apply the techniques of marketing in their jobs.

The perennial problems have always centred around customer behaviour and market segmentation and, indeed, these are extremely difficult concepts to grasp, even at the cognitive level. Even more worrying, however, is the blind assumption often made by top management that all the key marketing practitioners in an organization actually possess both the knowledge and the skills to be effective marketers.

The author has conducted a series of experiments in some of the UK's leading companies during the past two years, and has found that almost two-thirds of marketing practitioners do not know the difference between a corporate objective, a marketing objective and an advertising objective. Even fewer know what a logarithmic scale is and how it can be used in experience curves and matrices. Very few have heard of the Standard Industrial Classification and virtually no one has heard of PIMS. Very few even understand the significance of Benefit Analysis, let alone Benefit Segmentation. Out of 50 questions, the average score is about 20 per cent.

While these are only examples, and do not prove anything, it must be a matter of concern when thinking seriously about marketing planning, for without an understanding of at least some of the basic tools of marketing, the chance of coming up with strategies based on sustainable competitive advantage is slim.

Communication and interpersonal skills are also prerequisites for marketing planning success, since excellent marketing plans will be ineffective unless those on whom the main burden of implementation lies understand them and are highly motivated towards their achievement.

The principle then, is: ensure all those responsible for marketing in SBUs have the necessary marketing knowledge and skills for the job. In particular, ensure they understand and know how to use the more important tools of marketing, such as:

- information
  - how to get it
  - how to use it

- positioning
  - market segmentation
  - Ansoff
  - Porter
- product life-cycle analysis
  - gap analysis
- portfolio management
  - BCG
  - directional policy matrix
- 4Ps management
  - product
  - price
  - place
  - promotion

Additionally, marketing personnel require communication and interpersonal skills.

Lack of a systematic approach to marketing planning

Gorb (1978) talks about the differences between a hunter and a farmer in planning requirements. A hunter travels light, and needs stealth, cunning and know-how, whereas a farmer needs to plan ahead, buy seed, sow, harvest, interpret demand for the crops, and so on. Clearly, then, at the entrepreneurial end of corporate development, marketing planning as a formalized system is not likely to be seen as relevant because of the 'here and now' ethos.

Leppard and McDonald (1987) discuss the different kinds of planning system that are required by organizations. These range from very informal systems to highly formalized ones, with the degree of autonomy at the top or bottom depending of the organization's size and stage of development. They also devised an analytical tool for measuring an organization's stage of development to ensure that any marketing planning system is appropriate.

The point here, however, is that for all but very small, undiversified organizations, a marketing planning system is essential to ensure that things happen when they are supposed to happen and that there are at least some basic standards which must be adhered to. In the author's experience, even

where training has been carried out, the quality and usefulness of SBU marketing plans are so variable as to make headquarters co-ordination into a central document an impossible task. This is largely due to the different levels of intellect and motivation of participating managers.

It is essential to have a set of written procedures and a well-argued common format for marketing planning. The purposes of such a system are:

- to ensure all key issues are systematically considered;
- to pull together the essential elements of the strategic planning of each SBU in a consistent manner;
- to help corporate management to compare diverse businesses and to understand the overall condition of, and prospects for, the organization.

Failure to prioritize objectives

Even when organizations are successful in producing well-reasoned marketing plans, it is not uncommon to find in each marketing plan as many as 50 objectives and many more strategies. This is because of the hierarchy effect of a principal marketing objective leading to a number of sub-objectives, with each of these sub-objectives leading to further sub-objectives. It is rare, however, to find any kind of prioritization of these objectives, and even rarer to find any allocation of time resource to each. The result is that managers can, and do, get sucked into the day-to-day 'in tray' syndrome, which, in turn, results in the creeping non-implementation of the marketing plan.

The key role of senior management is to concentrate lower level management attention on factors that are both high leverage and actionable in order to get the essential jobs done effectively.

To prevent managers getting side-tracked by trivia, the author has found that it is helpful to get them to prioritize their next year's objectives using a time allocation planner. This is illustrated in Figure 8.4.

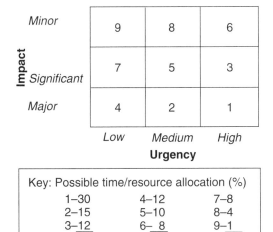

Impact			
Minor	9	8	6
Significant	7	5	3
Major	4	2	1
	Low	*Medium*	*High*
		Urgency	

Key: Possible time/resource allocation (%)

1–30	4–12	7–8
2–15	5–10	8–4
3–12	6– 8	9–1
57	30	13

Figure 8.4 *Objectives priority matrix*

The principle then, is as follows:

Ensure that all objectives are prioritized according to their impact on the organization and their urgency and that resources are allocated accordingly.

Hostile corporate cultures

During 1985 and 1986, Leppard and McDonald (1987) carried out a research study to attempt to provide an explanation for the widespread corporate resistance to marketing planning. This showed that the acceptance of marketing planning is largely conditioned by the stage of development of the organization and the behaviour of the corporate culture carriers. Thus it is that different modes of marketing planning become more appropriate at different phases of an organization's life.

That organizations experience different phases of life as they grow and mature, and that each phase has a different 'life-force', can be explained briefly as follows.

Essentially, an organization is a man-made product, and like all other products is subject to have a finite useful life cycle. Equally, the organizational life cycle can be extended, if it is managed astutely, just as with products or services. Therefore it is important to recognize when corrective action is required to renew the organization, and the nature of the appropriate action to take.

All organizations start life because somebody had a 'good idea' and the wherewithal to bring it alive. Sometimes the business idea proves to be the proverbial lead balloon and doesn't get off the ground. However, with good fortune, a following wind and sensible management, the organization can grow and thrive.

Indeed, its very success carries with it the seeds of destruction, because inevitably the organization outgrows the capabilities of the entrepreneur who gave it birth and was the single 'big brain' running things. One day, an extra customer, an additional order, another machine in the factory, one extra employee, becomes the straw to break the camel's back. The erstwhile busy owner-manager becomes over-loaded and can no longer cope. As a result, the organization stalls and can go into a tailspin (see Figure 8.5).

The solution to the problem would be for the owner-manager to take on some specialist staff and to delegate responsibility to them. However, for many entrepreneurs, to let go of even a single string is alien to them. They do not sit comfortably in a formally structured situation, for deep-down many of them are just not organizational men. They are hunters, rather than farmers.

So here we have an organization which has enjoyed a relatively trouble-free period of evolutionary growth being confronted with a major crisis. What happens next? There are three possible outcomes:

1. the organization fails;
2. the owner-manager learns to change his operating style;
3. a new strong leader appears on the scene.

Either of the last two outcomes enables the organization to extend its life cycle, but just as before, the next phase of evolutionary growth also brings with it the germ of the next crisis. In this way, an organization's total life can be depicted as a series of evolutionary

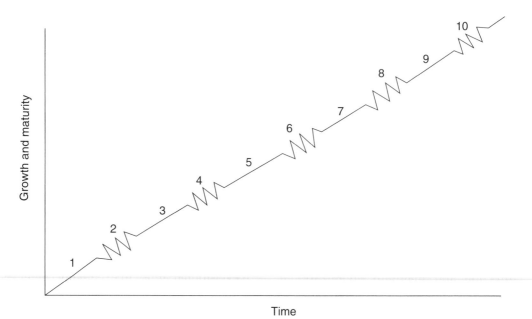

Figure 8.5 *The developing organization – the initial life phase*

growth phases, interspersed with periodic crisis points, as shown in Figure 8.6.

The levels on the diagram are explained below:

1. The first evolutionary growth phase can be termed the organization's 'creative evolution'. Its momentum is fuelled by the creativity behind the initial business idea, and the creative and flexible manner in which it responds to its business problems.

2. The first crisis is that of 'leadership', as we have seen.

3. The next evolution phase is bought about by a strong figure giving a 'directive'

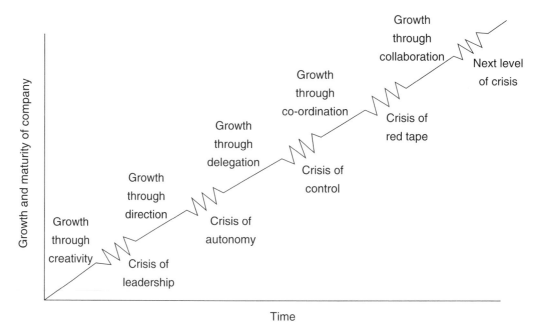

Figure 8.6 *Phases of organization growth and crisis*

lead. This person clarifies who does what and creates order out of the chaos. He will set up rules and procedures and, by doing so, alters the culture that was indigenous to the earlier phase.

4. The next crisis arrives when the directive leader no longer has the confidence of those working for him. As the organization has grown, so have those in specialist positions grown in expertise. The sales people know more about customers than the chief executive, the technologists are more in touch with the latest developments, and so on. The strong leader who could once give direction and maintain organizational momentum, no longer has credibility, he has lost touch. Thus the company is plunged into the 'autonomy crisis'. Whose hand should be on the tiller is the underlying issue.

5. The crisis is resolved by recognizing that the company's expertise must be tapped. Thus, more power and authority is delegated to key people throughout the organization and a period of 'delegated growth' ensues. Again, with the redistribution of power, the organizational culture changes in subtle ways.

6. As growth continues, those at the top of the organization are discomfited by feelings that the organization is getting out of control. The tail is wagging the dog, as it were. There is a 'crisis' about who is really in 'control'.

7. The resolution of this crisis comes about by establishing better 'co-ordination' between those at the top and those at the bottom of the organization. Again, the intention is to harness all the strengths.

8. Unfortunately, attempts to improve co-ordination lead to a proliferation of systems and procedures which eventually become counter-productive. Decision making is slowed down and people see themselves as subordinate to 'the system'. When this happens, the 'red

tape', bureaucratic 'crisis' phase has arrived.

9. The only solution, to offer a prospect of getting back on an evolutionary growth track, is to get rid of all the unnecessary trappings which have accumulated over the years. To rely more on open and spontaneous communications, for example, instead of memos written in triplicate, to recognize that it is people working together that achieves results, not impersonal systems. In striving to achieve yet another culture change, the organization moves into its 'collaborative evolution' phase.

10. As we have seen, each period of evolutionary growth eventually comes to an end, it seems (and this is only speculation) that the 'next crisis' might occur because people 'over-collaborate', that is to say, lose the ability to make individual decisions without con-sultation, or perhaps some form of col-lective 'group think' loses touch with the environment within which the organization operates. At present there is insufficient evidence to say with certainty what the next crisis, or what its succeeding evolutionary period will be. However, one thing is certain, human ingenuity will somehow prevail to extend the corporate life cycle even further.

With this type of overview of how an organi-zation grows and develops, it is obvious that it is at its weakest during the crisis phases. An alternative strategy which is sometimes employed by organizations when they reach these critical points is to 'put the clock back' – of course they cannot do this literally, but they can achieve an analogous results by divisionalizing, or breaking the organization down into smaller units. So, for example, an organization at the red tape crisis might rea-son that when it was smaller, it didn't require all these systems and procedures to co-ordi-nate and control activities.

Sometimes such a move can be successful, but generally it only delays the inevitable.

Continuing this example, managers who have adapted to a bureaucratic culture, often carry it with them into the smaller units. Perhaps the company only grows stronger in the long term by learning to overcome the crises as they arise.

The fact that some managers cannot easily let go of cultures that have served them well in periods of evolutionary growth, can sometimes explain why it is necessary to import a new chief executive at critical times. Perhaps there is a strong case to be made that you need the right kind of horses for the different (evolutionary growth) courses.

Can managers who have led a company down a particular path suddenly change track? Is it possible for frogs to become princes? Popular books would claim they can, because this is a much more optimistic message with which to sell copies. However, experienced practitioners and consultants would have some reservations.

If the business pressures on a company are great enough, intelligent behaviour will, of course, win the day, as in the cases of British Airways and Woolworth.

In the meantime, however, standardized, textbook type marketing planning cannot be imposed on all organizations with an equal chance of success, and most definitely not without the active support and participation of the culture leaders. Such participation must involve feeding back to those who have taken part in the process the total results of their efforts.

As a general rule, the marketing planning process should be matched to the organization life phases in this way.

- **Creative evolution** – marketing plans are generally absent, but a sales plan will be useful.
- **Directed evolution** – a systematic, top-down process will be most compatible with the corporate culture.
- **Delegation evolution** – a bottom-up marketing planning process.
- **Co-ordinated evolution** – a combination of top-down, bottom-up.

- **Collaborative evolution** – a more imaginative, less bureaucratic approach, perhaps only planning around key products or markets (remember the 80:20 rule!).

The final principle then, is as follows:

Marketing planning will not be effective without the active support and participation of the culture leaders. But even with their support, the type of marketing planning has to be appropriate for the phase of the organizational lifeline. This phase should be measured before attempting to introduce marketing planning.

Changing the marketing mindset ◼

A research project carried out by Cranfield School of Management on behalf of the Chartered Institute of Marketing (1994) identified a number of changes that are occurring within organizations to meet the rapidly changing and hostile business environment. These changes are all about becoming market driven, which is a prerequisite for effective marketing planning.

Strategic changes

- **Structure** – common to many of the articles on strategic change is the notion that the organizational structure of the marketing department has to be changed to accommodate the new business challenges. In effect, leading companies appear to be moving away from a formal, 'top-down', hierarchical structure, which is bureaucratic, but effective in terms of administrative costs as well as being risk aversive, in so far as everyone is directly accountable for their actions. In the past, this structure served companies well, but it is now being criticized because it impedes the creation of innovative ideas and it hinders the company's ability to respond quickly to market opportunities. In its place, a more flatter, flexible, 'open system' structure is being adopted, in which traditional job titles and responsibilities are being replaced.

- **Focus** – as companies become more global in their outlook, the effectiveness of controlling marketing operations from a centralized position is being questioned. Many companies are disbanding their central function and establishing multiple cores, comprising multifunctional, customer-facing teams. Potentially, the move to decentralization hinders marketing strategy cohesion. Companies overcome this problem in different ways: some use working groups, or 'task forces' (Unilever refer to them as category management teams), with representation from the various units, to steer strategic issues, others, such as Procter & Gamble designate 'lead countries' to take lead roles in projects and then to disseminate the knowledge to the other units. This enables companies to take a focused search for areas of competitive advantage. Increasingly, companies are looking towards strategic alliances, other 'lock-in' relationships, and more informal networks to expand their avenues for business growth.
- **Future driven** – to date, companies have assumed a largely reactive approach towards the way they conduct their business. There are signs that organizations are beginning to take a more proactive approach to the future and are becoming truly market driven. McKenna (1991) describes this as changing culture from the 'tell us what colour you want' school of marketing to 'let's figure out together whether and how colour matters to your larger goal' marketing. In essence, it implies moving towards a position of genuine involvement with customers and, where necessary becoming familiar with the customer's customer. It assumes a 'future backwards, market inwards' approach. Successful companies seemingly evolve with or in front of markets.

Operational and functional changes

Accompanying the strategic and philosophical changes is the need to implement changes at the functional level.

- **Professionalism** – there are many indications that leading companies are becoming more professional in their marketing operations in a number of different ways. They attach more importance to formal marketing training and qualifications and make greater use of marketing research and marketing planning, as well as heavier investment in marketing intermediary and internal analysis.
- **Market and performance assessment** – it is apparent that leading companies are moving away from discrete time assessments based around weekly, monthly or quarterly periods, towards continuous, ongoing monitoring and analysis, so that they can react quickly to market changes and prevent getting stuck in antiquated paradigms. Lazer (1993) thus described marketing as becoming a process of 'striving, but never arriving', of 'pursuing a journey, not reaching a destination'. In today's fast-changing marketplace, the traditional NPD process of getting an idea, developing a prototype, testing the market, and launching, is judged to be 'slow, unresponsive and turf-ridden' (McKenna, 1991). The alternative is to nurture continuous innovation fed by monitoring the market wants and competitive activity on an ongoing basis.

It is apparent that marketing success is a matter of doing the right things as well as doing things right.

Marketing planning: the way forward

The strongest message to emerge from the companies that took part in the

Cranfield/CIM study is that they are redefining marketing. Marketing for the excellent companies is now about customer service in a very special sense. The excellent companies are talking not just about satisfying present customer needs, but about anticipating the customer needs of the future and delivering them today.

This deceptively simple re-orientation is beginning to have the most profound impacts upon the ways in which excellent companies do business.

The introduction of a customer-orientated business philosophy across the whole organization is critical to effective marketing and business success. While many senior executives across different industries have come to accept that over the last decade, the stumbling block has been how to actually implement it.

Corporate cultures are impossible to change overnight; no one denies that. And this is borne out among the companies that we studied. Even successful organizations such as British Telecom admit that there are still some attitudinal barriers to overcome, before the marketing philosophy is embraced fully by all its personnel. The signs, though, are very encouraging; leading industrial companies are moving in the right direction – the supertanker is changing its course.

According to the study, there are a number of ways that help organizations achieve an overarching business philosophy centred on the customer. From the evidence it is clear that these mechanisms are being adopted. The first is customer focus through leadership; the cultural change has to be driven from the top. Both in the service and consumer goods companies studied, the preference was to bring in senior executives from outside the company to drive the cultural change.

The second mechanism that leading companies are adopting to become more customer focused is through the introduction of cross-functional mobility to their managers.

Company restructuring is the third mechanism to help break down inherent cultures and re-orientate around a customer focus.

Whether the primary catalyst to restructuring has been the need to become market-led, or whether it has been to respond to the business challenges (such as internationalization) that confront industry today, we are left with little doubt that leading companies are in the throes of major reorganizations. There is a firm belief in the companies that we studied that restructuring around customers is necessary, both to become closer to customers and to be able to respond quickly to their needs. Company structures are becoming flatter, as hierarchies are being delayered, and responsibilities are being devolved.

In many of the companies in the Cranfield/CIM study, a move was underfoot to restructure around markets. Currently, the standard practice is still to be organized around products and product categories. In industries where customer power has grown the quickest and become highly concentrated, leading companies are regrouping around key accounts and market segments, creating customer focus teams and equipping them with the necessary responsibility and authority. One company, AT&T Global Information Solutions, has created 23 Customer Focus Teams in the UK, as part of their restructuring, and has reduced the layers in its hierarchy to just three. This new organization structure is being adopted world-wide, with the aim of creating a culture of market awareness. The company is striving to reach a point where there are no more than two organizational levels between the customer and the service solution. They are supported by centralized, functional, specialist departments. In other companies, cross-functional teams were being introduced to take on special projects. There was every sign, in these cases, that they are having great impact and will assume a more permanent and mainstream role in the future.

In the companies that had adopted a marketing orientation, invariably marketing had escaped from the traditional marketing department. This was being reflected in its size. The lead taken by good marketing companies to smaller functional marketing departments looks set to be followed by others. Crucially, however, its influence is growing, not diminishing, as companies recognize the pivotal role it plays in two-way communication with customers and in delivering customer satisfaction against their needs. The future role of centralized marketing departments is seen increasingly as being split between the policeman of corporate identity and the ombudsman of the customer.

Accompanying restructuring, a strong feature of the good marketing companies studied was the heavy influence that the customer facing divisions were having on strategy formulation.

Unquestionably, the ways in which strategy was being developed were becoming more customer sensitive and dynamic. Strong direction was being provided from the top, but this tended to be in outline form. Strategic detail, as well as tactics, were being developed lower down, or, at least, away from central HQ.

Besides restructuring, the largest, single initiative in strategic marketing today is the current emphasis being given to building relationships with customers and even customers' customers. This was apparent in all of the case studies in the Cranfield/CIM project.

In order to achieve marketing excellence at an operational level, there were three distinct trends that were emerging among the leading companies, irrespective of their industry sector. The first was the renewed emphasis being placed on the collection, analysis and use of marketing information. In particular, the companies in the report were giving more emphasis on catching information which provides a better depth of understanding about their customers and their motivations to buy. Some leading companies believed that there is now too much emphasis being shown towards competitor analysis and benchmarking. By focusing on the competition, you can easily lose sight of the customer.

The second trend that is developing at the operational end of marketing, is the growing use and importance being given to performance measurement and monitoring. This is, beyond doubt, a feature associated with leading companies. The number and scope of performance measures are growing, as companies establish and fine-tune the measures they need to take in order to deliver customer satisfaction end-to-end. The measures are not restricted to assessing external customer satisfaction levels, but, increasingly, are becoming more sophisticated to cover the whole value chain, including internal customers.

The third and final trend that is helping leading companies to achieve marketing excellence is the investment made in the training and development of staff. All of the companies studied invested heavily in ongoing training programmes, to ensure that they possessed leading-edge skills and knowledge to defend their positions of competitive advantage.

The emergent marketing orientation

Finally, the Cranfield/CIM research suggested that there are certain key aspects to achieving a true marketing orientation. Some of these, such as leadership, reorganization and the move to process thinking, have already been mentioned.

The key to managing the change process to make an organization truly marketing and customer orientated seem to be leadership, flexibility and empowerment.

Leadership refers to the change driver within the organization and its visible commitment to the new philosophy, which must be at the very highest levels of the organization.

Flexibility means being prepared to accept change, not just as a one-off, but constantly. Given that the needs and wants of customers and consumers are constantly changing, truly marketing-led organizations cannot expect to change once and then to stay still. Flexibility must be built in to the organization by methods such as cross-functional working, so that customer wants can be anticipated.

Empowerment has two meanings for the market-led company, one internal and one external. Internally, it means encouraging the customer-facing teams to feed information back into the organization, particularly for the purpose of strategy development. Externally, it means allowing the customer-facing teams latitude to implement the strategy in the way that they believe will truly delight the customer. In order to do this, they will need not just to be empowered, but also to be equipped with the necessary marketing skills.

In essence, the emergent marketing orientation combines company-wide embracement of the marketing philosophy with the necessary functional skills to deliver the needs of customers.

We show in Figure 8.7 a matrix of marketing philosophy, on which we have plotted, in

Figure 8.7 The new marketing orientation

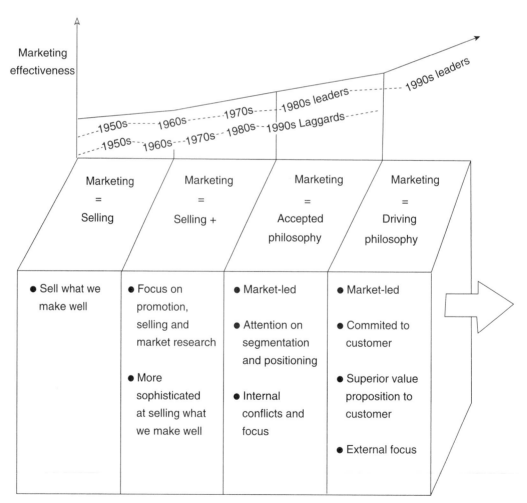

Figure 8.8 The evolution of marketing in the future. Source: Garda (1988)

diagrammatic form, the relationship between the adoption of marketing as a philosophy with the levels of marketing skills within the organization. Box 4 represents all that is worst in industry, i.e. a low marketing skills base and weak customer orientation.

Box 3 represents organizations that have recruited managers with excellent marketing skills, but which do not have an overarching marketing philosophy. In these organizations, marketing is likely to be tactical rather than strategic. In Box 2 we find organizations that have recognized the need to be market-led, but which do not yet have the marketing skills fully to achieve this.

It is organizations in Boxes 2, 3 and 4 that have led to the criticisms levelled against marketing in the past. In contrast, the excellent companies in the Cranfield/CIM study were either in Box 1, or moving rapidly towards it. For organizations in Box 1, marketing has a major contribution to make to business success.

Summary

In conclusion, it is clear that marketing, both as a philosophy and as a function, is still in its infancy. In part, difficulties in implementing marketing in industry have stifled its growth. However, the last section in this chapter has highlighted the steps that leading companies are now taking in order to implement marketing practice and the success they are achieving. It provides a route plan for others to follow. In excellent companies, marketing is now rapidly evolving into adulthood and will clearly be a major driving force in the late 1990s, for those companies that embrace it in the manner shown in Figure 8.8.

Clearly, marketing planning as a process cannot be successful unless the organizations practising it are truly market-driven.

References and further reading

Ansoff, H. I. (1977), 'The state of practice of planning systems', *Sloan Management Review*, **18**(1), 1–224.

Doyle, P., Saunders, J. A. and Wong, V. (1986), 'A comparative study of Japanese and British marketing strategies in the UK market,' *Journal of International Business Studies*, **17**(1), 27–46.

Glaser, B. G. and Strauss, A. C. (1967), *The Discovery of Grounded Theory: Strategies for Qualitative Research*, New York: Aldine Publishing Company.

Gorb, P. (1978), 'Management development for the small firm', *Personnel Management*, January.

Greenley, G. (1987), 'An exposition with empirical research into marketing planning', *Journal of Marketing Management*, **3**(1), July.

Kollatt, D. T., Blackwell, R. D. and Robeson, J. F. (1972), *Strategic Marketing*, New York: Holt, Reinhart and Winston Inc.

Lazer, W. (1993), 'Changing dimensions of marketing management – the new realities', *Journal of International Marketing*, **1**(3), 93–101.

Leighton, D. S. R. (1966), *International Marketing: Text and Cases*, New York: McGraw-Hill.

Leppard, J. and McDonald, M. H. B. (1987), 'A reappraisal of the role of marketing planning', *The Quarterly Review of Marketing*, **13**, Autumn, 1–7.

McDonald, M. H. B. (1982), *The Theory and Practice of Marketing Planning for Industrial Goods in International Markets*, Cranfield University PhD.

McDonald, M. H. B. *et al.* (1994), *The Challenge of Change*, Cranfield/CIM Research Report.

McKenna, R. (1991), 'Marketing is everything', *Harvard Business Review*, January–February, 65–79.

Thompson, S. (1962), *How Companies Plan*, AMA Research Study, No. 54, AMA.

Thune, S. and House, R. (1970), 'Where long range planning pays off', *Business Horizons*, **13**(4), 81–87.

9

Developing an effective brand strategy ___

Professor Leslie de Chernatony, The Open Business School

 This chapter considers the process which managers can follow to develop an effective brand strategy. It opens by clarifying the nature of brands and their value to corporations and customers. Many organizations are beginning to recognize that in today's more competitive environment they need to have a much clearer brand strategy for their existing brands. Others have identified opportunities for developing new brands and are going beyond the new product development process, augmenting these with new brand strategies. By following the systematic process identified in this chapter, managers should be better equipped to develop brand strategies which more effectively lever their existing brands, or enable them to gain a competitive lead for their new brands.

The nature of brands

Some managers consider brands as well-devised names, attractive logos and eye-catching designs that make their products or services stand out. This is but part of a brand. An analogy can be drawn between a brand and an iceberg. As a ship approaches the iceberg, the captain is aware that he is only seeing 15 per cent of the total iceberg. Likewise the name, logo and pack design are the visible parts of brands, evoking recollections of the added values that customers receive. These added values are a consequence of the unseen, unique corporate infrastructures, such as highly innovate R&D activities, modern production facilities and well-integrated logistics system. The extent to which these unseen aspects are orchestrated to add more value to the consumption experience than competitors, indicates the strength of brands.

The visible aspects of a brand are important, but to be a successful brand, customers need to instantly associate these with a unique cluster of benefits. The taxi firm owner who sticks 'A2B Taxis' on his fleet of cars is using the name to differentiate their commodity. However, to develop this into a brand, he needs to consider:

- what added value he provides beyond his competitors;
- whether he is adding value in ways that are relevant and highly desirable to his customers;

- whether competitors can rapidly emulate this; then
- how can he link the name to the added values, such that customers rapidly recognize extra benefits when seeing the name 'A2B Taxis'.

Thus brands are *holistic entities*. Powerful brands are the result of well-integrated management teams, aware of their brand's desired unique, added values and all working in a coherent manner to achieve this. Some organizations fail to recognize the importance of internal integration. They incorrectly believe they only have external competitors, when the reality is that some of their managers are pulling against others. For example, an insecticide producer, with a management team responsible for the wetter, northern region and another responsible for the drier, southern region are both pleased to capitalize on the reputation of their corporation. However, both continually lobby the production manager to adjust one of the ingredients to better suit their climatic conditions, and one team's gain is at the expense of the other team. With poor co-ordination this can lead to increasing frustration, internal animosity and ultimately, customer dissatisfaction.

We can pull on these points to clarify that a successful brand is:

An identifiable product, service, person or place, augmented through a coherent process, such that buyers, or users, perceive unique, relevant added values which match their needs most closely.

There are several key words in this definition. Brands have a distinctiveness which makes them *identifiable*. Many managers regard this distinctiveness coming solely from their firm's activities in packaging, advertising, or naming. However, they overlook two other sources that interact with these activities to make their brand distinctive. First, there is the way consumers perceive the brand. For example, even though the pack design team may have used a deep mauve colour to give their brand a distinctive, prestigious appeal,

some consumers may perceive it as rather dull and uninspiring. Secondly, there is the impact from consumers discussing brands with each other. Particularly for conspicuously consumed brands, consumers' conversations with their peer groups draws certain brands to their attention.

Practical tip

It is worth auditing the distinctiveness of your brand on a regular basis by asking your management team, your consumers and your consumers' peers how distinctive your brand is and why they express these views. Comparing each groups' views can better identify sources of strengths and weaknesses.

The principles of brand building evolved in the *product* sector, the best example of which is Marlboro, the world's most valuable brand in 1995, estimated to be worth US$44.6 billion. However, with the *services* sector now accounting for the largest proportion of most Western countries' GNP, many organizations are increasingly focusing on building their service brands. Branding principles are employed by agencies promoting individual *personalities*, for example politicians, pop stars and opera singers. *Places* such as cities, counties and countries are becoming increasingly concerned about conveying their brand benefits, for example when cities compete to host the Olympics.

When faced with two garages that are equally capable of servicing a car, consumers are likely to choose on the basis of price. However, one garage might be *adding value* by giving consumers complimentary sachets of car shampoo, while the other might collect and return consumers' cars. Both garages are adding value, since they are providing benefits beyond the core servicing. However, to the person who always uses automatic car washes, these complimentary sachets are less relevant. These are examples of tangible added values, but added values can also be intangible. For example, when choosing a car, research shows consumers consider the extent to which each brand reflects their personality. Consumers perceive added value through the way a particular car helps project their personality.

Importance of brands

One of the reasons for managers' interest in brands is due to their financial value. From the late 1980s, much publicized brand valuations, in particular the Nestlé valuation of Rowntree at virtually three times its stock market value, drew attention to the significant values of established brands. Many firms recognize the goodwill inherent in their brands and are increasingly interested in brand valuation exercises. Some argue that such brand valuations enable them to better reflect their corporations' true values. Others put their brand valuations on their profit and loss statements to protect themselves against aggressive take-over bids, while more sophisticated firms use brand valuation exercises to assess the attractiveness of alternative brand strategies.

Brands bring stability to firms. Managers are more confident in forecasting future income streams, through having respected relationships with their customers. Short-term crisis (e.g. illegal product tampering) can be more easily ridden out. High calibre employees are attracted to firms with powerful brands and, through their pride in being associated with prestigious brands, they feel more loyal to their firms.

Brands provide a basis for structuring firms and, for organizations with portfolios of brands, they facilitate the allocation of resources. They act as a means for identifying sources of costs and revenue. Data becomes more easily understood when presented in terms of brand performance among particular customer groups.

Powerful brands enable corporations, particularly global players, to 'glue' their disparate outposts together. Not only do they reflect particular promises to consumers, but

to employees they reflect desired standards of behaviour. Brands signify a corporation's culture, thus when the firm expands into more distant geographical markets, their brands unite employees by providing clear signs about beliefs, attitudes and behaviour. Powerful brands enable all employees to appreciate the corporate strategy their firm is following. Through their daily interaction with brands, employees understand far more easily the meaning of the sophisticated strategic terminology of senior managers.

Consumers appreciate brands because they simplify their choice decisions. They act as guarantees of consistent quality levels. Having the right sorts of brands enables consumers to integrate more easily with their groups. Brands reduce consumers' perceived risk when buying, making them feel more confident.

Clearly brands are valuable *assets* and therefore need nurturing through well-developed strategies, as is next considered.

It should be noted that this is an iterative process. For example, at the second step in this process, managers may have an objective of selling a particular volume of the brand to a specific consumer group, yet at the third step, the brand audit may indicate extremely entrenched, aggressive competitors likely to impede brand growth. Given this conflict, it is worth reconsidering the original brand objectives.

Following through this process is not an activity that should be delegated to one person. Rather this should be undertaken by a small team consisting of the key senior managers from those departments that are involved in brand building. Not only does this enable a total company perspective to be considered, but there is also a greater degree of commitment and ownership of the strategy.

The process of developing a brand strategy

Figure 9.1 shows a process by which managers can develop the most appropriate brand strategy.

Brand mission

Brand objectives

Brand audit

Brand positioning

Brand personality

Internal considerations

* relationships within the portfolio

* management structure

* systems to add value

Brand monitoring

Figure 9.1 *Developing brand strategy*

Let us now consider each step in detail.

Brand mission

Everyone working on the brand must be clear about the long-term rationale for their brand's existence. In essence, if the brand is to thrive, it must be driven by a desire to favourably change its target consumers' lives. Apple Macintosh provides a good example of a brand that challenged the dominance of major names, such as IBM, through its brand vision: man should not be subservient to machines. Since its founding in 1976, everyone in the Apple Computer Company adhered to the philosophy of refusing to sell complex, technical devices that make considerable demands on owners' intellect, but rather they wanted to develop and sell tools that enhance the productivity and creativity of people. Every employee conceived their approach to developing personal computers in terms of how they could build technology around their customers, rather than the other way round.

A brand can only thrive in a particular domain and the *brand mission* should make it clear not only how it is going to change users' lives, but also what types of users. A once dominant cement brand kept on losing market share since it was obsessed with its mission of being the architect's friend. What the firm had failed to recognize was the declining importance of architects in the house-building market. Instead of providing a high level of technical service to architects, it needed to reconceive its mission as the builder's price friend, and re-orient its thrust to gaining greater confidence among builders.

If a brand is to thrive by changing consumers' lives, it has to stretch the firm's employees. A classic example of this is the challenge presented by the CEO of Canon to his staff – take on the market leader in the personal copier market with a product that is significantly cheaper than the current model. Enthused by this stretching goal, the teams succeeded by radically changing their approaches. The CEO of a credit card company attributed part of the brand's success to the way he used the annual company conference to congratulate staff on last year's success, and within the mission of providing unsurpassed customer service, threw out daunting service improvement challenges for the coming years.

Once a mission has been crisply specified, managers need to assess its driving power by considering:

● What ideas will be challenged? In business-to-business brand marketing AMP foresaw a growth opportunity for its brand of connectors by encouraging its staff to no longer think of their connectors as pieces of plastic and metal on circuit boards, but rather as anything that provides connectivity, even between people. Redefining connectors enabled them to bring together new technologies, for example, sensors, optoelectronics and wireless components to provide better connectivity systems for their customers. In so doing though, managers faced the challenge of broadening their perspective to recognize a wider target market, to consider ways in which an expanded range could better solve customers' needs and to revise their approaches to customer service. Managers had well-established views about the nature of their competitors, but an expanded market opportunity necessitated them learning about a new set of competitors and forced them to reconceive ways of out-manoeuvring them.

- Is the brand's mission easy for everyone to understand and is everyone able to appreciate how they can contribute to achieve this brand mission? Even though the senior management team have a clear appreciation of their brand's mission, the terminology and the implications of this for more junior staff may not be that well understood. As such it may be wise to run a series of short workshops to communicate the brand's mission and to clarify how staff need to change in order to support it. This is particularly important for services brands, where the customer-facing staff play a major role influencing perceptions about the brand.

Brand objectives

Having formulated a view about how the brand will enhance consumers' lives, managers need to then set well-articulated, quantified *brand objectives*. At a minimum, this should specify sales levels for each target group. The brand's objectives are likely be influenced by the corporate objectives the firm has set itself.

A useful tool to help managers formulate their brand objectives, and to recognize

		Brand	
		Existing	*Extended*
Markets	*Existing*	Penetration	Brand development
	New	Market development	Diversification

Figure 9.2 *Adapted Ansoff matrix*

growth strategies, is the adapted Ansoff matrix, as shown in Figure 9.2.

In a situation where the corporate objectives are particularly demanding, the brand's team may believe that their current brand is unlikely to fully contribute to such goals by just appealing to the current group of buyers, i.e. the penetration quadrant. In this case, they need to consider further ways of filling the planning gap. One way is introducing the current brand to new groups of customers (market development quadrant); an alternative is to change the brand's characteristics but still appeal to the original customers (brand development quadrant). The highest risk is associated with the final route of significantly changing the brand and attempting to appeal to a new group of customers (diversification quadrant).

Let us consider how this has been applied. The Mars Bar mission appears to be: energize consumers through the enjoyment of chocolate. With more challenging corporate objectives being set for the Mars portfolio of brands, one way of Mars Bar making a greater contribution was following a strategy of appealing to a new group of consumers with only small brand changes (market development), For example, those people whose jobs demand a lot of energy, such as bricklayers. As such, the size of the Mars Bar was increased and in 1985 Mars King Size was launched, positioned to appeal to the new group, and not to cannibalize existing consumers from the standard Mars Bar. While a small brand change was made, the major difference was the new target market.

Continually interested in stretching the brand, Mars set even more demanding objectives, and to contribute to this, the Mars Bar managers filled the planning gap through brand development. Brand formulation changes resulted in the successful 1988 launch of Ice Cream Mars Bars which appealed to existing Mars Bar customers, increasing the overall sales of Mars Bar brands.

When setting brand objectives in terms of specific consumer groups, managers frequently characterize these groups using traditional segmenters. An alternative approach is to use the concept of segmenting consumers by their need states. When consumers buy brands, they choose to satisfy specific needs. For example, in a week, a housewife may buy a repertoire of yoghurt brands, since she is concerned with satisfying her cluster of need states. At the start of the week she might buy Marks & Spencer's yoghurt, as self-congratulatory indulgence, in addition to Mr Men yoghurt, to enhance her feeling of being a loving mother with her children. Later that week she may feel concerned about her weight and, aspiring for continual good health, buys Shape yoghurt. Through the use of consumer research, consumers' need states

can be identified, and given sufficiently large enough need-state segments, brand objectives can be set in terms of these segments.

Brand audit

To help formulate possible strategies to achieve the brand objectives, a *brand audit* needs undertaking. This can be structured by recognizing, from Figure 9.3, that a brand's strategy is influenced by five forces, i.e. the organization itself, distributors, customers, competitors and macro-environment forces. Some organizations do not use the services of logistics contractors or established distributors, since they supply their brand direct to their customers. These organizations are therefore not affected by this force.

Corporation

It is not unusual for an organization to be under-utilizing its brand through an inability to appreciate what is occurring internally. The *culture* of an organization, in other words its values and philosophies that guide staff in anticipating acceptable types of behaviour, has a strong influence on brand performance. A firm's culture evolves because of the firm's social structure and the systems it employs to encourage particular action standards, for example, displaying awards for excellence in customer service. Checking the brand's mission against the organization's culture can

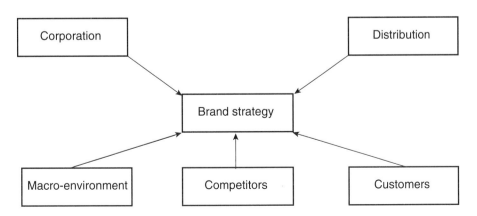

Figure 9.3 *Forces influencing brand strategy*

indicate the likelihood of brand success. Firms such as 3M and Microsoft have brand missions that focus upon continual innovation. Their corporate cultures support this through having minimal bureaucracy, encouraging experimentation, having good internal communication and publicly recognizing success. Mergers and acquisitions can affect brand performance since these are associated with changes in corporate culture.

Different departments may have different cultures, and significant differences may adversely affect the firm's brands. Furthermore, as stakeholders interact with several departments inside firms, where there are different cultures, these cause potential conflicting impressions about the brand.

When auditing the firm's culture, staff should be interviewed to appreciate their beliefs, values and attitudes. Through observation, or use of mystery shoppers, their behaviour can also be assessed. Having collected this data, it should be compared against an audit of the visual identifiers employed by the firm to achieve its corporate identity (for example, corporate logo, letter-headed paper, office design, reception area, etc.). This not only gives insight about the extent to which the corporate identity is in harmony with the firm's culture, but also helps when evaluating the congruence between the brand's mission and the cultural capability to meet this.

The heritage of the corporation needs appreciating since this can influence brand development. When Alfred Dunhill started his organization, he stipulated in 1907 that each Dunhill brand must satisfy the criteria: 'It must be useful. It must work dependably. It must be beautiful. It must last. It must be the best of its kind'. To this day this is still the case.

A firm's brands thrive because they focus upon blending the few core competencies that make the firm distinctive. For example, Swatch's distinctive competencies in watch design and production enables it to rapidly respond to changing consumer demand for novelty watches. The internal audit needs to identify the firm's core competencies and then start to consider how these could be used to meet the brand's mission.

Firms are increasingly aware of the need to adopt a relationship, rather than transaction, approach when dealing with their different stakeholders. Where there are well-bonded relationships, this enhances the ease with which brands can be built and sustained. Relationships occur through the interaction of staff with stakeholders and interviews need to be undertaken with staff to assess the strengths and weaknesses of the relationships they have.

Distributors

For those organizations using distributors, any brand strategy that is being considered needs to recognize, and support, distributors' objectives. Thus the first part of this section of the audit should ascertain for each distributor:

- their historical importance for each of the firm's brands and competitors' brands;
- their objectives;
- the strategies they are using to achieve these objectives;
- how the firm's brands and competitors' brands are helping them achieve these objectives;
- their positioning (more details about this concept are provided later in this chapter);
- the support that the firm, and its competitors, have provided to the distributor (e.g. discounts, merchandising, etc.);
- the strengths and weaknesses of the distributor;
- the criteria used by that distributor when deciding to stock the firm's brands, and how each of the firm's brands score on these criteria.

Without undertaking this audit, and using it to blend the brand strategy for the major distributors, firms are deluding themselves about the long-term viability of their brands. Using this audit, managers can better formu-

Table 9.1 *Power Analysis*

Brand C sales through distributors:		Share of different brands of office seats through distributor Q:	
P	37%	A	40%
Q	29%	B	28%
R	19%	C	12%
X	15%	Others	20%
	100%		100%

late brand objectives for each distributor. Consider the example shown in Table 9.1 for brand C, a well-designed office chair, competing against brands A, B and an array of smaller brands ('others') through office furniture distributors P, Q, R and X.

Some suppliers solely consider the left-hand side of Table 9.1 and may in particular acquiesce to the demands of distributors P and Q, due to these two distributors controlling two-thirds of the market. What should also be done though is the analysis on the right-hand side of the table, for *each* distributor. Since distributor Q accounts for 29 per cent of brand C's sales, *but* brand C only accounts for 12 per cent of distributor Q's sales of office chairs, brand C is more dependent on distributor Q than Q is on brand C. To escape from the position of retailer power, the managers of brand C need to consider ways of growing business for their brand through those distributors other than Q at a faster rate than is anticipated within distributor Q.

Another way to help prioritize brand development through different distributors is to use the brand strength-distributor attractiveness matrix, shown in Figure 9.4.

Managers need to first assess the strength of their brand proposition through each distributor. To do this they need to use the data from their audit, in particular focusing on the criteria each distributor uses when deciding to stock specific brands. Against these criteria they can then assess the strength of their brand through each distributor.

The second dimension, distributor attrac-

tiveness, needs considering. The brand's team needs to discuss and agree upon the factors that characterize attractive distributors, for example their turnover, image, geographical coverage, etc. From this they can then evaluate the attractiveness of each distributor.

The team are now in a position to plot onto the matrix the strengths of their brand when stocked by each individual distributor. Having done this, they can prioritize the investment behind the brand in each distributor. Those distributors in quadrant 1 on Figure 9.4 are high priority distributors, since the brand is particularly strong through highly attractive retailers. By contrast, the brand is consistently weak through those dis-

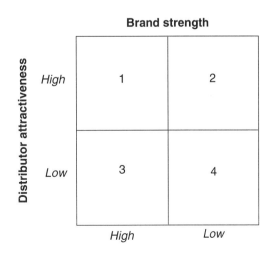

Figure 9.4 *Brand strength-distributor attractiveness matrix*

tributors in quadrant 4, which are not attractive distributors. Distributors in this quadrant are therefore lower in investment priority. In fact, one would question why such distributors are being used for the brand.

Customers

While brands start life in the form of a *brand plan*, they succeed because they exist as favourable impressions in customers' minds. Thus, while it is crucial to ensure that a coherent internal approach is adopted, it is also vital that any plans revolve around a clear understanding of customer behaviour and the role brands play.

The first consideration when auditing customers relates to identifying who is involved in the brand selection decision, then who uses the brand. In consumer markets, the purchaser is often the user, however, there are instances when this is not so. For example, breakfast cereals being bought by parents for consumption by their children. Where these split roles occur, the brand has to be positioned to appeal to both purchasers and users.

In business-to-business markets there are usually several different groups of people who have an influence on the purchase decision. Five roles can be identified for the members of the decision-making unit (DMU), i.e. users, influencers, buyers (those with formal authority to negotiate and place orders), deciders and gatekeepers (those controlling the flow of information to other members of the DMU). The challenge when formulating brand strategy is to identify the people playing these roles and then, by understanding the way firms go about selecting a new brand, tailor the communication of the benefits of the brand so these are relevant and understood by each person.

It should be realized that the influence of different people in the brand purchase decision varies over time and thus the audit should monitor this. An X-ray film supplier used to concentrate its branding activity towards radiologists' technicians in hospi-

tals. They failed to appreciate the impact of the UK government's changes to the NHS, particularly the increased importance of hospital administrators in buying decisions. Their main competitor shifted the focus of their branding activity to administrators, and increased their share of X-ray film sales.

To appreciate how the brand's benefits can best be communicated to consumers, the audit should assess the extent to which consumers become involved in the brand purchase decision and their perception of the differences between competing brands, Using these findings within the consumer decision matrix, in Figure 9.5, aids the identification of the most appropriate brand communication strategies.

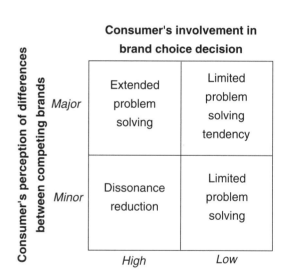

Figure 9.5 *Consumer decision matrix*

The majority of fast-moving consumer goods brands evoke limited consumer interest and involvement, due to their relatively low prices, and their high frequency of purchase. As a consequence, particularly where consumers perceive minimal differences between competing brands, their information search and evaluation is limited. Even when there are notable differences between competing brands, consumers are still likely to undertake limited search, as they do not feel more effort is warranted. Their decision

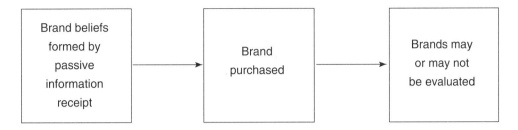

Figure 9.6 *Limited problem-solving decision process*

process is described as limited problem solving, and follows the process in Figure 9.6.

Whatever information consumers have about these brands will have been passively received, for example via a TV commercial that wasn't being paid much attention. A purchase is made when they realize the brand is out of stock at home. Evaluation, if any, takes place after the purchase. Typically, beliefs, attitudes and future intentions are the outcomes, rather than cause of purchase.

Brands that engender minimal consumer involvement need to be supported by promotional activity that stress very simple messages, which can rapidly be comprehended. The emphasis needs to be on a small amount of information, which has high consumer value. Packaging and point of sale material should not appear cluttered, and the brand names plus the core benefit should instantly be recognizable.

Where consumers are more involved in the purchase decision, and they perceive major differences between brands, they are more likely to follow an extended problem-solving process, as depicted in Figure 9.7.

In this process, consumers become aware of a need. For example, their car is becoming old, and they actively seek information. This is used, along with previous experience to evaluate competing brands. Emerging beliefs shape attitudes, and if sufficiently positive, a brand is selected and bought.

In this situation, the consumer appreciates information, but it should be realized that they soon become overloaded, and also have problems 'decoding' technical terms. Thus while more information can be provided, it should use terminology familiar to consumers and should focus on attributes relevant to purchase decisions ('crucial' rather than 'nice to know' information).

There are some brand purchases (e.g. carpets) where consumers initially are very involved, but they perceive minimal differences between brands. Their buying process, dissonance reduction, is shown in Figure 9.8.

Consumers feel confused and, without any firm beliefs, make a choice using a surrogate factor, for example trusting the salesperson's advice. Over time they gain more experience of the brand, and with their better understanding, they seek out information which supports their evolving beliefs, ignoring

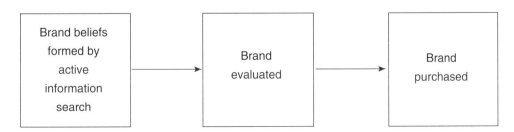

Figure 9.7 *Extended problem-solving decision process*

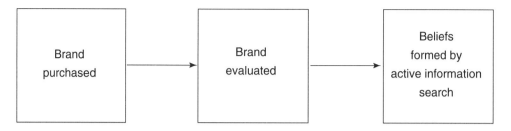

Figure 9.8 *Dissonance reduction decision process*

information that conflicts with their beliefs.

A twin push is needed for any brand communication in dissonance reduction. First, at point of sale, simple information needs to be presented, and sales staff trained to be 'brand reassurers'. Secondly, communications should be targeted at purchases after the event using advertising with the theme 'you've chosen well' or direct marketing to say 'congratulations'.

The business-to-business brand buying process is generally more involved than consumers' decisions and can be characterized by the flow chart in Figure 9.9.

While this is a demanding process, both in terms of information processing and time, after the first-time purchase of new products ('new task purchases'), organizational learning results in shortened search and evaluation procedures, for example when replacing trucks or needing further market research studies ('modified rebuy purchases'). After sufficient experience, systems will be in place that automatically place orders, particularly with suppliers' computers being networked ('straight rebuy'). In the new task purchase, the brand needs to be strongly supported by knowledgeable sales representatives, able to adapt their presentations to cope with different information needs from different people as they progress through this process. To ensure the smooth transition of the brand from new task purchase to a modified rebuy, the sales team needs to maintain close contact with the buyers, where possible amending their brand offering to better meet the needs of more experienced users. Having gained the user's confidence, effort needs to be directed towards encouraging the purchaser

to move to automatic electronic reordering.

Competitors

People rarely buy brands without comparing them against other brands. Brand audits therefore need to benchmark the current, or potential brand, against key competitors. Some competitor audits have an analysis of a large number of brands. While it is indeed laudable to have good databases, because

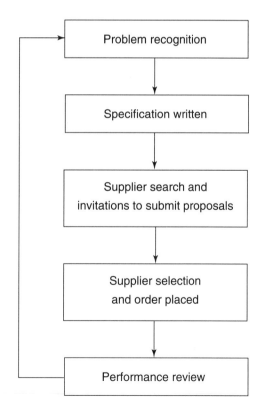

Figure 9.9 *Business-to-business brand decision process*

there are so many competitors tracked, managers are unable to remember all the data. Rather than causing confusion, interviews should be undertaken with current or potential consumers to identify those brands they consider to be similar to the firm's brand. This approach enables managers to focus on the key competitors.

Due to the pressure of work, managers are unable to spend as much time with consumers as they would like. Over time, they may lose sight of how consumers regard their, and competitors', brands. To avoid this danger, the brand audit should annually assess which brands managers believe they are competing against, and which ones consumers consider. By feeding these results back to the brand's team they can start to consider why they are becoming less synchronized with consumers and develop corrective action.

Everyone has a finite limit to the amount of information they can cope with. To overcome this problem people use simplification procedures, the most common of which is categorization. Thus, rather than having to make sense of a market in which 12 brands compete, people may instead interpret the market as four clusters of brands, each cluster having similarly perceived brands. Again to surface problems of managers losing touch with their consumers, having elicited the manager's view as to who is competition, these competitors need to be written on cards, given back to the manager who is asked to place them on a table, such that those competitors perceived as being similar to each other are placed in groups. By also undertaking this exercise with consumers, managers can be shown the extent to which their views about the competitive structure of the market reflect their consumers.

The competitor brand audit needs to address the topics:

- competitors' objectives;
- their strategies to achieve these;
- the strengths and weaknesses of their brands;
- their brand positionings and personalities

(covered later in this chapter).

From the information gained through this part of the audit, managers should start to ask themselves:

- How appropriate is the current strategy against the key competitors?
- How could the competitive strategy be improved?
- What competitive response could be anticipated?
- Would this be a rapid response and how intense would it be?
- How could we sustain the brand against the new competitive challenges?

Macro-environment

To complete the brand audit, managers need to understand what is currently going on in the macro-environment and what future trends are likely to emerge. Consideration needs to be given as to how the brand can capitalize on favourable external forces and protect itself against adverse forces such as:

- political forces;
- economic forces;
- sociological forces;
- technological forces;
- ecological forces.

Having investigated the impact of the corporation, distributors, customers, competitors and macro-environment on the brand, managers should be able to start to consider strategies for achieving the brand objective. The concern when developing these strategies is to register a favourable collection of perceptions in the consumer's mind, which add value to the consumption experience through them recognizing a distinctive performance advantage and an appealing, unique set of emotional benefits. There are numerous ways that the brand can satisfy consumers' rational, performance-related needs and managements' concern is to identify the most appropriate positioning strategy.

Even though the firm has devised a unique

functional benefit, which adds value beyond the core performance capability, competitors can emulate this. To sustain the brand, managers also add emotional benefits, for example providing reassurance, enabling consumers to feel more at ease with their peer groups, etc. One of the easiest ways for consumers to recognize these emotional benefits is through the metaphor of the brand as a personality. An effective brand strategy therefore not only adds value to the consumption experience through a well-conceived positioning, but also through a relevant, credible and appreciated *personality* being projected by the brand. It is more difficult to emulate a personality, than a functional benefit, particularly when the brand's personality is well linked to its positioning.

Brand positioning

In markets where consumers are faced with increasing choice, successful brands thrive because they have established themselves in their consumers' minds, based on the functional advantages they have beyond competitors. Thus, an effective brand positioning strategy should enable consumers to rapidly recognize what the brand does. For example, while Bang and Olufsen produce quality hi-fi systems, they are uniquely positioned, through their novel design, to appeal to the aesthetic needs of consumers. In the frozen ready meal market it is possible to distinguish between competing brands because they are positioned to appeal to health conscious consumers (Lean Cuisine), slimmers (Weight Watchers, Trimrite) and vegetarians (Linda McCartney). A six-stage procedure to develop a brand positioning strategy is shown in Figure 9.10.

The first part of this process may already have been undertaken in the customer part of the brand audit. If not, market research should be undertaken. This could involve looking through published market reports to enable managers to generate new ideas as to how the market could be segmented. More insight, particularly about consumers' need

states, can be obtained from qualitative research involving either depth interviews or group discussions.

The appropriateness of new ideas to segment the market can be applied at Stage 2. A structured questionnaire would need to be administered to current consumers and, depending on the brand objective, to new and lapsed consumers. Through quantitative research, they should be asked to rate different brands against different attributes and the data could be analysed to identify how consumers can be categorized.

At Stage 3 a workshop session with members of the brand's team should then be used, to identify the criteria to assess the attractive-

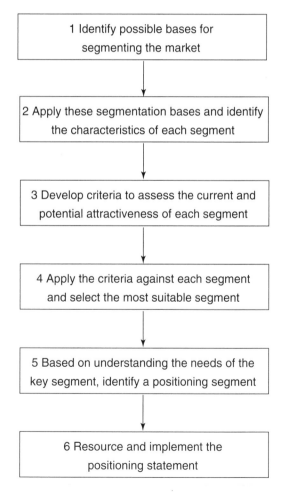

Figure 9.10 Developing a brand positioning strategy

ness of each segment. These may include the feasibility of tailoring the brand for particular segments, the likely competitive response, future growth and profitability. Having arrived at these criteria, they need to be applied to each segment and the most attractive segment selected.

The penultimate part can now be undertaken, since the firm should have a thorough understanding of the needs of its target group and, by involving its communications' agencies, positioning statements can be generated. These positioning statements should be unique, short, and convey the performance benefit using terminology familiar to consumers. If the positioning statements are well written they should indicate how marketing resources will need to be employed, thereby enabling managers to resource and implement the selected brand positioning.

Brand personality

To make sense of the plethora of competing brands, consumers use metaphors, for example describing a bank's staff as being 'like robots', since they can only deal with a limited range of enquiries and fail to take the lead in resolving problems. By so doing, their thoughts can be structured in terms of associations of the brand with something else. As noted earlier in this chapter, brands are clusters of performance and emotional attributes. One of the easiest ways for consumers to assess the emotional characteristics of brands is by drawing on their social experiences and conceiving the brand in terms of a specific personality which exhibits particular emotional traits. The challenge for the marketer is to:

- identify the emotional needs of the brand's target group;
- develop an appropriate personality to represent these emotions;
- use this brand personality to engender a particular relationship with customers.

Consumers' emotional concerns can be unearthed using in-depth interviews and group discussions, for example, by encouraging consumers to talk through their thoughts and feelings as they recount how they go about selecting, buying then using brands in the product field. Accompanying consumers when they go shopping, and being with them and their peer group as they consume the brands, provides further understanding about their emotional concerns.

Managers and their communications agencies should then be able to develop ideas about the personality their brand needs to have. As they work through possible alternatives, they need to ensure that there is a strong coherence between the rational, performance benefits depicted in the positioning statement and the emotional, psychological benefits conveyed by the brand personality. As consumers' perceptions about a brand's personality evolve through a blending of rational, emotional and sensual appeals, the aesthetic, texture, aroma, taste and sound components need tailoring to support the desired personality.

If the brand personality strategy is to be effective it should:

1. enable consumers to confidently express an aspect of their self to their peer group;
2. build a particular relationship between consumers and the brand.

People have a number of enduring perceptions, attitudes, feelings and evaluations of themselves, which are referred to as their 'self-concept'. They seek to protect and enhance their individual self-concept, doing so through buying brands that either reflect their actual self-concept, or their aspirational self-concept, or the concept of the self they wish to project when with a particular peer group. Thus when paying for petrol by credit card, a motorist may alternate between using his NatWest Mastercard, reflecting his actual self ('astuteness', using this card because it gives Air Miles) and his Barnardos Visa Card ('I hope to make the world a little bit better, knowing that some of the profit from this card goes to my preferred charity'). On another occasion, when paying for lunch, with a client, the same person may use their Porsche Visa Card to project a message about their success to their client. By understanding how the consumer uses the brand to convey their personality traits, the brand's personality can be more effectively developed.

A brand's personality becomes particularly powerful when it encourages a particular relationship between the brand and the consumer. In this sense, underlying the development work on brand personality is the assessment of whether this reinforces the desired relationship. There are numerous types of relationships that consumers can have with their brands, each of which draws on a particular type of personality. For example, in a world of continual change, some consumers want to have an emotionally based relationship with the brand, where they comfort themselves with it as they recall time-long traditions. A brand that capitalizes on this is Hovis. By contrast, in a world of change, some consumers find it difficult keeping up to date with personal computer developments, and have a tendency to buy a particular company's PCs because 'You can rely on them to continually incorporate new technology – buying a new PC becomes easier staying with this firm'. This type of relationship, that of trustful decision abdication, would be reinforced by a credible, youthful, dynamic personality, while the other relationship, that of comforting stability, would draw on a mature, kind-hearted, slowly spoken, homely character.

Internal considerations

Having progressed a long way towards developing an effective brand strategy, managers need to consider how this can best be supported. Specifically they should assess the relationship between the brand and the firm's other brands, the brand management structure most suited for managing this brand and the systems by which value will be added.

Relationships with firm's other portfolio of brands

It is rare to find an organization which has only one brand and therefore managers need to consider how their particular brand can contribute to, or capitalize on, any equity from the firm's brand portfolio. In essence managers need to consider whether:

- the corporation's name should dominate, i.e. a monolithic naming strategy (e.g. Virgin Cola, Virgin Direct Financial Services);
- the corporation's name should not be so dominant, but act as an endorser, i.e. endorsed naming strategy (e.g. Nescafé Gold Blend, Nescafé Alta Rica);
- there should be no call on the corporate name, rather the brand should stand alone, i.e. branded naming strategy as operated by Unilever and Procter & Gamble in the detergents market.

The monolithic naming strategy is most appropriate when the core values built by the corporation are ideal for the new brand, and also when the positioning of the new brand supports the wider perspective portrayed by the corporation. For example, the Virgin brand has always stood for challenging the status quo, particularly when consumers' interest have not been given too high a priority.

An endorsed naming strategy is particularly appropriate when the firm wishes to convey its size, stability and strength to various publics, for example retailers, financiers and suppliers. It allows the brand more freedom than a monolithic naming strategy, and tends to speed the brand's early adoption, reassuring consumers through corporate associations. There is a danger that as the brand becomes more established, it develops values which cause tension with the corporation's values.

A branded naming strategy is suitable in situations when the firm has undertaken a thorough segmentation analysis and they have several niche brands, uniquely appealing to each segment, yet positioned so they don't compete directly against each other. With such a tight focus, each of the firm's brands benefits from their own individual brand personalities. This brand naming strategy incurs high costs, since being unable to draw on any corporate heritage, investment is needed to establish the brand's credentials.

Structuring for brand management

Ensuring the success of the brand, necessitates an appropriate management structure. There are a variety of brand management structures. Traditional approaches either relied on a functional structure, with specialists dedicated to areas such as promotions or pricing, or allocated specific brands to individual managers. While these two approaches clearly identify internal responsibility, they do not encourage managers to adopt a total company perspective and tend to focus attention internally, making them less aware of evolving consumer needs, potentially stifling innovation.

Some firms have broken down this internal focus, by adopting a category management structure. More senior managers take responsibility for a related group of brands which constitute a particular category in the market, for example the shampoo category manager may have in their portfolio the cosmetic shampoos, anti-dandruff shampoos, and conditioner shampoos. Their responsibility is to grow the company's total share of the shampoo category, by liaising with the different departments to tailor their category to major customers' needs (e.g. different multiple grocery retailers). This forces managers to consider the needs of their retailers, who are less concerned about individual brand promotions and more interested in a strategy to promote the total category.

While the category management structure has strengths, it can be further enhanced by the integrator-functional specialist structure. Integrators are senior strategists taking responsibility for serving individual segments, channels or customer groups, working closely with a team of functional specialists, striving to create competitive advantage through world-class skills in a few functional areas. The integrators' strategic appreciation should enable them to identify, from an industry perspective, the drivers of profitability. They can then assess which segments offer the best opportunities and, working across their firm's value chain, develop more effective, customer-focused strategies. Leading cross-functional teams, these strategies can be optimally implemented.

A virtue of this structure is that the teams focus on processes that add value. Thus, the teams of integrators and functional specialists would be organized around processes such as building better customer service, growing stronger loyalty relationships and increasing brand equity.

Adding value systems

With a clear appreciation of the functional and emotional added values characterizing the brand, the firm needs to ensure that its processes are all adding the stipulated value. There are a variety of ways of checking to ensure this.

First, the management team need to undertake a value chain analysis. One way of doing this is to map all the activities involved between placing orders with suppliers, right through to the after sales service, when the brand has been sold. This should result in a flow chart which can be used in subsequent management workshops to identify:

1. how each activity is adding value;
2. whether any of the processes need re-engineering to more effectively add value;
3. whether some of the processes could be out-sourced to other organizations who have better core competencies than the firm, while not making the firm vulnerable.

Against each of the activities in the value chain, managers need to assess the costs involved. This information should then be used to consider whether the firm can reduce costs for each of these activities, while at the same time maintaining the quality. By involving managers from each department in this exercise, everyone becomes aware of how each change affects other areas. This should reduce the problem of a department identifying a cost saving, which results in a greater cost to another department and an overall net cost increase.

Having taken advantage of the implications from their value chain analysis, managers then need to broaden their horizons and consider their industry value chain. Just as their firm can be characterised by a value chain, so their suppliers and distributors have their own value chains. Each of these parties has competencies in particular processes as value is being added. However, some activities may be duplicated among the different parties. For example, market analysts in a manufacturing organization undertake forecasting exercises to guide production schedules and likewise analysts in the major retailers distributing these products devise their own forecasts to assess buying requirements. At open forums the different parties in an industry value chain can exchange information. Debate can then take place as to how they could better integrate their value chains, eliminating duplicated work and allocating specific activities to the parties with the greatest competencies.

Monitoring

Having developed and implemented an integrated brand strategy, managers need to monitor performance, making changes when this goes outside acceptable control limits. By referring back to the original objectives, monitoring systems can be devised.

One of the aims of an effective brand strategy is that over time, the strength of the brand should increase. This is best gauged using a tracking study, which at least evaluates the brand against its annual performance objectives. However, in addition it is worth assessing the emotional bond consumers

have with the brand by asking a sample of consumers questions about:

- perceptions of the brand's personality;
- views about the typical brand user;
- the relationship they have with the brand;
- the perceived culture of the brand's organization;
- how they would feel, and what they would do, were the brand to be withdrawn tomorrow.

Some measure of consumers' loyalty to the brand should also be considered. One way is to ask consumers how likely they would be to switch to a competing brand, which they respect, when the competing brand becomes 10 per cent cheaper.

Summary

- Commodities differentiate themselves by their names, while brands use names to enable consumers recall clusters of functional and emotional added values.
- Brands are powerful *assets* which have fiscal value, bring stability to organizations, provide staff with a clear indication of their expected behaviour and simplify consumers' purchasing decisions.
- An iterative process has been presented for developing a company-wide approach to brand strategy formulation.
- The process starts with the brand's mission, clarifying how it will favourably change the lives of a specific group of consumers. A brand's mission statement is particularly effective when it stretches employees, challenges their way of thinking and enables them to recognize how their roles contribute to achieving this.

- From the mission should emerge a series of quantified brand objectives.
- To appreciate how these objectives might be achieved, the impact of five forces on the brand need considering, i.e. those from organizations, distributors, customers, competitors and the macro-environment.
- With knowledge of these forces, managers can identify the most appropriate brand positioning, which clearly communicates their brand's functional advantage.
- Reinforcing this positioning, the brand is enrobed with a group of emotional values, communicated through an appropriate brand personality which encourages a particular relationship between consumers and the brand.
- To ensure that the brand strategy can be delivered, managers then need to find a naming approach which contributes to, or capitalizes on, any equity from the firm's portfolio of brands. The options include a monolithic, endorsed or branded naming strategy. Brand equity can be successfully grown through a well-conceived brand management system. This should blend the strategic skills of brand integrators and functional specialists, enabling them to design processes, through value chain analysis, which produce the required added values.
- Having followed this process and implemented the brand strategy, it needs monitoring and fine tuning to reflect changing circumstances.

References and further reading

de Chernatony, L. and McDonald, M. (1996), *Creating Powerful Brands*, Oxford: Butterworth-Heinemann.

de Chernatony, L. (1996), '2001 the brand management oddessy', *Journal of General Management*, **21**(4), 15–30.

de Chernatony, L. (1993), 'Categorising brands: evolutionary processes under-pinned by two key dimensions', *Journal of Marketing Management*, **9**(2), 173–188.

George, M., Freeling, A. and Court, D. (1994), 'Reinventing the marketing organization', *The McKinsey Quarterly*, 4, 43–62.

10

Strategic marketing networks _____

Professor Martin Christopher, Cranfield School of Management

Network organizations are constantly re-defining how the company can participate with multiple partners in the development and delivery of superior value to customers. They are defined by their customer base and their knowledge and skills, not by their factories and offices. Network organizations are the hallmark of the new marketing concept of the 1990s (Fredrick E. Webster, 1994).

 Of the many changes that have taken place over the years in the way in which organizations compete, perhaps one of the most significant has been the realization that the roots of competitive advantage lie not just within the single firm but are created through the relationships that exist within a wider network of suppliers, intermediaries and customers.

This new model of competitive advantage suggests that success in the marketplace is achieved through the ability to focus the combined resources of supply chain partners upon delivering value to customers at the end of the chain. Thus the ways in which suppliers' capabilities can be harnessed and integrated into the firm's own processes and, in turn, customers' processes, provide the basis for differential advantage.

These chains of mutually supportive organizations working to common agendas and shared strategic goals have come to be known as 'network' or 'virtual' organizations. A fundamental characteristic of a marketing network is that each entity within it will be focused upon a limited set of economic activities in which they have significant distinctive competence. There is now a widespread recognition that even the largest businesses will have only a few competencies in which they can claim real distinction. This recognition has led to an increasing concern by management to focus on the 'core business' and to 'out-source' everything else. Inevitably, as this process of retrenchment and out-sourcing gathers pace, the management of relationships between partners in the network becomes paramount.

Relationship marketing

The underpinning idea of a strategic marketing network is the notion of multiple partners linking together to form long-term relationships for *mutual* advantage. These relationships will not only be with suppliers and downstream intermediaries, but also with joint-venture partners and other forms of strategic alliances which will sometimes include competitors. Figure 10.1 provides some examples of the types of partnerships that are now becoming commonplace across a range of industries.

Managing these relationships is clearly a major priority in the network organization. It can be argued that the quality of the relationships in such a network becomes a major source of competitive advantage (or, conversely, disadvantage). Because of this there is now emerging a wider view of the marketing task within the business, a view that suggests that the management of partnership relationships is the real purpose of marketing.

'Relationship marketing' has been defined in a variety of ways but at its simplest it may be seen as a refocusing of the orientation of the organization to achieve preferred supplier status with customers through the sustained delivery of superior value. The achievement of this status, it is argued, is through the management of relationships with all the critical 'markets' of the firm – not just the end-user. This wider view of markets encompasses suppliers, employees, intermediaries and alliance partners.

A wider view of markets

Conventionally, the focus of marketing has been upon the customer and/or the con-

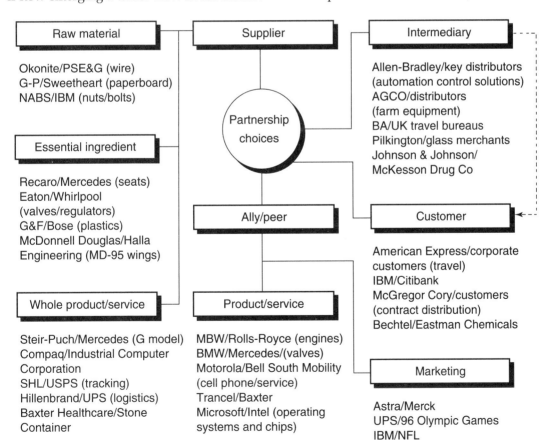

Figure 10.1 Partnership choices. Source: Dull et al. (1995)

Raw material
Okonite/PSE&G (wire)
G-P/Sweetheart (paperboard)
NABS/IBM (nuts/bolts)

Supplier

Intermediary
Allen-Bradley/key distributors
(automation control solutions)
AGCO/distributors
(farm equipment)
BA/UK travel bureaus
Pilkington/glass merchants
Johnson & Johnson/
McKesson Drug Co

Partnership choices

Essential ingredient
Recaro/Mercedes (seats)
Eaton/Whirlpool
(valves/regulators)
G&F/Bose (plastics)
McDonnell Douglas/Halla
Engineering (MD-95 wings)

Ally/peer

Customer
American Express/corporate
customers (travel)
IBM/Citibank
McGregor Cory/customers
(contract distribution)
Bechtel/Eastman Chemicals

Whole product/service
Steir-Puch/Mercedes (G model)
Compaq/Industrial Computer
Corporation
SHL/USPS (tracking)
Hillenbrand/UPS (logistics)
Baxter Healthcare/Stone
Container

Product/service
MBW/Rolls-Royce (engines)
BMW/Mercedes/(valves)
Motorola/Bell South Mobility
(cell phone/service)
Trancel/Baxter
Microsoft/Intel (operating
systems and chips)

Marketing
Astra/Merck
UPS/96 Olympic Games
IBM/NFL

sumer. The early development of the marketing concept was built upon the classic concept of a 'marketing mix' which sought to influence final demand through the four key levers of product, price, promotion and place. In the changed competitive environment of the late twentieth century new and more powerful determinants of marketplace success have emerged. While the goals of customer and consumer loyalty remain the same, the means of achieving them have altered. Instead of the limited focus on the final marketplace, the new paradigm of relationship marketing suggests that there are a number of other key 'markets' that must also be engaged and addressed.

In summary these are:

- **Suppliers**: without the closest involvement of suppliers in the innovation process and the means of meeting ongoing replenishment of demand the risk of failure to satisfy the needs of customers and consumers is heightened considerably.
- **Employees**: there can be no doubt that committed and motivated employees enable the company to achieve and maintain the highest levels of customer orientation. There is a growing recognition that 'our people are our brand'.

- **Intermediaries**: in so many markets today the power in the channel of distribution has swung towards the customer and in particular original equipment manufacturers (OEMs), distributors and retailers. Without their active support there is little prospect of long-term survival.
- **Alliance partners**: increasingly organizations are dependent upon the strengths of other parties who may contribute technology, financial support, logistics capabilities or access to markets. The more the trend to out-sourcing non-core competencies continues, the more will the creation and management of alliances become critical to success.

The marketing direction of the firm must be built upon an integration of mutually compatible and supportive strategies for each of these critical markets. In this way the foundation for long-term success in the ultimate consumer market is created.

Clearly the success of a network organization, by definition, will be highly correlated with how well it is able to integrate and co-ordinate the multiple relationships that comprise the network. This is the real task of relationship marketing. Figure 10.2 suggests that these markets, while individually dis-

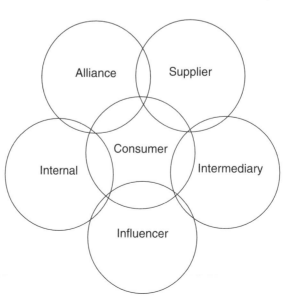

Figure 10.2 *Key relationships in a strategic marketing network. Source: Peck (1996)*

tinct, overlap and interact and must be managed holistically rather than separately.

It will be apparent that this 'relationship building' view of marketing is radically different from the so-called 'transaction' approach to marketing which traditionally has led to a market-share and volume-driven orientation within the business.

The supply chain

Traditionally, in the transaction-orientated organization, there was little integration between the firm and its upstream suppliers or its downstream customers. The tendency was for each entity in a marketing channel to seek to optimize its own position with only limited regard for the impact of its actions on other parties in the channel. Thus, there was little, if any, sharing of information on inventory status, future production plans or materials requirements. In some cases the climate in the channel was adversarial with conflict rather than co-operation the order of the day.

More recently there has emerged a realization that in markets that demand ever higher levels of innovation and responsive service – and all at a lower price – the traditional approach cannot achieve these goals. Instead, the model that is now gaining ground is based upon the recognition that most of the inefficiencies, and hence the costs, in the process of getting goods to the final market occur at the interfaces between firms in the channel. These inefficiencies and costs are manifested in the form of inventories held as buffer stocks, excessive lead-times due to lack of communication and poor use of capacity because of uncertainty of downstream requirements.

A significant pressure that is driving many firms towards supply chain integration is the realization that 'lean logistics' is a vital prerequisite for market responsiveness. Conventional inventory-based systems that sought to anticipate customer requirements through sales forecasts have been challenged by the advent of just-in-time, quick response solutions that rely on information rather than

reserves of inventory to meet customers' needs. The concept of the 'time-based competitor' is now firmly established and time compression in the supply chain, through the early capture of information on real customer demand, is a key element of this concept. As a consequence, the exchange of information between supply chain partners is a vital requirement if lean logistics and enhanced responsiveness to demand is to become a reality. This sharing of information is in reality the first step towards the real goal of process integration within the network organization.

The need for process integration

Perhaps one of the most profound changes in the way that organizations develop their competitive strategies is the realization that success in the marketplace is largely determined by how well those companies leverage their 'capabilities'. Capabilities are in effect the way things are done in the business or, more precisely, the processes that have to be structured and managed in order to achieve success in the marketplace.

A process in an organizational context may be defined as 'any activity or group of activities that take an input, adds value to it, and provides an output to an internal or external customer'.

The challenge to the organization is to break down the vertical, functional barriers that hamper integration and instead, become a horizontal, market-facing business. The driving force for this change is the recognition that it is *processes* that create customer value, not *functions*. Hence managing those processes that deliver customer value is the key to marketplace success.

What are the core processes that generate customer value and hence competitive advantage? While there can be some debate over a complete listing of core processes and the extent to which processes are universal to all businesses, the following are widely recognized as being of significance to most commercial organizations:

- brand development (including new product development);
- consumer development (primarily focused on building loyalty with end-users);
- customer management (creating relationships with intermediaries);
- supplier development (strengthening upstream and alliance relationships);
- supply chain management (including the order fulfilment process).

Network integration in its real sense is only achieved when the core processes of the members of the network are integrated. Process integration at this level requires joint involvement in product development, collective determination of priorities and goals for the supply chain and a complete transparency of information including costs.

Bringing about this alignment of processes between members of a network should be a key priority of marketing management. Clearly there is a need to break free from the conventional, vertically focused, functional organization and to move instead to a cross-functional, team-based orientation. Beyond this though is the requirement to engage other members of the network through a close linking of processes.

In the past there was surprisingly little regular, ongoing contact between buyers and suppliers. It was typically the salesperson who met a purchasing manager or equivalent to negotiate a 'deal'. Much sales training and courses in negotiation skills still tend to emphasize the essential 'win–lose' outcome of this approach. Not surprisingly the general atmosphere in this type of arrangement was often adversarial.

Network organizations have to abandon this confrontational mind-set and replace it with 'win–win' thinking. It should be emphasized that partnership does not necessarily imply 50/50 in terms of the gains shared. More often that not, there will be a lead partner who may benefit more than others in the relationship but the key idea is that there should be *equity* if not equality. In other words, all partners must share in the benefit and there should be no net losers.

Structuring these types of relationships in a hard, competitive world is no easy task. The frequently quoted example of how Wal-Mart, North America's biggest retailer, and Procter & Gamble, one of the world's biggest manufacturers of branded goods moved from a 'win–lose' to a 'win–win' mode provides some clues. First, co-operation needs to start from the top with a recognition of the strategic opportunities that process integration can provide. For example, the founder of Wal-Mart, Sam Walton, was personally involved in structuring the terms of the relationship with senior vice presidents from Procter & Gamble. He saw this type of arrangement as a way to improve both the efficiency and the effectiveness of the supply chain as a whole in that close co-operations could lead to less inventory, faster response and lower costs which supported the fundamental Wal-Mart strategy of 'Every Day Low Price' (EDLP).

The second lesson is that it is not sufficient to have a single point of contact between buyers and suppliers. Instead there must be **multiple contacts** at all levels of the core processes of the business. So suppliers' logistics people must work with the customers' logistics people, sales and marketing on the supply side must form teams with sales and marketing on the demand side and so on. Furthermore these buyer/supplier teams should be cross-functional and multidisciplinary. Figure 10.3 highlights the dramatic change from the traditional model – shown as two triangles that only connect at one point (the sales person and the buyer) – and the new model where there are multiple points of contact between corresponding people and processes within the network partners.

Information exchange binds the marketing network

A distinguishing characteristic of an effective marketing network is the value-added exchange of information between partners in the chain. In chains which lack the high level of integration that is a prerequisite for strate-

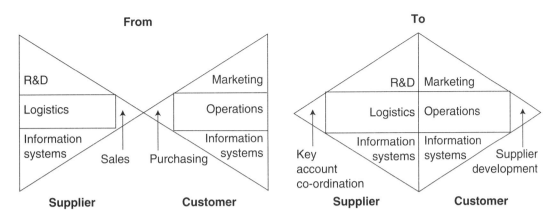

Figure 10.3 *Creating closer relationships with supply chain partners*

gic marketing networks there is little, if any, upstream visibility of real demand. For a supply chain to function effectively there is a requirement for information on end-user demand to be shared between all upstream parties. It is the ability to take demand information from a downstream partner and convert that into a proactive response that characterizes the integrated supply chain.

One of the best examples of this concept in action is provided by the initiative that began in North America but is now increasingly widespread known as 'Efficient Consumer Response' (ECR).

With ECR, information captured at the point of sale is shared with upstream suppliers so that early warning is gained of replenishment requirements. Acting upon this information the supplier can better schedule production and distribution and can make a 'just-in-time' delivery so that the retailer needs to carry only minimal inventory. The supplier benefits because the early notice of requirements enables them to improve capacity utilization significantly and the retailer benefits from higher service levels at less cost.

The logical extension of ECR is the move towards 'Vendor Management Inventory' (VMI) or Co-Managed Inventory (CMI) as some prefer to call it. The idea behind VMI is that replenishment becomes the responsibility of the supplier. Customers no longer place

orders on the supplier – instead they provide data (usually EPOS based) on sales and on-hand inventory. The supplier (vendor) now determines the shipping quantities and frequencies and the customer only pays for product when it is sold. Under this type of arrangement, there are clearly some profound implications for the nature of the trading relationship between the retailer and the supplier. The relationship must be partnership based rather than the traditional 'arm's length', even adversarial, arrangement that still prevails in many cases.

One of the most cited examples of the ECR/VMI revolution in North America is the relationship established between Procter & Gamble and Wal-Mart (North America's biggest retailer) which was mentioned above. The following benefits from their adoption of ECR/VMI have been reported (Poirier and Reiter, 1996):

Wal-Mart

- Warehouse inventory reduced from 19 days to 6 days.
- Inventory turns in the company increased from 19 to 60, with a one-time cash flow increase of up to $200,000 resulting from the lower amount of working capital tied up in warehouse inventory.
- Better utilization of distribution centre space.

- Reduced administration costs, through the use of electronic data interchange (EDI).
- Improved on-the-shelf service levels from 96.4 to 99.2 on specific products.

Procter & Gamble

- Improved customer service and satisfaction.
- Increased order volumes of up to 30 per cent.
- An increased market share of more than four points.
- Reduced distribution costs.
- An improvement of 4 to 12 per cent in vehicle utilization.
- A 60 per cent reduction in returns and refusals and a 20 to 40 per cent reduction in goods damage.

While there has been less progress in the adoption of this form of information-based partnership in Europe, there are growing signs that the benefits are being recognized. The major hurdle is one of 'mind-set' in that for decades there has been a view among buyers that says, in effect, that 'information is power – so why share it?'. Once this barrier can be overcome the opportunity for vastly more competitive supply chains will become a reality.

Supply chain competition and the extended enterprise

It was previously suggested that a new competitive paradigm is emerging as we enter the era of network competition. Whereas previously the competitive entity was the firm on a standalone basis, now it is the supply chain. In other words, competitive advantage is determined in large part by the way in which customer value can be created and enhanced by the more efficient and effective working of the supply chain as a whole. Quality products and services can be made available to customers in shorter time frames with higher levels of reliability and yet at less total cost as a result of supply chain integration.

The car industry provides a powerful example of how supply chain competition has replaced inter-firm competition. Companies such as Rover have now embraced the philosophy of the 'extended enterprise'. In the extended enterprise the aim is to create seamless, 'end-to-end' processes so that innovative products are created and delivered to market at higher levels of quality, in shorter time frames but at a price which in real terms in significantly less than it has ever been in the past. This is achieved through a number of means including:

- **Supply base rationalization** – In the 1980s Rover dealt with well over 2,000 suppliers of components, materials and services. In the 1990s that number was down to under 500. With the remaining suppliers Rover has established significantly closer relationships and is now looking to these suppliers increasingly to provide systems rather than components. For example, a single first-tier supplier will be responsible for supplying the complete dashboard for a particular model of car, complete with all the controls, displays and wiring ready for installation as a single unit – the whole unit being delivered on a just-in-time basis.
- **Supplier development programmes** – As with the majority of companies, Rover used to view the procurement activity as primarily a purchasing function tasked with buying at the lowest price. This would typically involve using more than one vendor to supply a particular component with perhaps an element of 'playing one off against the other'.

  Now, supplier development has replaced the traditional purchasing function. The idea behind this is that a cross-functional team of Rover specialists will work closely with suppliers to seek improvements in the suppliers' processes as well as in the interfaces with Rover's processes.
- **Early supplier involvement in design** – Much innovation in the car industry today is supplier originated. Such developments

as ABS (braking systems), engine management systems and improved suspension systems have come in large part from suppliers to the auto industry. By bringing these suppliers more closely into the vehicle manufacturer's new product development process it has been found that not only can innovation be continually embodied in new products but often that simpler, more cost-effective designs can be created.

It is now recognized that a significant proportion of the total cost of making and maintaining a car is 'designed-in'; the challenge now is to find ways of 'designing-out' those costs.

- **Integrated information systems** – The car industry was one of the first to go 'paperless' in the sense of using IT to provide the means of enhancing the flow of information both upstream and downstream in the supply chain. The use of electronic data interchange (EDI) coupled with the growing acceptance of the 'just-in-time' philosophy led to a realization that the benefits of a fully transparent information system could be considerable. Thus suppliers can now manage the flow of material into the plant on the basis of advance notification of Rover's production schedules. There are no orders, no delivery notes, no invoices – only a single source of information that provides the basis for a timely physical response which itself triggers a payment to the supplier.
- **Centralization of inventory** – The extended enterprise at Rover does not only include upstream suppliers but the downstream flow of finished product through its dealer network. Traditionally dealers carried a stock of cars which may or may not have matched the requirements of their customers. If a customer demanded a colour or an option that the dealer did not have, then a 'swap' would have to be arranged with another dealer who did have that particular vehicle. Now, instead, Rover has centralized the inventory and has taken responsibility for its

management. The dealers only have demonstration models, but they also have on-line access to the Rover supply system and can give the customer immediate confirmation of the availability of the car of their choice and when it can be delivered. For those vehicles that are not available from stock the dealer can enter the order directly into the Rover production schedule and the car is in effect made to order.

Managing the marketing network

The new competitive paradigm that we have described in this chapter places the firm at the centre of an interdependent network – a **confederation** of mutually complementary competencies and capabilities – which competes as an integrated supply chain against other supply chains.

To manage in such a radically revised competitive structure clearly requires different skills and priorities to those employed in the traditional model. To achieve market leadership in the world of network competition necessitates a focus on network management as well as upon internal processes. Of the many issues and challenges facing organizations as they make the transition to this new competitive environment, the following are perhaps most significant.

Network management issues

- **Collective strategy development** – Traditionally, members of a supply chain have never considered themselves to be part of a marketing network and so have not shared with each other their strategic thinking. For network competition to be truly effective requires a significantly higher level of joint strategy development. This means that network members must collectively agree strategic goals for the network and the means of attaining them.
- **Win–win thinking** – Perhaps one of the biggest challenges to the successful establishment of marketing networks is the

need to break free from the often adversarial nature of buyer/supplier relationships that existed in the past. There is now a growing realization that co-operation between network partners usually leads to improved performance generally. The issue then becomes one of determining how the results of that improved performance can be shared among the various players. 'Win–win' need not mean 50/50, but at a minimum all partners should benefit and be better off as a result of co-operation.

● **Open communication** – One of the most powerful drivers of change in marketing networks has been the advent of information technology making the exchange of information between supply chain partners so easy and so advantageous. Electronic data interchange (EDI) was an early precursor of the information highway that now exists in some industries enabling end-to-end pipeline visibility to become a reality. The textile industry in the USA has benefited tremendously from the use of shared information on sales which originates from the retail store but is then transmitted to garment manufacturer to material manufacturer to the manufacturer of synthetic fibre. With all parties 'singing to the same hymn sheet' a much more rapid response to marketplace changes is achieved with less inventory and lower risks of obsolescence. For network marketing to work to its fullest potential, visibility and transparency of relevant information throughout the supply chain is essential. Open-book accounting is another manifestation of this move towards transparency by which cost data is shared upstream and downstream and hence each partner's profit is visible to the others.

Process management issues

● **Focus on customer value creation** – Leading-edge companies have for some time been seeking to focus the organization around the management of the key processes of the businesses that deliver value to customers. This implies that there must be a clear understanding of what the value proposition is and how each process will contribute to the 'delivery' of that proposition. These fundamental business processes, referred to earlier in the chapter, must also be aligned with the processes of upstream and downstream partners. The role of marketing management in the new world of network competition is essentially to translate the overall network strategy into the specific strategies and implementation plans for the internal processes of the business. Process management will become the main differentiator and a key determinant of competitive advantage in these networks.

● **Cross-functional working** – Closely linked to the previously described model of the customer-focused process organization is the issue of how best to manage what are, in effect, cross-functional teams. There has been much discussion on the need to break down the functional 'silos' that have for so long dominated the corporate landscape. Yet at the same time there is still an ever-present need for functional excellence. In other words, even though the business needs to focus on process management, which by definition is cross-functional, those processes still need to draw upon the skills and resources of functional managers and their expertise. One company that has addressed this issue is Unipart, a supplier of components to the automobile assembly industry and after-market. The company has established 'Unipart University' to provide training at all levels in cross-functional working as well as investing further in developing functional excellence.

● **Performance measures** – One of the keys to success in developing an effective marketing network is the creation of appropriate performance measures – both for internal process management and for external process integration. Because of the tendency to manage what we measure, the measures chosen should reflect the 'horizontal' or cross-functional nature of processes rather than the narrow focus on 'vertical' or functional measures that has been so typical in the past. Appropriate process measures may include such dimensions as customer satisfaction, time-to-market, the costs of serving customers and order fulfilment lead-times. Ideally, these and other measures should not be limited for internal use only but should be extended across the supply chain. One strong reason for the need to implement supply chain wide measures is that the real opportunities for network competitive advantage exist primarily at the interfaces between partners in the network. Hence the need to set objectives for supply chain efficiency and effectiveness improvement and to establish appropriate key performance indicators to guide the search for improvement.

Summary

If these trends that we have observed towards the creation of strategic marketing networks continue, then the competitive environment of tomorrow will be significantly different from that of yesterday. The implications of this for management are profound and will require a fundamental reappraisal of the marketing task within the business. New skills will be required as the move away from functional specialization to process management gathers speed. In particular, the challenge to the organization will be to identify appropriate partners to join them in these strategic networks and to develop enduring relationships with them.

References

Dull, S. F. *et al.* (1995), 'Partners', *The McKinsey Quarterly*, No. 4.

Peck, H. L. (1996), 'The six markets reinstated and revisited', *Proceedings of the 1996 Marketing Education Group Conference*, Strathclyde.

Poirier, Charles C. and Reiter, Stephen E. (1996), *Supply Chain Optimization*, San Francisco: Berrett-Koehler Publishers.

Webster, F. E. (1994), *Market Driven Management*, New York: John Wiley.

11

The challenges of global marketing ———

Dr John Fahy, Trinity College, University of Dublin

 We are told that today the world is effectively a global village. Similar products and services are available in Manchester, Minneapolis, Melbourne and Manila. Large corporations such as BT and MCI are forming alliances which they argue will prepare them for the global challenges of the twenty-first century. New markets are opening up around the world and formerly protected national domains are increasingly being subjected to the full rigours of international competition. This chapter focuses on the issue of marketing across national borders. Its overall objective is to provide an understanding of the key challenges facing managers attempting to develop effecting marketing strategies for a globally competitive environment. Specifically, by the end of this chapter you should be able to:

- understand the key environmental forces driving global competition;
- assess the globalization potential of your industry;
- develop an appropriate marketing strategy for your firm;
- understand your sources of competitive advantage in a global marketplace.

International business is not new and trade has been taking place since the days of Marco Polo. However, recent decades have witnessed a dramatic growth in the scale and scope of world business fostered by growing levels of democracy, international trade agreements and developments in communications and technology. Rising income levels in many previously underdeveloped countries have created new markets for products and services. Decisions regarding the choice of location for production, R&D, retailing and customer service are increasingly being made on a more global basis. For example, the time differences between countries represent not a problem but rather an opportunity to be exploited. One firm in California provides a 24-hour toll-free service for its customers. At the close of business in Palo Alto, calls are diverted to Co. Kerry in the west of Ireland where they are handled by well-educated, English-speaking staff, who cost far less to employ than comparable workers in the California region. Moves toward economic union in Western Europe have forced managers to think about the competitive positioning of their organization at a pan-European as well as a national level. Firms in industries such as retailing, financial services and consulting have been rapidly forming alliances throughout Europe and beyond to ensure that they remain competitive in an environment where national borders are becoming less meaningful than before.

Effective marketing in the twenty-first century necessitates that the kinds of changes described above are understood and factored into the firm's strategic marketing decisions. Contemporary thinking on how to manage marketing activity across national boundaries has evolved over the years as the scale of international business has increased (see Figure 11.1). At one level, there are companies that are said to be engaged in export marketing. These firms typically retain all key operations in their home country and simply adapt and transport their products to foreign markets. This pattern is likely to be found in companies at an early stage of international development and may well be suitable where firms wish to grow their international operations in a slow and controlled manner. In contrast, at the other end of the spectrum, there are firms which treat the world as one global market, that are selective in where they locate value-adding activities and that look to provide products and services in the same way world-wide to a set of global customers. In between are a number of variants where firms are involved in many markets but adapt their strategies to suit those markets (international/multinational marketing) or seek to standardize practices on a regional basis such as those pursuing a pan-European strategy (regional marketing). Given developments in world business, firms are increasingly likely to find themselves adopting approaches which are located towards the right-hand side of the spectrum.

Irrespective of which of the approaches in Figure 11.1 best describes the firm's current marketing activities, several important steps need to be undertaken in order to devise **effective** marketing strategies which will meet the global challenges that firms have to face. In the first instance, managers must monitor and understand the key environmental trends changing the shape of world business. Second, it is important to consider developments that are specific to each industry and in particular to understand the extent to which the industry is becoming globalized. An analysis of these developments provides managers with an understanding of the factors critical to future success. Once such an understanding is gained, it is necessary to ensure that the firm's marketing strategy is appropriate given the industry conditions in which it operates. Finally, the company must identify and nurture its sources of competitive advantage to ensure its long-term position in the global marketplace. In summary, effective marketing strategy in a global environment involves understanding of the important trends in the environment, assessing of the globalization potential of the industry, developing appropriate marketing strategies and deploying unique resources to gain a competitive advantage (see Figure 11.2). We will now look at each of these elements in greater detail.

The global business environment ∎

Recent years have witnessed dramatic changes in the global business environment. In this section, some major global trends are documented which reflect the types of challenges to be faced by businesses as we enter the twenty-first century. Knowing how to respond to these challenges requires an

Figure 11.1 *Marketing approaches in a global environment*

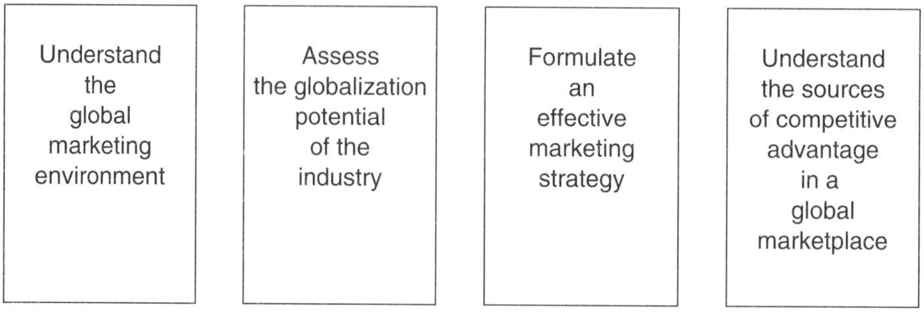

Understand the global marketing environment	Assess the globalization potential of the industry	Formulate an effective marketing strategy	Understand the sources of competitive advantage in a global marketplace

Figure 11.2 *Key issues in global marketing strategy*

understanding of how they have come about. The driving forces behind these global developments are documented as is their impact on a range of industries.

Some key trends in the global environment

Foremost among the developments in the global business environment has been the growth of international business, the shift in economic power to the Pacific Rim, the emergence of new competitive strategies, the development of segments of global customers and the rapid diffusion of innovations. A brief review of each of these trends follows.

The growth of international business

Evidence of the growing scale and scope of international business abounds. For example, since 1950, world exports of manufactured goods has risen by a factor of sixteen while world output has grown by only a factor of seven (Buckley and Brook, 1992). In 1993, developing countries attracted a record $70 billion in foreign direct investment (FDI), nearly twice the amount they received in 1991 and almost as much as the world's total FDI in 1986 (*Economist*, 1995). The composition of trade has moved from being predominantly primary products and natural resources to finished goods. In the 1950s, trade in primary products represented about 50 per cent of all world trade, but this per-

centage had dropped to less than one-third by the mid-1980s. The highest growth levels in international trade are now to be found in sectors such as chemicals, engineering products, computer equipment and road and motor vehicles. One consequence of this rapid growth in trade has been the emergence of some particularly powerful companies who dominate their industries and are able to exert significant leverage *vis-à-vis* host governments, local unions and suppliers. The United Nations estimates that the 100 largest multinationals, excluding those in banking and finance, accounted for $3.1 trillion of world-wide assets in 1990 or about 40–50 per cent of all cross-border assets (*Economist*, 1993). Their influence should not be underestimated. For example, a casual remark by a Toyota executive that they may reconsider future investment in the UK, because of the government's position on European integration, created intense political debate about the longer-term implications of Britain's policies on Europe.

The shift to the Pacific Rim

The balance of power in world trade has shifted dramatically eastward. If the World Bank's forecast for economic growth to the year 2020 is correct, China will overtake the USA as the world's largest economy and India, Indonesia, South Korea, Thailand and Taiwan will all join China in being among the world's top ten economies (*Economist*, 1994). This will mean a vibrant Pacific Rim region which cannot be ignored by firms in Western Europe and the USA as it is likely to spawn a new generation of global competitors. The impact of Japanese firms on sectors such as automobiles and consumer electronics has been well documented. It must be expected that tomorrow's global competitors will come from outside the traditional centres of power. All the indications are that this is taking place. Of the 7,000-plus MNCs operating in 1970, over half were from just two countries, namely, the USA and the UK. However, by 1993, the four richest economies in the world – the USA, Japan, Germany and Switzerland – accounted for less than half of all MNCs. On the plus side, developments in the Pacific Rim create tremendous market opportunities. These are to be found not only in rapidly growing economies such as China and Thailand but also in Japan which has traditionally been viewed as a very difficult market to enter. Recent research has documented important changes that are taking place in the country's distribution channels creating opportunities for Western manufacturers (Fahy and Taguchi, 1995).

New competitive strategies

One of the more distinguishing features of competition in a global environment is that the 'rules of the game' are never quite so clear. In domestic settings, competition is generally more predictable and competitive signalling between firms places limits on the types of strategies which may be pursued – such as the amount by which prices can be cut, before competitors will retaliate. Globalization has changed all this because firms from different parts of the globe are not necessarily familiar with the implicit rules. The arrival of Japanese manufacturers in Europe and the USA brought widespread accusations of product dumping and below-cost selling. Such accusations are rarely heard anymore as the basis of Japanese competitiveness in superior manufacturing techniques has become better understood. The decade of the 1980s saw determined efforts by Western firms to imitate Japanese manu-

facturing practices with limited levels of success due to the institutional and cultural factors that underlie them. In a global environment such domestic advantages will always exist and firms must seek to exploit those unique to their own country. For example, the disparity in world labour costs has been well documented. Labour costs in areas such as North Africa, Central and Eastern Europe and South East Asia are a fraction of what they are in Western Europe and the USA, seriously impeding the ability of firms in the latter regions to compete in labour intensive industries. A recent decision by Packard Electric, the subsidiary of General Motors which makes wiring harnesses for the automobile manufacturer, to close its operations in Ireland in favour of a location in the Czech Republic is typical of many recent decisions in a variety of industries. Effectively competing in a global environment necessitates an understanding of the bases for competitive advantage and an awareness of the kinds of new strategies being pursued by global competitors such as those documented in Example One.

The emergence of global customers

One of the most contentious debates in the global marketing literature has been the extent to which world markets are becoming more homogenous. In the cases of some industrial products such as, for example, aeroplanes, the argument is somewhat less relevant as these kinds of products have always had relatively few global customers with similar needs. It is in the consumer products and services businesses that the issue is hotly debated. Advocates argue that the world has changed due to the influence of technology and communications creating markets which show strong commonalities across national boundaries. The global reach of powerful brand names such as Coca-Cola, McDonald's, Mercedes, Gucci, Yves St Laurent, and so on are pointed to as evidence of this trend. Others contradict the view suggesting that even brands such as Coca-Cola and McDonald's must make adjustments to

Example One:
Mass customization – Japan's latest competitive weapon

The country that popularized lean production and Just-In-Time manufacturing appears to be upping the ante once again. The latest trend apparent in a number of industries is mass customization or the idea of mass producing tailor-made products. Impossible as it may seem, Japanese firms in industries such as men's clothing, bicycles and golf clubs are mass producing items to fit the sizes and shapes of their future owners (Westbrook and Williamson, 1993). For example, rather than purchase a ready-made suit, the customer simply selects the desired material and provides the necessary measurements. This information is passed to the production plant where parts of the suit are cut in parallel. This may even involve parts being made at different plants or by different firms. The completed product is assembled and dispatched to the customer within five days at off-the-peg prices. The system works on the compelling principle of selling the product before it is produced but it requires excellence in the firm's production and information systems.

many aspects of the marketing mix as they move from market to market. A mid-range position is that there are segments of the consumer market such as teenagers and business people who display a great deal of commonality across borders. A product such as the Sony Walkman is heralded as one which uniquely taps into these universal needs leading to its description as an 'electronic soft drink which is convenient, contemporary and universally appealing' (O'Reilly, 1992), Developing strategies which meet the needs of a global segment has many attractions in terms of cost efficiencies and the uniformity of the marketing message.

The rapid diffusion of innovations

One of the more discernible features of the modern business environment has been the shortening of product life cycles. In particular, this trend is observed in some high technology industries where, for example, the life cycle of many software products is down to a period of one year to sixteen months. Allied to this is the fact that innovations are also diffusing across national borders at a much faster rate. A notable example is in the consumer electronics sector (Ohmae, 1989). Black and white televisions had penetrated the

USA about twelve years before they did so in Japan and Europe. In the case of colour televisions the time lag was down to five to six years. The use of VCRs in Japan and Europe actually predated the USA by three to four years due to the popularity of cable television in the USA. In the case of compact discs, penetration was achieved in the USA only about a year before Japan and Western Europe and more recently satellite television is effectively broadcast simultaneously in the three regions. These trends have profound implications for the process by which firms grow internationally. Traditionally, firms have favoured a gradual rollout of products to neighbouring markets that have low economic and cultural differences. For example, Canadian firms tend to favour entry into the USA in the first instance in the same way that New Zealand firms favour entry into Australia. This incrementalist approach may be less appropriate in a world where knowledge about new products diffuses much more rapidly. Being successful on a global scale requires that firms examine the feasibility of a global launch or, at least, a simultaneous launch in major markets in order to avoid the risk of losing first mover advantages to a more nimble competitor.

The drivers of globalization

Taking account of the above trends requires an understanding of the forces driving them (see Figure 11.3). In broad terms, the drivers of globalization can be separated into those which are specific to particular firms and to those which are characteristic of the general external business environment. Chief among the latter are developments in technology and travel and communications, the convergence of income levels across the globe, growing levels of democracy, new trade agreements and the dominance of the English language. The major firm-specific drivers are the need to amortize major costs such as R&D, shortening product life cycles, the pursuit of economies of scale and the strategic intent of global competitors. We will briefly examine both of these sets of drivers.

External drivers of globalization

A number of macro-economic trends have played a significant role in the globalization of industries. Not least among these is tech-nology. The role of technology is significant both as an initiator and an enabler of globalization. Advancements in aviation have made international travel easier and cheaper allowing consumers to experience different cultures and to become much more diverse in the products and services they demand. Advances in the media, but particularly in television, have been significant in the dissemination of tastes and preferences across national borders. This has given rise to concerns regarding the impact of these technologies on local cultures. For example, Iran has banned the use of satellite television for precisely this reason. As well as creating global markets, technology has also enabled firms to manage their disparate international operations more effectively. Advances such as fax, teleconferencing, e-mail and the Internet has meant that business can be generated from remote locations and that communication, information transfer and reporting between organizational sub-units has become quicker, easier and cheaper.

An analysis of income levels throughout the world reveals the emergence of a global

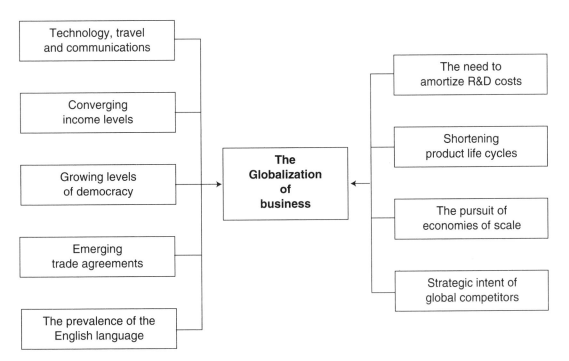

Figure 11.3 *The drivers of globalization*

middle class (*Fortune*, 1994). When middle class is defined as purchasing power parity of between $10,000 and $40,000, a very sizeable segment can be found in countries with low rates of per-capita GNP. For example, Venezuela has some four million people in this segment, Indonesia has 15 million, India over 30 million and China has some 83 million people who can be considered as middle class. These developments represent enormous opportunities for providers of consumer goods and services. When incomes surpass a $10,000 ceiling, Engels co-efficient comes into effect meaning that 70 per cent of this income is spent on disposable goods (Ohmae, 1985). Increasingly, the disposable goods purchased are the major global brands in cars, consumer electronics and cosmetics.

Political developments too have helped foster the globalization of business. The moves toward democracy in Central and Eastern Europe have dramatically altered product and factor markets in Europe. In the first instance, these developments have created large markets for everything from construction equipment to financial services to the provision of consulting services. Moves by companies such as Volkswagen who formed an alliance with Skoda in the Czech Republic reflect the attraction of the low-cost factors of production also available in the region. In Western Europe, politically driven moves toward economic union have done much to facilitate the pursuit of pan-European strategies. In keeping with the process initiated by the Single European Act in 1986, there has been a great deal of harmonization of business activity throughout Europe in the past decade. Many stumbling blocks have been removed in the physical movement of goods and the technical standards required for products and services. It is imperative that the potential side effects of these political developments on individual businesses be closely monitored as the case in Example Two aptly demonstrates.

Finally, the widespread prevalence of the English language greatly facilitates the conduct of international business. The emergence of an English-speaking management class throughout Europe has enabled firms from outside the region to locate in countries

Example Two: Lessons from the currency crisis of 1992

Since its foundation, the European Monetary System (EMS) had a turbulent history leading to its collapse after the currency crisis of 1992. A combination of events, most notably the cost of German reunification, recession in Britain and the rejection of the Maastricht Treaty by Danish voters brought about intense speculation and a sharp fall in the value of the British, Italian and Spanish currencies. The impact on firms trading in these countries was dramatic. For example, for many Irish firms, particularly in the food and clothing sector, Britain represented their most important export market. Many of these firms supplied large quantities of produce on a contract basis to supermarkets and department stores. Contracts and prices were typically drawn up well in advance of delivery. The sharp and unprecedented fall in the value of sterling efficiency wiped out the margins available to these exporters. On top of this, firms had to contend with the policy response of the government which had been to increase interest rates to stop speculation on sterling and other weak currencies. Firms trading internationally had to contend with the dual problem of losses due to exchange rates and the higher cost of borrowings, while those companies serving the domestic market also found themselves indirectly affected by the currency crisis through the effects of interest rate rises (Fahy, 1994).

such as Portugal or Greece without language becoming a barrier to the effective management of operations. Companies such as ABB which grew out of the merger of a Swedish and a Swiss firm and has operations in over 140 countries uses English as the official language of its meetings. The prevalence of English also enables efficiencies to be gained in advertising and communications activities. However, its popularity has been negatively received in some countries. For example, the Turkish government has recently ordered that it will ban radio and television presenters using American terms such as 'cool' and 'hip' and that it will fine shops that do not have their signage in the Turkish language.

Internal drivers of globalization

For many firms the competitive reality is that they must have a global presence in order to be able to compete. It was noted above that the life cycle of products is becoming increasingly shorter. For investments to be recouped, it is essential that the product be launched quickly in multiple markets or at a minimum in the key regions of Western Europe, North America and Japan (Ohmae, 1985). This is particularly true in industries such as pharmaceuticals where the cost of developing a new drug can reach phenomenal levels. Added to this, regulatory changes have reduced the period available to firms to recoup this kind of investment and competition from generic manufacturers has drastically reduced sales after patent expiration. Consequently, recent years have seen the global consolidation of the pharmaceutical industry through a series of alliances between major players. This has resulted in the industry being dominated by a small number of large corporations who have the facility to share R&D costs and who have a global market presence. The pursuit of economies of scale, particularly in upstream activities, has resulted in firms rationalizing assembly and production operations and locating in low cost centres around the world. Finally, many firms consider that it is necessary to become a world leader in order to

ensure future survival and prosperity. It has been noted that this kind of strategic intent or long-term goal of world leadership can be helpful in explaining the rapid growth of some of Japan's leading companies such as Komatsu and NEC (Hamel and Prahalad, 1989).

Practical tip

Nine key drivers of globalization have been identified, including technology, converging income levels, trade agreements, growing levels of democracy, prevalence of the English language, the need to amortize R&D costs, shortening product life cycles, the pursuit of economies of scale and the strategic intent of competitors. Examine how each of the nine drivers are affecting your business now and their likely impact by the year 2000.

In summary, the globalization of business is reflected in the world-wide scope of competition and in the potential to exploit converging world markets. To date, these changes have given rise to their share of winners and losers. Industries in many of the developed economies have been decimated by international competition. For example, in 1956, Swiss companies held over 50 per cent of the world market share for watches. By 1980, their share had fallen to one-fifth. In 1930, over 80 per cent of all cars produced were made in the USA. By 1980, US production accounted for only 20 per cent despite the fact that many Japanese-owned production plants were operating in the USA (Aliber, 1993). In contrast, organizations such as the Virgin Group appear to be going from strength to strength with a globally popular brand which appears to be able to stretch from travel to retailing to soft drinks to financial services. In the following sections, we review how firms can strategically respond to the challenges presented by the globalization of business.

How global is your industry? ▬▬

The foregoing discussion gives a flavour for the kinds of global challenges that today's firms have to face. However, responding to these challenges is not as difficult as it might first appear. Businesses need to remember the sound fundamentals of *strategic marketing*. The first step in an effective response is to fully understand the competitive dynamics in your particular industry. Industry analysis in a global environment must move beyond the examination of traditional dimensions such as the industry structure and the level of competitive rivalry. In particular, it must assess the extent to which the industry is becoming globally integrated. The pressures for global integration and local responsiveness (see Figure 11.4) impose different demands on the firm's marketing strategy. How to go about assessing the extent to which your industry is becoming global or remaining local is examined in the following paragraphs.

Pressures for global integration ─────

The presence of a number of factors in an industry makes the strategic co-ordination and the global integration of activities critical. These factors include the presence of global customers, customers with universal needs, the presence of global competitors, pressures for cost reduction, investment intensity and technological intensity. Take,

for example, the case of the automotive components business. It scores highly on all of these factors. Automotive original equipment manufacturers (OEMs) are by and large global players with relatively universal needs. Even though the automotive industry has emerged from the global recession in the earlier part of this decade, the current competitiveness in the industry means that manufacturers continue to exert considerable pressure on its suppliers to reduce costs. For example, Ford Motor Co. which buys in up to 70 per cent of its components has sought a five-year price freeze from its suppliers, asking them to absorb any increase in their costs whether caused by inflation or product improvements and breaking an industry tradition whereby the OEM automatically paid the supplier for an improved component. Large, global competitors are also emerging in the automotive components business. The Japanese firm, Nippondenso, which is Toyota's main supplier, generated over 1.3 trillion yen in sales in 1994 and has 23 production plants outside Japan. Some of these competitors are very global in their marketing orientation, such as Delphi Automotive Systems which promotes itself as having 190 locations in 31 countries enabling it to provide for an OEM's component, module and system needs. Finally, the production of components such as electronic control units or safety devices is highly technologically intensive while even the production of commodity parts such as springs, brackets and bearings

Pressures for global integration		Pressures for local responsiveness	
Global customers	☐	Differences in customer needs	☐
Global competitors	☐	Differences in channels	☐
Customers with similar needs	☐	Local substitutes	☐
Pressure for cost reduction	☐	Differences in market structure	☐
Investment intensity	☐	Host government demands	☐
Technology intensity	☐		

Figure 11.4 How global is your industry?

is investment intensive due to scale requirements.

Pressures for local responsiveness

In contrast, the existence of factors such as differences in customer needs, differences in distribution channels, availability of local substitutes, local market structures and host government demands may well impede integration efforts in an industry and require instead, product adaptation to suit local demands. In industries such as consumer food products, retail banking, healthcare, personal services and others, these pressures may be high. However, as noted earlier, many of the pressures for local responsiveness are being eroded. Differences in customer needs are being reduced through technology and travel while differences in market structures and distribution channels are being overcome through innovative strategies and practices. Host government intervention has traditionally been a major stumbling block to global integration through the desire to both protect local industry and to retain some control over the types of products and services available in domestic markets. However, the reduced influence of host governments is illustrated in Western Europe, where progress toward economic union has meant that European-wide standards are being implemented and

formerly protected sectors such as healthcare, aviation and financial services are being subject to foreign competition.

In summary, the first step in developing an effective global marketing strategy is to understand the nature of the pressures for global integration in your industry. To do so, it is necessary to monitor the strength of trends toward global integration or local responsiveness. If the balance is shifting in favour of integration, then the industry is likely to be moving toward the top left-hand corner of Figure 11.5. The factors critical to success in a global industry are likely to be significantly different to those in an industry which can be classed as local and the necessary adjustments in strategy will have to be made. For many firms the likelihood is that such an analysis will reveal that some parts of their business are becoming global while others are remaining local. This is not unusual and it is a trend that is to be observed in many businesses. For example, in the information technology industry, sectors such as terminals and PCs have become quite global due to the presence of large competitors, customers with universal needs, pressures for cost reduction and the existence of investment and technological intensity in the production process. In contrast, the Local Area Networks (LANs) and services sectors of the business remain quite local due to differences in market structures across countries

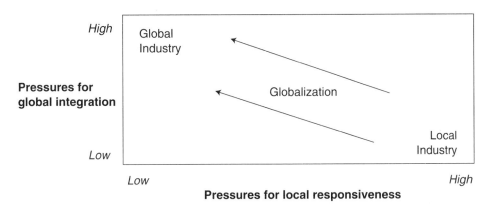

Figure 11.5 *Global integration versus local responsiveness adapted from Prahalad and Doz (1987)*

and differences in customer needs. Understanding the dynamics of your industry or the key sectors in it is a prerequisite for the development of an effective strategic response.

Marketing strategy in a global environment

Devising the appropriate marketing strategy in a global environment is a complex task. The basic strategic imperatives remain the same. The firm must understand its customers even though there may be differences between them from country to country. It must understand its competitors and be able to identify potential threats from new competitors. And the firm must exploit its resources to develop a marketing package that meets the needs of its customers. But the picture is complicated by the multiplicity of potentially conflicting goals and sources of advantage (Ghoshal, 1987). Firms operating across national borders have to balance the objectives of seeking to achieve efficiencies in their operations while managing the risks inherent in doing business across diverse markets as well as trying to exploit the potential to transfer learning and ideas between organizational sub-units. At the same time, firms can potentially leverage multiple sources of advantage such as exploiting scale economies or sharing investments and costs across products, markets and businesses. Typically, the marketing strategy of firms operating in multiple markets conforms to one of four distinct types, namely, the international firm, the multinational firm, the global firm and the transnational firm (Bartlett and Ghoshal, 1989). The strategic orientation of these types is documented in the following paragraphs.

The international firm

The marketing strategy adopted by the international firm is typical of that used by many firms at an early stage of their international development or by those operating from large domestic markets. All firms who oper-

ate across national borders are at an automatic disadvantage *vis-à-vis* local competitors. These disadvantages may take the form of the greater familiarity of local competitors with local market needs, the political and exchange rates risks inherent in international business and the travel and communication costs involved in running foreign subsidiaries. To overcome these disadvantages, international firms must be able to exploit their domestic competitive advantages whether it is lower costs, strong brand names or managerial skills in foreign markets. Therefore, international firms compete on the basis of their ability to effectively transfer learning from domestic markets to new foreign markets. In Porter's terms, they might be seen as competing on the basis of cost leadership or differentiation but in selected geographic segments of the market.

International firms typically see their domestic operations as being most important and their foreign activities as something of an appendage that may not be necessarily critical to the overall success of the enterprise. Therefore, the parent organization tends to take control of all the key marketing activities. The home country, which also typically hosts the R&D and design functions is seen as the key source for new products and new ideas. Subsidiaries are consequently dependent on the parent for flows of innovations and resources. Their role is generally confined to the implementation of plans developed at head office as well as the adaptation of products and other aspects of the marketing mix to meet local needs. Control is maintained by head office through a requirement on subsidiaries to meet sales and financial targets.

The multinational firm

In contrast to the international firm, the multinational firm pursues a quite different marketing strategy. Such firms place a premium on the differences between markets, adapting their products and strategies to suit local conditions. Therefore, multinational firms display a strong customer orientation that emphasizes the quality of response to local market needs. Its competitive advantages may originate in its home country but success in a global environment requires adaptation from market to market. Such a strategy is popular, for example, among consumer goods and services firms. A company such as McDonald's has been very effective in exploiting the competencies of its brand name and management systems throughout the world. But many aspects of its operations are adapted to local conditions, particularly, its menu items which range from beer in Germany to fish in Japan to the relative prices charged for its products which are highest in Switzerland and significantly lower in Russia and China.

The pursuit of a multinational strategy is often the outcome of how the firm has grown internationally. Many of Ireland's largest multinationals such as the Smurfit Corporation in the paper and packaging business, the Kerry Group in food ingredients, CRH in building materials and Glen Dimplex in the white goods sector have all grown rapidly through the acquisition of local firms in the UK, Europe and the USA. Though such acquisitions are usually followed by some level of rationalization, the acquired firms are usually allowed to operate relatively autonomously within certain broad financial targets. For example, Glen Dimplex has acquired some ten white goods companies in Europe and the USA including such brands as Belling and Morphy Richards. The white goods sector is one that exhibits strong pressures for local responsiveness (Baden-Fuller and Stopford, 1991) hence the company allows its subsidiaries considerable local autonomy though they must meet stringent financial targets. Subsidiaries tailor marketing strategies to suit local conditions and advantages are gained through effectiveness in meeting local needs.

The global firm

One of the major weaknesses of the multinational approach is that it creates the risk of large-scale duplication of activities across subsidiaries. Such duplication and the resulting potential for intense rivalry between subsidiaries can be very costly. In addition, multinational firms forego the opportunities for economies of scale which can be attained through the concentration of activities in world-scale locations. It is the pursuit of such efficiencies that is the driving force behind the strategy of the global firm.

The defining characteristic of global firms is that they emphasize standardization in marketing strategy. In an environment where the needs of customers are becoming increasingly homogenous, standardized or predominantly standardized products and strategies hold many attractions. Savings can be made by confining production to world-scale plants in low-cost locations. Significant savings can be made through the adoption of standardized promotion campaigns. For example, Gillette's 'the best a man can get' advertising campaign was run using the same message in nineteen countries saving the firm some $20 million in the process (Reisenbeck and Freeling, 1991). Further spin-off benefits that are to be gained from the standardization of strategy include global recognition and the uniformity of the message provided across markets.

Ford Motor Co. is very much an advocate of a global approach to its marketing strategy. On 1 January 1994, it announced that it was merging its North American and European vehicle businesses into a single grouping Ford Automotive Operations (FAO). Within FAO, product development, manufacturing and the firm's marketing and sales operations have been unified under a single executive to eliminate the costly duplication of activities. Of its five product categories, the production of four will be centred in North America with the production of small and medium-sized cars concentrated in Europe. And with the Ford Mondeo brand, the company is closer to the ideal of a globally standardized car than any of its competitors.

The transnational firm

Firms that pursue a transnational approach to their marketing strategy are in effect seeking to maximize the benefits of each of the approaches discussed above. In other words, these firms seek to balance the efficiencies of the global firm with the local responsiveness of the multinational as well as ensuring that there is an effective transfer of ideas, innovations and information throughout the organization. Such a multidimensional approach is consistent, for example, with the efforts of firms to simultaneously pursue both cost leadership and differentiation strategies. However, the difficulties in balancing the conflicting pressures of efficiency, responsiveness and the transfer of learning should not be underestimated and, to date, not many firms have been effective in doing it. One possible exception is ABB, the electrical products conglomerate. This firm operates under a complex structure. On one level, it is organized along the lines of a business area structure that champions a global strategy by rationalizing operations on a world-wide basis. However, this is counter-balanced by a country structure that seeks to maximize synergies between different ABB subsidiaries on a country-by-country basis. Therefore, the organization sees itself as being, simultaneously, big and small, global and national, centralized and decentralized (Taylor, 1991).

In summary, managers have a choice of four possible approaches when attempting to formulate the firm's marketing strategy. Each of the approaches emphasizes different customer and competitive orientations as well as different strategies and structures for the marketing organization. The choice of approach should be determined by both the nature of the industry and the conditions pertaining to the firm at a particular point in time. In other words, effective strategy in a global environment requires the existence of a 'strategic fit' between the organization, its strategy and the industry conditions in which it operates. In an earlier section, we outlined how the pressures for global integration in an industry can be assessed. Having understood the industry conditions, the firm must then evaluate its current strategy and establish if it is suitable given the present and likely future trends in the industry. It must also give attention to the question regarding which of the resources at its disposal are likely to yield a sustainable competitive advantage in the global marketplace. We now briefly address this question.

Understand your sources of advantage

An analysis of the competitiveness of firms in the global marketplace reveals that industry dominance has remained quite regional. For example, the top five aerospace firms in the world in 1995 namely, Lockheed Martin, United Technologies, Boeing, Allied-Signal and McDonnell Douglas are all US firms. Similar patterns can be observed across a range of other industries. In the brokerage business, the top four firms in the world are also US owned, in chemicals, three of the top five are German, the top two engineering firms in the world are French and the commercial banking and life insurance businesses are dominated by Japanese firms who account for six and eight of the top ten, respectively. Conventional discussion on the sources of competitive advantage tends to concentrate on factors that are specific to firms such as their research capabilities or their brand names. However, in a global environment, it is clear that the country matters also. Managers must therefore understand the interplay between firm-specific and country-specific resources in the attainment of sustainable competitive advantages in a global environment.

At any given time a firm is likely to have at its disposal a very large resource pool ranging from its plant and equipment, to its financial assets, its intellectual property and networks as well as the capabilities of its management and staff. Which of these resources are likely to be most important as a source of competitive advantage? A recent perspective, popularly known as the 'resource-based view of the firm', suggests that it is those resources which have the characteristics of *value, rareness, inimitability* and *non-substitutability* that will be the key sources of advantage (Barney, 1991). In other words, resources are important if they enable the creation of value for customers. In addition, they are only a source of advantage if they are rare and not possessed by all competitors in the marketplace. Furthermore, they must resist the efforts of competitors to duplicate them. Resources are difficult to imitate when they are complex, tacit, built up over time and protected by law. Consequently, tangible resources such as a firm's plant and equipment or its financial assets are relatively easy to duplicate and are not a strong source of competitive advantage. Even intellectual property that is protected by law is often rapidly imitated in international markets. It is the firm's intangible resources such as its relationships with customers, its culture and organizational practices and its technical know-how that tend to be the key sources of advantage because these resources are complex and difficult to imitate.

Many of the firm's intangible resources are closely related to its country of origin. In a more general way, countries at a given point in time will possess a stock of capabilities such as the level of labour productivity, communications and marketing infrastructures and its technological and organizational capabilities. Countries differ in their stocks of these capabilities because they are tied to the economic and institutional arrangements of the country and diffuse slowly across borders (Kogut, 1991). For example, the success of US biotechnology firms has been attributed to the unique mix of resources available in that country including government support for research in the field, an aggressive entrepreneurial culture supported by favourable capital markets and a high level of R&D expenditure. Therefore, in deciding how to compete internationally, firms must seek to deploy their difficult-to-imitate capabilities in ways that create value for customers across national borders. In particular, they should examine what country-specific resources can be exploited internationally as the culture-bound nature of these resources makes them a potent source of competitive advantage in the global marketplace.

Summary

- All the evidence points in the direction of the business environment becoming increasingly global and competitive. Some dramatic global trends can be observed, including the rapid growth in world business, the shift to the Pacific Rim, the pursuit of new competitive strategies, the emergence of global customers and the rapid diffusion of innovations.
- There are a range of forces driving the increased globalization of business. These include general factors such as technological changes which are manifest in travel and communications, converging income levels, international trade agreements, growing levels of democracy and the prevalence of the English language as well as the efforts by firms to amortize R&D costs, cope with shortening life cycles, pursue economies of scale and attain world market leadership.

- Marketing managers must assess the extent to which their particular industry is going global. Certain industries are likely to exhibit strong pressures for integration such as the presence of global customers with universal needs, global competitors and pressures for cost reduction. Others may continue to show crucial differences in customer needs, distribution channels and market structures.
- In developing their marketing strategies, firms may choose from one of four generic options, namely: international; multinational; global; and transnational strategy. Each approach places a different emphasis on customers, competitors and the planning and organization of marketing activity.
- Effective marketing strategy in a global environment necessitates that the firm understands the competitive imperatives of its industry and ensures that its strategy fits with these determinants of success.
- *Sustainable* competitive advantage in a global environment is only attainable where the firm deploys difficult-to-imitate resources in ways that create value for customers.

References and further reading ■

Aliber, R. (1993), *The Multinational Paradigm*, Cambridge, MA: MIT Press.

Baden-Fuller, C. W. F. and Stopford, J. (1991), 'Globalization frustrated: the case of white goods', *Strategic Management Journal*, **12**, June, 493–507.

Barney, J. B. (1991), 'Firm resources and sustained competitive advantage', *Journal of Management*, **17**, March, 99–120.

Bartlett, C. and Ghoshal, S. (1989), *Managing Across Borders*, London: Century Business.

Buckley, P. J. and Brooke, M. Z. (1992), *International Business Studies: An Overview*, Cambridge, MA: Blackwell Publishers.

Douglas, S. P. and Craig, C. S. (1995), Chapter 14, 'Developing global competitive strategy', *Global Marketing Strategy*, New York: McGraw-Hill.

Economist, (1993), 'Multinational: back in fashion', 326, 27 March, S4.

Economist, (1994), 'The global economy', 333, 1 October, S3-S4.

Economist, (1995), 'Multinationals: who wants to be a giant?', 335, 24 June, S12.

Fahy, J. (1994), 'Lessons from the currency crisis of 1992', *Irish Marketing Review*, **7**, 83–91.

Fahy, J. and Taguchi, F. (1995), 'Reassessing the Japanese distribution system', *Sloan Management Review*, **36**, Winter, 49–61.

Fortune, (1994), 'The big rise', 30 May, 40–46.

Ghoshal, S. (1987), 'Global strategy: an organizing framework', *Strategic Management Journal*, **8**, September–October, 425–440.

Hamel, G. and Prahalad, C. K. (1989), 'Strategic intent', *Harvard Business Review*, **87**, May–June, 63–76.

Kogut, B. (1991), 'Country capabilities and the permeability of borders', *Strategic Management Journal*, **12**, Summer Special Issue, 33–47.

Ohmae, K. (1985), *Triad Power: The Coming Shape of Global Competition*, New York: The Free Press.

Ohmae, K. (1989), 'Managing in a borderless world', *Harvard Business Review*, **87**, March–April, 152–161.

O'Reilly, T. (1992), 'Global marketing in the nineties', *Irish Exporter*, September, 34–36.

Prahalad, C. K. and Doz, Y. (1987), *The Multinational Mission*, New York: The Free Press.

Reisenbeck, H. and Freeling, A. (1991), 'How global are global brands?', *McKinsey Quarterly*, **4**, 3–18.

Taylor, W. (1991), 'The logic of global business: an interview with ABB's Percy Barnevik', *Harvard Business Review*, **69**, March–April, 91–105.

Westbrook, R. and Williamson, P. (1993), 'Mass customisation: Japan's new frontier', *European Management Journal*, **11**, March, 38–45.

12

Evaluating stakeholder principles in strategic marketing management ─────

Professor Colin Egan, Leicester Business School and Professor Gordon Greenley, Aston University Business School

 A theme that permeates the chapters of this book is the notion that strategic marketing can (and should) be considered within the framework of a planning process, i.e. in a formalized, structured and systematic fashion. As made clear by Malcolm McDonald in Chapter 8, a central tenet of marketing planning is that the starting point of the process is the formulation of clear objectives. This does, however, beg the question of whose objectives are they? We glibly talk about the company's objectives as if the organization is a living entity, divorced from individuals and groups who actually formulate the objectives and independent of other constituents who can help or hinder their implementation.

A series of questions draws attention to the scope of the issues that this chapter will address. Are a company's objectives the collective goals of the board, or of certain individual directors, or of certain groups of senior managers with particular vested interests? Are they formulated to satisfy the self-interests of individuals, the interests of the functions they represent or are they explicitly created to optimize company-wide performance? Are objectives set to satisfy the short-term dividend interests of the shareholders or the longer-term investment interests of future generations of employees, customers and more growth-minded investors? Do the objectives accommodate the needs and value systems of suppliers and distributors? Do they impinge on the profitability of direct and generic rivals? Are they designed to create profit at the expense of employee remuneration and job security? Do they confront government regulations? Do they compromise the safety or general welfare of local communities? And so on.

Defining stakeholders

The various groups of people and organizations that are directly or indirectly involved with any company are its stakeholders. A formal definition will aid our understanding:[1]

A stakeholder is any group or individual who can affect, or is affected by, the achievement of an organization's purpose.

The concept of stakeholder groups and the acknowledgement of their importance in a broad range of general management processes have long been recognized in the strategy literature. Despite this, research has remained fragmented, functionally biased and largely anecdotal. Human resource management focus on people, organizational behaviour sociologists examine trade unions, marketing prioritizes customers, financial management theorists research dividend policy and shareholder value, manufacturing researchers examine supplier relations, and so on. The structure of business schools reflects and reinforces these functional biases, as does the 'professionalization' of functional disciplines, each of which have their own institutes (for example, the Chartered Institute of Marketing which endorses this book). In this chapter we aim to provide a more *holistic* perspective, drawing on academic research where available and practical examples where appropriate. As may be concluded from the opening comments, there may well be more questions than answers as we develop the core themes of stakeholder principles throughout the chapter but this, in reality, should not be considered unusual for a concept which has only recently become a core rather than a peripheral topic of investigation. The functional priorities identi-

fied above are natural and it is not claimed that the researchers are ignorant of different perspectives. The reality is that any research project must have a clearly defined scope and while stakeholder issues have often been acknowledged they have rarely formed the focus of investigation.

From a more practical perspective, attention clearly needs to be given to the various interests of different stakeholder groups and how their interests should be addressed when creating strategic marketing plans. Indeed, every decision made in all aspects of strategic marketing will have an impact on some stakeholders, while the effectiveness of those decisions and the ability to implement them will be dependent on the influence of other stakeholders.

Categorizing stakeholders

As we will see throughout this chapter, there are a number of ways of categorizing the range of various stakeholders associated with a particular company. The first is to simply draw up a list of stakeholders, for example, advisors, competitors, consultants, customers, directors, distributors, employees, financial institutions, the general public, local communities, government agencies, managers, the media, marketing service agencies, retailers, shareholders, suppliers and unions.

This becomes more meaningful (and practical) if stakeholders are categorized into logical groups, i.e. categories where clusters of stakeholders have a collective impact on the company, for example:

- **Economic stakeholders** – those stakeholders that directly affect the economic performance of the company, such as customers, distributors, competitors, suppliers and trade unions.
- **Legal stakeholders** – those stakeholders that must be addressed for legislative reasons, for example, government agencies such as the Health and Safety Executive, the Monopolies and Mergers Commission, Customs and Excise, Inland Revenue, Companies House, and so on.

---

1 This definition is generally attributed to Freeman (1984), *Strategic Management: A Stakeholder Approach*, Boston, MA: Pitman, adapted here from Greenley, G. E. and Foxall, G. R. (1997), 'Multiple stakeholder orientation in UK companies and the implications for company performance', *Journal of Management Studies*, **34**(2), 259–284.

- **Ethical stakeholders** – those stakeholders which the company may feel it has a moral rather than legal obligation to address, for example, elements of the natural environment that are not directly covered by legislation (through 'green marketing'), charities, educational trusts and social welfare in general. A company such as The Body Shop prioritizes these, taking an ethical stance towards the planet and creating a marketing platform from this position.
- **Discretionary stakeholders** – those stakeholder groups which the company has a free choice in addressing as they are not classifiable into any of the above groups. Examples include the media companies, advisors and consultants, industry or product interest groups, local communities, local activists and, for some companies, trade unions.

Another common approach is to classify stakeholders as *primary* or *secondary* stakeholders. Primary groups are those whose continued involvement with the company are essential for its survival. Examples include:

- the shareholders and investors who provide financial resources;
- employees (and their unions) who provide human resources;
- customers and competitors who make markets by providing sales revenue and the incentive to improve products (effectiveness) and productivity (efficiency);
- suppliers and channel members who constitute the industry infrastructure;
- the government, whose laws and regulations must be obeyed and whose taxes must be paid.

Secondary groups are those who can affect or be affected by the company, but who do not enter into transactions with the company and are not essential for its survival. Examples include:

- the media;

- the local community;
- special interest groups which can favourably or detrimentally influence the image and reputation of the company;
- industry associations;
- etc.

The above classifications of stakeholders are relevant to the company as a whole but there are stakeholder groups whose interests are more closely aligned to the marketing department. Internally, examples include:

- the board of directors with respect to both short-term profitability and long-term product and market development;
- senior executives with respect to the market and financial performance of products;
- other departments with respect to information exchange and sharing;
- other departments with respect to the co-ordination of operations;
- other departments with respect to competition for resources.

Externally, examples include:

- customer segments;
- channel members such as selling agents, distributors, wholesales and retailers, i.e. where the company conducts business through transactions with intermediaries;
- channel members with whom the company has marketing relationships through formal and informal strategic alliances;
- marketing *facilitators*, such as market research firms, advertising and promotions agencies, PR firms, product design consultants, logistics advisers and marketing consultants;
- components and materials suppliers with respect to the company's product designs, new product development and customer benefit enhancement

Profiling stakeholder interests

Regardless of the classification of stakeholders, it is obvious that each group has very different interests. Having said this, a common factor among all stakeholder groups is that they expect their interests to be satisfied by the company. The very practical implications of this is that there are many demands placed on a company, including: sustaining high product benefits at low prices; long-term commitment to purchasing components and raw materials; increasing profits and, as a consequence, shareholder value; employee remuneration; fulfilment of all legal requirements; investments in environment protection; contributions to society; the provision of information to the media; being a 'good neighbour'. It is clear from this listing that many of these interests actually compete for resource and attention and some are obviously diametrically opposed. For example, the cost of developing new or enhanced products for customers may be in conflict with the profit expectations of the shareholders, especially if these take a short-term view of their investments.

Given this range and complexity of interests a natural question emerges as to the *legitimacy* of the interests of particular stakeholder groups. It can be argued, for example, that only shareholders and employees really have a legitimate claim to have their interests fully addressed as they have clearly committed an investment into the company. However, what is the extent of the legitimacy of customers' claims? As John Egan, CEO of British Airports Authority and formerly MD of Jaguar cars has noted:

Business is about making money from satisfied customers. Without them there can be no long-term future for any commercial organization.

To summarize the discussion so far, what appears at first sight to be a relatively straightforward issue becomes much more complex when we scratch the surface. The stakeholder concept, like many other 'common-sense' principles, has a variety of dimensions that must be thoroughly understood if the issues it raises are to be

effectively managed. In the sections that follow we address this challenge and provide a range of examples to illustrate the highly practical dimensions of a subject which, to many, appears abstract and unmanageable.

Managing stakeholder interests

There are two broad prescriptive approaches to how companies should address stakeholder issues (Greenley and Foxall, 1997):

1. The company needs to achieve a balanced approach that addresses its own values and needs and those of each of its stakeholder groups. The logic of this perspective is based on the argument that each stakeholder group has a particular part to play in the successful performance of a company and, therefore, such performance can only be achieved if all stakeholder interests are addressed. Plans should be established to optimize the satisfaction of all these needs, the ultimate goal being to ensure that no one particular set of needs dominates. Where equilibrium between the different set of needs or values is disturbed there should be a reallocation of resource to restore and subsequently maintain a balanced system. Maintaining a balance between these diverse and often conflicting needs is essential for long-term corporate success.

2. The second approach is grounded in more theoretical concepts and, although it might be more difficult to plan for in practice, it probably comes closer to the 'real world' than the previous approach! This perspective recognizes that different stakeholder groups will have different levels of power within their relationships with each other. It does this with reference to the economic logic that all firms, however large, must confront the basic issue of scarce resources. Since not all groups have similar 'legitimate' claims for equitable resource allocation then stakeholder interests should be prioritized

with reference to which particular groups have the strongest power base. In this scenario there will be inevitable trade-offs among stakeholders, for example, increasing employee remuneration and customer service levels is likely to result in reduced dividend payments to shareholders, particularly in the short term. In sum, rather than seeking a delicate balance whereby all stakeholders' interests are held in equilibrium, in this approach the company will make priorities and act accordingly.

From a marketing perspective, of course, the principle of consumer sovereignty suggests that the ultimate stakeholder power base rests in the freedom of choice enjoyed by customers. There are few statements in the chapters of this book which would argue against this basic marketing fact and it is generally accepted by marketeers that a sharp focus on prioritizing customer satisfaction will inevitably lead to the maximum long-term satisfaction of the interests of other stakeholders (with the exception of competitors!). The realities of markets and the intricacies of organizational life, however, ensure that the traditional marketing rallying call of 'the customer is king' has complex countervailing forces stacked up against it. Many of these forces are to be found rooted in the inherent contradictions which characterize stakeholder interests, thus ensuring that the topic is of central importance to our understanding of strategic marketing management as a complex economic and behavioural process.

An important contribution to the stakeholder concept from a marketing perspective was based on a critique of one of the most influential concepts in management thinking in recent decades, the so-called 'excellent companies'. We will evaluate this critique after first considering briefly the roots of the excellence movement.

In 1982 Tom Peters and Robert Waterman published an extremely popular and highly influential book, *In Search of Excellence*. The authors studied 43 companies and modelled a framework of excellence based on 'fit' between strategy, structures, systems, skill, staff, style and superordinate goals. Essentially the book was a showcase for McKinsey's strategic success model (the 'Seven S' framework) which claimed to provide a universal law for business prosperity. The '7S' framework was well received by both academics and practitioners and certainly seemed to make a valuable contribution to the understanding of organizational performance. Despite this, within five years more than half of the companies examined were in some difficulty and Tom Peters himself stated in a subsequent text that 'There are no excellent companies'. A cursory evaluation of the 7S framework highlights its most fundamental weakness, i.e. it pays virtually no attention to the fragile nature of the links between the elements, focusing instead on the 'soft S' of superordinate goals to provide a 'glue' which holds the framework together. In this sense, for example, the relationship between employees (staff) and managers (style) are modelled as harmonious rather than potentially conflictual. Structure is considered as coherent rather than, say, competitive (for scarce resources). Furthermore, no detailed evaluation of *external* forces is undertaken in the sense that we have outlined them in this chapter, for example, suppliers, distribution intermediaries, government agencies, and so on. Compounding this major weakness of the book was the attempt to 'pick' companies to fit the model, i.e. the framework was developed and then the authors went in search of '*who* were the excellent companies'. This is a fundamental weakness of much management research and a more appropriate question is raised here.

What are the excellent companies?

This question was raised by Professor Peter Doyle who charted the preoccupation with excellent companies to its roots in the late nineteenth century rather than the early 1980s (Doyle, 1992). Acknowledging the extraordinary impact of *In Search of Excellence* on management thinking, Doyle nevertheless questions its substance. He draws particular attention to the common treatment of excellence in the literature as a one-dimensional measure, noting that 'Excellence has become a popular exhortation and aspiration among managers, but it is a dangerous concept'.

Doyle calls for a recognition of a much broader range of stakeholder interests, including those of shareholders, managers, customers, employees, creditors, governments, suppliers, minority groups and local communities. He convincingly argues that the effective management of the multiple and often conflicting expectations of these interest groups is a key factor in ensuring organizational survival:

Managers should therefore not seek to excel on any single goal, but rather to look for a balanced performance over time on a set of goals. They should seek to operate in the tolerance zone which gives all stakeholder groups a satisfactory level of achievement.

This 'tolerance zone' of stakeholders and their expectations is shown in Figure 12.1.

The true measure of success, according to Doyle, is organizational survival and this, in turn, is a function of 'achieving a satisfactory

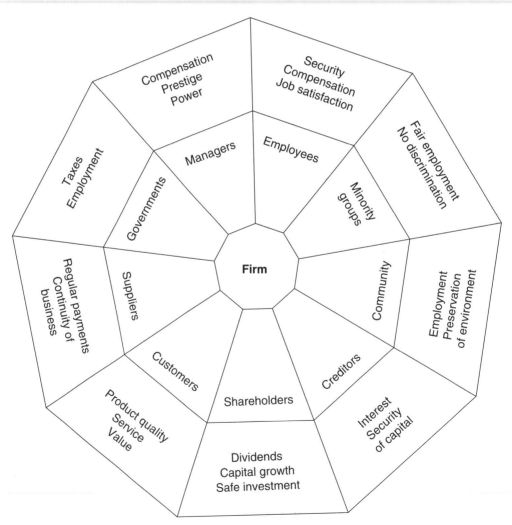

Figure 12.1 *The tolerance zone of stakeholder expectations. Source: Doyle (1992)*

level of performance across a multiple competing set of criteria'.

In the sections that follow we acknowledge the observations made by Doyle with regard to the diversity of interests which companies must address and take a perspective which in many ways confronts some of the basic tenets of strategic marketing management, particularly its more prescriptive elements. We combine practical examples and case studies with an examination of recent theoretical contributions to the understanding of stakeholder principles and, in the final sections, draw tentative conclusions regarding how these can be integrated within the strategic marketing process.

Mission, strategy and stakeholders: a practical perspective

Many companies have mission statements that formally recognize stakeholder interests. A good example is provided by the Dutch consumer electronics company Philips. Every employee (all 270,000!) is made aware of the company's mission as it is expressed through five values:[2]

1. Delight customers
2. Value people [employees] as our greatest resource
3. Deliver quality and excellence in all actions
4. Achieve premium return on equity
5. Encourage entrepreneurial behaviour at all levels

In the opening remarks to the company's annual report, the president of Philips, Cor Boonstra, draws a clear link between customer focus and shareholder satisfaction:

Philips has long been acclaimed as a leader in the world of electronic technology. But technological expertise is only part of the story of Philips. As our corporate values make clear, we seek to put people at the forefront of our efforts and improve the quality of people's lives. More than ever before, we are pursuing this goal not only through technology but in direct dialogue with our customers, leading to a level of business performance that is to the satisfaction of the shareholders.

The statement goes on to introduce the philosophy of the company as it is expressed in its global positioning statement, 'Let's make things better':

'Let's make things better' is a pledge we make to ourselves and to the world. We are eager to listen, learn and – together with our customers – create the exciting products and services of tomorrow.

This is a remarkable turnaround in intent for a company that has invented many of the technologies we use today but which has experienced a decade of appalling financial results. Indeed, Philips provides a classic example of the distinction made in Chapter 4 between invention and innovation, i.e. as a company it has achieved seminal technological breakthroughs but has consistently failed to fully commercialize and exploit its inventive genius with strong profit performance.

Philips famously misled its shareholders in 1990, announcing first that profits would be in line with expectations and then, within two weeks, admitting major losses. This led to a collapse in the company's share price from 60 guilders to as low as 15 guilders and it precipitated more than half a decade of mistrust among its shareholders. Until the arrival of Boonstra in late 1996 the share price rarely exceeded 65 guilders. As we write, the share price is 170 guilders having peaked at 190. This is an astonishing achievement in such a short period of time. Although Boonstra has made some key strategic moves since he took the helm their impact has yet to be seen and it appears that the confidence of the shareholders is firmly rooted in the honesty of Boonstra's statements. There is clearly a speculative element involved (for example, those expecting the company to be broken up) but the turnaround in perceptions among

---

2 This section is derived from the *Philips' 1996 Annual Report*. Citations are direct quotes taken from the report.

investors in general is still extraordinary. In a remarkable admission of the company's 'strategic sloppiness', Boonstra made the following comment in the president's message to shareholders in the company's annual report:

I [am] fully aware that we have had an extremely disappointing year ... Part of [our] decline was caused by gearing up our organization for growth which did not materialize. We were simply not quick enough in reacting to the market. We do not blame the markets, nor our competitors, but rather take full responsibility for our own lack of speed.

This really is an extraordinary statement to find in a company's annual report, where the normal approach of the chairman or president is to blame any number of external factors rather than their own incompetence! Boonstra goes on to describe how his philosophy of business is captured in a simple message printed on a sign which sits on his desk: 'The best marketing tool is profitability'. He concludes his president's message with the following comment:

The new élan of Philips is embodied in our 'Let's make things better' theme. This pledge is about continuously listening and working together to create better products, a better company and ultimately a better quality of life for the users of Philips' products. It is a tall order, but I expect all of us at Philips to deliver on this promise to our shareholders, our customers, our partners and ourselves.

We will return to the Philips case later on this chapter with reference to two categories of issues which it raises: (i) the inherent conflicts, from a stakeholder perspective, within the five values; and (ii) the emphasis on trust, an intangible concept which Boonstra makes very explicit in his heavy emphasis on the pledges promised to a broad range of stakeholders. In the meantime, our search continues for hard evidence relating to stakeholder principles and their impact and role within a strategic marketing perspective.

Stakeholders and the strategic marketing process: in search of evidence

There is surprisingly little empirical evidence relating to how firms actually address stakeholder issues, either formally or informally. Regarding formal approaches, this would involve including stakeholder issues in the company's mission statement (as in the Philips case) and in its strategic planning systems. As Malcolm McDonald indicates in Chapter 8, many firms are poor at formal planning anyway, so we might assume that incorporating stakeholder needs in formal plans is not the norm for most companies. Addressing stakeholders in an informal way would likely be consistent with a more reactive management style, for example, employees' needs are addressed when the union threatens to strike, retailers' needs are addressed when they threaten to de-list a company's products, customers' needs are addressed when they start to flock to a major rival! Such reactive management is extremely myopic but it does appear to be the norm in many companies.

Another issue that has had little investigation is whether or not a stakeholder orientation actually enhances or detracts from company performance. Given that significant resources have to be invested to balance the disparate needs of stakeholders this is obviously a very important question. Consider again the Philips' five values. Three specific stakeholder groups are directly mentioned: (i) customers; (ii) Philips' employees; and (iii) shareholders. Keeping employees and customers happy is potentially hugely expensive. For example, just how do we delight customers? Do we provide superb (and expensive) service? Do we offer high quality at very low prices? In reality, of course, it is extremely unlikely that any company can consistently delight its customers at all since a direct corollary of increasing customer satisfaction is a heightening of their expectations. The same is true of employees. As most human resource managers will agree, an enhancement in the benefits package this year very quickly becomes the norm and the base point for next year's negotiations. This leads to another important (and largely unresearched) question: does the degree of stakeholder orientation vary over time, for example, with reference to general market conditions? The case of IBM provides useful insights to this question.

Throughout the 1970s and early 1980s, IBM was famous for its commitment to lifetime employment. The company was noted for the fact that all managers had a placard on their desk which boldly stated 'Think!', the point being that executives had time on their hands to reflect and be creative. The fact that IBM enjoyed in excess of 70 per cent global market share of the computer market at the time afforded them the luxury of this human resource policy. From the mid-1980s onwards, however, IBM's strategic sloppiness was viciously exposed and the company spiralled into huge losses and came extremely close to the brink of commercial disaster. Not surprisingly, huge redundancies were made and the spirit of the lifetime employment message was lost forever. A *Harvard Business Review* cartoon captured the moment. A workman was pictured walking away with the Think! placard. In its place was a new message: Work! When Lou Gerstener, the new CEO, arrived with a brief to effect a corporate turnaround he gave a simple indication of his approach, letting it be widely known that the new company mission was: 'Don't think – execute'.

In a similar vein, it is widely believed that Japanese success is based on a culturally based collectivism and a management commitment to lifetime employment for all employees. While culture has certainly played a role in Japanese success, two things need to be noted: (i) 'lifetime' employment was a concession to militant unionism in the 1950s; and (ii) a huge second tier of sweat-shop-like components suppliers to the big-name Japanese manufacturing companies don't even recognize unions, let alone offer lifetime employment.

A very interesting example of the fragile nature of stakeholder relationships over time is provided by the industrial action precipitated by British Airways (BA) management in the summer of 1997. We will begin by examining two historical facts relating to the company:

1. As a state-owned company BA had a reputation for poor reliability and dreadful service. Staff morale was low and heavy deficits (losses) were the norm.
2. In preparation for privatization a huge turnaround initiative was put in place. Although some highly creative accounting by the government was used to make BA commercially viable, the major thrust of the initiative was to directly address the appalling service reputation by involving all employees, from pilots to baggage handling, in customer care training programmes.

The transformation of the company was dramatic and the case was used as an exemplar of service excellence in a best-selling US management book (Albrecht and Zemke, 1985). British Airways became the 'World's Favourite Airline' as well as its most profitable. Employees, customers, managers, unions and suppliers were all apparently happy stakeholders enjoying the sort of balanced equilibrium we discussed earlier.

The stakeholder bliss was shattered by what appeared at first to be a very innocuous managerial action, a decision to outsource some catering activities at the two London airports, Heathrow and Gatwick. Industrial action was threatened by the unions and was met by a very tough management response. The battle lines were clearly drawn and strike activity ensued. The remarkable characteristic of this case is not so much the strike itself but the hostility that characterized the unfolding events. Customers, probably the most loyal of any airline in the world, were greatly inconvenienced and extremely annoyed by the industrial action. Management were humiliated by the unions and heavily criticized by independent observers of their draconian methods, techniques that allegedly included the use of private investigators and video surveillance on striking workers. Employees, with an obvious pre-strike grievance, became embittered. Shareholders ultimately paid the bill for the dispute, an estimated £150 million. In a zero-sum game all stakeholders appeared to lose. The important point here relates to the fragile nature of stakeholder relationships. Time will tell whether or not employee morale (and trust) will be restored or whether customer loyalty is regained. Whatever the outcome among relationships with these two stakeholder groups, it is frankly inconceivable that long-term shareholder value will be enhanced by the outsourcing decision and its cost-cutting objective. The huge cost of the dispute is unlikely to be recovered, and this is the result of industrial action that, on the whole, was very predictable. In reality, it is highly likely that the outsourcing decision was the spark that kindled a broader range of stakeholder tensions as management prepared their globalization strategy for the twenty-first century. An interesting aside to this case is the decision by BA management to remove the Union Jack from the tailplane livery on all its aircraft and to replace it with 'global art'. This has caused an outcry among customers who, quite clearly, were not consulted. BA has become the butt of a thousand jokes and the new livery was very publicly rubbished by Margaret Thatcher, the driving force behind the initial privatization. Richard Branson's long running anti-BA campaign picked up the theme, immediately painting the Union Jack on Virgin Atlantic aircraft and running a huge press campaign with the simple byline: 'British – and Proud Of It!'

In general it is indisputable that managers should be allowed to manage and highly likely that, over time, strategic decisions will confront the fragile equilibrium which characterizes stakeholder relations. There are numerous examples. Intel alienated its largest single customer, Compaq, when it launched its 'Intel Inside' initiative and began marketing the benefits of Pentium processors for multimedia computing to end-

users. Compaq's anger was twofold: (i) the 'Intel Inside' logo created a commodity-type market wherein its own previously strong brand and the cheap Asian clones now shared the same 'beating heart'. Instead of seeing 'Made in Taiwan' on the back of the PC customers read 'Made in America' in the 'Intel Inside' badge on the front; and (ii) Compaq had a huge stockpile of 486 computers inventoried for the Christmas sale period. Intel, of course, refused to back down, reflecting its huge dominance of the global microprocessor market and an apparently strong endorsement of the 'Intel Inside' badge by end-users.

Another very good example of potentially conflicting stakeholder interests is the use by service organizations of 'mystery shoppers', i.e. people who pretend to be customers but in reality are preparing quite detailed performance reports on management and staff at service outlets. Mystery shoppers are the quality controllers of service industries, the guarantors of customer satisfaction and the implementation arm of corporate strategy. But they greatly alienate employees.

Another more abstract but equally fundamental example is the tachograph used in commercial vehicles, universally known as the 'spy in the cab'. This example adds a new dimension to the stakeholder story in the sense that it embraces government regulation. As with many such instances, this regulation may actually confront rather than satisfy stakeholder needs:

- the employer would be able to maintain a lower payroll if a smaller number of drivers were allowed to drive longer hours;
- any individual driver could have a larger pay packet if there were no restrictions;
- the economy would be more productive and national income would rise.

The goal of regulation here is to protect the driver from his employer (and even from himself) in the broader cause of road safety and therefore the welfare of the UK citizen.

This latter example demonstrates the broad scope of stakeholder principles, ranging from employer–employee relationships to the broader relationships between state, industry and society in general. It shouldn't be too surprising, then, that Labour's Tony Blair picked up on the stakeholder theme (which has been around the management literature for decades) to form the core of his Party's marketing campaign for the 1997 General Election. Blair leveraged the fundamental attraction of the stakeholder concept to tremendous effect, grasping the central principle that a broad constituency has an interest in, and a legitimate claim to, involvement in society and, in its purest form, empowerment. The phrase used to describe this principle in politics is pluralism, a philosophy that both recognizes and accommodates multiple interests. While pluralism is undoubtedly a laudable goal in democratic society it is not at all clear that it will translate into profitable business!

Recognizing that this fundamental 'marketing' question of profitability remained largely unanswered or at least unproven in the marketing literature, Greenley and Foxall (1997) undertook a study among managing directors and chief executive officers of large UK companies regarding the nature and degree of their stakeholder orientation and its impact on company performance. After preliminary research the authors identified five different constituents who they collectively described as multiple stakeholder groups: (i) unions; (ii) competitors; (iii) shareholders; (iv) consumers; and (v) employees. The research was broken down into two key components. First, the general proposition was made that there would be a positive relationship between having a multiple stakeholder orientation and strong company performance. Relative success was the key measurement used, i.e. how the companies involved in the research performed compared to their key competitors with regard to return on investment, market share, sales growth and new product launch success.

The second proposition investigated was the degree to which external factors would have an impact on a company's commitment to a stakeholder orientation. Factors taken into account were the degree of competitor hostility, the ease with which new companies could enter the market, the extent to which customer needs had changed in recent years, the rate of growth of key markets and the extent of technological change. The following list summarizes the key findings of the research:

- Companies who recognized and responded to multiple stakeholder groups typically had stronger performance than those with a lower stakeholder orientation.
- Other things being equal, companies should seek a balance in addressing stakeholder interests rather than selectively prioritizing their attention and resource allocation to specific groups.
- Factors in the external environment do have an overall negative impact on multiple stakeholder orientation. However, managers are not necessarily passive receivers of these forces and they can be successfully dealt with by formal planning systems, i.e. these external factors should be accommodated when developing strategic plans for addressing stakeholder interests.
- Where there are scarce resources optimization strategies for resource allocation among the diverse interests of stakeholder groups should be deployed.
- A single stakeholder focus does not enhance performance so, for example, the adoption of a customer focus at the expense of other stakeholder interests is not an optimal approach.
- Financial performance measures such as return on investment (ROI) are inadequate for addressing overall company performance in a multiple stakeholder environment.
- Market-based performance measures are more important than financial measures with reference to making decisions about stakeholder orientation.
- Competitive rivalry (an external factor) has the biggest impact on the effectiveness with which firms perceive they can

manage stakeholder interests for enhanced performance, although this will be less of a problem in a high growth context.

- In general, the findings suggest that relatively few companies successfully achieve an effective multiple stakeholder orientation for enhancing overall performance.
- Formal research is vital for effectively addressing the interests of multiple stakeholder groups since companies find these complex, diverse and difficult to plan for.

The key findings from this study support more general research into strategic management processes and marketing planning systems, i.e. that formalization and planning enhances performance but that most forms are bad at doing it! The authors summarize their research with the following comment:

Orientation to the interests of multiple stakeholders should be pursued, with some kind of optimisation in addressing their interests in strategic planning, based on an adequately researched understanding of their interests. However, consumers will receive priority within this overall orientation, as it is likely to be perceived that the needs and values of consumers are more susceptible to change, and are more difficult to understand, while failure to satisfy consumer interests will have more of an immediate impact on the company and its performance.

The research methodology and analysis was complex but the implications as identified in the above statement are clear. A customer focus remains paramount since customer needs are more likely to be volatile than those of other stakeholders, particularly in turbulent marketing environments. This was demonstrated in Chapter 4 when the topic of innovation was discussed. There it was shown that companies manage better in existing markets, where stakeholders are well understood, rather than in developing markets where, among other uncertainties, the boundaries of customer requirements and competitive threats are more opaque.

The Greenley and Foxall research gives some insights into the impact of stakeholder principles on strategic marketing planning and provides complementary reading for Malcolm McDonald's contribution on planning processes and systems (Chapter 8). However, as the authors acknowledge, like all exploratory research it does have limitations and further research is essential on the topic. But it can also be considered in association with additional streams of research emerging in the marketing literature as well as in combination with observations of leading edge marketing practice. In the next section we examine two key areas in marketing theory and practice where significant inroads into our understanding of the dependency dimension of stakeholder principles are being created.

Stakeholders and dependency

In earlier sections of this chapter the relationship between relative power positions and stakeholder management was described as the least tangible interpretation of stakeholder issues but it was also identified as providing the strongest explanation of the 'real world' of business management. The very concept of 'stakeholder' suggests a dependency relationship, a nexus that always has two associated dimensions: (i) conflict potential; and (ii) power plays. While this is formally recognized in the stakeholder literature a significant omission relates to the fact that such dimensions are not static, i.e. their intensity and relative strength change over time. There are other areas of research in marketing, however, which have examined these issues in some depth. In our conclusion to this chapter we leave the stakeholder literature and consider two significant developments in marketing theory and marketing practice: (i) the impact of the rapid accumulation of market power by retailers in the last decade or so and the impact that this has had on consumer goods companies; and (ii) the huge growth of interest and research into 'relationship management', a trend wherein organizations actually choose to increase their dependency on each other.

Power shift: the case of retailers[3]

Extensive retail concentration in recent years has shifted channel power into the hands of retailers, thus leading consumer goods manufacturers to experience high levels of dependence on a few giant retail groups. Predictably, retailers are using their immense buying power to play-off competing producers to enhance their own competitiveness and, indeed, to build their own brands. Their goal is to gain a continuous stream of concessions from manufacturers on a range of buying factors such as listing fees, prices, discounts, bonuses, rebates, credit terms, delivery schedules, batch sizes, promotional support, consignment stocks, and so on. In addition, they are pressing for the provision of own-label products to improve their own image, to garner strategic control and to enhance profitability at the expense of manufacturers. Retailers are also demanding product customization to build their own brand differentiation and to meet the changing requirements of their fragmenting customer segments. At the same time, smaller retailers have joined buying groups to strengthen their own purchasing power and/or they are targeting ever-tighter consumer segments and thereby increasing the pressures on manufacturers for product design proliferation.

In general, then, the economic environment of retailing has changed dramatically in recent years and incumbent firms are taking large shares of channel profits away from many manufacturers. The manifestation of this retail buying power has resulted in many producers being forced to offer lower trade prices while simultaneously incurring higher marketing costs. Consistent with our discussion of stakeholder power bases it is clear

that, from a manufacturer's perspective, the principal source of their current adversity is a dependency problem. Delisting of an established brand by just one of the major supermarket groups can lead to significant market share loss while failure to penetrate any of the major multiples with new products is highly likely to cause brand failure. By way of contrast, although a major retailer needs to stock market leader brands to satisfy customer demand, it can play off alternative suppliers who, facing their own fierce rivals, will be delighted to grasp the opportunity. In this context, then, most manufacturers are dependent on individual retailers but most retailers are not dependent on individual producers, a huge shift in power base over a relatively short time period.

Once again, economic theory strongly predicts this process. The economist J. K. Galbraith (1967) long ago drew attention to the theory of 'countervailing power' to explain relative shifts in market position:

... private economic power is held in check by the countervailing power of those who are subject to it. The first begets the second. The long trend toward concentration in industrial enterprise in the hands of a relatively few firms has brought into existence not only strong sellers ... but also strong buyers ... The two developed together, not in precise step but in such a manner that there can be no doubt that the one is in response to the other.

He saw this as an inevitable process and concluded that, in general, most positions of market power in the manufacture of consumer goods will be covered by positions of countervailing power.

Stakeholder power, then, and its use and effectiveness must be viewed in context. Perhaps the most significant aspect of power is the reaction of those who are affected by it and, in particular, their tendency to resist it where the achievement of their own goals are being threatened. We saw this clearly in the British Airways case earlier in this chapter and we can also make interesting propositions with relation to the Philips case study. In the 'Five Values' mission there is no mention of trade channels, a remarkable omission

3 This section is adapted from Shipley, D. and Egan, C. (1996), 'An evaluation of strategies for trade marketing', *Proceedings of the 1996 Annual Conference of the Marketing Education Group*, Strathclyde.

given the huge power now wielded by consumer electronic retail groups such as Carrefour, Kingfisher (Comet) and Dixons Group. Although Boonstra alludes to 'partners' in his president's statement, there is no explicit acknowledgement of distributors as either a route or barrier to market. The desire to delight customers while earning above normal returns can thus be seen to have two further weaknesses from a stakeholder perspective. First, as we have seen, retailers are exercising their power to demand more and more of the manufacturer's profit. Secondly, rivals such as Sony (including Aiwa) and Matsushita (Panasonic, Technics) also aim to delight customers and, to the extent that they can build stronger brands than companies such as Philips, they will secure the loyalty of the trade and win the ever tougher battle for retail shelf space.

It should be recognized that power of many consumer brands was historically built upon bullying tactics by manufacturers against retailers, including resale price maintenance, full-line forcing, allocation, refusal to supply, and so on. The erosion or absence of this power base in the contemporary environment undermines many attempts to build or maintain strong brands and demonstrates a stark reversal of manufacturers' fortunes.

Given this context, manufacturers need to formulate strategies to cope effectively in the management of their brands. In particular, they need strategies which (i) ensure that they obtain trade placement and (ii) which provide protection from exploitation arising in their unreciprocated dependence on major retail groups. The 'pull' strategies of the past that largely ignored channel members en route to market no longer suffice. Effective *trade marketing* is essential in this environment, a statement which simply recognizes a basic tenet of marketing, i.e. that companies should understand the needs and *preferences* of customers, in this case, those of the trade – a major stakeholder which has power and has demonstrated a willingness and ability to exercise it. In Chapter 10 Martin Christopher examined how Procter & Gamble are countering this power by working *with* the trade

to build a supply chain, or *strategic network*, which benefits both parties but equally makes them highly dependent upon each other.

Marketing as relationships: an industrial marketing perspective on stakeholder principles[4]

The increasing complexity of the industrial purchasing process and unprecedented changes in organizational markets are combining to radically alter the nature of exchange relationships in industrial supply chains. Key changes include the growing professionalism and sophistication of the purchasing management function, the internationalization of firms and markets and the impact of developments in information processing and communications systems on the way in which business is undertaken and supply chain relationships are managed. As supplying firms constantly seek business opportunities and new ways to service new markets, procurement professionals are increasingly demanding more from the purchasing process. For different reasons, but in an inexorable trend, both suppliers and buyers are seeking longer term relationships with each other, thus increasing their mutual dependency and transforming the impact of stakeholder principles on industrial marketing management.

Professor Martin Christopher and his colleagues (1991) have conducted extensive research into these trends and the impact that they have had on strategic marketing practice. They have demonstrated that a key task in the contemporary business environment is to secure long-term relationships of mutual advantage through building strong bonds between suppliers and customers. To meet this challenge companies should create inter-

---

4 This section is adapted from Egan, C. (1997), 'Relationship management', in D. Jobber (ed.), *The CIM Handbook of Selling and Sales Strategy*, Oxford: Butterworth-Heinemann.

nal co-ordination between customer service, marketing and quality control. Furthermore, to successfully enact the principles of what is described as 'relationship marketing', the superordinate goal of the business should be customer retention and every employee should have a close involvement in the marketing process. In Chapter 10 of this book Martin Christopher outlined the implications of this network-based multiple stakeholder philosophy from a strategic marketing perspective.

As a discipline, marketing is very good at describing the things which firms *should* do strategically to achieve competitive success. It tends to be less successful at dealing with the trickier task of *implementing* marketing programmes (see Chapter 13 for a detailed discussion of the issues). Having said this, a number of marketing academics have made significant contributions to the understanding of the factors involved in the *transition* from the traditional product orientation (self-interest) of companies to the 'resource' orientation which underpins the relationship management and stakeholder orientation (mutual dependency) to strategic marketing. Three mainstream 'schools of thought' have emerged (see Egan, 1997, for a description of the core principles of each):

1. The Nordic school of relationship marketing.
2. The collective writings of the Industrial Marketing and Purchasing group.
3. An integrative approach centred upon research undertaken at Cranfield University.

These streams of thought are increasingly converging and, taken together, their emphasis on matching internal marketing programmes with external marketing strategies provide a common agenda. All three schools recognize the importance of internal processes for partnership success and each approach acknowledges the sensitive impact of the 'atmosphere' which surrounds the relationship between two or more parties in a long-term exchange relationship. A common thread is the importance of networks and the emphasis on *internal* re-organization to secure successful *external* relationship management.

Many writers have argued that the network form of organizational behaviour is especially pertinent to markets which are characterized by sophisticated and rapidly changing technology and those which are exposed to continuous shifts in international trade and competition. In this context traditional organizational structures have failed to cope and the network of stakeholder partners has emerged as a superior form of organizational design. Here we encounter the notion that *organizational advantage* is a superior and more sustainable source of competitive edge than technological- or product-based competencies. In the case of networks, however, the challenge is to understand how successful inter-organizational relationships can be sustained and to evaluate the factors that deliver strong and sustainable performance over time. As we have seen elsewhere in this chapter, the equilibrium that binds the diverse needs of stakeholder groups is often very fragile indeed.

While the harsh realities of turbulent and discontinuous marketing environments are actually forcing companies to adopt a stakeholder perspective it must be acknowledged that, within many firms, managers remain extremely cynical about the possibilities of the relationship management approach. Stakeholder and relationship management concepts are extremely intangible and, like many 'soft' aspects of management, they often require fundamental attitudinal and behavioural changes before they are generally accepted within organizations. Partly in recognition of this problem, a group of researchers based at Cranfield University has developed a framework which embraces stakeholder principles but which also makes relatively abstract concepts accessible to practising managers. The next section profiles their contribution.

An integrated perspective on relationship management: the Cranfield six markets model

As mentioned above, a third approach to relationship marketing has been developed by a group of researchers at Cranfield University. A central thrust of this group's work has been to integrate the major dimensions of relationship management within a framework that they describe as the 'Six Markets Model'. This draws heavily on the stakeholder principles discussed throughout this chapter and it accommodates the growing complexity of industrial markets. The six categories of market are as follows (Millman, 1993):

1. **Customer markets**. This category is what is traditionally understood as a 'market' in the mainstream marketing literature. From a relationship marketing perspective the focus should be on building partnerships and the appropriate sales approach is via key account management.
2. **Internal markets.** In recent years there has been a growing interest in the concept of internal marketing, an approach that aims to transcend functional boundaries so that everyone in an organization has an awareness of their role in the marketing process. Internal marketing programmes are essential for transforming attitudes and beliefs within organizations and should form a central plank of any relationship management strategy.
3. **Supplier markets**. The move towards a much more strategic role for purchasing is forcing companies to recognize that the supply chain is the unit of competition. New technologies (such as Electronic Data Interchange) and inventory management systems (such as JIT) require a much more co-ordinated and cohesive approach to the management of buyer–seller relationships.
4. **Recruitment markets**. The basic premise here is that employee retention should be central to an organization's strategic direction and that employees should be seen as assets, particularly, but not

exclusively, those staff who interact with customers. The notion of 'moments of truth', whereby a customer's perception of a company is formed by multiple interactions with its employees, was an early attempt to draw attention to the need for excellent service quality among contact personnel. The emphasis here was upon careful selection, motivation and training of employees. Similarly, the highly successful 'Investors in People' initiative has brought many companies into an awareness of the power of strategic human resource management.

5. **Influence markets**. This is a recognition that opinion formers (e.g. journalists, analysts, academics) and reference groups (e.g. trade associations, regulators, lobbyists) can have a tremendous impact on general perceptions of a company. Word-of-mouth communications are very powerful and companies must try and shape these third party influences to create favourable impressions. For many companies public relations is taking on a much more strategic role, particularly as public scrutiny of business practice intensifies.
6. **Referral markets**. This category acknowledges the role of experts and professionals in shaping the decisions of purchasing organizations. For example, steel companies who would like to see the construction industry use a greater percentage of steel must persuade architects and structural engineers of the functional and aesthetic attributes of, say, tubes and pipes. More generally, the role of endorsement is critical and strong relationships with such 'influencers' can lead to enhanced credibility for the supplying firm and deliver much greater proximity to the specifications process. An important concept in the theory of relationship marketing is the notion of a 'loyalty ladder'. This describes how companies progress from seeking prospects towards developing a focus on customer retention, the ultimate goal being not only to have a loyal customer

but also to create a scenario where the customer is a strong advocate of the company.

The Cranfield research has made a valuable contribution to our understanding of how relationship marketing works in practice and it draws heavily upon the sort of stakeholder principles discussed in this chapter. Few deny the powerful nature of the relationship marketing concept or the emergence of stakeholder orientation as a new marketing paradigm. It is only by understanding the core business processes in more detail that we can hope to make it a sustainable and stable approach to business practice. In concluding the section on the six markets model we will present what the Cranfield group identify as 'an agenda for research', i.e. those areas which, upon investigation, will reveal more knowledge about this important topic. It is clear that the majority of these areas can and should be addressed by practising managers. After all, academics merely record and interpret what practitioners do in the first place! The following summary indicates the broad scope of required activity (Millman, 1993):

- Characterizing types of relationships and the frequency/quality of interaction in specific industry contexts.
- Developing external market scanning systems and internal information systems to support relationship marketing.
- Examining the nature of continuity and discontinuity of client/contractor relationships in project-based industries.
- In-depth studies of multi-level, multi-functional relationships in key account management and how these might best be integrated into existing/new organization structures.
- Exploring barriers to migration from transactional to relationship marketing.
- Developing accounting techniques for evaluating customer profitability.
- Understanding networking relationships driven by electronic data interchange.
- Assessing the potential for applying 'internal marketing' techniques to improve

core processes such as product innovation, marketing planning and customer service.

The clear importance of cross-functional integration in the traditional marketing philosophy sense of 'everybody does marketing' is consistent with other contributions to this book. More generally, the research agenda identified in the Cranfield research parallels that proposed in the broader based stakeholder literature. In the next section we briefly consider a common thread which permeates these contemporary perspectives on strategic marketing management.

Stakeholders and multiple relationships

Relationship management is making a tremendous impact on a number of broad fronts and, as we have seen, it is highly complementary with the stakeholder principles introduced at the beginning of this chapter. Central to the stakeholder concept is the notion of multiple relationships and there is a strong ethical underpinning to its practical foundations. Applying this perspective to relationship marketing, Takala and Uusitalo (1996) argue that, for such an approach to be successful, there are two essential conditions:

1. A relationship is a mutually rewarding connection between the provider and a customer, i.e. both parties derive benefit from the contact.
2. Parties have a commitment to the relationship over time.

As we have mentioned elsewhere, the importance of commitment is central to a long-term partnership approach but in practice it is very difficult to measure, i.e. it is a 'soft' aspect of management, intangible yet of critical importance. Takala and Uusitalo (1996) have gone some way to make the notion of commitment more tangible, identifying three key components:

1. stability;
2. sacrifice;
3. loyalty.

Stability is a central issue since it balances the conflicting interests of different stakeholders. They go on to argue that a stable relationship presupposes trust and that, fundamentally, it is only mutual trust which can be the cornerstone of successful relationship marketing activities. There is much debate about the characteristics of trust in social science theory but, where consensus exists, it tends to relate to the intangibility of the concept. Having said this, research demonstrates that trust is used by managers as a proxy for a broad range of issues associated with strong and long relationships. In this sense, the *feeling* of trust is essential to establishing an atmosphere of mutual co-operation. Figure 12.2 presents a summary of the key dimensions of trust.

What many of the dimensions of trust indicate is that achieving a feeling of trust is fundamentally a function of time. In this sense, a manager will describe a relationship of trust with reference to *cumulative* positive experiences. The emphasis on cumulative indicates that trust is a long-term issue and that it must be built up over time. Similarly, a key factor that will allow trust to emerge is the 'atmosphere' within which the relationship develops. A positive atmosphere is essential for a trusting relationship, i.e. a climate created by a joint philosophy of co-operation. A negative atmosphere, meanwhile, is typical where conflictual relationships are the norm. It is essential, then, that effort is put into building an atmosphere of co-operation to secure the stability of long-term stakeholder relationships.

The notion of trust can be applied to a broad range of marketing concepts. For example, *brand loyalty* is underpinned by cumulative satisfactions, a trust relationship that can pass through many generations. In the brand example, however, the relationship is with an inanimate object which manufacturers have managed to standardize. Interpersonal relationships, meanwhile, have the added dimension of *variability*, i.e. they are marred by the inconsistencies associated with human behaviour! This explains why trust relationships

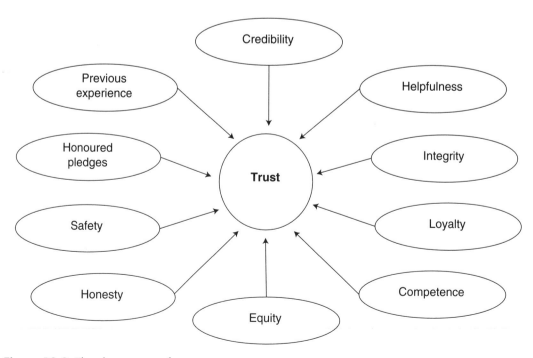

Figure 12.2 *The dimensions of trust*

must be managed, a *process* that also recognizes that any relationship where people or organizations rely on each other has a dependency dimension. The generally accepted solution involves a recognition of this dependency and a positive outlook on dealing with it for mutual advantage, i.e. an adoption of a philosophy of partnership.

Summary

Stakeholder principles are unusual in management theory in the sense that they have been discussed in the literature for many years but have attracted very little serious research, certainly not in the holistic sense we have tried to present here. Perhaps the most famous case and certainly the earliest was the Hawthorne experiments undertaken in a General Electric plant by Elton Mayo. In this research it was convincingly demonstrated that simply involving factory workers as passive subjects in experiments would significantly enhance their productivity. These experiments founded the Human Resource Movement and provided a major setback to the rationality of scientific management. Remarkably, research on stakeholder principles since the Hawthorne studies has remained functionally biased, as we mentioned in the opening remarks to this chapter. Hopefully a more eclectic research stream is emerging, if only in response to developments in strategic management processes and marketing management practice which are forcing ever greater mutual dependencies on stakeholder groups.

Tentative evidence has been put forward in this chapter that a structured and systematic planning approach to managing the diverse and often conflicting multiple stakeholder interests surrounding a company will have a positive impact on strategic marketing performance. However two caveats have also been firmly drawn. First, delusions of stakeholder equilibrium are very often and very easily shattered in turbulent marketing environments. Secondly, since long-term relationships will only survive in an atmosphere of trust, careful consideration should be given before responding to environmental turbulence with short-term, knee-jerk reactions, particularly if these are likely to breech a hard-earned stakeholder equilibrium.

References and further reading ▬

Albrecht, K. and Zemke, R. (1985), *Service America!*, New York: Warner Books.

Christopher, M., Payne, A. and Ballantyne, D. (1991), *Relationship Marketing*, Oxford: Butterworth-Heinemann.

Doyle, P. (1992), 'What are the excellent companies?', *Journal of Marketing Management*, **8**(2), 101–116.

Egan, C. (1997), 'Relationship management', in D. Jobber (ed.), *The CIM Handbook of Selling and Sales Strategy*, Oxford: Butterworth-Heinemann.

Galbraith, J. K. (1967), 'The concept of countervailing power', in B. E. Mallen (ed.), *The Marketing Channel: A Conceptual Viewpoint*, New York: John Wiley & Sons.

Greenley, G. E. and Foxall, G. R., (1997), 'Multiple stakeholder orientation in UK companies and the implications for company performance', *Journal of Management Studies*, **34**(2), 259–284.

Millman, T. (1993), 'The emerging concept of relationship marketing', *Proceedings of the 9th IMP Conference*, University of Bath.

Peters, T. J. and Waterman, R. H. (1982), *In Search of Excellence*, New York: Harper and Row

Takala, T. and Uusitalo, O. (1996), 'An alternative view of relationship marketing: a framework for ethical analysis', *European Journal of Marketing*, **30**(2), 45–60.

13

Implementing marketing strategies _____

Professor Nigel Piercy, Cardiff Business School, University of Wales

 The goal of this chapter is to focus attention on some of the very real problems faced by managers in driving marketing plans and strategies through an organization to the marketplace. First, the problems in ignoring or assuming away implementation and execution issues are discussed, and warnings laid down about the potentially severe penalties in misreading a company's commitment to a marketing strategy and its real capabilities of delivering that strategy effectively to the market. The agenda for addressing the implementation issue is shown to have three major components: managing *processes* inside the organization to achieve a better match between marketing strategies and corporate commitment and capabilities; developing a *strategy of change* inside the organization and with its external partners in the form of an internal marketing strategy; and managing *execution* to achieve effective implementation. We examine a simple tool for evaluating the existence and the different types of implementation problems on which management attention should focus – Strategic Gap Analysis. Possible sources of implementation barriers – the causes of strategic gaps – are examined. Finally, the chapter lays out the requirements for a systematic and structured approach to developing effective implementation strategy in marketing, as a necessary parallel to formulating marketing strategy. This approach involves examining managing strategy processes in a more integrated way, so implementation is a central issue, not an after-thought; the development of a coherent strategy of change to support marketing strategies; and applying appropriate execution skills and behaviour-based management approaches to achieve the effective implementation of marketing strategies.

The implementation issue in strategic marketing cannot be avoided. Indeed, some would go as far as to say that implementation is strategy – on the grounds that without a systematic management approach to the execution of plans and strategies, they simply will not happen, and so remain ideas which never become strategy in any real sense. Others suggest that implementation is *different* to strategy – it is the difficult part – they argue that finding out what a company needs to do in its markets is easy, it is putting new things into effect that is difficult. Whichever view is taken, to ignore implementation when we look at marketing strategy is to ignore an important part of the reality which executives face.

There is no need, however, to make implementation issues complex or abstract – this defeats the object. Our focus is quite simply described as 'making strategy work', and identifying the things that are needed to get from the plans to the action. There is a problem, however. While executives and organizations have become increasingly aware of theories of marketing strategy and the technical tools of market analysis and strategic market planning, there has been much less attention given to the processes involved in *executing* plans and strategies. The result has been described by one authority as executives being 'strategy-sophisticated' but 'implementation-bound', and this seems to be a familiar situation in many companies. In short, we need to do far better in responding to the executive's question: 'we know what marketing *is*, but how do we *do* it?'

The urgency of this topic is underlined by the frequent failure of marketing plans, and the strategies they represent, to reach the marketplace and achieve the results promised. The underlying problem is that in most situations marketing strategies have to survive in a corporate and organizational environment, which may provide fundamental barriers to successful change.

In fact, we can identify two underlying issues in implementation: the way in which the processes we use to generate plans and strategies actually create implementation problems; and the execution skills that are needed to translate plans into reality in an organizational context.

The way we approach the implementation issues here is:

- to examine the common and dangerous organizational dichotomy between strategy formulation and implementation, which is mainly a question of processes;

- to compare the problems of managing processes better to avoid implementation problems emerging, with the need for change management and execution skills to win commitment and support for the strategy in the organization;
- to describe strategic gap analysis as a practical way of identifying implementation problems and their sources;
- to examine what is required to manage the key processes better to avoid the emergence of implementation barriers;
- to build a structured approach to developing strategies of change that support marketing strategies, focusing on the use of strategic internal marketing, where appropriate;
- to identify key managerial execution skills as a critical resource and to underline the potential importance of behaviour-based management approaches to effectively and successfully implement marketing strategies.

Implementation versus strategy in marketing

Traditionally, implementation has been regarded as what follows after new market strategies have been created, plans have been written, approval has been obtained, and what remains is simply a matter of telling people what to do and waiting for the results to happen.

If we think about implementation, then we see it as the logistics of getting things organized:

- we focus on developing the organizational arrangements needed for the new strategy – allocating responsibilities across departments and units, and maybe creating new organizational structures where necessary;
- we allocate resources in the form of budgets and headcount to support the activities underpinning the strategy to the appropriate part of the organization;

- we produce 'action lists' and 'action plans' and do presentations to tell people the way things are going to be done, and;
- we develop control systems to monitor outcome performance in sales, market share, profit, and so on, to evaluate the success of the strategy, and to take remedial action if things are not turning out how we wanted them.

There are some very substantial problems in approaching the implementation in this way. First, it is illogical to plan strategies that are not firmly rooted in the organization's capabilities, and yet we seem to set up planning systems to do precisely this. Second, organizational arrangements and resource allocation are important, but on their own they are very weak, and usually very slow, approaches to the organizational change inherent in many new strategies. Third, outcomes such as sales, market share and profit, are what we want to achieve, but the driver of these outcomes is likely to be the behaviour of people in the organization who impact on what the customer receives in service and quality, which suggests we should focus on the behaviour not just the outcomes.

The dangers of separating implementation from strategy formulation

Organizational processes which treat implementation as an after-thought when the real work of generating innovative strategies and writing strategic plans has been done, are counter-productive for a number of reasons.

The 'dichotomy' between strategy formulation and implementation that exists in many organizations is fraught with dangers:

- it ignores or underestimates the potential link between market strategy and a company's unique implementation capabilities and weaknesses – strategies should logically exploit the things we are good at doing, and avoid dependence on the things that our competitors do better;
- more generally, it risks ignoring the competitive advantage which may be

> **Practical tip**
>
> It is easy to underestimate how serious the consequences may be of designing robust and well-researched innovative market strategies that are a poor fit with our capabilities, systems and policies. We have described in some detail the failure of a market segmentation strategy in a commercial bank (Piercy and Morgan, 1993). This failure was because an innovative, new segmentation scheme based on customer benefits was incompatible with the organizational structure, information systems, and culture of the company. Reading through this case example may provide some new insights into our own problems with new market strategies.

achieved by identifying and exploiting the organization's core capabilities and competencies in each market, by reflecting the views of the 'professional planner' in the corporate ivory tower, not the understanding of those who are working in the marketplace concerned;
- it encourages a weak linkage between strategy plans and operating plans – strategies which cut across operating plans and budgets and do not fit departmental plans are likely to be ignored and undervalued inside the organization;
- it ignores the hidden but often highly significant 'inner workings' of the organization – the culture and how it shapes people's behaviour; boundaries between functions, regions and organizational interest groups which may provide barriers to communication and co-operation, and the role of the powerful and influential in the organization;
- it may prevent a company from ever exploiting 'time-based' market strategies, or from realizing first-mover or pioneer advantages in a market – traditional approaches to implementation are too

slow and cumbersome to support fast change in market strategy. For example, in markets where the most important competitive advantage comes from the company's ability to execute effectively a succession of appropriate, but increasingly short-lived, strategic initiatives, then traditional approaches to planning and strategy and implementation provide an insurmountable barrier to market success;
- it ignores the practical problems of understanding the real capabilities and practical problems faced, as a company moves into operating through a network of collaborations and strategic alliances with other companies.

These arguments suggest that the first, and perhaps the most fundamental, long-term issue that we need to address is how to manage planning *processes* in the organization to integrate strategy with implementation, to exploit our corporate capabilities to the full.

Organizational structure and organizational change

To rely on organizational design and resource allocation systems to achieve the implementation of marketing strategies rests on two key assumptions. First, it assumes that these things can be changed and that we have the power to change them, as well as the time. Second, it assumes that these issues will resolve problems of organizational change and achieve the commitment and support of the people in the organization. Many academics and practitioners suggest that, in reality, organizational change requires far more than this.

This suggests that our attention should focus on the *strategy of change* that is needed to achieve the implementation of marketing strategies. *Internal marketing* is one approach to building this type of structured approach to implementation.

Outcomes and behaviour

Strategies are designed to lead to achieving the outcomes that matter to the organization:

sales, market share, profitability, competitive positioning, and so on. It is right that we should measure the outcomes that matter to us, and evaluate the progress of our strategy. However, this is very different from the issue of what drives those outcomes. In taking implementation seriously our attention should focus not just on the outcomes we want to achieve, but also on the behaviour that we need from people in the organization, to deliver those outcomes. This suggests a very different focus for management attention and often a very different approach to management. In essence, part of our approach to implementation requires us to give attention to the *execution skills and behaviour* that are needed to make the strategy happen.

Process management and execution skills

The argument above suggests that there is a need to consider both process management and execution skills in implementation. The difference is that managing the strategy process has the goal of integrating implementation and change issues with the market strategy, with the goal of avoiding the emergence of implementation barriers. On the other hand, execution skills are concerned with how to manage a way through the change problems and barriers that stand in the way of market strategy. While these are different approaches, they are not mutually exclusive, and in most practical situations we will need to give attention to both.

The reasons for this are suggested in Figure 13.1. The implementation scenarios suggested are four: *Weak Implementation*, where the management of process and execution skills are inappropriate to drive a market strategy; *Management-Driven Implementation*, where the emphasis is on leadership and control by management to put a strategy into effect and to overcome problems which may exist; *Implementation-Driven Strategy*, where the emphasis is on exploiting the capabilities of the existing organization and adapting

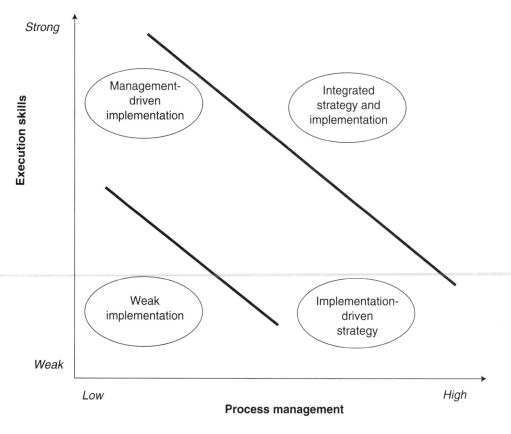

Figure 13.1 *Execution skills versus process management in marketing implementation*

strategies to 'fit' with this reality; and *Integrated Strategy and Implementation*, which achieves implementation by both managing key processes and applying management execution skills.

The *Weak Implementation* scenario is largely based on managers assuming that once plans and strategies are written, then people will go away and make them happen. Some managers make these assumptions implicitly in how they approach things, and then get upset when their edicts and commands are not put into effect or are implemented half-heartedly or haphazardly. Any market strategy that matters to an organization deserves to have implementation taken more seriously than this.

The *Management-Driven Implementation* scenario is probably closest to the traditional view of how things should be managed. The emphasis is on line management to take charge, to overcome obstacles, to lead, to coerce, and to make things happen – it relies on high quality management execution skills to overcome implementation barriers. It is fast to put into practice and in the short term may achieve change, but it lacks longer term effectiveness in sustaining change.

The *Implementation-Driven Strategy* scenario is where the focus of market strategies is dominated by exploiting existing capabilities and skills in the organization, mainly by adapting market strategies to 'fit' with the organization's existing competencies. This is also fast to be put into effect, and will keep implementation costs low. It is weaker in achieving strategic change because the emphasis is on exploiting what we already have and not upon developing new capabilities – this is fine until the point when our capabilities do not provide what the market wants, i.e. our strategy becomes outdated by market change.

The *Integrated Strategy and Implementation* scenario is the ideal to which we aspire. Implementation is not an issue because it is fully integrated with the market strategy, and we are not forced to cling to existing skills and processes, because part of developing strategy is developing the appropriate processes, structures, skills and capabilities to drive the strategy. It is slower to achieve and expensive, and in the short term not outstandingly effective. It is probably the only route to long-term sustained strategic change. It is also the scenario we understand least well, and find rarely in practice. We will assume, however, that this is the situation to which we aspire.

The characteristics of these different implementation scenarios are summarized in Table 13.1. A good question for the executive to raise at this point is which of these scenarios sounds most like how we do things in our company, and how can we improve the way we do things?

Strategic gap analysis

One way to challenge the implementation issue in a company is through a simple strategic gap analysis. This is a way to find out if we have implementation problems, and if so the sources of the barriers that we have to confront.

The approach is simple and the underlying model is summarized in Figure 13.2. The reasoning is straightforward. Strategic intent is what the managers and planners and strategists think the business is about in a specific market (the strategy, the plan, and so on). Strategic reality is what the business is really about in that same market. Strategic gaps are simply the difference between the intent and the reality. The important thing to ask is why those strategic gaps exist, whether they can be removed, and where that leaves the market strategy.

The stages to go through to conduct a strategic gap analysis are as follows:

● Identify the market in question and summarize the marketing strategy that is in place or is planned for that market.

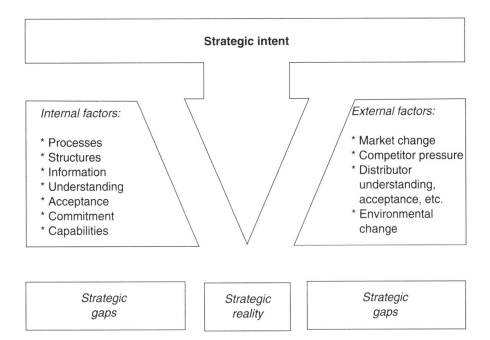

Figure 13.2 *Strategic intent versus strategic reality*

Table 13.1 *Implementation scenarios*

	Weak implementation	Management-driven implementation	Implementation-driven strategy	Integrated strategy and implementation
Characteristics	Ignore implementation	Focus on the management of execution and behaviour	Focus on exploiting the capabilities and matching organization and matching them with new strategies	Building implementation and strategy together
Timing	N/A	Fast	Fast	Slow
Cost of implementation strategy	None	Medium	Low	High
Ability to manage strategic change	None	Short term: high Long term: low	Short term: low Long term: low	Short term: low Long term: high
Implementation effectiveness	None	Medium	High	High

- Translate the marketing strategy into the operational requirements that are necessary to make the strategy real, e.g. products and services, pricing and value, marketing communications, distribution, and strategic positioning, which defines the strategic intent.

Practical tip

If we find it impossible to summarize in a few words the strategy for the market – then we probably do have a strategy. If we cannot identify what the strategy has to mean in practical operational terms, then how can we expect people in the company to execute the strategy? If this is what we find, then the problem is one of developing a clear and coherent strategy, not blaming people for having weak implementation skills or resisting change.

- Then ask what has actually been achieved in each of these same areas to define the *strategic reality* – it works best if this information comes from a different source, such as salespeople, distributors, or even customers.
- The comparison between the strategic intent and the strategic reality indicates the *strategic gaps*, i.e. the differences between what we need to have for the strategy to work, and what we actually have.

The strategic gaps which are found in this analysis define the implementation problem, and the sources of the gaps indicate where action is needed, or in extreme cases why the strategy will not work. Strategic gaps may come about for any of the following types of reason:

- Gaps may exist because there are substantial internal barriers faced, which may vary from shortages of resources, key skills, or necessary processes to support the strategy in reality, or more covert obstacles such as the political resistance to change in the organization.
- Gaps may exist because line managers do not accept the validity of the strategic intent – there is no 'buy-in' or commitment to the strategy, or because they do not understand or take seriously the strategy itself.
- Gaps may exist because the strategic intent is out of line with real corporate capabilities, i.e. the strategy asks for performance that is beyond the scope of the existing organization and planners have not recognized this shortfall.
- Gaps may exist because planners did not have a good understanding of the reality of the marketplace in which the strategy has to be executed.
- Gaps may exist because the issue of implementation has not been addressed in any systematic way – things are expected to happen because they have been put in the plan, but they do not happen or they are done badly.

Depending on the conclusions we draw from our analysis, we are likely to need to consider different approaches to the implementation issue. These may vary all the way from reformulating the marketing strategy to get a better fit with internal capabilities and external change, to internal communications to win support for the strategy inside the organization, to developing coherent programmes of managerial action to improve execution of the strategy.

In fact, underlying this analysis is the making of a real judgement about the need for strategic change in a company's market position – can we prosper by continuing to do the things we do now, or do we need a radical 'stretch' in our strategy to achieve more and perform better? For example, consider the model in Figure 13.3, which raises the question of whether we need 'strategies for stretch or more of the same?'

The judgement we make here is likely to be highly indicative of the type of implementation barriers we face and the approaches

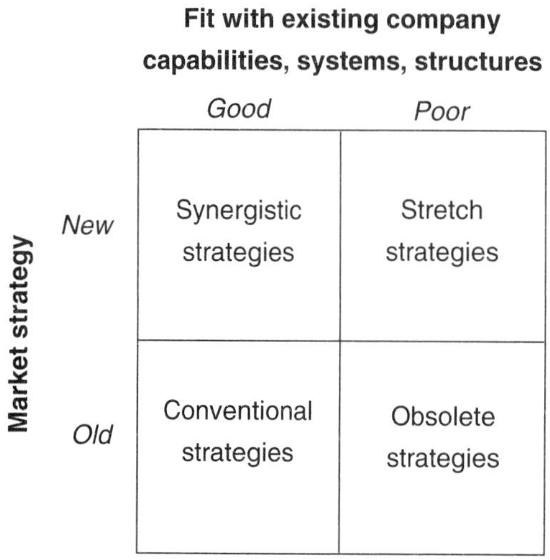

**Fit with existing company
capabilities, systems, structures**

	Good	*Poor*
New	Synergistic strategies	Stretch strategies
Old	Conventional strategies	Obsolete strategies

(*Market strategy* shown as vertical axis label)

Figure 13.3 *Strategies for stretch or more of the same?*

needed to develop an effective implementation strategy.

Where our market strategy is essentially a continuation of the type of approach we usually take – i.e. 'conventional strategies', it follows there is probably going to be a good fit with the company's capabilities, and relatively few new implementation problems. An example of this type of strategy from the retail sector is the development of growth from increased market share through sales promotion, new product launches, price positioning, and so on. The implementation tasks here are probably mainly concerned with action planning, resource allocation, internal communications and the day-to-day leadership skills of line management, i.e. what we have described above as management-driven implementation.

On the other hand, look at the case of 'synergistic strategies'. This is where we have developed new market strategies to achieve the things we need in the external market, but they are designed around existing company capabilities and systems. We may be doing new things – but they are the things we know how to do and have the resources to do. An example from the retail sector is the move of major players such as Sainsbury and Tesco into petrol retailing and financial ser-

vices – entry into different product markets based on customer franchise and retailing skills. Here the scenario is what we have described as implementation-driven strategy, and implementation barriers are likely to be small. Implementation strategy may be about no more than resource acquisition, action planning and internal communications, so that managers know what the new strategies are.

What is more worrying is where our plans and strategies are relatively conventional for the company, but have a poor fit with company capabilities, systems and structures – critical people have left, we have been left behind by the competition, or perhaps the market has changed in its requirements. Then we are left attempting to drive 'obsolete strategies', which are familiar but no longer appropriate to the company. A classic example was the determination of Encyclopaedia Britannica to continue selling books through direct selling, when the market was moving to CD-ROM for this type of published material. The problems then are surviving the short term with what we have got (management-driven implementation), but as quickly as possible developing new strategies to cope with new realities.

This leads to the case of 'stretch strategies' – the new things we need to do to perform in the external marketplace, but which are unfamiliar and currently do not fit well with the company's capabilities and systems. An example of this type of strategy is provided by the move of computer companies from selling technology to relationship-based marketing of solutions to customer problems, involving huge changes in culture and priorities. These strategies may be the only route to marketplace success – but only if we can execute them effectively. It is here where we need to think about what is needed to achieve the integrated strategy and implementation scenario we described earlier. In this situation, we may need to think not just about what we have to do to develop organizational learning and changing internal systems and structures to implement the strategy, but also about what we have to do to develop a programme of organizational change, and ultimately how we manage the processes of strategy building to win commitment and support for new strategies in the first place.

Practical tip

Bear in mind the importance for marketing implementation of building links with other functions. For example, many of the issues we need to confront in managing implementation may need skills and experience that are available in human resource management. In many service situations, personnel policies for selection and recruitment are as much a product design issue as are engineering or technical service content decisions. For some leading companies, building a collaboration here has proved an effective route to managing marketing implementation effectively. It should not, however, be used as a way of abdicating responsibility.

The situation we face, the strategic gaps we identify, and the degree of 'stretch' in our market strategy will dictate which of the following areas we need to consider most urgently:

- *managing processes* to develop ownership and commitment to change;
- our *strategy for change* in the organization;
- the *execution* skills needed by managers in the company.

Managing processes for effective implementation

Process refers to the way in which we make decisions and develop programmes of action inside companies. Critical processes in this present context are market planning, marketing budgeting and marketing control – i.e.

the ways in which we develop our market strategies, allocate resources to them, and evaluate their success. The argument is that the way we design and manage these critical processes will have a major impact on the quality of the strategies we produce and, most important, the chance that they will be implemented effectively and driven through the organization.

There are many examples of market strategies that fail not because they are weak strategies but because they fail other tests:

- they do not fit with an organization's culture, and the people do not support them and make them effective;
- they are not supported by key management players, perhaps because they involve unwelcome change or because they compete with other projects for resources;
- they do not fit existing planning and budgeting systems, and so 'fall in the cracks' and fail to become formally recognized in the company or to get the resources they need;
- they do not sit well on the existing organization structure of departments and units, so are neglected or given only lip-service, and fail through lack of ownership.

These types of problem are unlikely to be solved through management advocacy, presentations, internal communications to *tell* people they way things should be done, or management sabre-rattling. They are unlikely to be overcome by tighter control systems and budgeting, or re-organization. These are the types of barriers that drive us to look at the process issue in marketing implementation.

Evaluating process in this context means looking at three related components of planning budgeting or control: the techniques, systems and procedures used, i.e. the *analytical dimension*; the attitudes, beliefs, commitment and ownership of the people involved, i.e. the *behavioural dimension*; and, the organizational context in which we have to operate

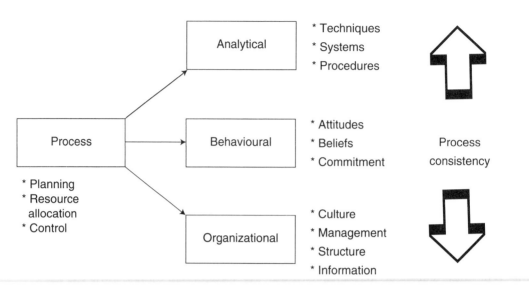

Figure 13.4 *Components of process*

in terms of cultures, management, information, and structure, i.e. the *organizational dimension*. This view of process is summarized in Figure 13.4, to provide a checklist of issues to consider, and also to make the point that we need to think also about the consistency of these different dimensions of processes of planning budgeting and control.

The significance of managing and changing key processes should not be underestimated. Our understanding of process management is not complete, but it is clear that we can produce highly undesirable effects in a company if the result of our efforts is a high degree of inconsistency between different dimensions of process. For example, consider the situations in Figure 13.5, for our market planning process.

Clearly, where we would like to be is in the top-left corner, where planning techniques and formalization are 'state-of-the art' and 'best practice', and at the same time the organization – management and employees – are fully supportive. Then we have 'effective planning', and implementation problems are likely to be minimized. However, experience suggests that this situation is rare. The other extreme is 'ineffective planning', when techniques and systems are crude and unsophisticated and do not generate the strategies we

need, but there are few implementation problems, because no one in the organization takes much notice of the plans we produce anyway.

More difficult yet are the other situations. 'Planning frustration' describes the situation where the techniques we have for planning strategy are weak and ineffective and yet the organization is crying out for new strategies. 'Planning conflict' arises where we have the systems and techniques to identify the way

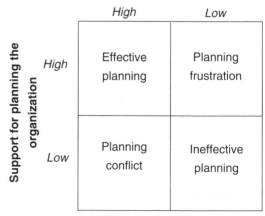

Figure 13.5 *Planning process problems*

forward, but the organization does not support change. Either of these situations is potentially very harmful – executives planning new strategies are either frustrated because they do not have the systems to build the strategies they need, or are thrown into conflict with management and the rest of the organization, because they have found the way forward, but not the support in the organization to put things into effect. Both represent a lack of consistency between the dimensions of the planning process. Both represent situations where implementation problems are likely to be different but substantial.

Indeed, overcoming process problems of this type may require us to do exactly the opposite of what is normally advised in marketing textbooks and by consultants. Figure 13.6 suggests that it is easy to assume that the answer to the problem is to train and educate people in systems and analytical techniques to make the process more effective – i.e. to get from 'planning frustration' to 'effective planning'. On the other hand, observation suggests that what we actually find is that systems and techniques often do little to win the 'hearts and minds' of people in the organization – i.e. really all we do is go from 'ineffective planning' to 'planning conflict'. The

Planning techniques and formalization

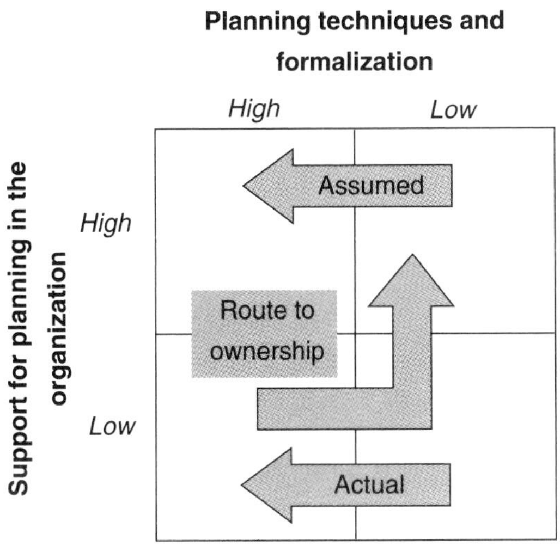

Figure 13.6 *Overcoming planning process problems*

route to 'ownership' may require us to give up some of our planning process sophistication and to devote more effort to winning support within the organization, and then to rebuild sophistication.

However, the underlying point is that managing process to improve implementation effectiveness requires us to think about all the dimensions of the process and to manage them consistently. This suggests that our agenda for managing process should address the following issues:

- **Systems and techniques** – have we provided the people who matter with the tools they need to identify and test new market strategies, to identify the resources needed, and to identify the key success factors against which performance should be evaluated, through training and development and investment in systems?
- **Behavioural dimension** – have we thought through how we will win people's support to get their 'buy-in' and commitment to new programmes of action, do we have involvement from the functions and

departments whose co-operation is needed to make the strategy work, do we have participation from all those whose insights can enrich our strategies and whose 'ownership' is important to their success?

- **Organizational setting** – is what we are doing compatible with the real organizational context; do we have the support of the powerful in the organization; what have we done to build bridges across the major organizational boundaries that stand in the way of our strategies, such as identifying liaison roles and forming cross-functional teams where needed; is the strategy process well co-ordinated to the personnel policies of the organization in terms of management development and career pathing?
- **Consistency** – have we done all this in a balanced and consistent way, so that the people we need to involve have the appropriate tools to do the job, and we are not forced into conflict with the rest of the organization?

This is a demanding agenda, but the evidence is that it is the one that matters if we are to manage process to avoid implementation barriers that prevent the market strategies we need to be effective from reaching the marketplace. If the alternative is that we produce new plans and strategies that are executed poorly and half-heartedly so they never achieve what they should, then perhaps the process management agenda will be seen as less demanding.

A strategy for change

The next step in addressing the implementation issue in strategic marketing is to recognize that market strategies may require a high degree of change in the organization, if they are to be implemented effectively. This suggests that we need to think in terms not just of action planning, but in how we manage that process of change. Experience suggests it is simply not enough to write brilliant market plans and to expect the rest of the

organization to be so awed that they automatically give us their support.

Practical tip
Recent research by 3i (a venture capital company) suggests business success is closely related to the ability to manage change – sales and profit growth go to those who react quickly to market changes and have a high proportion of sales from new products. British companies are criticized for their lack of attention to the motivation, team work and training that underpins the ability to manage change successfully. It may be useful to see what lessons can be learned from those in our industry who seem to be able to implement change effectively – what do they do, and how does it work?

Building a coherent and effective strategy for change around our market strategy will benefit by considering the following issues:

- Have we tested the market strategy, with the people who will be expected to implement it, for its completeness, practicality and their support (and adapted it as needed)?
- Have we evaluated whether people in the company see the need for change and whether they are willing and capable of making the changes needed?
- Have we thoroughly screened our market strategies for implementation barriers?
- In other words, have we considered the internal market for the strategy as well as the external market and planned our internal marketing to match our external marketing?

Testing the strategy

A first point to consider is who we usually blame for the implementation problem when it occurs. It is obvious – it is the operations

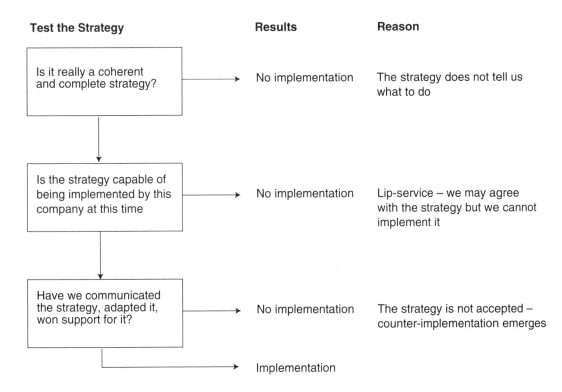

Test the Strategy　　　　**Results**　　　　**Reason**

Is it really a coherent and complete strategy?　→　No implementation　The strategy does not tell us what to do

Is the strategy capable of being implemented by this company at this time　→　No implementation　Lip-service – we may agree with the strategy but we cannot implement it

Have we communicated the strategy, adapted it, won support for it?　→　No implementation　The strategy is not accepted – counter-implementation emerges

→　Implementation

Figure 13.7 *Testing marketing strategies*

people who never produce just what we want; or it is the sales people, who never seem to get behind new products and markets; or maybe it is the finance people who mess up the pricing. On the other hand, maybe it is us. Maybe the heart of the problem is the people who produce plans and strategies without testing them against the people who matter, before casting them in tablets of stone.

Figure 13.7 suggests that we should ask some searching questions about the robustness and practicality of the market strategy, before blaming others:

- Is it really a coherent and complete strategy – if it does not tell people what to do, they are unlikely to do anything.
- Is it capable of being implemented – do we have the resources, skills, systems, experience, capabilities and will to drive the strategy: if not we are likely to get little more than lip-service.

- Have we communicated the strategy and won support for it – if not, then the best that can happen is that we are ignored, but more likely we generate the powerful force of counter-implementation in the company, i.e. a dogged and pervasive determination among all concerned that whatever we want, we are not going to get it (a force never to be underestimated as a management capability).

Consensus about the need for change

Related to the question of the technical robustness of our market strategy and the support it has among the people in the organization who matter, is the issue of change itself. The underlying question is whether the people in the company accept the need for change, and whether they are willing and capable of changing in the way needed.

Figure 13.8 summarizes some of the situations we may face here. In situation I, people

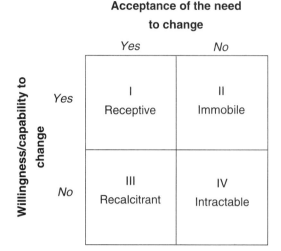

Acceptance of the need to change

Figure 13.8 *Consensus about the need for change*

accept the need for change and they are willing and able to change. Where people are 'receptive', then the implementation issue may be largely one of communications and reinforcement, and line management execution skills.

In situation II, people show every sign that they are willing and able to do the things needed to make the strategy work, but they just do not accept the need for change, so they do not change – they are 'immobile', not hostile, just not committed. Here the challenge is to find ways of building the view that change is needed, to unleash people's capabilities to do new things in new ways. The problem is that simply telling people they need to get their act together has generally proved ineffective in changing their minds. Building consensus about the need for change and the direction of change may be about managing the strategy process to get 'buy-in', rather than telling people.

In situation IV, we face the largest problem of all – the people who matter do not see that there is a need to change and they are not willing or able to change either – the 'intractables'. These situations describe the most severe implementation scenarios. We have to build a perception of the need for the new strategy as well as overcoming the pres-

sure to the status quo. This may involve a huge effort, or the need to find ways to work around these people instead of through them.

Situation III is in many ways the most intriguing. This is where the people concerned accept the need for change – they are likely to give chapter and verse about all the things wrong with the organization and the way it does its marketing. They are 'recalcitrant' because they know we should change – they just are not willing or able to change. Where there are entrenched 'defensive routines' and commitment to maintaining the status quo, we may need to think about what we have to do to break people free of this inertia and give them the systems they need to work differently.

There are no easy, 'off-the-shelf' ways to deal with these different situations, for the moment it is enough to recognize that if we do not even bother to uncover the organizational reality, and just go ahead with a new strategy, it is likely to perish.

Screening strategies for implementation problems

One way of building these insights into our strategy planning is shown in Figure 13.9. This suggests that we should look at implementation issues early, i.e. when we are building the strategy, not later when we are committed to a particular course of action. Some companies now require that this be done as part of the planning process alongside the analysis of the external markets, competition, and SWOT analysis.

The goal is to get down to the detail of what the requirements are for each part of the strategy to happen, and to identify the problems we face – what resources have to be freed from other uses, whose objections have to be overcome, whose support is needed, what bargains have to be struck inside the company, and so on. Much of this analysis requires us to think in terms of the key players involved – i.e. the people we need to 'buy-in' if the strategy is to succeed, in top management, in marketing, in other departments, in service and maintenance, and so on.

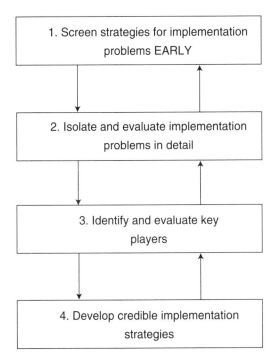

1. Screen strategies for implementation problems EARLY

2. Isolate and evaluate implementation problems in detail

3. Identify and evaluate key players

4. Develop credible implementation strategies

Figure 13.9 *Screening strategies for implementation problems*

The output is a statement of what we have to change inside the company if the strategy we want is to be delivered effectively – including the costs and time delays involved. The outcome will either be that we have a better view of whether the strategy is really attractive when we have evaluated the change costs inside the company, or we may have to conclude that the strategy simply cannot be delivered by this company at this time at a reasonable cost. If this is our conclusion – better to draw it while we are planning than later after we have tried to make the strategy work and failed.

Strategic internal marketing

One approach that has been used successfully in some companies to turn that implementation strategy into reality is strategic internal marketing. This means applying the same planning and analysis to the internal market (of managers and employees and distributors) as we do to the external market of customers and competitors.

> **Practical tip**
>
> It is often a mistake to believe that internal marketing has to be sophisticated. If the tasks we need to achieve are simple, then the methods we use may be simple. For example, in one study we found that the critical issue for some companies is simply to market customers to employees – i.e. to make employees aware of the things that matter to the paying customer. This involves things such as newsletters and customer days and customer visits, not sophisticated communications (Piercy, 1995). This may be worth considering before planning and costing internal marketing.

> **Practical tip**
>
> Bear in mind that it is easy to be convinced that there is no implementation problem, when we see the enthusiasm of the management team who have developed the strategy, and the promises of the enthusiastic audiences at our strategy presentations. We should try asking the same people two weeks later, when the bells and whistles have been forgotten and the cold light of day has been seen. This is usually a much better indication of the implementation problems we really face.

Figure 13.10 suggests one way that this can be built into the strategy process. The model suggests that we approach market planning in the conventional way – we examine mission, set marketing objectives, audit our capabilities and market opportunities, and develop marketing strategies and tactics. This turns conventionally into a programme of marketing action – our product positioning against the competition, our price terms and position, our marketing communications

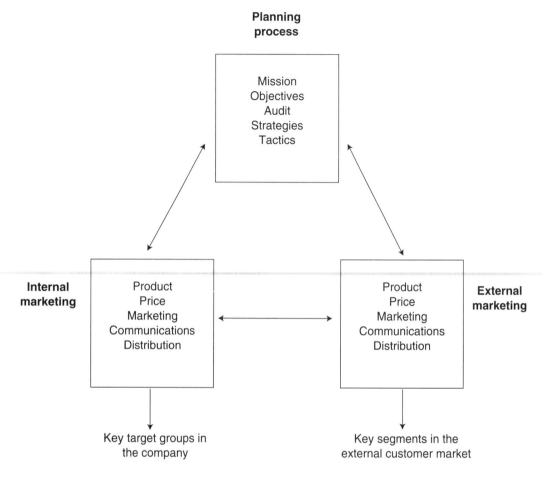

Figure 13.10 *Internal and external marketing strategy*

activities, and our investment in distribution and service.

However, we add a further strand to this conventional approach to developing market strategies. We ask what has to be achieved inside the organization for that external marketing programme to be effective? (See the points above for approaches to this). We can use directly parallel terms and forms of analysis, but the key differences are as follows:

● **The internal market** – this is all those people and groups inside the organization, on whose efforts, support, commitment and co-operation we depend for the external market strategy to work,

Practical tip

Do not make the mistake of confusing internal marketing with internal selling, and do not believe it is the perfect answer to every problem of implementation and change. Remember that marketing focuses on the customer's needs not the seller's – we may have to listen and adapt the strategy to make it acceptable to the internal market. Internal marketing has proved effective in some companies, but no marketing of any kind achieves total success.

who we may divide into key targets in just the same way that we segment the external customer market.

- **The 'product'** – at one level, in the internal market the product in question is the plan or strategy we are trying to drive and the challenge is to ensure that it is understood and accepted, but at another level the product is about the change and disruption associated with the new strategy, as it is perceived by the people affected.
- **The 'price'** – this is not the costs from our point of view, but what the people inside the organization have to pay, if our strategy is to work – in terms of learning new skills, giving up other projects, transferring resources, and so on.
- **The 'communications'** – are about the internal communications that we use to inform and persuade people inside the organization to understand and support the strategy, ranging from the presentations and written communications we develop, to personal interactions and social networking.
- **The 'distribution'** – is about the channels of communication that we can use to win support for the strategy, including written media, presentations and the like, but also through deeper issues such as participation in key decisions and company-wide issues such as evaluation and reward systems.

The goal is that for each conventional external market strategy we drive forward, we should have an internal marketing strategy that tells us about the degree and types of change needed inside the organization and what this will cost. In fact, experience shows that sometimes when we look at the real costs of organizational change (i.e. the budget needed for internal marketing) needed to make a market strategy work, the only conclusion is that the market strategy is too expensive, and we need to think again. However, it is better to see these costs at the planning stage, than to find out about them later, when there is no alternative but to per-

severe with an increasingly unattractive strategy.

None of these approaches is perfect. However, what they provide is a practical framework for understanding and evaluating the costs of change which are normally hidden away in a market strategy, and planning a strategy of change to back up the market strategy. In the real world we are never going to get such issues totally right. This suggests that we should not neglect the importance of acquiring and deploying managers' execution skills, i.e. their ability to make things happen.

Managerial execution skills

However well developed and researched are our marketing strategies, and however carefully we evaluate implementation issues and build implementation strategies, one critical resource we should not ignore is the ability of our line managers to put plans into effect – their execution skills. Quite simply, however much strategy we talk and however many plans we write, in reality, the way the strategy implementation process is managed at an interpersonal level is likely to be a critical determinant of implementation success. In fact, in many cases it is true that managers' personal skills of leadership and action may have to substitute for having the right structures and administrative policies – because external markets often change faster than companies can respond with their formal systems.

One way of looking at managerial execution skills is as follows:

- **Interacting skills** – this refers to how a manager behaves and influences the behaviour of those around him/her, and includes leadership by example and setting the standards by providing a role model, as well as bargaining and negotiating and using power to get the rights things to happen. In most organizations, the managers who have superior interacting skills are well known for their bias for action and getting things done.

- **Allocating skills** – this is about how a manager sets the agenda for others by budgeting time, money and people around the highest priorities to achieve implementation, even if this is at the expense of 'fair play' and administrative 'neatness'. In some cases this may even involve 'cheating' the system to get things done, and reward those who perform – even if this is not formally approved behaviour.
- **Monitoring skills** – refers to how the manager develops and uses feedback mechanisms that focus on the critical issues for success, rather than just the information provided by the company's information systems. This may involve face-to-face discussions, participation in key tasks, and coaching, more than score-keeping and awarding penalties.
- **Organizing skills** – in the sense not of designing formal organizational arrangements, but of networking and arranging and fixing things to achieve the right kind of action.

The importance of these issues is that managers' execution skills represent a hidden but vital resource for strategy implementation. This is a resource we need to consider when we look at the internal market and ask questions such as what are we really good at doing here, and who do we need on our side to make the strategy happen?

In fact, there is a deeper significance to management behaviour as well. One of the lessons we have learned in the management of sales is that 'behaviour-based control' is one of the keys to effectiveness. Modern approaches to selling frequently emphasize relationship selling and the building of competitive advantage from close collaborative relationships with important customers – this is the direct counterpart to the trend towards relationship marketing strategies (see Chapter 10 for a full discussion of these strategic networks). This raises the question of how sales operations can be changed from

a focus on sales targets and volume driven by transactions, to emphasize customer satisfaction and customer relationships. Research suggests that one critical lever for implementing this change lies in sales manager activities. Highly effective sales organizations do not simply manage outcome performance achieved by salespeople (sales, profit, market share, and so on), they manage the behaviour of salespeople (particularly their adaptiveness in selling, their teamwork, their sales planning activities, and their performance of sales support activities).

In effective sales organizations, sales managers spend more time and effort on the following types of activities:

- **Monitoring** – in terms of observing salespeople in the field, carefully reviewing call reports, watching the day-to-day activities of salespeople and advising them.
- **Directing** – mainly involving participating in selling activities, being involved in training and developing salespeople, and being seen to help salespeople develop their potential.
- **Evaluating** – appraising the professional development of salespeople and the quality of their selling and non-selling activities, as well as simply judging sales results.
- **Rewarding** – providing regular feedback and rewards (often non-financial) linked to results (frequently the quality of work not just the quantity).
- **Coaching and communicating** – adopting a role as the coach, communicator and facilitator, rather than the traditional role of keeping score and allocating financial rewards, and providing a role model through active participation in field sales activities rather than following the traditional command and control model of sales management.

These management activities characterize the most effective sales organizations – those who outperform their competitors and their own targets for sales, profit, market share and customer satisfaction. Not only does this suggest that customer satisfaction drives sales and profit, not the other way around, it also underlines the fact that the behavioural performance of salespeople drives their outcome performance – the key becomes managing the behaviour not just the outcomes.

This defines a very different role for the sales manager – coach and communicator instead of commander and score-keeper – but it seems the key to transforming the sales force from order-takers, 'lone wolf, road warriors', and persuaders, into the 'outsource of preference' for customers with whom we want a sustainable, collaborative relationship, based on teamwork and customer focus.

This example underlines the key role of line management in achieving the execution of important marketing strategies such as relationship marketing. The challenge seems to be to make the transition from relying on management-driven implementation to integrated strategy and implementation (see Figure 13.1). Nonetheless, in the meantime we should not underestimate the importance of management skills (or the lack of them in some cases) in driving forward the strategies in which they believe.

This leads to a distinction between how we manage the way in which plans and strategies are developed to minimize implementation problems – managing the process – and management execution skills to get things done. Uncovering the relative importance of these two related issues for an organization can be done through a strategic gap analysis, which contrasts the strategic intent in our market plans and strategies and the strategic reality of what we actually have, and asking why these strategic gaps occur. This can help us decide whether the problem is one of managing the process better, developing a coherent strategy for change in the organization, or improving managerial execution skills.

We saw that management execution skills are a critical resource in achieving the implementation of marketing strategy, and this should not be underestimated. However, the chapter concludes by suggesting some of the broader issues that are important to avoiding the emergence of implementation problems and barriers, rather than trying to solve them when they do occur.

The issues to consider as a longer-term strategy for avoiding the emergence of implementation problems, include the following:

Practical tip

Much of the analysis and model building in strategic marketing is rightly concerned with developing a 'better' strategy than the competitors to achieve competitive advantage and superior performance. One neglected question to add to this analysis is: what are we good at doing? In some situations we may find that a less sophisticated strategy that we know we can implement effectively is superior to the more innovative and sophisticated strategy that we execute badly.

Practical tip

Do not assume that everyone in the company wants to participate in building market strategies. Some will. Some may be positively hostile. Some may not care one way or the other, as long as we leave them alone. Participation and consultation may need to be part of our internal marketing effort to win this concession from the people in the company we need to be involved. Do not forget – the need is ours not theirs.

- **Participation in the strategy process** – if the key to effective implementation is the commitment of managers to new strategies, then one challenge is to think how we manage their participation in the identification and development of market strategies. This may be the route to achieving 'ownership' and commitment to change, or at the very least getting the 'buy-in' of the powerful and reducing the resistance to change.

Practical tip

One approach to building this strategic understanding is to involve more people from different parts of the company in studying the marketplace and interpreting its trends – environmental scanning – as part of building market strategies. The tools for achieving this are described in Piercy and Lane (1996)

- **Strategic understanding in the organization** – if company culture is not just 'the way we do things here' but also 'the way we look at things here', then avoiding the emergence of implementation barriers may be about what we do to allow people to learn about the market and customers and competitors for themselves to shake their critical assumptions and simplifications, rather than just what we tell them.
- **Champions and leaders** – committed individuals lie at the heart of effective implementation. Often organizations pretend they do not need them, or actively discourage them. The question is what do we do to nurture the change agents and to align them with the strategies that matter to the organization.
- **Shaping the strategy process** – traditional strategic marketing planning starts with

---

Practical tip

One way of emphasizing the need for change agents to managers is for top management to let it be known that they will not read any plan for anything unless the front page identifies the people who have ownership and are determined to make it work, and are prepared to stand up and say so. (This has to be the people responsible for implementation not for plan writing).

---

our mission and goals, works through analysis, and ends with statements of strategies, tactics and actions plans. It may be that this is quite wrong. Maybe planning strategies should start with how line managers understand the outside world and the company's capabilities and work back from that to develop strategies that managers believe in.

- **Liaison mechanisms** – where the critical implementation problems and strategic gaps come from the problems of interfunctional co-ordination and co-operation, then one answer may be to establish liaison roles and units to foster the needed cross-functional collaboration.

Practical tip

A way of involving line management more directly in market strategy and achieving ownership by changing the shape of the planning process is described in Piercy and Giles (1990). This may be worth examining for some ideas in how to reshape planning processes to exploit line management capabilities and win their commitment.

- **Career paths and management development** – lastly, one important long-term route to effective implementation of market strategies may lie in more effective collaboration with human resource management specialists. For example, if the crucial needs are for broader perspectives among managers, cross-functional understanding, collaborative relationships crossing organizational boundaries, and the reinforcement of effective managerial behaviour, then approaches may involve job rotation schemes, cross-functional teams driving specific projects, career paths and management evaluation that supports strategic change, and management workshops to address the problems of strategy implementation high and low in the organization.

Summary

This chapter has made a case that one of the key weaknesses we see in strategic marketing is that implementation is not taken seriously enough – the effort goes into research and analysis to produce market strategies, and we assume that things will get done. This *dichotomy* between strategy and implementation is dangerous both in leading directly to implementation failures, but also in leading to inferior strategies that ignore one of the most important capabilities of an organization – the ability to get things done, and to do some things better than others. Most traditional approaches to implementation do little to address either of these concerns.

The chapter has also addressed the issues that managers need to consider in gaining the *implementation* of marketing strategies. The problem arises because all too often organizations separate the planning and formulation of market strategy from the question of implementation. This dichotomy is harmful because it leads to many of the implementation failures that companies experience – the brilliantly conceived strategy that just never seems to happen – and because it cuts planners off from the reality of what a company is good at doing.

Traditional approaches to implementation in marketing strategy are inadequate, because they are concerned only with the mechanics of organizational structure and administrative arrangements, not the realities of organizational change. The real problem has three aspects: getting better at managing the process of strategy development to avoid the emergence of implementation barriers; accepting the need to plan organizational change alongside market strategies; and, focusing on critical managerial execution skills. Strategic gap analysis is one way of deciding what the most critical implementation issues are for a particular company and a specific market strategy.

Managing the key processes of planning and resource allocation requires the balance between techniques and formal systems, the beliefs and attitudes of the people involved, and the nature of the organizational setting.

Developing a strategy for change involves us in testing the robustness of our market strategy with the people who will have to drive it and understanding whether those people genuinely see the need for change and have the willingness and ability to change the way things are done. In short, we should screen market strategies at the earliest stage for implementation barriers, to identify ways around the barriers or to reject the strategy in question. One way of putting a strategy for change and implementation into effect is strategic internal marketing, where we use our skills and analysis in the internal market as well as the external market.

However, implementation success is also concerned with key managerial execution skills. Implementation involves skills in interacting, allocating, monitoring and organizing to work around barriers and put things into effect. Behaviour-based management control approaches have proved effective in the implementation of relationship-based market strategies.

At the broadest level, the effective implementation of market strategies may involve longer-term issues such as: participation in the strategy process; strategic understanding in the organization; the role of champions and leaders; the use of appropriate liaison mechanisms, and collaboration with human resource management to create appropriate career paths and management development approaches that support strategic change.

References and further reading ▬

Bonoma, T. V. (1985), *The Marketing Edge: Making Strategies Work*, New York: Free Press.

Cespedes, F. V. (1991), *Organizing and Implementing the Marketing Effort*, Reading, MA: Addison-Wesley.

Giles, W. D. (1991), 'Making strategy work', *Long Range Planning*, **24**(5), 75–91.

Piercy, N. (1996), 'The effects of customer satisfaction measurement: the internal market versus the external market', *Marketing Intelligence and Planning*, **14**(4), 9–15.

Piercy, N. (1997), *Market-Led Strategic Change*, 2nd edition, Oxford: Butterworth-Heinemann.

Piercy, N. and Cravens, D. W. (1996), 'The network paradigm and the marketing organization: developing a new management agenda', *European Journal of Marketing*, **29**(3), 7–34.

Piercy, N. and Giles, W. (1990), 'The logic of being illogical in strategic marketing planning', *Journal of Services Marketing*, 14(3), 27–37.

Piercy, N. and Lane, N. (1996), 'Marketing implementation: building and sharing real market understanding', *Journal of Marketing Practice: Applied Marketing Science*, **2**(3), 15–28.

Piercy, N. and Morgan, N. A., (1991), 'Internal marketing: the missing half of the marketing programme', *Long Range Planning*, **24**(2), 82–93.

Piercy, N. and Morgan, N. (1993), 'Strategic and operational market segmentation – a managerial analysis', *Journal of Strategic Marketing*, **1**, 123–140.

Piercy, N. and Peattie, K. (1988), 'Matching marketing strategies to corporate culture', *Journal of General Management*, **13**(4), 33–44.

Piercy, N., Cravens, D. W. and Morgan, N. A. (1997), 'Sources of effectiveness in the business-to-business sales organization', *Journal of Marketing Practice: Applied Marketing Science*, forthcoming.

14

Looking to the future: marketing in the twenty-first century

Professor Peter Doyle, Warwick Business School

This chapter looks at the role of marketing the twenty-first century. It begins by looking at the causes of the increased criticism of marketing in the 1990s. One cause has been the new economic environment, which makes the marketing positioning strategies of recent years look increasingly irrelevant. Another has been the orientation of marketing departments towards line extensions rather than genuine new product development. Finally, traditional marketing has been undermined by the reshaping of competition from firms to networks. Marketing is radically changing both in the numbers employed and in how, and where, they work. Marketing in the twenty-first century will increasingly be about the management of internal and external networks geared to achieve core business processes.

The 1990s did not prove a good decade for marketing. Through the 1980s it had appeared to be the all-conquering discipline. In 1991 a lead article in the *Harvard Business Review* entitled 'Marketing is Everything' concluded: 'in the 1990s, all the critical dimensions of a company are ultimately the functions of marketing'. Five years later the sentiment was changed entirely. A recent report by McKinsey was entitled 'Marketing's Mid-life Crisis' and argued that marketing departments are 'often a millstone around an organization's neck'. A study by Coopers and Lybrand concluded that the marketing department is 'critically ill'. Research by the Boston Consulting Group found that 90 per cent of major companies claimed to have restructured their marketing departments. Even Unilever and Procter & Gamble were abolishing the job of marketing director.

Observers point to several symptoms of marketing's decline. Most significant has been the apparent decline in the market share and profitability of manufacturer brands. For example, retailer private label has pushed the share of manufacturer brands from over half to under one-third of food spending in the last decade. At the same time margins have been eroded by a decline in brand premiums (estimated by Booze Allen to have dropped from 25 per cent to 17 per cent) and a rise in below-the-line spending to obtain retail shelf space. It appears that the retailer rather than the marketer now more often controls the consumer franchise. Second, marketing departments have been criticized for their lack of innovation. While there has been an enormous proliferation of line extensions, it is difficult to find examples of really significant new products or services that have emanated from the marketing function in recent years. Finally, marketing appears to have lost its primacy to other disciplines. The ideas that shaped businesses in the 1990s – TQM, JIT, business re-engineering, strategic alliances – had their origins in other functional areas.

The marketing problem

Studies show that the roots of a marketing failure lie in two areas. First, marketers defined the subject as a functional discipline rather than an integrative business process. Marketing directors have sought to make marketing decisions rather than share responsibility for satisfying customers with cross-functional teams. Unfortunately, the only decisions where marketing has sole responsibility tend to be tactical: promotions, line extensions and superficial positioning policies. The real strategic decisions that do determine competitive advantage: product innovation, total quality, service and cost structures are inherently controlled outside the marketing function. Second, marketers have not adapted to the new type of competition that today pits networks rather than single companies against each other. To create the outstanding value markets now demand, managers have to work with other members of the channel to reshape the entire economic chain. The price paid or value received by the final consumer depends not just upon the manufacturer's value chain but also on the efficiency and effectiveness of its suppliers and distributors. In fact, virtually every major innovation in the last decade has been based upon a new company reconfiguring the entire economic chain rather than on reshaping its own costs or processes.

The marketing the of the 1960s through the 1990s with its emphasis on marketing as an autonomous function led to the idea that the discipline was about tactical, and generally superficial, segmentation and positioning

rather than real innovation and the creation of sustainable competitive advantage. Such segmentation and positioning could be controlled primarily from the marketing function, it required little support from other parts of the economic chain, and it could often produce short-term gains. This marketing strategy was one that economists refer to as capturing 'the consumer surplus'.

The principle is illustrated in Figure 14.1. If a company is charging a single price for say, its brand of whisky, the optimal price might be P1 and the revenue the company receives is P1BQ1. However, some consumer segments (e.g. rich Japanese tourists, yuppies, etc.) would have been prepared to pay more than others. This revenue lost is the consumer surplus P1AB – potentially a very large amount. The obvious strategy is to price discriminate – to charge higher prices for those who are willing to pay more, say P1 or P2. The problem is, of course, that even affluent customers will not be willing to pay a high price when the same product is sold alongside at a low price. The marketing solution to this became branding and line extensions. For example, Johnnie Walker had as its core brand of Scotch whisky Red Label at £9. The company then launched in the 1980s a series of line extensions to successfully capture consumer surplus: Johnnie Walker Black Label at £16, Swing at £30, Blue at £90, and so on.

This type of segmentation and positioning strategy became the epitome of marketing in the 1980s and 1990s. Line extensions became a cheap substitute for genuine new product development. American Express added to its

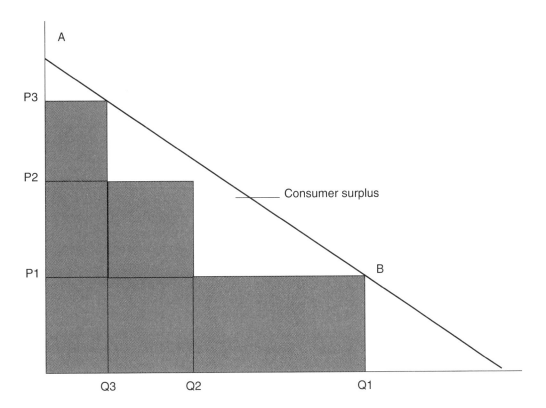

Figure 14.1 *Price and product differentiation*

green card, gold and platinum cards at higher prices. Castrol added to its core GTX brand, premium GTX2 and GTX3 extensions. Banks launched a 'premier' service aimed at their high net worth customers. Industrial companies also tried to join in, segmenting customers by price sensitivity. Many firms also segmented downwards to block competitors entering the market. For example Kodak added a low price Fun Time brand alongside its familiar premium Gold. Tesco added a discount Value Line alongside its regular own-label range.

Such strategies depended upon two conditions both of which became undermined in the highly competitive environment of the 1990s. First, these strategies required the core brand – Johnnie Walker or American Express – to convey significant monopoly power, consumers would pay more for them than generics. Second, the line extensions must be substantially differentiated so that discrete

market segments could be maintained – consumers would not trade down from Black to Red. For many brands the first assumption began to erode under the combined impacts of more price-orientated consumers, new high-value retailer own-label products and reduced investment by manufacturers in brand support (for example in the USA estimated brand advertising dropped from 70 per cent to 25 per cent of total marketing spending in the past 10 years). The second condition was often vulnerable because the premium line extensions rarely offered tangible benefits above the regular or core brand. The chairman of Guinness (owner of Johnnie Walker) admitted this, saying:

We have massive amounts of research which show that people cannot tell the difference between one Scotch and another. Although they swear total allegiance to one product and would never dream of drinking Brand X, in blind tastings Brand X is more often than not what they select.

In these circumstances it is hardly surprising that line extensions at prices four and five times that of the core brand were often not durable players in the market.

The way conventional marketing strategies fail is illustrated in Figure 14.2. Here three brands or line extensions operate in a segmented market: a discount brand, a regular brand, and a premium brand (e.g. a generic film, Kodak Fun Times, Kodak Gold). This typical market structure has been rocked by three changes in the 1990s. First, many customers have traded-down from the premium brands. They have concluded that the modest quality differences don't justify the generally substantial price premiums demanded. Next, segmentation and positioning strategies have been hit by new competitors who have fundamentally reconfigured value chains through their entire channel. One type can be termed price-value competitors: these offer customers high quality products at prices substantially below the 'positioned' brands. They achieve this by management re-engineering not only their own operations but also the costs of the entire economic system. Total costs are often reduced by 30 per cent or more. Two examples of price-value competitors are Direct Line Insurance and the Lexus division of Toyota. By looking at the whole

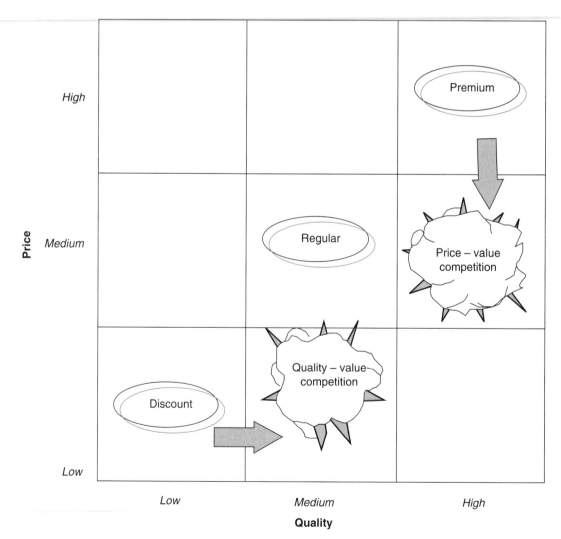

Figure 14.2 New high value competitors in segmented markets

economic chain Direct Line was able to replace a vast army of middlemen and cut the total cost of providing high quality insurance by 40 per cent. Within two years it dominated the market and had revolutionised the industry. Toyota, similarly took a total systems view of the value chains of suppliers, its own primary and support processes and the costs of its distributors and agents when it designed its luxury Lexus models. By knowing and managing the costs of the entire economic chain rather than its costs alone it was able to enjoy a cost advantage of 50 per cent over the market segment leader, Mercedes.

The other type of innovator can be termed a quality-value competitor. Here the integrated value chains are restructured to provide higher levels of quality rather than low prices. Marks & Spencer, Virgin Airlines and The Body Shop are examples of this type of competition. All eliminate functional boundaries (none have marketing directors or conventional marketing departments), focus on the three core value-adding activities of innovation, effective operational processes, and customer support, and build networks which design-in quality from the beginning to the end of the entire economic chain.

The difference between the 'marketing model' and the new competition is that the former have concentrated on exploiting differences in price elasticities between customer segments; the latter have sought to create demonstrable value advantages in terms of major cost savings or superior quality. Many market segmentation and positioning strategies proved vulnerable to the new competition because they depended on customers lacking the information and incentive to purchase rationally. The newcomers built core competencies that allowed them to create often dramatically superior value.

Measuring performance

In comparing the new price-value and quality-value competitors with the market segmentations and positioning approach, the *measures* of performance need to be defined.

The most widely used criteria of success are profit measures. But profits as a measure of performance are subject to a host of well-known practical and strategic weaknesses. In practice, they are easily and commonly manipulated by managers to produce misleading results. Different, and perfectly legal, methods of accounting for depreciation, stock valuation, research and development, foreign currency transactions and especially different choices of accounting for acquisitions can change accounting losses into big reported profits and vice versa. Worse, short-term profits and long-term competitiveness in the market are generally antithetical. It is very easy to achieve remarkable improvements and profits by curtailing investment, chopping R&D and brand support, and raising prices – but the inevitable result is a long-term erosion of the company's market position.

Another common performance measure is market share, but again there are problems. Defining the relevant market is always ambiguous and subjective. Also, market share depends on factors additional to the quality of the company and the strategy it pursues. Market share can always be bought by sacrificing margins or acquiring competitors. Saatchi and Saatchi, for example, built a dominant market share in the advertising industry this way, but as they, and others, have discovered, share built around financial engineering tends to be a very temporary achievement. Share can also be a result of inherited advantage rather than current competitiveness. One example is BT's pre-eminent position in the British telecommunications market. More generally, current market share is the result of strategies and brand investments made by past generations rather than those made today.

The most appropriate measures of current performance are those provided directly by customers – customer satisfaction and customer loyalty. Customers satisfied with the value being provided will buy again and this provides the basis for future market share performance and profitability. Many important studies in recent years have quantified the high costs of dissatisfied customers on both future market share and future profitability. Relationship marketing and customer loyalty are now at the forefront of modern marketing management. The key task of management is to focus on those activities that create customer satisfaction and loyalty: the ability to deliver high quality products and services at a competitive cost. These are the core value-adding processes; they are about efficient and effective operational processes, servicing customers and innovation.

Determinants of performance

The importance of selecting the appropriate criteria to measure performance becomes clear when one seeks to explain it. A major determinant of variations in profit performance is the industry in which the company competes. As Professor Michael Porter explained, structural differences – the number of competitors, barriers to entry and the relative power of the organizations constituting the distribution channel, make average profits in some industries and much higher profits in others. The *Fortune 500* listing neatly illustrates this: of the ten most profitable companies in the world, eight are prescription pharmaceutical companies. Businesses operating in such industries as building and construction, distribution, engineering, textiles and clothing have returns on average of under one-quarter that of pharmaceutical companies. Thus variations in absolute profits are often little to do with the competitiveness of the firm or its management. Even variations in relative profitability within an industry are rarely explained by such factors. More important tend to be accounting policies and the relative preferences of management between short-term profits and long-term market competitiveness.

In explaining differences in market shares: BA versus Virgin, Coke versus Pepsi, etc., differences in acquired resources are the major factor. These are of three types. First are windfall gains that enable a company to acquire dominant market position without having to strive for it. For example, BA's market share strength is largely the result of it being handed, on its privatization, the overwhelming proportion of landing slots at Heathrow, the world's busiest international airport. BA's management is luckier, not better, than Virgin's. The second cause is past investments in brands. Coca-Cola's market share today is the result of hundreds of millions of dollars being invested in brand support in each of the last 50 years. Even if Coke ceased to invest today, it would be years before its market share would begin to erode dramatically. The third factor is past strategy, which may have left current management with scale economies, experience advantages and distribution channels which competitors can only surmount by innovations which change the rules of the game.

To build tomorrow's performance, management need to focus on measures of how to satisfy customers today. Customer satisfaction is primarily a function of how well the value experienced by customers compares with what they expected and what they perceive they could have obtained from a competitor. To create high performance, management has to resolve three issues. First, there is the strategic issue of determining what products and markets to focus efforts on. A key question here is whether the achievement of high levels of customer satisfaction and loyalty will translate into high profits and share. As noted, there are clearly industries with structures where even highly customer-orientated businesses earn poor returns. Of course, industry structures are not static, and change can transform the fortunes of the better competitors. Nevertheless, some industries are best avoided unless management are confident they can innovate to transform the value chain of the industry like First Direct did in banking, Direct Line in insurance, or Toyota in luxury cars.

Second, management need to identify those capabilities to invest in – what are the 'key factors' which lever high levels of perceived value? A vast amount of research has built agreement on what the general answers to this are, namely the firm's specific skills and its ability to motivate its people to energetically harness these skills to deliver superior value to the customer. Core competencies today are based upon specific knowledge that resides in the organization's staff and the systems that it has developed. For example, Marks & Spencer delivers superior value through its unique skills and systems in supply chain management. It controls costs and quality not only in its own operations but also in the firms which distribute to the stores, which manufacture for it, their subcontractors, and even the ultimate growers of the raw materials. 3M's competency is built on its specific knowledge of substrates, coatings, adhesives and various ways of combining them. Casio's core competencies are in miniaturization, microprocessor design, material science and ultra-thin casings. These skills provide companies with the raw material for providing superior value and continuous innovation.

Skills are only half the story, however, the organization also needs to have what Hamel and Prahalad call 'strategic intent' – the ambition and commitment to use these skills to delight the customer with products and services which are demonstrably superior in value. In the early post-war years British manufacturing companies had comparatively high levels of skills but fatally lacked a management and workforce motivated and committed to pull together to provide world-class performance. What builds this strategic intent? Again there is broad agreement about what is required and what the best companies do. First, the organization has to demonstrate a commitment to the security and development of its employees that ranks at least equally to that of its shareholders. Recognize that unless you look after your staff, they are not going to look after your customers. Second, create structures which break down functional barriers, flatten organizational levels, empower front-line staff and focus efforts on the three core value-adding processes of operations, customer support and innovation. Third, top manage-

ment should provide leadership by reinforcing these values and offering a vision of what the organization will become.

However, there is a further extension of strategic intent that the marketing literature has not yet reflected. Today competition is increasingly between networks rather than standalone businesses. 'The winner' as Professor Kotler noted 'is the company with the best network'. In other words, management has to be concerned with building the right conditions, not only within its own organization, but also within the other organizations that constitute its value-adding network. As in so many areas of management, Marks & Spencer has pioneered this still rare type of leadership. Companies working with Marks & Spencer are expected to follow its guidelines on providing good working practices, to open up their organizational procedures and practices to review by Marks & Spencer management, and to share in the vision of providing outstanding quality and value to customers of the stores.

By exploring customers, competitors and their own performance, management have to identify the key skills they require to build competitive advantage. Then, in a rapidly changing environment, they have to invest in them to ensure they stay at the forefront and remain continually relevant.

Building core capabilities

What has changed substantially in recent years is our understanding of how these skills are acquired and developed. Three eras can be identified. The first might be termed the era of *scale and specialization* which characterized the aspirations of firms up to the 1970s. The objective was vertical integration – the leading companies such as Ford, ICI, IBM and Unilever sought to own the key channel resources and to internalize, via large specialized developments, all the skills necessary to run the business effectively. Unilever, for example, owned plantations in Africa, refined its own oils, manufactured all its products in its own factories, and distributed them through its own vehicle fleets. It had a head office, containing not only a huge multi-level marketing department, but its own advertising agency, a major market research organization, an economics department bigger than many universities, a sophisticated management consultancy organization, and so on.

In the 1980s many of these companies ran into big problems. Increased competition sharply eroded gross margins forcing them into radical programmes of asset disposals and the elimination of support activities. Not only were these organizations too costly, but functional demarcations and bureaucracies detracted from a customer focus, disempowered front-line employees and slowed the pace of decision making. Finally, these vertically integrated organizations proved resistant to the quickening pace of change in technology, markets and channels – they carried too much baggage from past environments.

The subsequent downsizing and delayering might be termed the 'Lopez era' – after one of its most famous proponents. Dominant partners in the channel broke explicit or implicit contracts with both internal stakeholders, notably employees and outsiders – suppliers or customers. They sought to boost their own profits by exploiting their monopoly power to reduce the prices they paid or increase the prices they charged. For example, in the 1980s, General Motors under Mr Lopez confronted its suppliers with demands for 30 per cent or more price discounts to maintain the business. In the UK, in the same period, BTR built a £11 billion conglomerate with a formula of acquiring companies with strong positions in niche markets and then confronting customers with demands for higher prices. BTR's strategy in its industrial markets was analogous to the segmentation and positioning strategies being played in many consumer markets by the likes of Guinness, American Express and others – the objective being to raise margins by exploiting differences in price elasticities.

Like scale and specialization, these new exploitive strategies proved non-sustainable.

First, because core capabilities were being neglected, the companies were not enhancing their ability to offer superior value to customers. Second, because internal and external relationships were being fractured, strategic intent – the motivation and commitment of staff and channel members to the success of the enterprise, was dissipated. Carefully developed economic and social networks – the very bases of a firm's competitive advantage were destroyed for short-term gains. Finally, many of these firms discovered the obvious point that long-term supply and demand elasticities are greater than short term. Customers and suppliers that can be exploited because they are temporarily 'locked-in' to a relationship usually find ways in the longer run to build new, more valuable relationships. In the 1990s, both General Motors and BTR among others, became casualties to this longer term backlash.

During the 1990s, it became clear that *network competition* was an essential characteristic of successful businesses in dynamic environments. Companies were moving from a confrontational to a partnership culture in which members of the channel had normally, long-term contracts to work together to reduce total system costs or bring new products to market. They understood that while Lopez-type confrontational tactics could reduce component costs, their impact on total system costs was small. What had a much bigger impact was to redesign the whole process to lower total manufacturing or marketing costs. Similarly while segmentation and repositioning tactics had in the past often produced temporary margin gains; in today's low inflation, high competition environment, the only sustainable way of gaining price increases was by being the first to bring new, higher value products to the market. These strategies required co-operation rather than confrontation.

Effective networks offer companies five crucial advantages in their pursuit of competitive advantage. First, managers attend to the whole value system, rather than the relatively small component of the firm's value

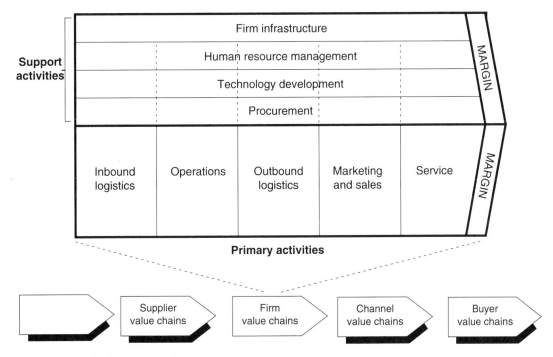

Figure 14.3 *The firm in its value system*

chain (Figure 14.3). This offers much greater scope for re-engineering cost reductions and quality enhancements. Second, it enables the organization to extend its skill base and substantially enhance its capacity for innovation. New products in most industries increasingly depend upon skills in a widening range of technologies. Companies can no longer master these skills alone; instead they rely on collaborative networking. European businesses now depend on partners to provide 20 per cent of the R&D, in Japan the figure is close to 60 per cent. Networking also allows firms to move faster, which is particularly important now with first-mover advantages becoming an increasingly key determinant of long-term profitability and share. For example, the British company, Glaxo, built a £1 billion business for its new product, Zantac, in the USA by an alliance with Swiss company Roche which allowed it access to Roche's 1000 person sales force. Networking also offers financial benefits: it increases sales per employee; raises return on assets and transforms fixed costs to variable costs so making

earning streams more stable. Finally, by outsourcing to members of a network, activities are almost invariably performed at lower cost and with higher quality. This is because unlike internal support services, the products of network members are continually market tested – if customers are not happy they can move elsewhere.

Marketing relationships

The objective of business in the twenty-first century will be to create *relationships* with customers which support future profits and growth. Customers no longer need to accept shoddy quality products or high prices in most markets. Strong customer satisfaction and loyalty depends on the value they receive from suppliers. Marketing managers need to appreciate that such value is not under the control of the marketing department. It is a function of the relationships between people within the firm and across the organizations with which the firm deals.

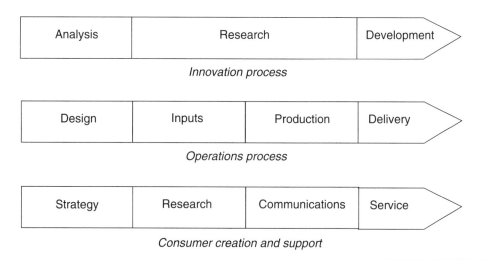

Figure 14.4 *The core processes of the organization*

Core processes of the organization. While an organization conducts a multitude of processes it is useful to group the *core* processes which create value for customers into three sections (Figure 14.4). The first is the innovation process – as Drucker concluded, 'every organization, not just business, needs one core competence: innovation'. Without a steady stream of new products the organization will find its prices and sales being driven relentlessly down. Second, the business needs an efficient operations process – it has to be able to produce and deliver products that meet world-class standards of cost and delivery. Third, it needs an effective process for identifying and communicating with potential customers and supporting and servicing current ones. It is processes that add value, not functions and departments.

Horizontal, cross-functional teams. This new focus redefines the firm around horizontal, cross-functional processes rather than vertical, functional tasks. Each of these processes depends upon teams of people with the necessary skills – from R&D, marketing, production, finance, working together for a common goal: satisfied customer. Functional boundaries and hierarchies are counter-productive: they add unnecessary overhead costs, slow processes down and orientate the business to low value-added functional initiatives rather than to real projects which generate major improvements for customers. Much of the observed downsizing and restructuring of marketing departments is aimed at creating this new focus. It is an effort to make organizations more customer-focused, not less. It recalls an observation made by Drucker over 20 years ago:

Marketing is so basic that it cannot be considered a separate function within the business. Marketing requires separate work ... but it is, first, a central dimension of the entire business. It is the whole business seen from the point of view of its final result, that is, from the customer's point of view ... concern and responsibility for marketing must, therefore, permeate all areas of the enterprise.

Networking relationships. Not only departments such as marketing have to co-operate with other specialists in the organization but increasingly they must share processes with others outside the organization. In an era of rapidly changing markets and accelerating technology, companies no longer have the skills inside the organization to conduct closed core processes. The innovation process in fast-track companies sees technological alliances with competitors, suppliers, consultancies, partnerships and consortia playing an increasing role in coming up with new products. Similarly, outsourcing relationships increasingly dominates the operations processes of leading-edge companies. More are saying, 'if there are businesses out there with more expertise than us in design, low cost manufacture and distribution – let them undertake the processes for us if we can co-ordinate for the benefit of our customers'. Customer creation and support has long relied on external parties – advertising agencies, market researchers and other specialists, but here again the reliance is growing and expanding into new areas such as strategy development, service and support. The ability to build and sustain external and internal networks has become the crucial management skill – it is the engine for developing core capabilities, sustaining strategic intent and is therefore the value-generating process of the organization.

In the 1990s this concept of relationship marketing was hailed by academics as a fundamental reshaping of the field', and a 'general paradigm shift'. Tomorrow's market-driven companies are seen as located at the centre of networks of functionally specialist organizations given cohesion by a common vision, mutual commitment and trust. So the paradox of business in the future is that to be a successful international *competitor*, the firm also has to be a committed and trusted *co-operator*.

Figure 14.5 suggests a general framework for relationship marketing that permits the

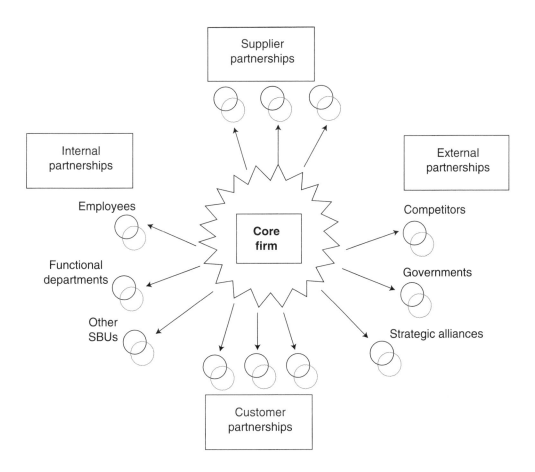

Figure 14.5 *The core firm and its partnerships*

integration of the key concepts of core capabilities, strategic intent and value creation. There are four types of networks. First, there are the core firm's partnerships with suppliers of raw materials, components and services (such as advertising and research). Effective relationships here permit not only high quality inputs but also JIT and TQM objectives. Second, there are partnerships with customers. These include final consumers and channel partners. The first two types of network relationships comprise the firm's supply chain. Next there are external partnerships with competitors, strategic alliances and governments to achieve technology development, core marketing or global alliances. Last, there are the firm's internal partnerships with stakeholders which include employees, functional departments and other SBUs within the organization. Good relationships with employees are important to achieve strategic intent, with other functional departments to build strong core processes, and with other SBUs to achieve synergies and share skills.

Causes and symptoms

The prophets of marketing's demise have focused on two features. First, they have invariably concentrated on fast-moving consumer goods (FMCG). Second, they refer to such indications as the growth of private label, the erosion of brand premiums and the decline of 'brand advertising' which McKinsey consultants called, with alarming ignorance, 'the very basis of modern marketing'. But these two features are merely symptoms of much broader changes reshaping businesses that are having effects not only on marketing departments but also on all other functional areas.

The primary cause is the changing business environment. The shift in the balance of power from manufacturer to trade customer in FMCG, which has exercised commentators, is just one isolated aspect of these changes. More fundamental has been the shift to a new era of lower inflation and lower

security of employment which has made consumers less willing to accept price increases and purchase premium line extensions of uncertain value. Alongside this has been the continuing high rate of technological change that has had the effect of first commoditizing then obsoleting the products of companies that are not staying ahead. On top of these changes has been ever-growing tougher international competition offering high value in terms of lower prices, higher quality, or both.

The response of companies has increasingly been to re-engineer around core processes – innovation, operations and customer relationships. This has meant delayering, merging of departments (e.g. sales and marketing) and downsizing to cut costs and enhance effectiveness. For example, British Telecom expects re-engineering and focusing around core processes to cut its costs by 50 per cent! Reuters claims to have reduced its debt collection from 120 days to 38, increased invoice accuracy by 98 per cent and can now deliver new services in 15 minutes. Not surprisingly, marketing departments have not remained unscathed by these dramatic changes.

The fundamental requirement of all efficient core processes is the sharing of the tasks among cross-functional, fully responsible teams. The aim is to eliminate the delays and politics of handing work-in-progress, back-and-to between departments and up-and-down hierarchies for approval. In such environments go-it-alone marketing projects get short-shift. Where marketing specialists fail to demonstrate commitment to the new order and fail to build up trust, not surprisingly the team members generally decide to do the work without them, after all the basic marketing ideas are soon learned and the specialist skills can be bought when required. In such cases the marketing department becomes redundant to the firm.

Pressures to cut fixed costs, to improve core processes, to acquire new skills and to rapidly adapt to new technologies and market opportunities are shifting companies away from confrontational transactions and vertical integration to partnerships with external and internal parties. These not only include members of the firm's supply and distribution channels but also competitors, employees and other business units. Competitiveness requires co-operation. Marketing is impacted here because many departmental jobs such as brand managers look archaic in the new process-driven organizations, while other specialisms such as market research, advertising, public relations or sales promotion look more effectively conducted by outside partners. All the changes point to smaller marketing departments staffed by a few generalists with big responsibilities for achieving results through teams of internal and external partners.

Implications for marketing

These changes do not necessarily predict any decline in the number of marketing professionals employed. In fact, the increasing complexity of the communications and marketing scene is more likely to increase the demand for such expertise. But these changes will change where they will work. Charles Handy described the twenty-first century firm as a 'shamrock organization' consisting of three leaves. The first is the 'professional core': the managers who run the business. This would be a relatively small, flat organization made up of full-time professionals, largely with general management skills. The next group is the 'contractual fringe': these are individuals and organizations that are subcontracted to manufacture or do professional services such as public relations or advertising. The third group is the 'flexible labour force': these are the people who do not have long-standing contracts with the firm, but are hired as and when needed. These can be low-grade casual workers but there may also be specialist agencies such as consultants, market researchers or new product design units. What is happening to marketing jobs is that they are beginning to move dramatically from the shrinking professional core to the contractual fringe and flexible

labour force. More and more specialist marketing jobs are done by individuals – often past employees of the core firm – or small specialist organizations working on a contractual or occasional basis for the firm. Sometimes the relationships will be long-term continuing ones, other times they will amount to the creation of 'virtual organizations': intense, but short-term marriages that dissolve once the task is complete.

Successful people prefer this newfound freedom. Many of these will be self-employed entrepreneurs, working from home, commuting electronically, and away from the office bureaucracy. For the core firm the advantages will be eliminating fixed costs, paying for marketing services only when they are needed, and buying in specialists who will survive only if they provide the results that are needed.

What about those marketers who remain inside the 'professional core'? In general, the core will consist of qualified, high performing professionals, technicians and managers. They will have relatively higher security and higher pay – although both will increasingly depend upon results. One downside is that they will work a lot harder. Handy refers to the $\frac{1}{2}$ x 2 x 3 phenomenon: firms of the future will employ half as many people, paid twice as much, doing three times as much work. The other downside is that the historical career patterns will disappear: with fewer layers there will not be the rungs of the ladder to climb. Career development will be horizontal: managers will progress by working on increasingly important cross-functional processes, for example, first looking after small new projects and then leading on to major innovative initiatives.

Tasks of the new marketing

The tasks of this small marketing group at the centre will be a mix of the old and the new. But all will have the ability to work in teams with other professionals as a key requirement. Whether the marketer is a leader on these teams will depend upon the nature of the task and his or her skills, style and attitude.

Advocate of Customer Orientation. One task that will still be essential is for the senior marketing manager to be the champion of the marketing philosophy. He or she should be an internal educator – getting people to understand that the objective of all the change and restructuring is to provide customers with what they want – to delight the customer. The primary task now – as it was always meant to be – is cross-disciplinary: the aim is to get the non-marketing specialists to appreciate the primacy of being market driven.

One of the most underestimated tools for creating a marketing culture is the introduction of regular measures of customer satisfaction. Marketers have to encourage the company to create a system whereby consumers are regularly and systematically asked to rate the major elements of the products and services provided. Customer satisfaction should be the major criterion for judging the success of the firm's processes and for evaluating and rewarding personnel at all levels.

Assessing market attractiveness. Another key task that should engage the marketing manager is the strategic choice of markets and segments where the firm will compete. This choice will depend first on an assessment of the firm's core capabilities and resources: where does it have a competitive advantage? Secondly it will depend on analysing the structure of the industry – will high customer satisfaction lead to high returns on investment? In some markets, the power of distributors, long-term excess capacity and the lack of entry barriers make even market-driven companies inadequately profitable.

Determining the core strategy. Core strategy defines how the firm seeks to create a competitive advantage: how can customers be encouraged to choose its offer rather than those of rivals. It is about defining the appropriate skills to create and sustain customer preference. 'Competitive advantage' involves two concepts: the noun refers to the benefits the customers want; the adjective refers to the requirement, not just to be good, but to be better than the firm's competitors. Developing a long-term core strategy therefore requires two types of analyses. The first is a thorough customer analysis. Marketing management need to provide a detailed understanding of how the market is segmented, what benefits customers want and how purchasing decisions are made. It also needs to explore how these wants and buying patterns are likely to move over time with shifts in technology and the competitive environment. Marketing professionals have developed a variety of models such as multi-attribute choice models, conjoint analysis and market mapping to assist such analysis.

The second type of analysis required is a competitor analysis: what are the key success factors in the industry and how does the firm compare to its competitors? Again there are a number of techniques available including marketing audits, SWOT analyses, value chain comparisons and causal analysis. Putting together the insights from the customer and competitor analyses should provide the basis for formulating a clear core strategy.

Internal networking. Marketing in the last decade ran into problems because it tried to be too functionally autonomous. This often resulted in low value-added line extensions and promotions substituting for real innovation and impacts on the company's value chain. Essentially the marketing failure was a failure in networking. In the next decade marketing managers will have to work more effectively as team players: proactively putting teams together and co-operating with other functions to enhance the core processes of innovation, order fulfilment and customer service. Functional boundaries in the 'professional core' will be seen as irrelevant and general management, process skills will become much more prized.

External networking. It is in the external networking that the major change occurs from the conventional view of marketing. It will no longer be true that most of the marketing is done by people inside the firm. Key decisions will be how to position marketing in the total value chain. Which activities should continue to be done internally? Which are better brought in? Which should be undertaken with a strategic partner? The criterion will be which solution provides the most effective and efficient core processes.

External networking in the future will be much more proactive and offer great opportunities for managers with marketing skills. In the past, marketing has been about exploiting opportunities generated from the firm's own capabilities and processes. Tomorrow's marketing managers will be scanning more broadly and looking at any organization with capabilities or resources that offers synergies that can be exploited in the market. These external resources might be new products, alternative distribution channels, manufacturing capabilities, or more generally, knowledge that can be exploited together.

Motivation and relationships. Marketing people will remain central if they are effective at creating and maintaining networks. What skills will this require? For external networks power is an important determinant of what the firm can gain. Power is a function of such attributes as the relative size of the firm, the rewards it can offer, its expertise and prestige. But for internal networks in particular, this is not enough. To suggest to colleagues that marketing is a more powerful or important function than theirs will invariably rebound. More important in creating and sustaining productive relationships is commitment and trust. Commitment means marketing managers demonstrating that they have an enduring desire to work through the internal teams and external partners. Trust means proving to partners that your word can be relied upon. Commitment and trust often require new forms of behaviour from marketing managers. They mean subsuming individual flair and decisiveness within group processes. It means involving others, listening, and sharing information from the beginning. It involves recognizing that great ideas

about enhancing core processes – innovation, operations and customer relationships are likely to come from any area of the organization and its partners.

Summary

During the last decade marketing appears to have been under increasing pressure. One cause has been the change in the environment that has led many firms to consider radical downsizing, delayering and re-engineering around core processes. Marketing, along with other departments, has been subject to cuts and restructuring as part of these changes. But marketing managers have also not adapted well to the new competitive climate. Perhaps boosted by the popularity of marketing in the 1980s, they have often tried to remain aloof and autonomous from these developments. This has resulted in marketing not making an effective contribution to the new focus on core processes. Instead, line extensions and new forms of promotion have hampered attention being given to real new product development, enhanced operational processes and comprehensive customer and service relationships.

This resistance has been bad for both marketing and the organization. It results in marketing management being marginalized and other functions spearheading the changes. It is dangerous for the firm because without the marketing input, the re-engineering taking place can erode the customer focus and become technical or cost driven. A firm today is always part of the total supply chain and broader network of organizations. Firms that are not customer led, not expert in understanding the needs of the market, become dominated by other organizations in the network with superior knowledge. When this occurs the value added shifts and the firm becomes a commodity subcontractor. This has happened to many FMCG firms supplying the top retailing groups. Now the retailer controls knowledge of, and access to, consumers. Marketing will become more important in the future: increasing competition will ensure this. The issue is where it will be located in the network, which parts will be maintained in the 'professional core', and which will be bought in. Certainly the numbers maintained in the professional core will continue to shrink. The continuing impact of marketing will depend on how effective the managers network both internally and externally to achieve the new marketing orientation.

References and further reading

Doyle, P. (1994), *Marketing Management and Strategy*, London: Prentice-Hall.

Hamel, G. and Prahalad, C. K. (1989), 'Strategic intent', *Harvard Business Review*, May–June, 63–76.

Hammer, M. and Champy, J. (1993), *Re-Engineering the Corporation*, London: Brealey.

Handy, C. (1990), *The Age of Unreason*, London: Arrow Books.

Mandel, M. J. (1996), *The High-Risk Society: Peril and Promise in the New Economy*, New York: Times Business Books.

15

A strategic view of the future of the marketing professions

Professor Michael Thomas, University of Strathclyde

 The term 'tail-end Charlie' was used in the United States Air Force to describe the poor fellow who sat beyond the tail plane of a Flying Fortress, whose loneliness was accompanied only by a machine gun. In the height of battle alas, Charlie was often unheard and unnoticed, and frequently dead. I hope that writing the last chapter in this volume does not place me in the role of tail-end Charlie. There are a lot of pilots flying this particular machine, so bringing up the rear is an unenviable task. However, I am still alive and my machine gun is loaded.

In contemplating the future of the marketing profession, I am going to address two rather distinct topics.

One topic addresses the issue of accountability. I believe that unless the marketing profession becomes more sophisticated in demonstrating that what it does constitutes value added it will live in the shadow of the manufacturing function which has clearly demonstrated in the last decade that it knows how to cut costs and still produce quality products and services. This is a micro-economic issue.

The other topic is a much broader one, and focuses on the macro-economic environment. I will raise the issue of post-industrial, post-modern society, and speculate that we may be moving into a period where many of the assumptions we make about strategic marketing may have to be questioned. How the profession addresses this challenge may determine its future.

Before I discuss accountability, let me summarize my philosophy, by contrasting market-driven behaviour with what I will call internally orientated businesses (Table 15.1). It concisely encapsulates my philosophical approach.

Table 15.1 *Contrasting market-driven business with internally orientated business*

Market-driven business	Internally orientated business
Segment; by customer applications and economic benefits received by the customer.	Segment by product.
Know the factors that influence customer-buying decisions; focus on a package of values that includes product performance, price, service, applications.	Assume that price and product performance/technology are the keys to most sales.
Invest in market research and systematic collection of sales reports to track market changes and modify strategy.	Rely on anecdotes and have difficulty disciplining the sales force to provide useful reports.
Treat marketing investments in the same way as R&D investments.	View marketing as a cost centre with little of the value associated with an investment.
Communicate with the market as a segment.	Communicate with customers as a mass market.
Talk about customer needs, share, applications and segments.	Talk about price performance, volume and backlogs in orders.
Track product, customer, and segment P&Ls and hold junior managers responsible for them.	Focus on volume, product margins and cost allocations among divisions; junior managers not held accountable due to the 'political' nature of allocations.
Know the strategy, assumptions, cost structure and objectives of major competitors.	Think of distribution channels as conduits.
	Know competitive product features.
Management reviews spend as much time on marketing and competitive strategy issues as on R&D, sales and human resources.	Marketing not reviewed outside of budget time.

Accountability

In Chapter 14, Doyle argues that the task of 'the small marketing group at the centre' will be:

- to advocate customer orientation, and to get the cross-marketing specialists to appreciate the primacy of being market driven;
- to assess market attractiveness, so that the choice of markets and segments will exploit fully the organization's competitive advantage and enable management to understand how, within the industry served, to deliver high customer satisfaction;

- to determine core strategy, that is exploiting competitive advantage, by thorough customer analysis leading to effective market segmentation, and by competitor analysis which will enable the group to define key success factors;
- to network internally, to remove once and for all marketing as a functionally autonomous group living within a marketing silo;
- to network externally through close co-operation with all other management functions;
- to create and maintain networks which Doyle regards as a central skill for marketing people.

That is a very valuable agenda and itself begins to suggest how 'success' might be measured.

Doyle and Hooley (1992) have done valuable empirical work on performance measures. They explored eleven propositions:

- **Proposition 1**: A distinction can be drawn between long-term market-share driven companies and short-term profit-driven companies.
- **Proposition 2**: A significant percentage of British companies will be in a 'transitionary' phase shifting from a short-term profit to a long-term share orientation.
- **Proposition 3**: Market-share orientated companies are more likely than profit-orientated companies to be customer led. Share-driven companies are less likely to be product or sales led.
- **Proposition 4**: Long-term share and transitionary companies will be more likely than the counterparts to adopt a marketing orientation as a corporate philosophy.
- **Proposition 5**: In the transitionary companies marketing can be expected to increase in importance in the near future more rapidly than in the short-run profits companies and even the long-term share companies.
- **Proposition 6**: In the long-term share companies marketing will generally enjoy a higher status compared with other functional areas than in the short-term profit companies. Transitionary companies might be expected to fall between these extremes.
- **Proposition 7**: Long-term share-orientated companies will exhibit closer working relationship between marketing and the other functional areas.
- **Proposition 8**: The major objective of the short-term profit companies will be more associated with productivity improvement and survival compared with the more expansive objectives of the other companies.
- **Proposition 9**: The long-term share and transitionary companies will adopt a more proactive approach to the future while the short-term profit companies are likely to be more reactive.
- **Proposition 10**: Long-run share and transitionary companies are likely to adopt a greater degree of marketing planning than their counterparts.
- **Proposition 11**: Short-term companies will more often measure performance in terms of profit while the market-share driven companies will more often measure performance in terms of market share.

Their conclusions should be noted:

Three different strategic orientations were observed among a large sample of British companies. The orientations were associated with different attitudes towards marketing, marketing relationships and strategic outlooks.

Attitudes

The short-run profit-orientated companies are more likely to adopt a product orientation ('make what we can and sell to whoever will buy') and see marketing as primarily a sales support function confined to the marketing department. Their CEOs are more likely to see marketing as 'really selling', and the role of marketing will have been least changed in the last five years, and is expected to change little in the next five.

By contrast, the long-run share-orientated companies are characterized by a marketing orientation ('marketing is identifying and meeting customer needs') adopted as a guiding philosophy for the whole organization. This is echoed by their CEOs who see marketing as 'an approach to business that should guide all of the company's operations'.

The transitionary companies share many of the characteristics of the share-led companies, though to a lesser extent. The major discriminators of this group centre around the increased importance attached to marketing (both over the past five years and expected in the next five) and in their willingness to 'adjust products and services to meet market needs if necessary'.

Marketing relationships

Two issues were explored: the status of marketing compared with the other functional areas, and the extent to which marketing and the other functional areas work together.

In the profit-led companies marketing was more often seen as of lower status than financial, personnel, production and even sales. In both share-driven and transitionary companies marketing enjoyed a higher status, and working relationships were reported to be much closer (i.e. marketing is not just confined to what the marketing department does). In the market-share orientated companies in particular, a more balanced status for marketing was noted.

Performance

Contrary to expectation, the market-share driven companies were not found to pursue market-based goals at the expense of short-run financial performance, but rather to reconcile the two. This reconciliation has resulted in companies that not only perform well today but promise to continue to perform well in the future. The transitionary companies share many of the characteristics of the longer run share-orientated companies and perhaps promise a brighter future for British industry.

Again, their propositions and conclusions point to a framework for measuring performance. I do note with interest that Doyle in this book (in the section on 'Measuring performance') expresses some doubts about market share as a measure of market performance, and emphasizes his preference for performance measures related to customer satisfaction and customer loyalty.

McDonald in Chapter 8 refers to the Cranfield/CIM (1994) study, and says this about market and performance assessment:

It is apparent that leading companies are moving away from discrete time assessments based around weekly, monthly or quarterly periods, towards continuous, ongoing monitoring and analysis, so that they can react quickly to market changes and prevent getting stuck in antiquated paradigms.

A year after the Cranfield/CIM study, CIM (1995) sponsored research done at Bradford, which led to its advocacy of a Marketing Excellence framework. Its components are worth stating:

Marketing strategy

- There is an extensive awareness of the need for external analysis and review of the company's competitive and marketing position.
- There is a systematic process for the collection and use of marketing information.

- Staff at all levels are actively involved in the collection of market information.
- There is a well-defined strategic marketing planning process.
- There are explicit strategies for developing and managing strategic alliances.
- Resources are explicitly developed by reference to competitive information.
- Organizational structures reflect the marketing strategy.
- The company culture is marketing orientated.

Quality strategy

- Top management is committed to quality.
- The company has a long-term commitment to improving quality.
- The company has a culture that underpins quality.
- The company uses systems, tools and techniques to monitor and control quality.

Innovation

- New product development is seen as a critical business process.
- Systematic approaches are used in new product development.
- External stakeholders are consciously and deliberately involved in new product development.
- Product and process development are simultaneous considerations.
- Cross-functional teams are consciously and deliberately involved in new product development.
- New product development is time driven.
- Quantified goals are established to manage and control new product development performance.

Customer development

- There is a conscious and explicit approach to segmentation, targeting and positioning.
- The company explicitly manages through relationship marketing.

- The marketing programme is regularly adjusted to reflect and anticipate customer needs.
- The company has an explicit programme to develop strategic partnerships with distributors, agents and other intermediaries.

Branding

- There is a clear understanding of the role of brands throughout the business.
- Branding is seen as a source of strategic competitive advantage.

Supply chain management

- Supply chain management has a strategic role.
- There are explicit systems in place for managing suppliers.
- The company and its suppliers share the same strategic vision.

Manufacturing strategy

- Manufacturing's strategic role is explicitly recognized.
- Manufacturing investment is determined by explicit reference to market needs and competitive strategy.

Note: 'there is a systematic process for the selection and use of marketing information', and the reference to specific goals and explicit systems.

Thus far we have identified both qualitative (QL) and quantitative measures (QM). Most of the observations quoted so far are QL. That is, of course, a problem facing marketing professionals. It is the charge frequently levelled at marketing professionals by finance directors and accountants. Are marketing professionals averse to QM measures? I think not, though I admit that the profession has not been active and articulate in promoting QM, mistakenly in my view. In addition to the standard ratio analysis tools that are easily applied to marketing activities, there is a good literature on marketing pro-ductivity analysis, and I plead that marketing professionals proactively use quantitatively based productivity measures. Only when we can demonstrate that marketing does create value added merely in the minds of consumers and customers, and that investment in marketing activities yields returns substantially greater than the input values, will we be able to argue our case for marketing as an investment rather than as a cost.

Market information systems of high quality are not hard to design. There are a number of market response models available. Database marketing allows for precise targeting and customer feedback monitoring. Internet-based marketing with the heady promise of one-to-one interactive marketing is already accessible to those brave enough to try it.

Marketing professionals can rationalize the company's offerings in a number of very productive ways. Make versus buy will force companies to focus on where they add value. Reducing product proliferation becomes possible by detailed analysis of product-by-product contribution and profitability analysis. Matching product lines with market segments is what matters. Increasing brand equity may be achieved more productively by umbrella branding. Advertising expenditures remain exposed to criticism as long as objectives based budgeting and task is unused. Unbundling advertising creation and placement may yield important cost savings. Hard analysis of sales promotional expenditures reveal that too much money is spent inventivizing loyal customers, too little on winning customers away from the competition. Pricing remains a very poorly managed function, maybe because accounting assumptions remain unchallenged. Dynamic pricing requires market-based not cost-based pricing systems. Services need to be unbundled regularly to expose the hidden costs of unvalued free services.

In managing marketing personnel, insist on zero-based budgeting in order to assert the primacy of objectives setting. Link remuneration schemes to hard measures of both effectiveness and efficiency. Productivity is about both effectiveness (doing the right thing) and efficiency (doing things right). Use activity-based costing so that the links between actual operating costs and revenues are clear.

If we fail to come out as far as productivity measurement is concerned, I fear we will be marginalized.

The macro-economic environment

There is one scenario that says the discussion in the previous section on accountability is akin to making music while hell is freezing over. We live in interesting times. We live in times that are a changing so fast that even the paper world that brings you this book is obsolescent and that if we have any good ideas they should have gone down the World-Wide Web long since.

I have written elsewhere about Advanced Marketing Capability (Shaw and Hood, 1996)

and in that Chapter I ask a number of fundamental questions about where marketing and the marketing profession is going (pp. 192–194). I have also proposed in the chapter that marketing professionals, if they are to be heeded, must become very adept at building bridges to the future (Table 15.2).

These arguments, however, are in a very real sense culturally rooted. We must live in a global economy, and we must be aware of the need to be culturally sensitive. The rest of the world does not see the world as we tend to see it. I can make the point easily by contrasting the Anglo–American world view with the German–Japanese view (Table 15.3).

Table 15.3 dramatically illustrates the sources of short-termism which has too frequently destroyed British companies. It illustrates the roots of contrasting government attitudes toward enterprise. It may explain why technology and science are closer to servicing enterprise in the Pacific Rim than in Britain. It is the contrast between long-term

Table 15.2 Advanced marketing capability – the bridge to the future

	Today's business	Pre-empting the future
Intelligence gathering	Collect data about existing markets and competitors	Create insights about emerging markets and competitors develop 'early warning signals' capability
Strategy formulation	Employ technology for today's competitive advantage	Exploit technology for reformulating the strategic vision of the business paradigm shift
Idea creation	Screen new ideas to fit to existing business	Nurture ideas for creating new business opportunities
Innovation	Reduce time to market	Create new products and new markets
Technology development	Boost performance of today's technology	Exploit the potential for leapfrogging into new technologies
Technology sourcing	Tap and enrich the existing network	Set up new networks

Table 15.3 *Contrasting the Anglo–American world view with the German–Japanese view*

	UK and USA	Germany and Japan
Time factor	Early industrializers	Late industrializers
Development strategy	Innovate across a broad front of entrepreneurship and management	Catch up in technological sectors seen as the most valuable
Historical role of governments	Generally ignorant of new business developments. Interfere after the fact to 'reform' wealth creators, who have adversarial roles to regulators	Genrally informed about strengths of leading economies. Co-operate before the fact to facilitate industrialzation playing a constructive role
Education	Extremely broad and generalist, with stress on pure science and management studies	More focused on successful technologies and science applied to key sectors
Economies	Divided between macro-economies (the whole economy) and micro-economies (the individual firm)	Organized around meso-economics (the dynamics of particular industries and sectors)
Social policies	Left behind in the leads to innovate. Government may seek to reimpose social 'burdens' on business retroactively	Included in concerted efforts to industrialize. Government sees social benefits as key to winning popular consent.
Development philosophy	*Laissez-faire*, free-trade and Anglo-American empiricism toward what markets demand, eschewing grand designs or 'picked winners'	Managed competition, early protections, and teleology – a logic of ends – already accomplished by leading economies. Target key niches, 'pick teachers'
Transition from feudalism	Slow and largely complete. Industry built on middle-class values of individualism and self-interest	Rapid and partly unfinished. Industry built on collective concepts of feudal obligations and reciprocities
Approach to financing industry	Domination by shorter-term equity markets and risk-taking profit-orientated individuals with high uncertainty, limited knowledge, fleeting relations	Domination by longer-term bank financing and lower-risk industry-orientated institutions with lower uncertainty, deeper knowledge, closer relations

Source: Hampden-Turner, C, and Trompenaars, A. (1993)

science and technology driven solutions (the leapfrogging technologies of Table 15.2) and quick fix tactical solutions.

We need to extend this dialogue, however. All those countries – the USA, the UK, Germany, Japan are capitalist according to conventional wisdom. I have spent much time in the last decade in Poland, before the fall of communism and intensively since then. There is glib talk about the fall of communism and the triumph of capitalism. What have we learnt since the fall of the Berlin Wall?

I think what we have learned is that capitalism has not necessarily triumphed because, at the moment of capitalism's triumph, the majority of European countries, and the traditionally developed economies, were moving on into post-industrial, post-capitalist society.

I shall try to define more clearly what I mean by that statement, but I will first state my hypothesis. It is that we are all engaged in economies that are transforming not from communist to capitalist, but in economies and societies that are struggling with the realities of moving from industrial to post-industrial, from primarily manufacturing-based economies, to primarily service-based economies; from industrial to post-industrial society; and to societies and economies ruled by professional élites, who are replacing both the capitalist barons (according to Marx) and the nomenklatura. These professional élites are for the most part the products of higher education. What we have learned since the Wall fell, is that we have not begun to define our responsibilities for the future shape of society, yet what we do, or fail to do will have a crucial influence on the future shape and direction of each and every society in which we live – it is that factor that links East and Western Europe, Europe with North America, and all of us with Japan, Singapore, Hong Kong and the other Asian tigers. We are all societies ruled by professional élites, societies that will succeed or fail only in so far as they invest in human capital. We live in a post-capitalist, post-communist world, because the real controlling resource is no longer capital, no longer land, no longer labour, but *knowledge*. Instead of capitalists and proletarians, the classes of post-capitalist society will be on the one hand knowledge workers (the professional élites) and on the other, service workers.

What is meant by post-capitalist, post-industrial society?

Think of these characteristics:

1. **Steeply rising living standards and expectations**. Far from universal in developed societies, but certainly in the West, even the disadvantaged have a level of security unimaginable a hundred years ago. In Eastern Europe, perhaps with the notable exception of President Havel, no one questions the desirability of trying to achieve living standards demonstrably present in the European Union.

2. **The decline of manufacturing and the rise of service industries**. Post-industrial society is characterized by a movement away from agriculture and manufacturing (particularly as a source of employment) to non-material production. Table 15.4 illustrates the point.

3. **In general, the meritocracy run post-industrial societies**. The managerial classes are meritocrats. The people who run state sector enterprises, the public sector establishment, the bureaucrats, are members of the meritocracy. They are all, certainly in the West, highly educated and consider themselves to be 'professionals' – they typically value membership of a profession above their current employment. Politicians are generally a reflection of this development – few politicians in the West come from the working class – they tend to be middle-class meritocrats.

4. **The advancement of women**. Professional expertise is no longer monopolized by men, though male chauvinism is still virulent. Ironically the former Soviet system placed fewer barriers in front of women than did most Western societies with the exception of Nordic capitalism.

Table 15.4 *Percentage of workers in employment sectors (1993)*

	Agriculture	Industry	Service
EUR 15	5.6%	31.5%	62.8%
USA	3.0%	24.0%	73.0%
Japan	6.0%	34.0%	60.0%
Canada	4.0%	22.0%	73.0%
Russia	13.8%	39.5%	46.7%

5. **The growth of government**. Despite both the collapse of state socialism, and a decade of Reaganite/Thatcheristic attacks on government, the fact is that central governments' control over expenditure of GNP in all developed countries shows few signs of curtailment. In most Western countries about 40 per cent of GDP is channelled through the state.[1]

6. **The welfare state**. Public expenditure on social services, social security, health and education as a percent of GNP shows little sign of decreasing, privatization programmes notwithstanding. Though welfare spending is frequently denounced, even the affluent show both public and private enthusiasm for pensions, health services, policing, infrastructure construction and higher education. Decent medical treatment, decent housing, a clean environment and access to higher education for all appear to be generally regarded as the cornerstones of a civil society.

7. **The dominance of big corporations**. We are currently observing the apparently unstoppable advance of big corporations. The statistics behind this statement can easily be assembled. In the UK, the 200 largest companies account for 85 per cent of total manufacturing output, six supermarket chains account for 66 per cent of all grocery sales, four banks dominate deposit banking, twelve insurance companies dominate the market. Similar statistics can be mobilized for Japan, the USA and Finland. Big corporations are run by meritocrats.

8. **The emergence of the global economy and global financial markets**. The global co-operations just discussed, have been catalysts in creating the global economy, the great global corporations have assets in excess of many nation states, they are tending to dominate the development process, their brands are household icons across the globe. The 100 largest corporations (excluding banking and finance) are located exclusively in the developed world, 29 in the USA, 16 in Japan, 12 in France, 11 in Britain, 9 in Germany. Singaporean, Hong Kong and Korean companies are competing for placement in this list of the top 100 companies. We have hardly begun to understand the significance of these organizations that, in many cases, are more powerful than many sovereign states.

Global financial markets, lubricated by modern information technology enable banking and investing to take place 24 hours a day and 365 days a year, with the attendant risks of currency speculation and stockmarket gyrations.

9. The last characteristic of post-capitalist society is the one I want to concentrate on – it is **the centrality of higher education to the future of that society**. Professional society, the society of professional élites encourages this development, since all professionals are by definition people in

---

1. The figure for the UK is exactly 40 per cent (*Financial Times*, 6 November 1996).

whom capital has been invested – a trained workforce is a *sine qua non* of post-capitalist society and education is expensive (but if you think it is expensive, then try ignorance).

I want to argue that post-industrial, post-capitalist society, will not be anti-capitalist, or anti-industrial, it will be a society based on knowledge, a society where real wealth, real value will be added by knowledge workers – the professional élites. Productivity and innovation will define success for nations as well as for (global) companies, success will manifest itself in wealth created essentially by knowledge workers, wealth that will have to be redistributed in order to sustain a civil society. I say this because the society I am contemplating will consist primarily of knowledge workers and service workers – the service workers will not have had successful access to higher education, the knowledge workers will have succeeded.

It may help to see from where we have come.

- The *Industrial Revolution* represented the transforming of society by technology.
- The *Productivity Revolution* enabled manufacturing workers to gain a greater share of the wealth created in and by manufacturing – we have so far done little to address the question of the productivity of service workers (the contracting out of service work by many government agencies is a crude attempt to start the process). The productivity revolution – knowledge being applied to knowledge – is in fact contributing to the destruction of the industrial labour force in developed economies, since sophisticated computer controlled manufacture is more productive than labour applied to machinery.
- The *Management Revolution*. All organizations require professional management, non-business organizations maybe more than business organizations – universities more than hypermarket chains, opera houses more than McDonald's. The

bottom line imposes a discipline on business managers absent in many not-for-profit organizations. Knowledge is the resource of management.
- The *Organizational Revolution*. We are now in the middle of that revolution. Every organization in society is under challenge and scrutiny. We are redesigning Yugoslavia; we are privatizing formerly state-run organizations; we are questioning the way we are governed; we are re-organizing Europe; we have re-organized world trade; we have re-organized world financial markets; we want to re-organize the United Nations. We live in a world where we are increasingly prepared to abandon the established, the customary, the comfortable, the familiar – whether it be products or services, skills, the organizations to which we belong, even human and social relationships. Organizations are in constant flux because innovation requires change in the way we do things, and presently we live in a science and technology driven world. Knowledge changes fast and it has never before changed faster – today's certainties become tomorrow's absurdities.

And who is it that energizes this process? Knowledge workers, the professional élites, are the leading edge of innovation.

Marketing professionals, as members of this élite stand challenged to face up to the many questions that impinge upon the future development of post-industrial society.

1. Do we actively debate the nature of social responsibility in the field of marketing?
2. Do we as marketing professionals, contribute to the definition of organizational social responsibility?
3. Do we ourselves have a clear view of the nature of civil society?
4. The productivity of knowledge may be decisive in the future economic and social success of each of our countries.

Making knowledge productive is a management responsibility, hence a marketing management responsibility.

It has been said that the past decade has not been kind to marketing. McKinsey has been forthright in its criticisms of the marketing profession's performance (Brady and David, 1993 and George, Greeling and Court, 1994). While always recognizing that leading consultants have a vested interest in change for change's sake, I find their views well informed. Their views on both the past failings of marketing and their opinions as to where marketing is going are worthy of note, even if the note is controversial.

George *et al.* see marketing professionals in the future organized around integrators and specialists, organized through teams and processes, not through functional or business structures.

The integrators, senior line managers, will completely displace traditional brand and product management. They will understand the real drivers of profitability throughout an industry sector's value chain. They will pursue a truly cross-functional agenda, they will develop partnerships with major customers, they will explore more efficient supply chain options. They will be aligned with customer needs, by segment and account, not with products or brands. Integrators will be supported by specialists, with truly analytical and technical marketing skills, in areas such as integrated marketing intelligence gathering and analysis, in pricing strategy, in measuring promotional effectiveness, in advertising and direct marketing.

As companies move beyond transactions based models of marketing to truly relationship based models, the traditional boundaries between the company and its customers on the one hand, and its suppliers on the other, will fade. Marketing operations will look like confederations of specialists, led by integrators, all joined together to meet customer needs more effectively.

At this moment in time, I anticipate continuing speculation about the future of the mar-

keting profession. In the macro-economic context, the future orientation of post-industrial society is a matter for debate. Despite short-term reassurances that we may continue to do business as usual, a debate has begun, particularly in Western Europe as to how the European Union, with unemployment averaging about 12 per cent of the workforce, will evolve and function in a global market economy where many of the hitherto competitive advantages of these economies are being eroded out of existence. The USA has lower unemployment (circa 5 per cent) though its highly developed service sector may explain the statistic. The Asian Tigers benefit both from focused sector development, government patronage and paternalism, and from targeted educational systems, but they are already beginning to show the stresses and strains of second stage development (manufacturing migrating both to China, and to first world market centres). What we cannot be sure about is whether the first world market economies will continue to grow on the basis of expanding demand for goods and services, or whether some form of acquisition fatigue will set in – consumption fatigue, taxation fatigue, and failure to develop a just and civil society in which the knowledge workers' ability to generate wealth will result in an en-feudal society in which the majority are beholden to the wealthy minority. In such a society marketing will have lost its *raison d'être*, since twentieth-century capitalism has laid its claim to legitimacy by placing the consumer at the heart of its value system.

As I complete the writing of this chapter, I have received a communication from the Marketing Science Institution in Boston, inviting contributions to a Special Issue of the *Journal of Marketing* (for publication in Autumn 1999, no evidence of short-termism here). The issues to be addressed are as follows:

1. **How do customers and consumers behave?**
   Much marketing thinking is guided by the belief that customers are rational value

maximizers. What do we really know about how choices are made and exchanges consummated, in an era of proliferating choices and rapid technological and social change, and how these choices are influenced by persuasive efforts? What do we know about understanding customers needs – current, latent and emerging?

What are the most appropriate models for describing and explaining the processes of search, preference formulation and choice, and the resulting customer experience? Why are customers satisfied or dissatisfied, loyal or defectors? Further, what do we need to know about the influence of social trends, demographic shifts, and market reforms on individual behaviour?

2. **How do markets function and evolve?**
   The concepts of market segmentation, positioning, and product life cycle are central to marketing. Yet serious doubts have been raised about the validity and utility of these foundation concepts. Are they adequate to the task of describing and explaining the function, structure, and evolution of contemporary markets, or are new concepts and models needed? Issues that need to be addressed include: are market boundaries distinct and stable, or shifting and overlapping? Is segmentation meaningful when it is possible to address and respond to segments of one? How do new products diffuse into new markets? How are patterns of market growth and evolution shaped by the forces of globalization, rapid information diffusion and competitive consolidation? How do vertical market structures shift, and how does value flow between levels?

3. **How do firms relate to their markets**
   In today's complex and dynamic global environment, firms increasingly relate to one another in the multiple roles of customer, competitor, and collaborator. This raises questions concerning how firms should and do relate to their customers (and by extension, to their customers' customers), to their suppliers

and partners, and to their competitors. Marketing thought is shifting from an emphasis on transactions and acquisition to relationships and retention. Meanwhile, developments in information technology and networks facilitate interactive communications and help tighten relationships. There is a pressing need to understand the sources and implications of these evolving forms of linkages: why do the parties participate, how are conflicts resolved in a web of relationships, and how do they evolve and adapt in global markets? How will electronic commerce and interactivity transform markets?

Co-operative relationships are also changing the competitive landscape. Suppliers, customers, channels and even rivals are entering into alliances and partnerships, greatly extending the complexity of inter-firm relationships. How will increasingly disaggregated firms manage the total value or supply chain? What competitive advantages are gained, and how are they sustained? A related issue is how do firms come to understand and anticipate the reactions of competitors? How should they deal with the emergence of competition?

4. **What are the contributions of marketing to organizational performance and societal welfare?**
   The role and value of marketing has been repeatedly challenged. Within the organization there have been pointed queries about productivity of marketing expenditures, the appropriate organizational role and influence of the marketing function and the contributions to financial performance.

   Where and when do marketing processes and activities need to be performed? There is also wide acceptance of the value of a marketing orientation to the organization. What is known and should be known about how this orientation is achieved and leads to better performance?

   From a societal perspective, what is the net contribution of marketing societies and economies as a whole? What criteria should be used to judge the societal value? Who are the stakeholders? What theories and evidence can be used to objectively examine both the benefits as identified by its advocates and abuses seen by its critics? How might society seek to preserve the benefits and minimise the negative aspects?

And finally…

I can think of no better way of concluding my chapter: MSI's view of what constitutes major issues facing marketing, and hence the marketing profession exactly coincide with mine. We must await the autumn of 1999 with eager anticipation, unless of course, hell freezes over in the meantime.

References and further reading ■

Bradford Management Centre in association with the Chartered Institute of Marketing (1995), *Manufacturing – the Marketing Solution*, May.

Brady, J. and Davis, I. (1993), 'Marketing's mid-life crisis', *McKinsey Quarterly*, 2, 17–28.

Cranfield School of Management in association with the Chartered Institute of Marketing (1994), *Marketing – the Challenge of Change*, May.

Doyle, D. and Hooley, G. I. (1992), 'Strategic orientation and corporate performance', *International Journal of Research in Marketing*, **9**(1), 59–73.

George, M., Freeling, D. and Court, D. (1994), 'Reinventing the marketing organization', *McKinsey Quarterly*, 4, 43–62.

Hampden-Turner, C. and Trompenaars, A. (1993), *The Seven Cultures of Capitalism*, New York: Doubleday.

Piercy, N. F., 'The effects of customer satisfaction measurement: the internal market versus the external market', *Marketing Intelligence and Planning*, **14**(4), 9–15.

Piercy, N. F. and Morgan, N. A., 'Customer satisfaction measurement and management: A processional analysis', *Journal of Marketing Management*, **11**(8), 817–834.

Shaw, S. and Hood, N. (eds) (1996), *Marketing in Evolution*, London: Macmillan.

Sheth, J. N. and Sisodia, R. S. (1995), 'Feeling the head, Part I and II', *Marketing Management*, Fall, **4**(2).

Thomas, M. J. (1996), 'Marketing Adidimus', in S. Brown (ed.) (1996), *Marketing Apocalypse*, London: Routledge.

Thomas, M. J. (1996), 'The changing nature of the marketing profession and the implications for requirements in marketing education', in S. Shaw and N. Hood (eds), (1996), *Marketing in Evolution*, London: Macmillan, 190–205.

Thomas, M. J. (1997), 'Consumer market research – some post-modern thoughts', *Marketing Intelligence and Planning*, **15**(2).

Index